Baldrige Award Winning Quality

Tenth Edition
Covers the
2000 Award
Criteria

How to
Interpret the
Baldrige Criteria
for Performance
Excellence

Mark Graham Brown

Productivity, Inc.
P.O. Box 13390
Portland, Oregon 97213-0390
United States of America
Telephone: 503-235-0600
Telefax: 503-235-0909
E-mail: info@productivityinc.com

Printed in the United States of America

Library of Congress Cataloging-in-Publication Data Applied for

ISBN 1-56327-232-6

05 04 03 02 01 00   6 5 4 3 2 1

CONTENTS

INTRODUCTION

Thirteen years after their initial publication, the Malcolm Baldrige Award criteria continue to be the best set of guidelines for running an effective organization. Each year, more organizations adopt the criteria to evaluate their progress toward excellence and high performance. Not only have most businesses adopted the Baldrige criteria, but they are being used by all branches of the military, many federal government organizations, schools, and healthcare institutions. Although the number of applicants for the national Baldrige Award have been fewer than 50 for the past few years, state-level awards based on the Baldrige criteria have flourished. New Mexico, for example, received 99 applications for its state quality award in 1997! Appendix A of this books lists the state awards based on the Baldrige criteria.When this book was first published in 1990, it was the only book available on the Baldrige criteria. Now there are at least 20 books on the award criteria, and hundreds of articles have been published. The Baldrige criteria are now even similar to the European Quality Award criteria. The benefits of this are that there is now one global set of standards on how to run an effective organization.

The Growth and Decline of the Quality Movement

The Malcom Baldrige National Quality Award program was started in 1988 to promote total quality management, or TQM, as an increasingly important approach for improving the competitiveness of American companies. In the past thirteen years, what started as a major business fad has become integrated into the fabric of the way many organizations do their business. Some elements of TQM have become standard in many organizations, including the use of statistics to analyze data, documentation and improvement of key work processes, pulling together employees into teams, and investing in employee education and training. Other aspects of the TQM movement have faded away. One lesson we have learned in thirteen years is that focusing on any one aspect of performance is an unhealthy way to run an organization. A number of companies focused too much effort on quality, and too little on other such factors as profits, new product development, or employee morale. Quality is important in any organization, but so are a number of other factors. Some early Baldrige winners later got into financial trouble even though they had excellent quality. Focusing on defect removal and customer satisfaction does not lead necessarily to improved business performance.

The Baldrige criteria have always been non-prescriptive, supposedly. In other words, the criteria do not provide a checklist or prescription indicating how to run an organization. However, in the early days, the criteria did require or prescribe a quality program that included a mission statement, quality values, quality plans, quality training, quality teams, and quality results. In 1995, the authors of the Baldrige criteria removed the word "quality" from all parts of the criteria and replaced it with "performance". This was much more than a simple word change — the entire focus of the Baldrige Award changed. The old focus was on defect-free products/services and satisfied customers. The focus for the last five years has been on balancing all aspects of organizational performance, including profitability, safety, growth, market share, employee morale, innovation, and a variety of other factors. The new focus has caused the criteria to get much tougher than they were in the early days. I have heard executives from several companies that won Baldrige Awards in the first few years say they could not come close today to earning the 750+ points generally needed to win.

The folks at NIST who revise the Baldrige criteria have done an excellent job not including the latest business fads in the criteria. You will not find words like "6-sigma", "e-commerce", or "re-engineering" in the criteria. Being immune to fads has allowed the Baldrige criteria to be accepted widely across the world as the best model for assessing organizational health.

Do Big Corporations Still Follow the Baldrige Model?

Many Fortune 500 corporations in the last few years have dropped the internal Baldrige-based award programs they started in the early 1990s. IBM, AT&T, Baxter Healthcare, Westinghouse, and others have eliminated internal Baldrige Awards in recent years. The U.S. Air Force, the first branch of the military to conduct Baldrige assessments, stopped doing them in 1998. Many of these organizations found that the assessments cost millions of dollars each year, and that there was little evidence the companies improved as a result of the Baldrige assessments. I worked with a large aerospace company for seven years doing Baldrige assessments, and the company did not improve. These assessments failed to lead to improvement because the Baldrige evaluation was a sideline project conducted by a quality department, and the feedback was never incorporated into company strategic plans. Separate Baldrige improvement plans were prepared but never seemed to get executed. Other organizations found that their units became better at playing the Baldrige game; hiring consultants to help write their application and prepare for the on-site visit. Scores went up from year to year, but the organizations really did not become healthier.

The failure of many of these internal Baldrige assessments is in the implementation, not the criteria. Many of the companies that have dropped their Baldrige assessment efforts did so prior to 1997 when the focus of the criteria shifted to business results. It would be difficult to receive a high score on the 2000 criteria without a solid business plan and financial results. Many executives believe that the Baldrige award is still about TQM, and they have moved on to other approaches. The Baldrige office has not done a good job of communicating this change in focus to corporate America.

Ritz-Carlton and Solectron — Two-Time Baldrige Winners

Winning one Baldrige Award is tough enough, but two companies have won the coveted award twice! The Ritz-Carlton hotel chain won the award the first time in 1992, and again in 1999. When they won the award in 1992, critics complained that the company was not profitable, and that good quality is easy when you charge $300 a night. The Ritz Carlton was owned at the time by a company that also owned the Waffle House restaurants, which are on the other end of the economic spectrum from the Ritz-Carlton. A greater number of people can afford to eat at the Waffle House, however, and that part of the business was profitable enough to help keep the Ritz Hotels going.

As the Baldrige criteria changed over the years, so did the Ritz-Carlton. Marriott bought the major share of the company some years ago, and Marriott was concerned about the lack of profitability in most properties. Management at the Ritz-Carlton convinced Marriott to leave them alone, and they continued to follow the new Baldrige model that emphasizes financial results along with customer satisfaction and quality. I spoke with one of the vice-presidents from Ritz-Carlton several years ago who informed me that the Ritz-Carlton had become the most profitable division of Marriott. The Ritz-Carlton has done exactly what the new Baldrige criteria call for: demonstrate a balance between financial results and customer and employee satisfaction. Ritz-Carlton did not trade quality for financial results; it has managed to retain the exceptional service that won the award in 1992 while achieving profitability.

Solectron is another two-time Baldrige winner that has had amazing success. The company has grown from about 1,800 employees when it won its first Baldrige Award in 1991 to around 26,000 today, with manufacturing facilities all over the world. Solectron's stock has risen over 1000% and is picked continually by analysts as a strong investment. The company, which manufactures circuit boards and electrical components, is so successful that it opened a store in the outlet mall in Milpitas, California for recruiting new employees! Solectron has not had the profit problems that Ritz-Carlton needed to surmount to win a second Baldrige. The challenge for Solectron has been maintaining its strengths and systematic approaches as it experiences explosive growth domestically and internationally. Solectron won its second Baldrige Award in 1997, and continues to show stellar performance when compared to competitors. The company looks at the Baldrige assessment process as one of the biggest consulting bargains out there. A similar evaluation by one of the big consulting firms would cost over $100,000, compared to the few thousand dollars it costs to apply for Baldrige. Solectron uses the feedback from the Baldrige application process to improve the company each year.

Beyond the Headlines—The Real Payoff of Using the Baldrige Criteria

The bad news about Baldrige winners and finalists seems to make it to the front page, whereas the good news ends up in small print in the back of the paper. The real test of whether or not the Baldrige criteria are a road map for running a better company is whether companies that win the award are better off financially than those that do not apply for the award.

Business executives who dismiss the Baldrige Award as a trophy whose acquisition is more driven by CEOs' egos than by a desire for improved performance need to take a look at the business results of Baldrige winners. The National Institute of Standards and Technology, which administers the Baldrige, reports that a hypothetical Baldrige Index has outperformed the S&P four years in a row. Although the S&P has had its best performance of the 20th century in the last few years, Baldrige winners that are publicly traded outperform the S&P by a 3 to 1 margin. Baldrige winners showed a 395% return, whereas the S&P showed a 149% return during the same period. In previous years, before the stock market took off in 1997, Baldrige winners had outperformed the S&P by about a 5 to 1 margin. Among the companies that won the award is stellar performer Solectron, whose stock increased over 500% after winning their first Baldrige Award in 1991. Solectron used the Baldrige criteria as a road map for designing its company, which it originally purchased for about $150,000. Solectron is also the only company to win the Baldrige twice. They are growing so rapidly that they have rented a store in a mall in Milpitas, California, for recruiting new employees. The company has gone from 1800 employees in 1991 to about 22,000 today!

More Evidence That Following Baldrige Leads to Business Success

Armstrong, the Lancaster, Pennsylvania, firm that manufactures flooring, furniture, and related items has been doing Baldrige assessments of its business units for the past several years. Former V.P. Bo McBee, who served as a Senior Examiner for Baldrige, reports on research in his company that shows a clear correlation between scores on Baldrige assessments and the profitability of a business. In other words, units that do well on Baldrige, tend to also do well on their business results. Armstrong's Building Products Operations became one of 2 companies to win a Baldrige Award in 1995.

Solar Turbines of San Diego is another company that has found success by following the Baldrige criteria. The company began using the Baldrige criteria for self assessment in the early 1990s, and applied for the Baldrige-based California Quality Award several times to receive external feedback on their health as a business. Solar, which manufactures large turbine engines, has about $1 billion in sales and customers all over the world. The company, which is a division of Caterpiller, used the feedback they received from California Award Examiners each year to improve their performance. Originally, they received a Bronze Award, and went on to win Silver and Gold Awards in California. Winners of a Gold Award in California often go on to win a Baldrige the next year. 3M Dental Products was the only gold winner in 1996, went on to win a Baldrige in 1997. Similarly, Solar went on to win the Baldrige in 1998. The company was hoping to be a Baldrige finalist, and ended up receiving the award last year.

Scores were so high for Solar partly because their business results are quite impressive. The company spends 13% of its revenue on R&D each year, which is triple the industry average, and up 10% from what Solar spent in 1995. Along with impressive sales, profits, and market share growth, Solar clearly stands out as a company that treats its employees well. 86% of employees rate the company as a good place to work, which is 32 percentage points higher than the average U.S. business. Incentive pay for employees has also increased from 7.6% of salary in 1994 to 10.4% in 1997, as the company has become more efficient. On-the-job injuries and worker's compensation claims also show reduced levels and trends over the last four years. Solar is a prime example, of how a company has used the Baldrige process to find areas for improvement, over a number of years, to go from being a good company to become one of the best in the world.

The Baldrige Award Has Served Its Purpose Well

In spite of all the criticism about fairness in judging, and whether or not meeting the criteria predicts financial success, the Baldrige has done more to improve the quality of U.S. products and services than anything that has come before it. Quality is now something that almost every company in America is working on. The biggest benefit of the Baldrige criteria is that we now have a common framework for making sense out of all of the theories, tools, and approaches that are part of running an effective organization. We have a common language and a common way of understanding where to apply all of these theories and techniques. Another benefit of the Baldrige has been that companies are now sharing and talking to one another to help one another get better. This sharing and helping almost never occurred five years ago—companies kept to themselves, and shared only those practices that they were certain would not help a competitor. The Baldrige Award has been successful beyond the greatest expectations of its founders. It has given rise to 18 similar awards in other countries, 5 of which are modeled exactly on the Baldrige criteria. Most states in the U.S. have either established their own quality awards or have an effort underway. Through these "baby Baldriges," the approach is being deployed even more pervasively than through the Baldrige by itself. In fact, the existence of state-level quality awards is one of the primary reasons why Baldrige applicants dropped from around 100 in previous years to around 50 or less per year during the past five years or so.

Interpreting the Baldrige Criteria

One problem for users of the Baldrige Award criteria is that they can be difficult to interpret. The criteria are written to be very general, because they must apply equally to both service and manufacturing organizations, and they must apply to organizations ranging in size from a few hundred employees to many thousands. Because the criteria are so general, they are difficult to interpret. The other thing that makes the criteria hard to use for assessment is that they are non-prescriptive. In other words, they don't tell you how you should run your organization. In my work as a management consultant and as a Baldrige Examiner, I've encountered many instances where people had difficulty interpreting the Baldrige criteria. Other examiners and quality improvement consultants I've spoken to report similar observations.

The purpose of this text, then, is to provide readers with a better understanding of the Areas to Address that make up the Baldrige Award criteria. The book is designed to aid organizations that are actually preparing an application for the Baldrige Award, as well as the many organizations that will be using the award criteria as a way of improving their quality improvement efforts.

How to Use This Book

Generally, there are two types of uses for this book:

1. As a guide for individuals who are responsible for coordinating or actually writing a Baldrige Award application or an application for a state award.

2. As a tool for individuals who wish to audit or assess their organization using the Baldrige Award criteria, or who wish to apply for an internal award based upon the criteria. Individuals who are responsible for developing assessment and improvement plans based upon the Baldrige criteria will also find the book useful.

The specifics of the book are directed primarily toward the individuals of the first category, with information provided on how to write various sections of the Baldrige Award application. Chapter 1 provides general information on understanding the 2000 Award criteria. Chapter 2 explains how to write an application. Chapter 3 explains how the seven categories of criteria work together as a system, and covers the overall themes carried throughout the criteria. Chapter 4 includes information on the scoring scale. The next seven chapters cover the seven main categories in the Baldrige criteria. Each of these chapters includes an overall explanation of the main category and definitions of the Examination Items and the Areas to Address. Also provided are sections entitled "What They're Looking For Here," which describe the criteria as seen by the Examiners. This section is followed by a listing of "Key Indicators," or evaluation factors, provided to further assist you with the interpretation of the criteria. Naturally, I assume that those companies seriously considering challenging for the Award have had systems in place for several years and that their use of this text is to help them best represent their systems and demonstrate compliance with the Baldrige criteria.

This information is also helpful to individuals using the criteria for the second purpose. For this second type of user, the various "indicators" that are listed for each of the 27 Areas to Address are helpful in devising Baldrige-based audit instruments and in developing plans rooted in each of the seven categories in the Baldrige criteria. Chapter 12 explains how to plan for a site visit by Baldrige examiners. The final chapter outlines alternative assessment approaches and how to use such assessments as an input to your strategic planning process.

A complete copy of the 2000 Award Criteria and Application Forms and Instructions are included in Appendix B. If you are not already familiar with the criteria, I suggest that you quickly review them as a means of preparing for reading and working with this text. For the purpose of actually applying for the award, you should familiarize yourself with *all* the information in this book and the criteria booklet. A copy of the criteria is available free of charge through the National Institute of Standards and Technology, Route 270 and Quince Orchard Road, Administration Bldg., Room A537, Gaithersburg, MD 20899-0001. It is also found on the Baldrige web site at: http://www.quality.nist.gov

How the Information for This Book Was Compiled

The information in this book was compiled on the basis of my experience as a Baldrige Award Examiner from 1990 through 1992. My experience as an examiner enabled me to review actual applications, discuss the examination process and award criteria with numerous other examiners, and participate in the Examiner Training Workshop in which examiners are trained to interpret the criteria. I also served as the lead judge for the California version of the Baldrige Award from 1994 through 1996, and continue to conduct training for potential examiners in California. The text is not an official publication of the National Institute of Standards and Technology, and the suggestions and opinions in it are my own.

The information in this book also draws upon my consulting experience, in which I help companies develop their own improvement processes based upon the Baldrige criteria. I have been consulting with companies such as Ford, IBM, Motorola, Unisys, Cargill, Ericsson, as well as the U.S. Army, Coast Guard, Navy and Department of Energy.

Additional Notes to the Reader

Because the Baldrige Examiners are not allowed to disclose any information contained in award applications, all of the examples used in this text are fictitious. Some are based upon actual applications but are thoroughly disguised so as to protect the anonymity of the applicants. Some companies have volunteered or have made public specific information about their experiences in challenging for the Award. These companies have been mentioned by name.

Future Volumes

Revised and updated editions of this work are planned for each year, assuming that the Baldrige Award criteria continue to be revised and improved each year. Suggestions on how we might improve the 2001 version of this book are welcome, and should be directed to:

Mark Graham Brown
c/o Productivity Inc.
A Division of The Kraus Organization Limited
444 Park Avenue South, Suite 604
New York, NY 10016

Chapter 1

Understanding the
Malcolm Baldrige
National Quality Award

The Malcolm Baldrige Award is the highest honor any business can receive, and after 13 years has remained very difficult to win. As the criteria have changed over the years, the Baldrige has become an award for overall effectiveness of an organization, as opposed to an organization that simply has high quality products/services. The Baldrige process allows winners and nonwinners alike to receive feedback on how well they meet the criteria. The overall purpose of the Baldrige Award application and award process is to strengthen the competitiveness of U.S. companies. According to the 2000 criteria booklet, the award process plays three additional roles:

- *To help improve performance practices and capabilities.*
- *To facilitate communication and sharing of best practices information among U.S. organizations of all types.*
- *To serve as a working tool for understanding and managing performance, planning, and training. (p. 1)*

The dual goals of the Baldrige criteria are to improve value to customers, which results in marketplace success, and to improve overall financial and company performance to meet the needs of shareholders, owner, and other stakeholders. Baldrige winners have shown that it is not necessary to trade off financial results for satisfied employees or customers. Baldrige winners have demonstrated that they can achieve exemplary financial results, delight their customers, and provide their employees with a good work environment. This balance is what the 2000 Baldrige criteria are all about.

The 2000 Baldrige criteria are quite different from earlier versions of the criteria. The Baldrige program is evolving toward an overall model of how to run a successful business. The criteria are much less detailed in prescribing particular approaches such as TQM or teamwork. More emphasis is placed on the results an organization has achieved than in the past. In the 2000 criteria, 55% of the points are linked to a company's approaches and the deployment of those approaches. The other 45% of the points are for the results the company achieves. The Baldrige model is becoming more like the European Award, where the breakdown is 50/50, between results and approaches.

The people that run the Baldrige Award have done an excellent job over the years in listening to business leaders and looking at what has worked and not worked. Benchmarking, reengineering, problem solving teams, quality planning, and a variety of other management programs turned out not to be the silver bullets that some of us thought they were a few years ago. The Baldrige criteria have reflected those lessons learned, and tried to refrain from jumping on the bandwagon with some of these fads. However, many of the trappings of TQM programs were very much a part of the early Baldrige criteria. The word *quality* was first removed from the criteria in 1995, and continues to be absent in 2000. More information on the changes to Baldrige for 2000 may be found later in this chapter.

The existence of the Baldrige Award is based upon Public Law 100-107, which creates a public-private partnership designed to encourage quality from American companies. The Findings and Purposes sections of Public Law 100-107 state that:

1. The leadership of the United States in product and process quality has been challenged strongly (and sometimes successfully) by foreign competition, and our Nation's productivity growth has improved less than our competitors' over the past two decades.

2. American business and industry are beginning to understand that poor quality costs companies as much as 20 percent of sales revenues nationally and that improved quality of goods and services goes hand in hand with improved productivity, lower costs, and increased profitability.

3. Strategic planning for quality and quality improvement programs, through a commitment to excellence in manufacturing and services, are becoming more and more essential to the well-being of our Nation's economy and our ability to compete effectively in the global marketplace.

4. Improved management understanding of the factory floor, worker involvement in quality, and greater emphasis on statistical process control can lead to dramatic improvements in the cost and quality of manufactured products.

5. The concept of quality improvement is directly applicable to small companies as well as large, to service industries as well as manufacturing, and to the public sector as well as private enterprise.

6. In order to be successful, quality improvement programs must be management-led and customer-oriented, and this may require fundamental changes in the way companies and agencies do business.

7. Several major industrial nations have successfully coupled rigorous private-sector quality audits with national awards giving special recognition to those enterprises the audits identify as the very best; and

8. A national quality award program of this kind in the United States would help improve quality and productivity by:

    A. Helping to stimulate American companies to improve quality and productivity for the pride of recognition while obtaining a competitive edge through increased profits;

    B. Recognizing the achievements of those companies that improve the quality of their goods and services and providing an example to others;

    C. Establishing guidelines and criteria that can be used by business, industrial, governmental, and other organizations in evaluating their own quality improvement efforts; and

    D. Providing specific guidance for other American organizations that wish to learn how to manage for high quality by making available detailed information on how winning organizations were able to change their cultures and achieve eminence.

The Award is managed by the National Institute for Standards and Technology (NIST), which is part of the Department of Commerce and is named for Malcolm Baldrige, who served as Secretary of Commerce from 1981 until his tragic death in a rodeo accident in 1987. His managerial excellence contributed to long-term improvement in efficiency and effectiveness of government.

The actual award is quite impressive. It is a three-part Steuben Glass crystal stele, standing 14 inches tall, with a 22-karat gold-plated medal embedded in the middle of the central crystal. This prestigious award is presented to winners by the president of the United States at a special ceremony in Washington, D.C.

WHO CAN WIN THE AWARD?

The award program is set up so there can be a maximum of 9 winners each year—three large manufacturing companies, three large service companies, and three small businesses, which may be either manufacturing or service. In previous years, the award was limited to two recipients in each category, so one additional winner in each of the three categories is possible in 2000. This may, however, not make much difference because there have never been even two winners in each category. In 1999, there were two large manufacturer winners, two service companies, and no small businesses.

Fewer big companies seem interested in winning the prize, but most of these large corporations continue to use the Baldrige criteria to assess and improve their businesses. Ford, AT&T, 3M, Johnson & Johnson, Ericsson, Cargill, and most of the world's most successful companies use Baldrige to assess their health and identify opportunities for future improvement.

AWARD WINNERS: 1988 to 1999

1999 Award Winners

Manufacturing
STMicroelectronics
Carrollton, TX
Sunny Fresh Foods
Monticello, MN

Service
Ritz-Carlton Hotel Company
Atlanta, GA
BI
Minneapolis, MN

1998 Award Winners

Manufacturing
Solar Turbines, Inc.
San Diego, CA
Boeing Airlift and Tanker Programs
Long Beach, CA

Small Business
Texas Nameplate
Dallas, TX

1997 Award Winners

Manufacturing
3M Dental Products
St. Paul, MN
Solectron Corporation
Milpitas, CA

Service
Merrill Lynch Credit Corporation
Jacksonville, FL
Xerox Business Services
Rochester, NY

1996 Award Winners

Manufacturing
ADAC Laboratories
Milpitas, CA

Service
Dana Commercial Credit Corp.
Toledo, OH

Small Business
Custom Research, Inc.
Minneapolis, MN
Trident Precision Manufacturing, Inc.
Webster, NY

1995 Award Winners

Manufacturing
Corning Telecommunications
Products Division
Armstrong Building Products
Operations
Lancaster, PA

1994 Award Winners

Service
AT&T Consumer Communications
Basking Ridge, NJ
GTE Directories
Dallas/Ft. Worth, TX

Small Business
Wainwright Industries
St. Peters, MO

1993 Award Winners

Manufacturing
Eastman Chemical Company
Kingsport, TN

Small Business
Ames Rubber Corp.
Hamburg, NJ

1992 Award Winners

Manufacturing
AT&T Network Systems Group
Transmission Systems Business Unit
Morristown, NJ
Texas Instruments, Inc.
Defense Systems & Electronics
Group
Dallas, TX

Service
AT&T Universal Card Services
Jacksonville, FL
The Ritz-Carlton Hotel Company
Atlanta, GA

Small Business
Granite Rock Company
Watsonville, CA

1991 Award Winners

Manufacturing
Solectron Corp.
San Jose, CA

Zytec Corp.
Eden Prairie, MN

Small Business
Marlow Industries
Dallas, TX

1990 Award Winners

Manufacturing
Cadillac Motor Car Company
Detroit, MI
IBM Rochester
Rochester, MN

Service
Federal Express Corp.
Memphis, TN

Small Business
Wallace Co., Inc.
Houston, TX

1989 Award Winners

Manufacturing
Milliken & Company
Spartanburg, SC
Xerox Business Products and Systems
Stamford, CT

1988 Award Winners

Manufacturing
Motorola, Inc.
Schaumburg, IL
Westinghouse Commercial
Nuclear Fuel Division
Pittsburgh, PA

Small Business
Globe Metallurgical, Inc.
Cleveland, OH

APPLICATION AND EVALUATION PROCESS

Applicants for the Baldrige Award must write up to a 50-page application (down from the 70 pages allowed in 1996) that explains how they run their business and present the business results they have achieved. The report is divided into seven sections, corresponding to the seven categories of criteria for the award:

1. Leadership	(12.5%)
2. Strategic Planning	(8.5%)
3. Customer and Market Focus	(8.5%)
4. Information and Analysis	(8.5%)
5. Human Resource Focus	(8.5%)
6. Process Management	(8.5%)
7. Business Results	(45%)

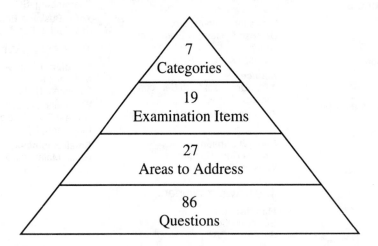

Figure 1.1: Hierarchy of Award Criteria

Each category is weighted according to its importance in the overall evaluation. As you can see, category 7 is worth almost half the points, whereas most of the other categories are only worth 8.5% each.

The seven categories are further broken down into 19 Examination Items, which are themselves broken down into 27 Areas to Address; and 86 Questions; see Figure 1.1.

The application report needs to address each of the 27 Areas to Address and 86 Questions separately. All Areas to Address should be covered by all organizations. However, an applicant does not lose credit if one or more Areas to Address do not pertain to his/her business. If an item is not relevant, the applicant must explain why, however. With the changes made to the criteria for 2000, it is highly unlikely that one or more of the Areas to Address will not be applicable to an organization. Chapters 5 through 11 of this book explain each of the criteria in detail, so that you can better understand what the examiners are looking for.

Evaluation

Figure 1.2 depicts the four-stage review process that occurs once an organization has submitted an application.

In Stage 1, all applications are reviewed by at least five members of the Board of Examiners. The board is composed of approximately 250 examiners selected from business, professional, and trade associations; universities; and government. All members are recognized experts in the fields of business or organizational improvement. When assigning board members to review applications, the experience and industry background of the examiner are matched to the applicant, provided that there is no conflict of interest. Examiners with manufacturing backgrounds receive applications from manufacturing companies and examiners with service industry experience receive service company applications. Board members must follow strict rules regarding the confidentiality of applications, and must agree to abide by a code of ethics, which includes nondisclosure of information from applicants. Examiners are not even allowed to reveal the names of companies that have applied for the award.

In Stage 2, the scored applications are then submitted to a Senior Examiner who reviews the variability in scoring, identifies major discrepancies, and schedules a consensus meeting. Much like a jury, the examiners must reach consensus on your score. A consensus meeting is held via conference call or in person, and is led by a senior examiner. Senior examiners are responsible for supervising the team of examiners

---

STAGE 1: INDEPENDENT REVIEW AND EVALUATION BY AT LEAST FIVE MEMBERS OF THE BOARD

STAGE 2: CONSENSUS REVIEW AND EVALUATION FOR APPLICATIONS THAT SCORE WELL IN STAGE 1

STAGE 3: SITE VISITS TO APPLICANTS THAT SCORE WELL IN STAGE 2

STAGE 4: JUDGES' REVIEW AND RECOMMENDATIONS

Figure 1.2: Four-Stage Review Process

assigned to review each company. A recommendation is made as to whether or not a site visit is warranted. A panel of judges decides whether or not to accept the recommendation, or to have the application reviewed by other examiners.

Of the 1,000 points possible to earn on an application, the majority of applications receive scores of less than 500 points. As a general rule, if an application receives a score of 601 or above, the organization is considered to have made it to the semifinals, and might qualify for a site visit. The 600 or above points is not a hard rule about who receives a site visit, only a general guideline based on what's happened in the past. During a site visit, Stage 3, a team of five or more examiners spends approximately three to five days in your facilities touring, conducting interviews, and reviewing data and records. Applicants are asked to make introductory and concluding presentations. The site visit is similar to having an audit done. The purpose of the site visit is to verify and clarify the information included in your written application and to resolve any issues or uncertainties that came up in reviewing your written application. The examiners may have accepted what you said in your written application at face value, but now they want to see proof of your claims.

The findings of the site visit are summarized in a site visit report that goes to the Baldrige Award judges for the Stage 4 review. It is during this review that the judges decide which applicants they will recommend in each category to be award winners. The panel of judges makes its recommendations to the National Institute of Standards and Technology, which makes final recommendations to the U.S. Secretary of Commerce. Those serving as judges are known nationally for their expertise in the quality field and have typically served as examiners or senior examiners in the past.

At the end of the calendar year, feedback reports are sent out to all Baldrige Award applicants. Regardless of the score, each applicant receives a detailed feedback report that summarizes the strengths and weaknesses identified by the examiners in their review of the application. Feedback reports are probably the most valuable result of applying for the award because they provide very specific information on the areas in which you excel and the areas that you need to work on. In fact, the feedback report is probably the best bargain in consulting services that you could buy. It costs $4,500 for large companies to apply for the Baldrige Award and $1,500 for small businesses. For that fee, you get five to six highly trained quality experts to review your company and prepare a detailed analysis of its strengths and weaknesses. If you wanted to purchase this service from an outside consulting firm, it may cost between $10,000 and $25,000, depending upon the size of your organization and the number of consultants involved. So, for $4,500 you receive a wealth of valuable information. In fact, many organizations realize that they are far from being at the level required to win the Baldrige Award, but apply anyway. That way, they can find out exactly where they need to focus their improvement efforts in the next few years.

WHAT THE EXAMINERS ARE REALLY LOOKING FOR

The three factors (or "evaluation dimensions") that the Baldrige Examiners look for in each section of an application are your:

- Approach

- Deployment

- Results

Approach refers to the processes you use to run your organization. Clearly there are certain themes that the Baldrige people look for in your approach:

- The degree to which the approach is logical given your business

- Focus on continuous improvement

- The appropriateness and effectiveness of the methods, tools, and techniques to the requirements

- The degree to which the approach is systematic, integrated, and consistently applied

- The degree to which the approach embodies effective evaluation/improvement cycles

- The degree to which the approach is based upon research that is objective and reliable

- The indicators of unique and innovative approaches, including significant and effective new adaptations of tools and techniques used in other applications or types of businesses

Deployment refers to how well your approach has been executed. It is possible that an organization has an exceptional approach, but it has only been implemented in a few areas. Some of the overall indicators for assessing deployment are:

- The appropriate and effective application of the stated approach to all product and service features

- The appropriate and effective application of the stated approach by all work units to all processes and activities

- The appropriate and effective application of the stated approach to all transactions and interactions with customers, suppliers of goods and services, and the public

Results are clearly *not* asked for in six of the seven Baldrige categories. In fact, one of the big changes in 1997 was that results are only asked for in Category 7.0: Business Results, which breaks out into the following items:

- 7.1 Customer Focused Results

- 7.2 Financial and Market Results

- 7.3 Human Resource Results

- 7.4 Supplier and Partner Results

- 7.5 Organizational Effectiveness Results

Some specific factors that are examined when evaluating results are:

- Current and past performance levels

- The demonstration of sustained improvement or sustained high-level performance

- Demonstration of cause/effect between company approaches and results

- The rate/speed of performance improvement

- The breadth and importance of performance improvements across units, products, service

- Significance of quality improvements to the company's business

- The performance levels relative to appropriate competitors, comparisons, and/or benchmarks

Each of the 27 Areas to Address that are described in Chapters 5–11 of this book is identified as to whether it pertains to approach, deployment, or results (see brackets [ ]).

RESPONSIBILITIES AND BENEFITS OF WINNING THE BALDRIGE AWARD

Winning the Baldrige Award may be the dream of a number of companies' CEOs and executives. However, winning brings with it a great deal of responsibility. One price of winning is that you must share your approach to quality with others. As an award winner, you will be inundated with requests for information, tours, etc. Everyone will want to know how you did it, how much money you spent implementing total quality management, how much time it takes, and how they can take what you have done and apply it to their own companies. According to an article in the April 23, 1990, issue of *Fortune,* Richard Beutow, Motorola's vice president for quality, made 352 speeches to conventions and corporations, and answered requests for information from over 1,000 companies (p. 109). All of the award winners report similar interest and responses. So if you win, you must be prepared to share your secrets of success with the world, and be prepared to devote several full-time people to the task of responding to requests for information on how you won the Baldrige Award. According to Janet Fit of *USA Today:*

> *For some companies the onslaught can be overwhelming. "We've traveled tens of thousands of miles and made thousands of presentations," says Winston Chen, president of Solectron until he retired in March. Solectron won in 1991. "It's actually quite a bit of a burden. We chose to only do what we could afford to do."* *(October 19, 1994, p. 4-B)*

The benefits of winning, however, far outweigh the costs. Winners are allowed to publicize the award as much as they want to their customers. Xerox, for example, includes the Baldrige logo on all of its correspondence and product literature. This does wonders for promoting their image as a quality company. Motorola has taken similar advantage of the opportunity to advertise its quality achievements. Winners receive a great deal of peer recognition from other executives, competitors, and the entire business community. Winning is probably the best thing that can happen to a company to promote a positive quality image. Another benefit of winning is the impact the award has upon employee morale. Employees of Motorola, Xerox, Ritz-Carlton, Federal Express, AT&T, and the other award winners have long known that they worked for a quality company. But did the world know? Winning the award tells their business relations, neighbors, relatives, friends, and competitors that they work for one of the best companies in the world.

WHAT'S NEW IN THE 2000 CRITERIA

The core criteria have not changed at all in the 2000 edition of the Baldrige Award. The categories, items, areas to address, and questions are the same as in 1999, word for word. Some subtle changes were made to the definitions of the categories and to the items, but the changes are very minor, improving clarity rather than changing focus. I usually devote an entire chapter to annual changes, which are often substantial. In 1999, I updated nearly 100 pages to reflect changes in the criteria. The fact that NIST has made no changes to the criteria for 2000 indicates that the Baldrige criteria have become a mature system. In some of the previous years, changes were made for what appeared to be the sake of change. For example, what used to be an "a" and "b" area to address was moved into a single "a" without removing any of the words. Such changes, which do nothing to improve the criteria, often occur in any document written by a committee.

In 1999, the criteria underwent a fairly heavy copy edit and all the criteria were turned into questions that must be answered by the applicant. The wordy sentences with eight commas, three semicolons, and four subpoints are still found in the criteria from time to time, but they are far less prevalent than they used to be.

Core Values

Although the criteria have evolved into a tight system needing few updates, other parts of the criteria booklet issued by the government have not enjoyed the same evaluation and improvement cycles. In the 2000 criteria, changes have been made to the core values and concepts upon which the Baldrige model is based. The new set of core values, which is described in Chapter 3, better represents the new criteria. The old version of the core values retained some of the TQM flavor from previous versions of the criteria. The new core values are much more business focused and less prescriptive about the approaches Baldrige examiners expect to see in an organization.

There are still 11 core values, but a number of the old ones have been replaced with improved versions. *Visionary Leadership* replaces the old *Leadership,* which was always too generic and intuitive. The authors of the criteria removed *Customer-Driven Quality* and replaced it with *Customer-Driven.* This change was made to acknowledge the fact that customers might be driven by many factors other than quality, including low price, delivery, or selection. The 2000 criteria replace the old *Continuous Improvement and Learning* with the new *Organizational and Personal Learning,* which sounds even more like buzzwords than the old version.

Some other changes to the core values are more substantive. The old *Valuing Employees* has been changed to *Valuing Employees and Partners* to reflect the importance of treating as true partners suppliers and other collaborating groups. *Agility* replaces the old *Fast Response,* which was much narrower in its focus. The best companies today need to be agile, capable of changing business practices as the environment changes. Two new core values have been added to the 2000 version of the criteria: *Managing for Innovation* and *Systems Perspective.* Two others remain the same as they were in 1999: *Management by Fact,* and *Public Responsibility and Citizenship.* Although the remaining two core values, *Focus on Future* and *Focus on Results and Creating Value,* have changed slightly, the changes are more word-smithing than anything substantive in what is being required of organizations that do well against the criteria.

Additions to the Glossary

The Baldrige criteria always have contained a number of technical terms and management words that were difficult to understand by many. The following new terms have been added to the 2000 glossary to help the reader to determine their exact meaning: *analysis, approach, deployment, empowerment, results, strategic objectives,* and *systematic.*

Category and Item Descriptions

The criteria booklet contains two different versions of the category and item descriptions. The actual criteria with all the areas to address and questions can be found between pages 9 and 26 of the 2000 criteria booklet, which appears at the back of this book. This is the part of the criteria that did not change from 1999 to 2000 and is the part from which an application is written. A more detailed explanation of the seven Baldrige categories and the items appears on pages 30-43. This information is similar to the main text of this book, in that it is an explanation of each section of the Baldrige criteria, why it is important, and what is being asked for. This section of the 2000 Baldrige booklet has been revised and is much easier to understand than in previous years. Each item description is broken down into subheads, defining its *Purpose, Requirements,* and *Comments.* Breaking the information down into these three sections makes the criteria much more understandable and is a good improvement over the 1999 text.

Chapter 2

Preparing an Application
for the Baldrige Award

Preparing an application for the Malcom Baldrige Award is a great deal of work. In fact, the time invested in creating this 50-page proposal is what intimidates many potential applicants. Although the size of the application was reduced from 70 to 50 pages several years ago, most applicants go through at least four or five drafts before sending off the final document to Washington, D.C. Some state award programs have been sensitive to the time commitment for preparing a full 50-page application and have developed separate categories for organizations just getting started using the Baldrige criteria, and asked for a 25 page or less document. Arizona is one of the state quality award programs that pioneered this abbreviated award, and the process is now being used by other states such as California and New Mexico.

The quality level of Baldrige Award applications varies considerably. Some are expertly written, contain only pertinent information, and are printed in four colors, so they look like an annual report. Others are poorly written, are missing information, and are typed on an old typewriter. The quality of your company is being judged based upon the quality of this report, so it is crucial that the application report be complete, clear, and error-free. In this chapter, I outline some major issues on how the application should be written and provide guidelines concerning mistakes to avoid when preparing your application. Examples are provided to help illustrate what to do and what not to do.

As a special note to readers, I suggest that the information provided in this chapter be reviewed in conjunction with the information contained in the 2000 Criteria and Application Forms and Instructions for the Malcolm Baldrige National Quality Award. Reproductions of these documents appear in the back of this text. An original set is available free of charge from the National Institute of Standards and Technology (see Appendixes A and B).

GENERAL OUTLINE OF THE MAJOR COMPONENTS OF THE APPLICATION PACKAGE

Your 2000 application package must contain all required forms including (1) the Eligibility Determination Form (which must already have been approved); (2) the Application Form; and (3) the Site Listing and Descriptors Form. These forms are available in the 2000 Application Forms and Instructions booklet, as are complete instructions on how to prepare them.

Your application package must also contain an application report. The application report consists of a 5-page overview of your business and a 50-page document that is generally divided into seven major sections, corresponding to the seven categories of criteria. In this document you must respond to and address all of the Examination Items and Areas to Address as presented in the criteria. If you are in the small business category your written document is limited to 50 single-sided pages (the 5-page overview is not counted as part of the page limit). This 50-page limit includes charts, graphs, tables, and any supporting materials you decide to attach to your application. The examiners are very strict on this guideline. If your application report contains 60 pages, the Baldrige administrators will probably tear off the last 10 pages before sending the application to the examiners to review. It will be very difficult to respond to all of the criteria within 50 pages, so you may need to employ a ruthless editor.

You may also be required to submit Supplemental Sections as a part of your application report. According to the Award Criteria, these are required when the applicant is a unit within a company that is in many different businesses. The Award Criteria booklet at the back of this book provides more details on this.

The major components of your application package should be organized into logical and clearly defined sections, such as:

- Application and Other Forms
- Overview
- 1.0 Leadership
- 2.0 Strategic Planning
- 3.0 Customer and Market Focus
- 4.0 Information and Analysis
- 5.0 Human Resource Focus
- 6.0 Process Management
- 7.0 Business Results
- Supplementary Sections (if required)

HOW TO WRITE THE APPLICATION

The way most internal users and award applicants approach writing the application is to form seven teams to work on each of the seven sections in the application. A project manager oversees the effort and attempts to edit the final document to make it appear as if it were written by one person. Although by far the most common approach, it is also the reason why most internal users and award applicants receive such low scores. *Using seven teams and/or individuals to work on each of the seven sections in the application is a major mistake.*

The seven categories of Baldrige criteria work together as a *system*. They are not seven independent factors. One of the most common problems appearing in Baldrige applications is what I call "disconnects." Disconnects are inconsistencies between sections. For example, an applicant might report in section 4.1 that they collect data on three different measures of customer satisfaction, but include no goals for these measures in section 2.2 and no graphs of results in section 7.1. *All seven sections need to be consistent and work together as a system.*

So, how do you ensure that all sections work together effectively? One answer is to have one person write the entire application. Although this is not feasible in many large and complex organizations, it has been done. Marty Smith, of New England Telephone, was the primary author of that company's Baldrige application. Marty had a committee that assisted in gathering information in writing the application, but he did the majority of the project coordination and writing himself. Several small companies that have won Baldrige Awards submitted applications written primarily by the CEOs.

In most large complex organizations it simply is not practical to have a single person write the application, so some type of team must be formed. But if forming teams around each of the seven Baldrige categories is not the way to organize the effort, how should it be done? A recent client of mine put together an application for the award by forming teams as follows:

TEAM A: Section 1.0 Leadership
TEAM B: Section 5.0 Human Resource Focus
TEAM C: Sections 2.0 Strategic Planning and 4.0 Information and Analysis
TEAM D: Sections 3.0 Customer and Market Focus and 6.0 Process
        Management
TEAM E: Section 7.0 Business Results

Sections 1.0 and 4.0 in the Baldrige system are the easiest ones to work on independently of the other sections. The approach of dividing into the five teams as listed above worked fairly well in this case, but Teams C, D, and E had to work closely with one another. Team E (results) did not write its sections until the planning and measurement team (C) finished its section.

Another organization I worked with organized two small teams and one large team to prepare their Baldrige Award application:

TEAM A: 1.0
TEAM B: 5.0
TEAM C: 2.0, 3.0, 4.0, 6.0, 7.0

This approach also worked well and helped to ensure that the seven sections flowed together well. Granted, the third team that had five sections had a lot of work to do, but it was a larger team than the other two and was prepared for the bigger effort.

MANAGING THE APPLICATION DEVELOPMENT PROJECT

Regardless of how you choose to put together teams to write the application, you will undoubtedly need a steering committee to oversee and approve the application, as well as a project manager to coordinate the effort. The steering committee should consist of 4 to 7 executives, including the CEO and his/her direct reports. These individuals may not have any involvement in writing the application, but they should provide access to any data needed by those writing each section and review the completed report. The steering committee members allocate resources to write the application and make any decisions regarding policies and the divulgence of confidential information. Steering committee members should plan on attending a minimum of two 4- to 8-hour meetings and spending an additional 6–8 hours reviewing various sections of the application.

Once the steering committee has been formed, select a project manager. In some organizations, the vice president of quality is chosen. In others, a function manager or director fills the position. The job this individual currently has is not important. What is important is that this individual have a good overall knowledge of the entire organization, know quality concepts, have good rapport with other managers, and pay great attention to detail. The project manager is responsible for seeing that the individuals working on various sections of the application meet their deadlines and adhere to key quality standards. The project manager serves as the liaison between the steering committee and a group of representatives from the teams who will make up an award application committee.

The number of people who participate on the award application committee will depend upon the size and complexity of your organization and how you decide to divide into teams. Figure 2.1 depicts a typical structure of the teams/committees that work on preparing the Baldrige application.

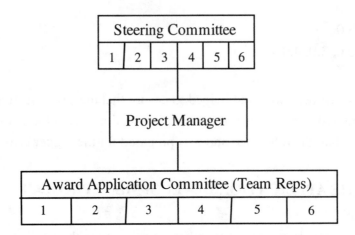

**Figure 2.1: Typical Organization Structure for
Baldrige Application Committee/Team**

Select people to work on the award application committee who are knowledgeable of the area/category they have been assigned and possess excellent writing skills. This will consume a great deal of time over the months that it takes to polish the application, so it is important that their bosses release them from some of their other responsibilities.

It is also a good idea to form a team of individuals responsible for editing and formatting the various sections of the application, creating graphics, doing word processing, and coordinating the reproduction and binding of the application. These tasks are time-consuming, yet important. And it is important that the application look good and be error-free. The leader of the application production team should be a member of the award application committee and attend all key meetings.

The first task on the project manager's and the award application committee's agenda is to hold a meeting to create a project plan for the development and production of the application. A project plan is a detailed list of tasks, resources, estimates, and deadlines. It specifies the person(s) responsible and the amount of time allocated for performing each task. This serves as the basis from which a project can be built. The project plan can be created during a meeting facilitated by the project manager. An example of such a plan is shown in Figure 2.2. The numbers listed in the columns represent the time estimates (in days) for the various people who will work on the application. The plan presented is based upon using a seven-person award application committee. Time estimates apply to each person on the committees, and are based upon the assumption that quality assurance systems are already in place.

Project Plan
Baldrige Award Application

Tasks	Responsibilities & Time Requirements						Schedule
	PM	AAC	PROD	EDIT	SC	REV	
1. Project Planning Meeting							
a. Prepare for meeting	0.75	-	0.25	-	-	-	
b. Conduct/attend meeting	1.0	1.0	-	-	-	-	
c. Write Project Plan	1.0	-	1.0	0.25	-	-	
d. Review/Revise Project Plan	0.25	0.25	0.25	-	0.25	-	
2. Conduct Interviews and Gather Data	2.0	3.0	-	-	-	-	
3. Write First Drafts of Application Sections	2.0	2.5	5.0	4.0	-	-	
4. Review First Drafts	-	-	-	-	1.0	1.0	
5. Complete Mock Evaluations	0.5	-	-	-	-	2.0	
6. First Draft Feedback							
a. Assemble Reviewers' comments and evaluations	2.0	-	1.5	1.0	-	-	
b. Conduct/attend Feedback Meeting	2.0	2.0	-	-	-	-	
c. Document meeting outputs	1.0	-	2.0	-	-	-	
7. Write Second Drafts of Application Sections	1.5	1.5	-	3.0	-	-	
8. Production of Application Report							
a. Prepare and conduct/attend Production Planning Meeting	1.0	-	0.5	-	-	-	
b. Produce artwork, graphics, and printing specifications	1.5	-	4.0	0.5	-	-	
c. Printing of Final Award Applications	0.5	-	1.0	-	-	-	
9. Review Final Materials, Complete Forms, Prepare Overview, and Submit Application	1.5	0.5	1.5	0.5	0.5	-	4/3
TOTALS (days)	18.5	10.75	17.0	9.25	1.75	3.0	

KEY		
	PM = Project Manager	EDIT = Editors
	AAC = Award Application Committee	SC = Steering Committee
	PROD = Production/Graphics	REV = Reviewers

Figure 3.2: Project Workplan

As you can see in Figure 2.2, the plan includes a detailed list of tasks for each committee member or subcommittee. This plan is the project manager's tool for tracking the progress of the committee members. Many applicants don't bother to create such a plan and end up missing deadlines or having to race around at the last minute to complete the application in order to get it out by the June 1 deadline.

The best way to approach the application report is to look at each Examination Item and Area to Address separately. For each one, make a list of the data or resources needed for reference in order to prepare your response. For any Area to Address that asks for trends or data, you should also make a list of the graphs or charts you will need to prepare. This can be done in the committee meeting by listing the information on flipcharts, as demonstrated in Figure 2.3.

If you are working with several subcommittees, it may be necessary to assign information-gathering tasks to specific individuals. At the conclusion of the initial

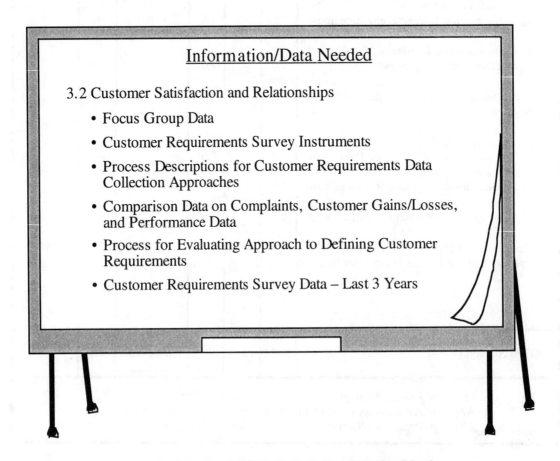

Figure 2.3: Example Flipchart From a Planning Meeting

meeting, the project manager should formalize the project plan and distribute it to all award committee and steering committee members.

Gathering the information necessary to write the various sections of the Baldrige Award is the most difficult and time-consuming task. Rarely will an organization have all the data needed readily at hand. Some data may not exist anywhere in the organization and may need to be collected. A number of departments and individuals within the organization may need to be contacted to collect all of the information needed to write each section of the application. The biggest problem experienced by committees working on the Baldrige application is lack of cooperation from other employees and managers who must dig up the information or data needed. This is one of the reasons that it is important to have high-level individuals on the steering committee. If the CEO or one of the vice presidents calls a manager to ask him or her where the data are that you requested in order to write your section of the award application, you can bet that the delinquent manager will get the information quickly.

All first drafts of sections of the application report should be turned in to the project manager, who will review them for accuracy, completeness, and clarity. He or she will return the edited copy of first drafts to the committee members who wrote them. The writers will then make the corrections suggested by the project manager and resubmit the application sections. If the project manager is satisfied that all of the necessary changes have been made, the material will be turned over to an editor who will edit the grammar, consistency, headings, readability, and other factors. After the sections have been edited, they will be turned over to production for word processing and preparation of graphics.

Once the report has been produced, internal copies should be prepared and distributed to the steering committee members and other key managers and technical professionals for their review. It is also a good idea to give the application to a few relatively new employees who have industry experience but little knowledge of the organization. These individuals can review the manuscript and the practices of your organization more objectively.

In addition to having many different people review the application and provide their feedback, it is also a good idea to train a group of people to actually evaluate the application against the Baldrige criteria. This might be a group of outside consultants or a group of your own employees. Whoever you select to perform this evaluation should be familiar with the Baldrige criteria and be objective in their evaluation of the organization's application.

Feedback from reviewers and evaluations of the application should all be returned to the project manager by a specified date. After assembling and summarizing all of the comments, suggestions, and scores of the evaluators, the project manager should plan a two-day meeting with the award application committee to review the feedback and discuss changes and additions needed to each of their sections, as well as any overall comments that pertain to all sections. As each section is reviewed, the project manager should record the changes needed in each Area to Address to satisfy the reviewers' suggestions and to improve on the scores given during the mock evaluation.

Following the meeting, the committee members revise their assigned sections based upon the action items and suggestions outlined in the meeting. Final drafts are submitted to the project manager for review and to the editor for final editing. The entire application should then be given to production so that the layout, cover, tabs, and any other aspects of the final document can be designed. Some applicants custom-design a cover and special tabs for their applications, but this is definitely not necessary. In fact, an application that looks *too* slick may make the examiners suspect that the applicant is perhaps substituting flash for substance. Final artwork is then done, the materials are thoroughly proofread, and the application is printed and bound.

Then, the tough part comes—the waiting. Applications are due on June 1 and you won't receive feedback for several months. This can be very frustrating, but the review process takes a long time.

Figure 2.4 provides a graphic representation of the major steps involved in completing an application. The exact process you use will no doubt vary somewhat from this. A mock evaluation by people trained on the Baldrige criteria is an important step that you should not leave out. Many organizations don't do this because they lack time or expertise. Lack of time shouldn't be a problem if you prepare the application far enough in advance. Lack of expertise is no excuse either. Universities and professional associations such as the American Society for Quality and the Association for Quality and Participation offer workshops on how to interpret the Baldrige criteria.

HOW TO WRITE THE APPLICATION REPORT

The main reason for writing this book is that many applicants and others using the Baldrige Award criteria misinterpret what the Areas to Address are requesting. Reading Chapters 5–11 of this book and using them as a reference when writing your responses to each of the 27 Areas to Address should help you to interpret the criteria accurately. In writing your report, it is important that you don't make the same mistakes made by many of the previous Baldrige Award applicants.

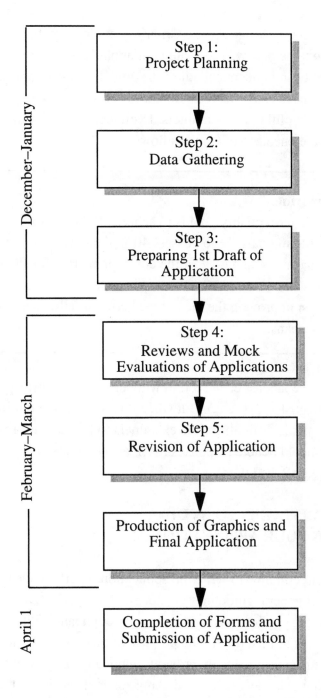

Figure 2.4: Application Development and Production Process

Pages 46–50 of the 2000 Baldrige Award Criteria provide some fairly specific instructions and advice about the best way to write your application. Make sure that you read these pages thoroughly and understand all of the guidelines. An important guideline that bears repeating is to make sure that you reference each section with the appropriate numbers and letters. It is helpful to the examiners if you include the Examination Items in your response, for reference. An example follows.

2.2 Strategy Deployment

2.2a. Anacon's long-term quality goal is to achieve 100% customer satisfaction. Some related long-term goals are to possess 40% of the domestic market for automated teller machines, and 60% of the domestic market for POS terminals. One of the requirements we must address is to improve the reliability of our products. We need to work on improving the mean time between failures as well as our overall product lifespans.

Several applicants have labeled each section with a number to correspond to the Examination Item (e.g., 4.2, 2.1, etc.). But when this is done without indicating *letters* for the Areas to Address, it is difficult for the examiners to find the information that pertains to each Area. You should denote responses to Areas by underscoring the Item/Area number and letter [e.g., 2.2a(1)].

TEN COMMON MISTAKES TO AVOID WHEN WRITING YOUR APPLICATION

The general guidelines on how to write the application report are clear and well written. However, sometimes general guidelines are not enough to effectively guide performance. Judging by some of the applications received, many applicants either misunderstood the guidelines or chose not to read them. The purpose of this portion of the book is to list and explain some of the mistakes made by previous applicants. By reviewing this information, you should be able to avoid making some of the errors that others have made in the past. I have listed and discussed 10 of the most common mistakes in the pages that follow. Some of these are minor errors, but most are mistakes that may cost you a large percentage of the points that otherwise might have been earned for a particular item.

Some of the information in this section is based upon the Baldrige Award Criteria. Other information is based upon my own and other examiners' experience in reviewing applications.

Mistake #1: Reiteration of Words From the Criteria

This is a technique that can enhance your score only if the examiner is not paying much attention to what he/she is reading. Examiners all have other jobs, so frequently they must review the applications in the evenings, after a long day of work. If your response includes some of the same words from the criteria, at first glance, it sounds like your response meets the criteria well. An examiner who is tired might just skim your response and give it a high score because it "sounds good." However, you must remember that up to six different examiners review each application. For every one or two who give you a higher score because your response includes words from the criteria, there will be others who will take points away for this. Repeating the criteria in your response is unnecessary.

Mistake #2: Use of Examples Rather Than Descriptions of Processes

This commonly occurs when the applicant does not have a systematic process to describe. A typical response starts out with a general statement such as: "We identify customer requirements in a variety of different ways." This is then followed by a detailed example of one situation where customer requirements have been identified. The problem with responding this way is that it doesn't tell the examiners how you identify customer requirements. If you do not describe a well-defined process in your response, chances are that you do not have a process, and customer requirements are identified in a casual and unsystematic manner. Whenever the criteria ask about processes, respond with a fairly detailed description of a step-by-step process or with a detailed flowchart.

Mistake #3: No Examples When They Will Help to Illustrate a Process

This is just the opposite of Mistake #2, using an example as your response. Including an example or two helps to clarify a flowchart or process description. Examples add interest and credibility to your process descriptions; just be certain that you have adequately described the process(es) before the example is used. When you use examples, make sure that you label them as such, and explain whether or not the situations you described are typical. Remember that the examiners have never seen your company and may not even be very familiar with your industry. Examples help to paint a picture for the examiner, making it easier for him/her to understand how your processes and approaches work.

Mistake #4: Lack of Specificity

Of all the mistakes made by applicants, this is the most common and the most severe. Answering all of the 27 Areas to Address thoroughly within 50 pages is tough. It is obvious that many applications have been ruthlessly edited to include only the most necessary information. Often, too much information is eliminated. A vague and general description of a process will earn few points from the examiners. An example of a non-specific response is shown in the following box.

2.2b(2) How do you follow up with customers on products/services and recent transactions to receive prompt and actionable feedback?

We pride ourselves at MGB Industries at being proactive in our approach to managing relationships with our customers. With our own sales force and our field representatives, we are in almost constant contact with our various customers to ensure that we are consistently meeting or exceeding their expectations. This sometimes daily telephone or face-to-face contact has allowed us to forge strong bonds with our customers, making it likely that we will be their supplier of choice for years to come. One example of this is Willow Manufacturing, who has been a customer of ours for the last 21 years.

There is nothing particularly wrong with what is said in this example. The problem is that the response is vague and nonspecific. It also includes an example of an isolated incident, rather than describing a system or process. The response is about as long as the criteria, and not enough information is provided to adequately judge how well the applicant is doing on this Area to Address. When a response is vague or nonspecific, examiners are taught to assign a low score. You don't need to provide pages and pages of information in response to each area. However, a sentence or two is usually not enough.

Mistake #5: Presenting Data on Only a Few Performance Indices/Measures

This is also a very common occurrence, and one that will cause you to lose a significant number of points. If you collect data on over 20 different indices of performance and report on only five or six of them, the examiners might assume that you have chosen to report on only the measures for which your performance is good. Data not reported are often assumed to be negative. In one case study used to train the Baldrige Examiners, the applicant claims to have 160 indices that are used to measure performance. Yet, the application presents data on only three or four of these indices and says nothing about performance levels for the other 150+ measures. Although it may not be practical to present data for 160 indices, a great deal of information can be summarized in a table or chart. Examples of how to do this are presented in Chapter 12: Interpreting the Criteria for Business Results.

Mistake #6: Too Many Cross-References to Other Sections

According to the directions in the 2000 Award Criteria, you should:

Cross-reference when appropriate.

> *Each Item response should, as much as possible, be self-contained. However, some responses to different Items might be mutually reinforcing. It is then appropriate to refer to the other responses, rather than to repeat information. In such cases, key process information should be given in the Item requesting this information. For example, employee education and training should be described in detail in Item 5.2. References elsewhere to education and training would then reference, but not repeat, this detail. (p. 47)*

The criteria further explain that you should not repeat information included elsewhere. You can cross-reference information if it will help enhance your response to a particular Area to Address. Make sure that you cite the page number, the Examination Item (number), and the specific Area to Address (letter). For example:

> *"Additional information on our overall approach to human resource management is presented on page 28, in section 5.1a."*

You should minimize the amount of cross-referencing that you do, however. It is very frustrating to the examiners to have to constantly flip back and forth from section to section. Because each of the Areas to Address is designed to stand on its own, it should not be necessary to cross-reference very often.

Mistake #7: Responding With Words When You Should Respond With Data

All of the Areas to Address in Category 7, ask for trends and results. Any time you see the words "trends," "results," or "data" in the criteria, this should be your clue to make sure your response includes graphs and data. It is surprising that this is misinterpreted, but applicants sometimes describe a *process* when the criteria specifically ask for *trends (data)*. Or, they give a narrative summary of their results with no graphs or statistics. A narrative summary of the information included in graphs is good, but it is not a substitute for hard data.

Mistake #8:   Responding With Information That Is Not Relevant to the Area to Address

This is also one of those mistakes that occurs quite frequently in the applications. It seems that either the applicants misunderstand some Areas to Address or that they understand them but have little to say in their response. Rather than admit something like: "We have not identified a process for tracking the degree to which customer requirements are met," applicants respond with some quality jargon that may seem good at first glance. But in reading it a second or third time one realizes that the response has nothing to do with what was asked for in the Area to Address.

An example of a response that is unrelated to the Area to Address is shown in box 2.2b(2) (following).

2.2b(1) What processes, measurement methods, and data do you use to determine customer satisfaction and dissatisfaction? Include how your measurements capture actionable information that reflects customers' future business and/or potential for positive referral. Also include any significant differences in processes or methods for different customer groups and/or market segments.

Customer satisfaction is our number one priority at Baker Industries. Every employee is expected to meet customer expectations for timely service and high quality products. We work in a collaborative fashion to systematically identify the ever-changing demands and expectations of our customers, and find ways of meeting those demands. Our quality and levels of customer satisfaction are unsurpassed in our industry, and continue to improve each year.

The Area to Address asks you to explain how the organization measures customer satisfaction. The example in the box does not discuss how customer satisfaction is measured. It only includes various "well written" phrases, which is typical of an application submitted by an organization that does not have the data to respond to an area. A response such as the one in the example would not earn any points, because there is no information that tells the reader how the company segments its customers and measures customer satisfaction.

Mistake #9: Use of Too Many Acronyms

I was once interviewing a man from AT&T on a consulting project, and I asked him to describe a particular process he was involved with, without using acronyms in his description. He just stuttered and couldn't explain the process without including a myriad of acronyms. Use of acronyms is very frustrating to the Baldrige Examiners. Everyone in your company may know what certain company-specific acronyms stand for, but the Baldrige Examiners won't. Spelling out what an acronym stands for the first time you use it will not solve the problem either. An examiner will forget and have to refer back to previous sections to recall what the CASE or AIP programs are. Avoid acronyms entirely if you can. This is tough for many large companies that have an acronym for every process, document, and program. An example of an acronym-laden response is shown in the following.

Our CEO, CIO, and CQO all strongly support the TQM effort at BMI through the initiation of a variety of programs such as the CCF (Customers Come First), AQP (Assessment of Quality Processes), and PTM (Participative Team Management). Our IIS and OEM Divisions have thoroughly implemented QFD using a variety of QITs (Quality Improvement Teams).

Many Baldrige applicants include a 2- to 3-page glossary of acronyms in their application. This is very frustrating to examiners. An application ought to be written in plain English without having to put a three-word title or three-letter acronym on every program and process.

Mistake #10: Use of Too Much Industry or Management Jargon

This irritates many of the Baldrige Examiners because it appears as though you are trying to impress them with your vocabulary. The application should be written at a fairly low reading level, about the same level used in an annual report to shareholders. It should not be written like a college textbook or a technical paper for a professional journal. Use of complicated words and jargon should be thoroughly discouraged. The Baldrige Examiners are probably as unfamiliar with your industry jargon as they are with your acronyms. To eliminate jargon, it is a good idea to have someone outside of your company, or new employees, review the application before it is finalized.

Even though the Baldrige Examiners may be familiar with management jargon such as "Balanced Scorecard" or "Activity-Based Costing," it is best not to overuse these terms either. Write the application as if it were to be read by shareholders or the general public. A tenth- to twelfth-grade reading level is appropriate. This is the same level as a magazine such as *U.S. News and World Report.*

Similarly, you may want to avoid using trendy management words and phrases such as

- Reengineering
- Intrapreneuring
- Cross-functional management
- Participative team process
- Delayering
- Outsourcing

- Value engineering
- Best-case scenario
- Competitive advantage
- Right-sizing
- Empowerment
- Performance-based management

TEN RULES TO USE WHEN PREPARING GRAPHICS FOR YOUR APPLICATION

Up to this point we have been discussing the writing style of the application and common mistakes made when preparing the written response. Let's now turn our attention to graphics, which are also a big part of the application. So many of the applications contain poor and hard-to-read graphics that this subject warrants separate treatment and guidelines. I have outlined ten rules to keep in mind when preparing and discussing graphics in your application.

Rule #1: Explain Graphics in the Text

Some applicants have responded to an Area to Address that asks for data by simply including a graph, with no explanation of what the graph shows, or what kind of results are shown. A graph or chart should never be included without at least some explanation or reference in the text of your application. For example, you might say something like:

> *Figure 7.1a presents a summary of our major quality results compared to our foremost competitor: DMI. As you can see, we are superior to them in each of the six measures of quality results depicted in the bar graph.*

Always explain what the graph represents and summarize the conclusions that can be drawn from the data depicted on the graph. Even though it may seem obvious, the examiner may miss the significance of certain data unless you call attention to it.

For example:

The data in Figure 7.8 show that our levels of customer satisfaction have improved by over 80% in the last two years. We have shown steady improvements over each of the last five years.

Rule #2: Don't Duplicate Information From Graphics in the Text

This is just the flip side of the first rule. Graphics should be explained and referenced, but the information contained in them need not be duplicated in the text that accompanies them. This is simply a waste of valuable space and an insult to the examiner's intelligence. Figure 2.5 shows what *not* to do when explaining graphics.

As you can see in the graph below, the levels of customer satisfaction began at 78% satisfied in 1994, rose to 83% in 1995, dropped back to 79% in 1996, and rose again to 86% in 1997. In 1998, levels of customer satisfaction rose to 88% and to an all-time high of 92% so far in 2000.

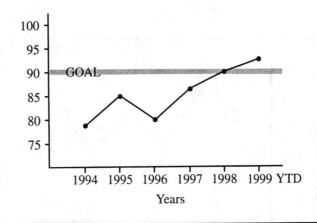

Figure 2.5: What *Not* to Do When Explaining Graphics

Rule #3: Don't Include More Than Two Lines of Data on Any One Graph

In an attempt to conserve space, some applicants have tried putting four or more lines of data on a single graph. This is also done in an attempt to show interrelationships among different quality indices. You should never include more than two lines of data on a single graph. Figure 2.6 shows the right and wrong ways to present data graphically.

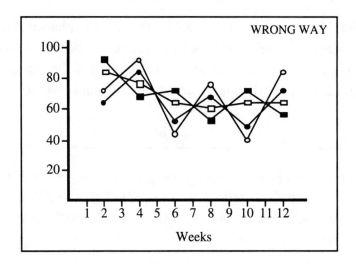

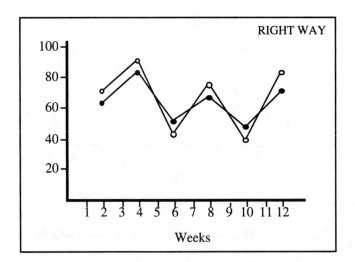

Figure 2.6: Put No More Than Two Lines of Data on a Graph

Rule #4: Graphs Should Depict Goals or Targets

A graph without a line to indicate a goal or target is very difficult to interpret. Target or goal lines should be drawn on all graphs to indicate how close actual performance is to desired performance. Figure 2.7 presents an example.

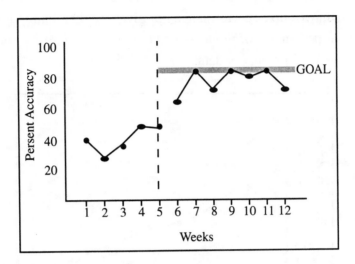

Figure 2.7: Goals Should Always Be Shown on Graphs

Rule #5:   Graphs of Performance Indices Should Show Improvement Using an Ascending Line

We are all taught that results are better when the line on a graph slopes up, representing an upward trend, and that a negative trend is indicated by a downward sloping line. Yet many applicants report positive quality results using negative indices such as number (or percent) of errors. Wherever possible, quality data should be presented in a positive fashion, so the line moves up as performance improves. Rather than graphing errors, graph the number or percentage of products *without* errors. Figure 2.8 shows the right way and wrong way to graph quality data.

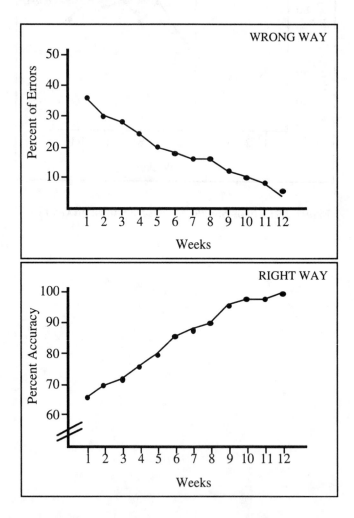

**Figure 2.8: Graph Desired Performance So Improvements
Appear as an Ascending Line**

Rule #6: Scales on Graphs Should Be Set Up to Show Maximum Variability in the Data

For your own benefit, it is important that you set up performance scales on graphs to show the maximum degree of change or variability in quality performance. For example, if customer satisfaction ratings are done on a percentage scale, you would not set up the scale from 0 to 100%, unless there were that much variability in the data. If scores over the last five years have ranged from 80% to 95%, you might set up the graph with a scale that goes from 70% to 100%. As you can see in the "Wrong Way" example in Figure 2.9, very little variability is seen in the data scale on the graph from 0 to 100%. The second graph with the smaller scale, however, shows a great deal of variability.

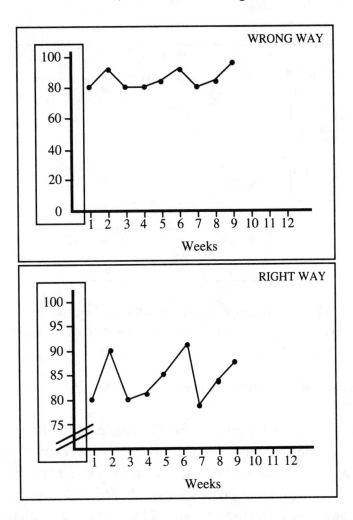

Figure 2.9: Setting Up the Scale for Performance on the Vertical Axis

Rule #7:   Separate Baseline Data From Postimprovement Effort Data

Baseline data are those on levels of performance before a countermeasure or change has been introduced to improve performance. In many of the Areas to Address it is important that you demonstrate a cause–effect relationship between improvements in results and the introduction of improvement efforts or programs. In order to do this, you need to show performance levels both before and after you began your improvement effort. When depicting the data on a graph, separate the two phases using a dotted vertical line and do not connect the last baseline data point with the first postimprovement data point.

Figure 2.10 shows a sample graph that depicts the impact of goals and feedback on the percent accuracy.

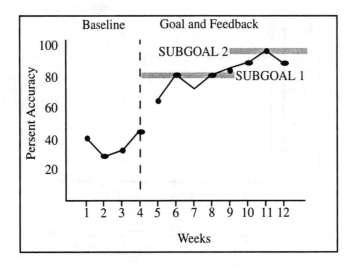

**Figure 2.10: Graph Showing Baseline Performance and
Percent Accuracy After Goals Were Set and Feedback Began**

Rule #8: Use Standard Graphing Formats

Use of strange or exotic graphing formats should be discouraged. Several applicants included graphics that this examiner, for one, had trouble interpreting. Almost any type of quality data can be presented using either a bar graph or a line graph. Bar graphs are most effective when comparing summary data. Line graphs are most effective for showing trends and for showing data over time. Figure 2.11 shows a line graph that has been appropriately labeled.

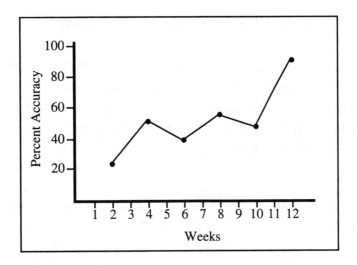

Figure 2.11: Line Graph Appropriately Labeled

Other acceptable formats include pie charts, cumulative line graphs, and scatter diagrams. Examples of these formats are shown in Figure 2.12.

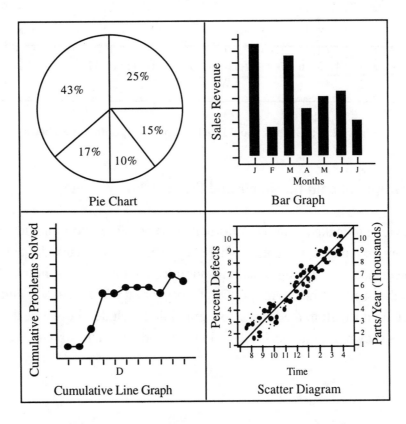

Figure 2.12: Various Ways of Graphing Performance

Rule #9: Graphs Should Be Clearly and Specifically Labeled

Every aspect of the graphs included in your application should be appropriately and completely labeled. The two axes should indicate the quality dimension that is being depicted and the measure of time. Goals and subgoals should be labeled, along with the phases in your quality improvement efforts. An example of an appropriately labeled and easily read graph is shown in Figure 2.13.

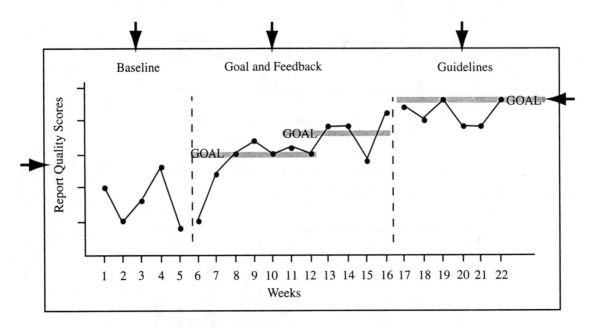

Figure 2.13: Graphs Should Be Clearly and Specifically Labeled

Rule #10: Graphs Should Be Simple and Free of Clutter

Some people tend to make a graph as informative as possible. Pointing out significant increases or improvements, indicating where key events have occurred that have impacted the data, and including other relevant information are thought to help the reader interpret the data better. This seems good in theory, but it often results in cluttered graphics that are difficult to read. A sample graph that includes a great deal of information is shown in Figure 2.14; it is cluttered and very hard to read.

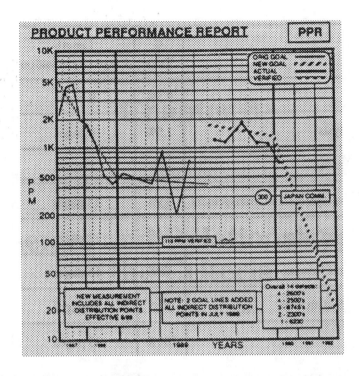

Figure 2.14: Graph Is Cluttered and Very Hard to Read

This graph includes four different lines, too many notes, and scales that are very difficult to read. The spacing between years is unequal, as is the PPM scale on the vertical axis. Furthermore, we don't know what PPM means, nor whether the scale is number of defects, ratio of defects, or something else. In general, this graph represents a perfect example of what *not* to do when preparing your own. It violates at least four of the ten rules we have discussed.

LENGTH OF APPLICATION REPORT SECTIONS

You are allowed a maximum of 50 single-sided pages. These limits do not include the five-page overview, the table of contents, tab dividers, and covers. Appendixes and attachments are included in the 50-page limit, however. In deciding how much space to allocate for each of the seven sections of the report, you should keep in mind the weight given to each of the categories. The Business Results (7.0) section is worth almost 50% of the evaluation, so it should be allocated the most pages. A suggested breakdown of the number of pages to allocate for each of the seven sections of the application report is as follows.

CATEGORY/SECTION	% Value	Suggested Length
1.0 Leadership	12.5%	6 pages
2.0 Strategic Planning	8.5%	4 pages
3.0 Customer and Market Focus	8.5%	4 pages
4.0 Information and Analysis	8.5%	4 pages
5.0 Human Resource Focus	8.5%	5 pages
6.0 Process Management	8.5%	5 pages
7.0 Business Results	45%	22 pages
TOTAL	100%	50 pages

PRODUCING THE FINAL COPY OF THE BALDRIGE APPLICATION

The appearance of the application is not formally one of the criteria by which it is evaluated, but appearance does give the examiners an overall impression of your organization. If the application is sloppy, poorly laid out, and includes typographical and other errors, this doesn't portray a positive image about the company's level of quality. The appearance of the applications ranges from corner-stapled applications that have been typed on old typewriters, to application reports that have been typeset, printed on expensive paper, and include four-color photos and graphics throughout.

It is certainly not necessary that the application include color photos or that it be typeset. Most laser printers and desktop publishing packages can produce written materials that look as good as those that have been typeset—for a fraction of the cost. The 2000 Application Forms and Instructions provide specifics on the type style and size that must be used in the application. Be sure to review this information before writing your application.

The Baldridge officials also discourage using 3-ring binders for your application. I suggest using a Cerlox plastic spiral binding. With this type of binding, the application can be opened flat on a desk and does not take up much space or hinder movement.

Be certain to include a table of contents, and to separate each of the seven main sections of the written report with tab dividers. I also suggest that pages be numbered sequentially within each tab, and that graphics and exhibits be integrated into the text and not placed at the end of each section or in appendixes. Finally, material should be printed on both sides of each page to lessen the bulk and weight of the application.

Chapter 3

Key Themes and Relationships Among the Criteria

THE BALDRIGE BURGER

The diagram on page 6 of the 2000 Baldrige criteria booklet, reprinted below, shows how the various parts of the criteria work together as a system.

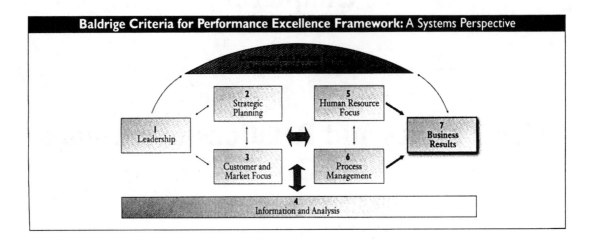

This diagram is called the "Baldrige Burger" by many because it resembles a hamburger. Parts of it make sense, and parts of it are confusing. There is one box for each of the seven Baldrige categories, which makes sense. Box number 4 is stretched out to become the bottom bun, I assume to illustrate how information and analysis are critical to the other six categories. The problem I have with the Baldrige Burger is that leadership is the first box, rather than the customer. Leaders have been known to lead their organizations off a cliff by not being attuned to the marketplace. The Baldrige model is customer driven, not leadership driven. In my diagram on the next page, you will see that the customer is the first box, not the leadership. Leaders need to review market research to decide on company mission, vision, and other factors. The second problem with the Baldrige Burger involves the top bun. The words in the top bun read *Customer and Market Focused Strategy and Action Plans.* Plans are part of Category 2, so it would seem that they would be addressed there. One could put Category 2 as the top bun, since strategic planning cuts across all other categories the same way information and analysis does. However, that would leave a lopsided burger with only three boxes as the "meat" in the middle.

The diagram that follows is graphically boring, but seems to capture the system nature of the Baldrige criteria better than the Baldrige Burger. The two diagrams are mostly the same, showing inputs, processes and outputs. The only substantive difference is that I show customers rather than leadership as the beginning of the system. Both diagrams show the importance of all seven categories working together as an organizational performance system to drive the right results.

THE BALDRIGE CRITERIA AS A SYSTEM

The Baldrige criteria are made up of seven Categories, which are further divided into 19 Examination Items and 27 Areas to Address. While each of the seven Categories is evaluated separately, there are relationships (or "linkages") between the seven and they function together as a system.

As you can see from Figure 3.1, the "input," or beginning, of the Baldrige assessment is not Leadership, but customers and their requirements. Baldrige suggests that an organization needs first to define its customers and markets, and then identify what is important to each of those groups of customers. Customers and their requirements are asked for in Item 3.1 of the Baldrige criteria. Once markets and needs have been identified, the company can develop its mission and direction, which is what is asked for in the Leadership (1.0) section. Once the mission and direction of the organization have been defined, you need to identify measures of success. Measures are asked for in Section 4.0, Information & Analysis, and Item 3.2b, Customer Satisfaction Determination. Short- and long-term goals and strategies then need to be developed, relating to each of the performance measures. Planning is asked about in Section 2.0 of Baldrige. Based upon the goals and improvement strategies outlined in the organization's plans, you need to develop systems/processes: Section 5.0 asks about human resource systems; Section 6.0 asks about work processes in the direct and indirect areas of the organization; and item 3.2a asks about the processes used to manage relationships with customers. All of these systems/processes should work together to produce business results (7.0) for the organization and its customers.

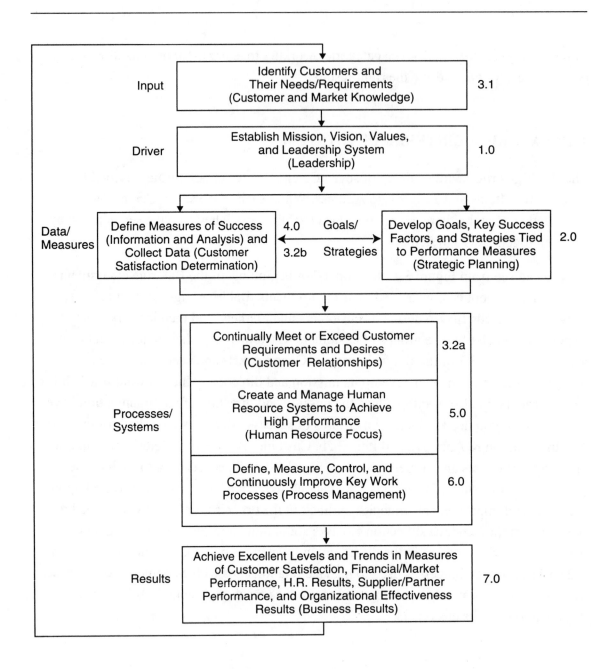

Figure 3.1: The Baldrige Criteria as a System

CORE VALUES IN THE BALDRIGE CRITERIA

Although there are 27 Areas to Address and 86 individual questions in the 2000 Baldrige criteria, a few common themes or "core values" underlie many of the items and categories. This section of the book explains each of these core values. Additional information on these themes or values may be found on pages 2-5 of the 2000 criteria booklet, which appears at the end of this book.

Visionary Leadership

Every effective organization starts with a visionary leader. Herb Keleher of Southwest Airlines, Jack Welch of General Electric, Steven Jobs of Apple, Bill Gates of Microsoft, Jeff Bezos of Amazon.com, and other respected CEOs have clear visions of what they want their organizations to become, and they manage to translate that vision into strategy. Many organizations today lack a clear vision and end up with a strategy cluttered with such buzzwords and phrases as world-class, value-added, and customer-focused. These jargon-laden visions often indicate a management team that has not figured out where they want the organization to be in the future. A vision should be clear enough for employees to understand, and it should inspire them to want to help the organization achieve it.

The values of an organization that define its culture are also linked to the values of the CEO and other senior executives. Everyone watches the behaviors and decisions of the executives to learn what is considered appropriate and inappropriate behavior in the organization. One of the values of Southwest Airlines, for example, is a sense of humor. CEO Herb Keleher has a great sense of humor, and has been careful in selecting other executives and employees at all levels that have a sense of humor.

Executive commitment to the Baldrige process is a key criterion for success, as well. In the 10 years that I have been working with business and government organizations to use the Baldrige model to drive improvement, nearly two-thirds of those organizations have not improved much as a result of Baldrige assessments. The one-third that has dramatically improved has a common characteristic — executive commitment and involvement. Consider an example of the former president of the 1998 Baldrige winner, Don Ing of Solar Turbines of San Diego: Solar made major improvements in its processes, and worked to further deploy good practices as a result of feedback from several rounds of applications for the California Baldrige Award (administered by the California Council for Quality and Service [CCQS]). Ing used the feedback from the state award process to develop strategic plans and processes to lead his company from a score in the 300s to winning the Baldrige Award in less than five years. The entire leadership team at Solar became believers in the Baldrige process and was actively involved in the improvement efforts.

Customer Driven

Being customer-driven or customer-focused is something most organizations today talk about but is something few do well. The foundation of a customer-driven organization is solid market research providing information on the factors that influence customer-buying behavior. Quality used to be a differentiating factor in some industries, but not today. The car industry, for example, is one in which quality products are assumed, rather than being the competitive advantage it was 20 years ago. Market research is so difficult because customers and potential customers often have a hard time articulating what is most important to them. Leading companies today have adopted creative methods for determining the factors that most influence customer buying decisions. Daimler-Chrysler, for example, rides around with customers for hours in their cars and gets them to talk about what they like and do not like about the cars.

Part of being a customer-driven organization is determining desired customer groups. Years ago, many organizations spent huge sums of money to drive up customer satisfaction, and found that it did nothing to improve sales or profits. The Baldrige criteria do not suggest that you need to build relationships with all customers. Smart organizations figure out which the most important customers are, and do not worry about getting all customers to be loyal. Solectron, a two-time Baldrige winner that manufactures circuit boards and electronic components, managed to improve dramatically sales and profits while reducing its number of customers. It is hard for a growing organization to turn away business, but often this is the best strategy for ensuring profitable growth.

The frustrating part of trying to be customer driven is that customer needs and priorities seem to change constantly. A company finally figures out what customers want, and then they change their priorities. The Internet and other new technologies have changed dramatically customer expectations and priorities for many things in life, such as how we buy books or get information from others. Part of what the Baldrige criteria look for is an organization that is flexible enough to adapt and change as customer requirements change. Ritz-Carlton, another two-time Baldrige winner, keeps an extensive database on each guest that includes information on their preferences and special requests. The process required to keep the database up-to-date is even more impressive. Ritz customizes aspects of its service to the guests preference, such as making make sure you always get fat-free milk with your cereal, or that the Ritz employees refer to you by first name, or that you have SPF 30 sun block waiting by your favorite chair at the pool. Understanding what customers want is enough of a challenge, but being able to act on those demands quickly is the mark of an exceptional organization.

Organizational and Personal Learning

This is what author Stephen Covey calls "sharpening the saw." Organizations and employees need to continually improve their knowledge and skills and have ways of sharing lessons learned with each other. The "learning organization" is another buzzword that gets talked about a great deal, but is rarely practiced well. Larger organizations have a bigger challenge to learn from one another. Big organizations get chopped up into smaller units, facilities, and departments, often having little opportunity to learn from one another. A company that does this well is Cargill. Cargill, the largest privately owned firm in the world, is the first food company to win a Baldrige Award. Its Sunny Fresh Foods egg business captured a Baldrige award in 1999. Cargill has used the Baldrige criteria to drive improvement in its companies for over seven years. Each year it holds a conference that is attended by over 500 employees from around the world to share best practices. It also publishes a book of best practices each year called *Cargill Gems* that summarizes the best practices gleaned from the 100 or so applications for its internal Baldrige-based award. Sharing lessons learned in a company of over 100,000 employees in all parts of the world is a challenge, which Cargill does well.

Along with organizational learning, the Baldrige criteria also focus on individual learning. Motorola, the first Baldrige Award winner, has always been a role model for other companies when it comes to employee education and training. The Motorola University remains one of the best facilities of its kind in the world. However, you do not need to be a major corporation with its own university to emphasize employee learning and development. A company called Momentum Textiles, which I predict will be a Baldrige winner in a few years, has an extremely sophisticated and successful approach to training and development, and it does not even have an HR manager, let alone a corporate university. The company, a distributor of fabrics for office furniture and commercial interiors, has less than 100 employees and is number two in market share. The company defines a curriculum for each job, and detailed development plans are prepared for each employee once a year. The company relies on outside resources such as public workshops, college courses, and technical schools to meet some of its training needs, and makes use of structured on-the-job training to satisfy other developmental needs. Motorola and Momentum have in common a focus on continually improving employee knowledge and skills. The theme of continual learning is found throughout all sections of the Baldrige criteria, not just in the human resources section. Each approach/ deployment item asks for evidence of evaluation and improvement of processes and approaches showing evidence of learning.

Valuing Employees and Partners

An increasing number of organizations today rely on employees and suppliers or partners for success. Organizations that depend on the latest manufacturing equipment for success are becoming fewer and fewer today. Even such capital-intensive businesses as steel mills, paper mills, and airlines are finding that employees and suppliers give them the edge over competitors. Southwest Airlines stands out as a role model for the wonderful culture it has created. The company is extremely careful about each person it hires, making sure it has the right mix of skills, ethics, and personality traits to ensure the culture is maintained. It also values its employees and treats them like they are members of a big family. The company was listed last year in Fortune as one of the best to work for in America, and it consistently beats most competitors in safety and on-time performance.

Companies that truly value their employees often do creative and sometimes weird things to show their devotion to their workforce. For instance, Southwest has great parties, and Baldrige finalist MBNA has a department that plans weddings for employees and another department that arranges funerals for relatives of employees. Another Baldrige finalist, Appleton Papers, teaches employees that family and personal lives always come before the job. The company has about 2% annual turnover, while other paper companies often have more than 30% annual turnover.

Suppliers and vendors also need to be valued and treated like partners. Many organizations still treat suppliers as if they cannot be trusted, and foster an adversarial climate. For example, the federal government has been farming out a greater amount of its work to outside companies. However, although the outside companies do the work at a fair price, the government often employs an army of federal agents to do "program oversight." Such oversight entails watching the suppliers so they follow all the rules and do not cheat the government. Much of this oversight is not necessary, and a number of government employees I have spoken with suggest that their jobs are nothing more than white collar welfare.

Private industry has done a better job of partnering with its suppliers and vendors. Shea Homes in Phoenix has narrowed its list of contractors to about 50, which it uses to build several thousand homes a year in Arizona. The suppliers fill out abbreviated Baldrige applications. Shea evaluates suppliers against the Baldrige criteria and provides consulting to help them improve their businesses. Several of the suppliers have won Arizona Quality Awards, and Shea Homes has won state awards in both California and Arizona. By partnering with the contractors that build the homes, 76% of the homes built build by Shea had zero defects — an 8% improvement from last year.

Strategic alliances are important to many organizations today, as well. Forming alliances with similar companies or those that provide a related product/service often allows both companies a stronger presence in the market. United Airlines "Star Alliance," for example, is a partnership with other airlines around the world. Aligning with the wrong partner can spell disaster for a company, however. It is important to develop specific criteria for selecting other organizations with which to partner.

Agility

The second section of the Baldrige criteria asks about strategic planning. While it is important to have a strategic plan, it is also necessary sometimes to scrap the plan two months into the year and take a different direction. Agility, a characteristic found in many Baldrige winners, means that the organization can quickly adapt to changing competitive, technological, or customer factors. One of the things that has made Nokia number one in market share in the cellular phone business is its fast new product development cycle. Nokia designs and introduces new products in about half the time it takes its major competitors. The trick is to improve cycle time for R&D and new product introduction without sacrificing quality and thoroughness. Another cellular phone manufacturer worked hard to improve it's new product design timeliness and found that a large number of its phones were failing after two years.

Being the first to market something new can make all the difference in the world. A competitor can often do a lot to capture a huge share of the market just by being first with a new product or service. Barnes&Noble.com is working hard to catch Amazon.com, but Amazon remains far ahead and it is unlikely that B&N will catch them in the near future. Changing from a bricks and mortar chain of bookstores to selling books on the Internet is a drastic change, the type of change that most companies would struggle with. Sears is trying to undergo similar changes with Sears.com to sell appliances on the Web. Most people would not classify Sears as a particularly agile organization, but it is doing what it can to adapt to changing customer shopping patterns. Sears has hired a team of talented and creative outsiders to run Sears.com. Whether or not people will buy washing machines on the Internet remains to be seen.

Focus on the Future

Another core value in the Baldrige criteria is the focus on identifying future customers, markets, technologies, and other factors that might impact the business. Doing a good job on today's requirements and today's products may not ensure an organization's long term survival. Part of the job of senior executives is to search out new opportunities for the business. Opportunities might consist of companies to buy, others to partner with, new markets to enter, or new products or services that might expand a company's offerings. Cisco is clearly focused on the future. The company has acquired more than 40 new firms in the last five years, and continues to show outstanding results. One of its core competencies appears to be finding and acquiring the right companies that allow it to become larger and stronger without distracting the company from its mission, or changing its culture.

1999 Baldrige winner Sunny Fresh Foods is another organization that does a good job focusing on the future. Sunny Fresh supplies McDonald's with all the liquid eggs used in scrambled egg products. One of the factors that helped Sunny Fresh earn the contract with McDonald's (a very demanding customer) was its record of exceeding the new food safety regulations that came out a few years back. Sunny Fresh, as well as other Cargill businesses, gained an edge on many competitors by exceeding new food safety requirements before anyone else. One might think of the egg business as one that would not change much from year to year, but Sunny Fresh has proven that a food company needs to focus on the future as much as its high tech counterparts in other industries.

Managing for Innovation

Winners of the Baldrige award are often characterized as innovative companies. 1997 winner 3M Dental Products is known for innovation. 3M is known all over the world for its innovative products in a number of fields. Innovation is not just the job of research and development, either. Employees in all functions need to be encouraged to be innovative. Risk taking and innovation are cultural values that are hard to find in many big companies today. They may have become large and successful because some creative and innovative people had a great idea at one time, but big companies tend to lose that entrepreneurial spirit as the founders retire and the size of the corporation increases.

Maintaining a culture of risk taking and innovation in a large company with thousands of employees takes work. Apple seemed to have lost its creative edge for a while, but is back stronger than ever with Steven Jobs in charge, creating some of the most innovative new computing products to come along in quite a while. Chrysler also has a wonderfully innovative culture. Chrysler cars over the last few years have been the most creative designs in the market. The Prowler, Viper, and even the flagship 300M are among the most beautiful and interesting looking cars any car company has designed. Ten years ago Chrysler was known for building boring nondescript cars. (Remember the Chrysler K car?) Today the company leads the world in creative new car designs. By teaming up with the engineering at Mercedes, the marriage of these two companies should make them a formidable force in the world market. Companies such as Apple, 3M, and Chrysler should be studied to see how large corporations can create a culture that rewards innovation.

Management by Fact

This is probably the most difficult of the Baldrige core values to follow. What it says is that the Baldrige criteria expect a company to put more science into how they run their organizations. Baldrige expects organizations to systematically gather data on the right variables, to analyze those data, and use them to make decisions, and plan improvements. The level of analysis expected by the Baldrige Examiners is much more sophisticated than one normally sees in a business. Selecting the right performance measures in the first place should be a fairly scientific process, linked to business strategy and strategies of competitors. Once an organization has developed a good balanced set of metrics, it needs to conduct research between leading and lagging indicators, and between hard and soft measures. For example, very few organizations can show a link between customer satisfaction scores and future business, or between customer satisfaction and profits. Understanding these links and using the correlational data improves the accuracy of decision making.

Public Responsibility and Citizenship

Because the Baldrige judges expect winners to be role models for the world, it is important that the company be a good corporate citizen. A well-rounded organization is not unlike a well-rounded individual who should balance the priorities of work, family, charity, and personal interests. Many big corporations donate a lot of money and time to charities and community groups. However, most are completely reactive, waiting for someone to knock on their door and ask for a check or some other donation. Writing a lot of checks is not what this value is about.

Smart organizations select a few beneficial charities to support that will help the community and also help their image. For example, Baldrige finalist Haworth, donated several million dollars to Western Michigan University to build the Haworth Business School. They could have divided the money among 20 different charity and educational organizations, but this would not have had much impact. Haworth draws many new employees from this university's business program because it is in nearby Kalamazoo. McDonald's is another organization that is more proactive and strategic in their approach to community support and public citizenship. Ronald McDonald House is a charity the company created to help families with children in the hospital. This doesn't hurt their image either because McDonald's caters to families with small children.

Focus on Results and Creating Value

Baldrige used to be a prize for the companies who did all the right things. Quality gurus told us in the 1980s that U.S. companies need to spend less time watching the bottom line, and more time thinking about quality, customers, and employees. Just about every organization jumped on this quality bandwagon to some extent. Many found that the effort did nothing to improve bottom-line results. In fact, just the opposite occurred in some companies. Quality and customer satisfaction improved, but expenses also went up, and profits came down. The 2000 Baldrige criteria expect a balanced focus on all kinds of results, including financial performance. Emphasis now is on balance between short and long-term performance, ensuring long-term survival and success. About half of the points in the Baldrige criteria are based on the results an organization achieves, so Baldrige is not just about doing the right things, it is about getting the right results.

An orientation toward specific types of results is also important. An analysis of the market, the economy, competition, and a number of other factors should help the company to decide its driving forces for success in the next 5 to 10 years. It might be increasing their market share, decreasing prices and operating expenses, or any number of things necessary to be a leader in the markets they serve. Results-oriented organizations need to show flexibility in pushing for different results from time to time, as situations change. One year, profits might be the most important index, and the next year it's safety and environmental performance.

Systems Perspective

As I explained in the beginning of this chapter, the seven categories of the Baldrige criteria work together to form a system of organizational performance. One of the core values of the criteria is the alignment of all the pieces of the organizational systems. Large organizations typically have great difficulty in ensuring that all units and locations are properly aligned with the corporate vision and goals . Some units of large organizations I have worked with work at cross-purposes with each other, or even compete against each other. It is OK that different parts of an organization have different approaches. In fact, the Baldrige criteria encourage the tailoring of approaches to the nature of the business in each unit. However, it is also important to look at all of these units or locations as part of a larger organization that has its own goals and objectives.

One of the major reasons applicants for the Baldrige Award lose points in the approach/deployment sections is that breaks or inconsistencies exist between various parts of their performance system. The various items and areas to address in the Baldrige criteria relate in many ways to other items and areas to address. A common inconsistency involves multiple process improvement teams working on projects that in no way are connected to the company's strategic plan. Another common inconsistency is to find no connection between the overall strategic plan and various lower level activities such as the technology plan, human resource plan, marketing plans, and so forth. Finding and correcting these inconsistencies are important to winning a Baldrige Award. Read the next section of this chapter carefully, have someone evaluate your draft application to identify any of these breaks, and get them fixed before the final draft is prepared. Finding and correcting these inconsistencies are not just important for the sake of a good Baldrige assessment. These breaks end up wasting valuable resources, and often send mixed messages to employees about the behavior the organization expects of them. Finding an organization that has all of its sub-systems aligned is quite impressive, and is something one finds in all winners of the Baldrige Award.

KEY RELATIONSHIPS AMONG THE SEVEN CATEGORIES

Although each of the 19 Examination Items is given a separate score and evaluated independently, performance on one item clearly affects performance on other items. Something that the Baldrige Examiners routinely do is to look for what I call "disconnects" or missed linkages among items in different categories. The more of these missed linkages that are found, the more likely it is that an applicant will receive a low score. A lack of consistency across the categories and items shows a system that is flawed, or at least an application that was not well planned and written. In the next few pages I will discuss the linkages that should be addressed for each of the seven categories, and the common "disconnects" that I have found in the Baldrige Award applications I've reviewed in the last few years.

How to Check for Consistency Between Baldrige Items

Although it's important to understand the major relationships among the various Baldrige items, there are so many of them that it can get confusing. In a related book by another Baldrige expert, interrelationships are defined between each of the 19 Baldrige items, using a graphic with arrows from one item to many others. This information may be interesting for Baldrige scholars, but has little practical use. Baldrige examiners simply don't have the time to check for consistency between one item and the 10 or 15 others that may relate to it when reading an application. A good application takes between 16 and 24 hours to review and score as it is, and this endless checking for consistency between most items would add many hours of time to the review process. Rather than identify how each Baldrige item may be even slightly connected with others, I have chosen to discuss only the most important interrelationships. These are the relationships that could have a major negative impact on your score if inconsistencies are found.

1.0 Leadership—Key Relationships With Other Criteria

Compared with other sections of the criteria, the Leadership category is fairly independent. There are, however, a few things to check for overall consistency. The approach senior leaders use to communicate values and direction (1.1a(1)) needs to be consistent with the communication and work systems described in section 5.1 of the criteria. If you rely on teams to do a lot of the work in your organization, for example, the leadership system needs to support this approach. Similarly, 1.1a(2) asks about how leaders create an environment that encourages empowerment, learning, and innovation. Your response to this item needs to be consistent with 5.1, where you might also discuss empowerment and innovation, and 5.2 that looks at employee education and training. Your answer to 1.1a(3) that asks how leaders set future direction and find new opportunities should be consistent with the overall company approach to strategic planning discussed in 2.1.

1.1b asks about how executives review organizational performance. The answer to these questions should be consistent with the answer to questions in 4.2 (that ask about analysis of data) and consistent with questions in 6.1 and 6.2 (that ask about process analysis and improvement). Question (3) in 1.1b asks about priorities for improvement and opportunities for innovation. The answer to this question should correspond to 2.1b, where you must outline your strategic objectives.

Item 1.2, which asks about your efforts in the areas of public responsibility, ethics, and environmental performance, should correspond with the results you present in section 7.5, which asks for organizational effectiveness results. If you have developed metrics for environmental performance, ethics, or other measures of public responsibility, you will want to list these metrics in section 1.2, and present data on these measures in section 7.5 of your application. Similarly, you will want to set targets or goals for these company responsibility and citizenship metrics and discuss these goals in section 2.2, where you outline your strategic plan.

2.0 Strategic Planning—Key Relationships With Other Criteria

2.1 asks about the process you use to develop your annual and longer-term business plans. 2.1a(2) asks about how you use information on current and future customer requirements to develop appropriate goals and strategies. The information in this section should correspond exactly with the response to 3.1a, which asks about your targeted customers and their requirements. In this section, you need to explain how you use the market research data on customers and their priorities to develop plans and strategies. 2.1a(2) also asks about information on the competitive environment that is used during the planning process. Information on your competitors should be presented in section 4.1 of the application, and should be well integrated with your response here. Area to Address 2.1a(2) asks about how supplier/partner capabilities are considered during the planning process. Your response to this portion of the criteria should be consistent with the information on your supplier/partner management process found in section 6.3.

Your approach to strategy deployment (2.2a) should be consistent with your leadership system, described in section 1.1, as well as your overall performance management system, which would be described in section 5.1. The approach you use to track performance against plans should also closely match the approach you use to analyze performance data, which is found in Item 4.2.

Section 2.2 is where you outline your goals and strategies for both the long and short term. Your goals or targets that you list in 2.2a should link directly with the performance metrics you identify in section 4.1. This is a common area where disconnects or inconsistencies are found. If you list something as a measure in section 4.1, you should make sure that targets and improvement strategies are presented in 2.2a. The overall vision of the company for the long term should also correspond with the information on the company niche or mission that might be outlined in the response to Item 1.1. The improvement strategies that you discuss in 2.2a might also correspond to the processes you elect to improve in sections 6.1 and 6.2. Many good companies use the strategic plan as the driver of process improvement activities. This helps ensure that process improvement activities are linked to the company's goals and plans.

Your human resource plans that you present in 2.2a(2) should present goals or targets that are linked to your HR strategies, which are outlined in section 5.0. The HR systems that you discuss in sections 5.1 through 5.3 should be consistent with the HR goals and targets that you outline in your response to 2.2a(2).

Area to Address 2.2b asks for information on where you project your performance to be in the next five years, relative to major competitors. Your response to this item should be consistent with the information you present on your major competitors in item 4.1a. Both responses should address the same competitors.

3.0 Customer and Market Focus—Key Relationships With Other Criteria

Item 3.1a(1) asks about your targeted market segments and the requirements of each group of customers. This information should be consistent with the factors that you evaluate when discussing how you measure customer satisfaction in section 3.2. If you divide customers into three distinct segments in 3.1, because of their unique requirements, then you should probably measure customer satisfaction in three different ways in section 3.2. Customer requirements outlined in 3.1a should also be consistent with internal requirements and standards described in 3.2a.

Your approach to prioritizing customer requirements and using this information to design new products and services [3.1a(3)] should link well with your process for new product/service development outlined in 6.1a. Your response to these two Areas to Address should be fairly close in content, and may require some cross-referencing.

3.2a asks about how you make it easy for customers to contact your organization and do business with you, and how you handle and track complaints. Service standards should be consistent with any targets or goals you set in section 2.2. Your system for tracking complaints should link to your market research processes described in 3.1a, where you discuss customer requirements.

3.2b asks about the approach used to measure customer satisfaction. Your response to this section should expand upon a briefer description of customer satisfaction measures presented in section 4.1. Item 4.1 asks about your overall performance metrics, including how you measure customer satisfaction. Your response to 3.2 should go into more detail on the methods used to measure customer opinions and buying behavior as a way of gauging their overall satisfaction. The customer satisfaction measures discussed in 3.2b should also be consistent with the results you present in section 7.1. If you identify six different customer satisfaction metrics in 3.2b, you should present data on all six of these metrics in section 7.1. In discussing how you obtain information on customer satisfaction levels of competitors, you might want to reference back to 4.1, wherein you discuss approaches for gathering all types of data on competitors.

4.0 Information and Analysis—Key Relationships With Other Criteria

This section is all about data. The performance metrics that you list and discuss in section 4.1 should be directly linked to the company strategy, vision, and key business drivers, outlined in section 2.2. In fact, you should see targets set for each metric, and strategies outlined in 2.2 to hit or exceed the targets. In section 4.1, the examiners are evaluating whether or not your performance metrics are the right measures. One way of ensuring this is to make sure that they are closely linked to your overall strategies for success, and your business plans (2.2). The measures that you identify in section 4.1 should also be the metrics on which you present data in section 7.0. The overall performance measures you identify in section 4.1 should also be linked to the process metrics identified in section 6.0. The process metrics should support the overall performance measures used on your company scorecard. The metrics you identify in section 4.1 should also be linked to the analyses you do on the data in section 4.2.

Item 4.1 also asks about data you gather on competitors, the industry, and benchmark organizations. The types of data you gather on your competitors should be linked to your overall strategy and key success factors. For example, if you decide that having the lowest prices in the market is one of your strategies, you would want to gather data on competitors pricing on a regular basis. The types of companies and processes that you choose to benchmark or compare yourself to would also link in to your overall business strategy (2.2) and the processes you select for improvement (6.1 to 6.3). Data on your competitors and other comparative data should be presented on the graphs you include in section 7.0. Without comparative data on the graphs, it is impossible for examiners to evaluate your levels of performance. All graphs of results should include comparative data. A low score in this item, or a lack of competitor and comparative data, will have a dramatic negative impact on your score in section 7.0.

Item 4.2 asks about the approach used to review and analyze performance data. This write-up should mesh well with 2.2a(5), which asks about the approach for deploying your plans. The focus of 4.2 should be more on how data are analyzed rather than simply how they are reviewed. Data analysis approaches should also be consistent with the company approach for analyzing and correcting problems. For example, if the company employs a particular process analysis and improvement model that is discussed in section 6.1, this analysis model should be referenced in 4.2. Aggregation of individual metrics into an index may also be discussed in section 4.2. If this is done, the Examiners will expect to see data on this index somewhere in section 7.0. If you have established correlations between performance measures (e.g., customer satisfaction and repeat sales), graphs showing these correlations should be presented in section 7.0. Your response to section 4.2 should be consistent with your answer to 5.3c, which asks about how you establish correlations between measures of employee well-being and health and overall company performance. You might mention some of these correlations in 4.2, and go into more detail in 5.3c.

5.0 Human Resource Focus—Key Relationships With Other Criteria

As with section 1.0, this section on human resource development is fairly independent. I have already mentioned the link between 2.2b, which asks about your human resource plans, and the HR processes described in this section of the criteria. It is also important that your leadership system described in Item 1.1 links well to the overall performance or work systems described in section 5.1. Your compensation and recognition programs described in 5.1b should be linked to the company strategies and goals listed in Item 2.2, and the overall performance measures identified in Item 4.1. The examiners will look for inconsistencies between what you measure and what you write. For example, if you write about growth in market share as a critical success factor, and a primary performance measure, and pay executive bonuses for profit rather than market share growth, this would be seen as a negative. Similarly, if you write about the importance of teamwork and cooperation as a key part of your success strategy, and have a recognition and compensation system that is strictly based on individual performance, the examiners would see this as a problem.

Also important here is the link between your work systems and your overall business strategy (2.2). It is important that the approaches you use to ensure consistent performance from your people are aligned with the company mission, vision, and values. HR practices such as performance appraisal systems and annual raises based on seniority often contradict stated company philosophies or values.

Item 5.2 asks about employee training and development. What is important here is that your training and development priorities link to your overall business strategies and to the work systems you have defined in Item 5.1. It is also important that your leadership training is integrated with your leadership approach described in Item 1.1. Training on process analysis and improvement should link well to section 6.0, and training on customer relationship management should be consistent with your response to Item 3.2.

5.3 is about safety, employee well-being, and satisfaction. Safety and employee satisfaction goals and measures listed in Items 2.2 and 4.1 should be referenced here. Safety and employee satisfaction results should be presented in Item 7.3, and should be consistent with the measures and targets identified in this section. Any overall safety and employee satisfaction measures that are part of your company scorecard and that are mentioned in Item 4.1 should also be consistent with the information presented in this item.

6.0 Process Management—Key Relationships With Other Criteria

Section 6.0 asks about how the company manages its key work processes to ensure consistency in its products and services. Item 6.1 is fairly broad and addresses new product/service development, as well as the production and distribution processes. Most of the organization's key work processes fall into this item. In looking at how you respond to 6.1a, which asks about new product/service development, the Examiners will look for correspondence with 3.1, which is about market research. Baldrige Examiners want to see a company that uses current and future customer requirements as drivers of new product/service development. You may find that you need to refer back to your answer to 3.1 in preparing your response to item 6.1a. Your response to 6.1a should also be consistent with your overall planning process described in 2.1. In fact, planning for new products and services may be a key part of your future success strategy. Thus, 2.1, 2.2 and 6.1a should be well integrated.

6.1b asks about how you manage and improve your key work processes. Your response to this item should be consistent with your overall strategy and any key success factors identified in Item 2.2. Process standards and measures identified here should also be consistent with customer requirements (3.1) and with targets or goals identified in your business plan (2.2). Your approach to process analysis and improvement should be consistent with the data analysis approach defined in Item 4.2. The processes you select to improve should link well to your company strategy (2.2). Benchmarking or other sources of comparative data described in Item 4.1 should also be cross-referenced in this section, if you use these data to drive process improvement.

Item 6.2 asks about how you manage and improve your support processes. The write-up to this section should be consistent with the approach used to manage and improve processes that was defined in 6.1. Many Baldrige applications refer back to 6.1 and explain that the same approaches are used to manage and improve all processes in the company. This is perfectly acceptable and quite common. It is important that external customer requirements, which are identified in 3.1, be used to help design and improve support processes (6.2). Thus, there may be a link between 3.1 and 6.2a(1). As in 6.1, there should be a link among overall performance measures in 3.1, comparative/ benchmark data in 4.1, and the process measures and performance improvement activities defined in 6.2. Benchmarking is often used as a way of setting improvement targets and improving processes in indirect or support areas as well.

The last item, 6.3 in Category 6.0, asks about how you select and manage the performance of your suppliers and business partners. The measures and standards that relate to supplier/partner performance should link to customer requirements identified in Item 3.1. The supplier/partner standards should also link well to your internal process standards and measures identified in Items 6.1 and 6.2. The processes, product, and services that you choose to purchase from outside companies or partners should also be consistent with your overall strategy defined in Items 2.1 and 2.2, and the capabilities analysis you mentioned in Item 2.1. Analysis of employee competencies described in Item 5.2 might also be a reason for using outside suppliers or partners to perform certain work. Measures of supplier performance might also appear on a company's overall scorecard, which is defined in Item 4.1.

7.0 Business Results—Key Relationships With Other Criteria

This is the most important category in the Baldrige criteria. The data you present in this section should be consistent with the performance measures you identify in Items 4.1, 3.2, 5.0, and 6.0. All of these sections ask about performance measures. It is important that you present data on most of the measures you list in other sections. Goals or targets identified in Item 2.2 should appear on the graphs and charts in section 7.0. Data on competitors, industry, and benchmark companies from Item 4.1 should be presented on performance graphs to illustrate your levels of performance. This is extremely important in demonstrating how good your results are compared to others.

SUMMARY OF KEY RELATIONSHIPS AMONG THE CRITERIA

When Reviewing These Criteria	Check for Correspondence With These Criteria
1.0 Leadership	
1.1	2.1, 2.2, 3.1, 4.2, 5.1, 5.2, 6.1, 6.2
1.2	2.2, 7.5
2.0 Strategic Planning	
2.1	1.1, 3.1, 4.1, 4.2, 5.1, 6.3
2.2	1.1, 3.1, 4.1, 4.2
	5.1, 5.2, 5.3, 6.1, 6.2, 6.3, 7.0
3.0 Customer and Market Focus	
3.1	3.2, 6.1a
3.2	2.2, 3.1a, 4.1, 4.2, 7.1
4.0 Information and Analysis	
4.1	2.1, 2.2, 4.2, 6.0, 7.0
4.2	2.1, 4.1, 5.3, 6.1, 7.0
5.0 Human Resource Focus	
5.1	1.1, 2.2, 7.3
5.2	1.1, 3.2, 5.1, 6.0, 7.3
5.3	2.2, 4.1, 7.3
6.0 Process Management	
6.1	2.1, 2.2, 3.1, 4.1, 4.2, 7.5
6.2	2.1, 2.2, 3.1, 4.1, 5.2, 7.5
6.3	2.1, 2.2, 3.1, 4.1, 6.2, 7.4
7.0 Business Results	
7.1	2.2, 3.1, 3.2, 4.1, 4.2
7.2	2.2, 4.1, 4.2, 6.1
7.3	2.2, 4.1, 4.2, 5.1, 5.2, 5.3
7.4	2.2, 4.1, 4.2, 6.3
7.5	2.2, 4.1, 4.2, 6.1, 6.2

Chapter 4

Understanding the
Baldrige Award Scoring Scale

According to a major quality consultant's data base from a survey they conduct on the Baldrige criteria, "corporate America" rates 560 points out of the 1000 on the Baldrige scale. An organization I consulted with scored themselves at 700/1000 on a Baldrige self-assessment survey, and was shocked when they got knocked out of the first round upon actually applying for the Baldrige Award. The truth is that most companies think they rate much higher on the Baldrige scale than they really merit. If corporate America were really at an average level of 560 on the Baldrige scale, U.S. products and services would be beating everyone else's in quality.

THE TRUTH

The truth is that corporate America is nowhere near 560 points on the Baldrige scale. If we define corporate America as including small and large service and manufacturing companies, corporate America is really around 250 points or less. As a Baldrige Examiner, I evaluated a company once that received a score of 26 points out of 1000. Another Examiner gave an applicant 60 points out of 1000. These are companies that thought they had a chance at winning a Baldrige!

MISINFORMATION

One of the major reasons for this gap between where companies think they are and where they really stand on the Baldrige scale is the popularity of surveys as a means of self-assessment. I've written one myself that has been published for the last five years in the June issue of the *Journal for Quality and Participation*. If you review the advertisements in any of the quality journals, you can find ads for at least half a dozen companies with surveys that claim to tell you "where you really stand" on the Baldrige scale. The problem with all of these surveys, not excluding my own, is that they are all based upon internal company opinions and self-report data. Consequently, they are all questionable measures of your status on the Baldrige scale. Some of them look very scientific. They are computer scored and you receive a detailed report showing you a variety of different breakdowns of the data. But no matter how many computers are used or how many data comparisons are done, much of it is doubtful because it is based upon people's opinions of themselves and their work. People tend to think that they are further along applying the Baldrige principles than they really are.

Using one of these surveys to assess your Baldrige status is like filling out a questionnaire to determine your level of health and physical fitness, rather than going to a hospital or clinic and actually getting a physical. A survey is an inexpensive method of determining where you stand, but chances are you will not get an accurate assessment. Companies such as Johnson&Johnson, 3M, Motorola, and Cargill use a more thorough approach to evaluation against the Baldrige criteria by simulating the Baldrige Award process. Applications are prepared and scored just like they are in Baldrige, using internal and external Examiners that have been through several days of training. Some of these organizations even conduct site visits of the best scores to validate the information contained in the written application. An approach like this is likely to give you a score that is within 10% of the score you would receive if you actually applied for the Baldrige Award.

HOW DO BALDRIGE APPLICANTS AND WINNERS SCORE?

When you look at the breakdown of scores over the last few years, you find that most of the Baldrige Award applicants score less than 600 points out of a possible 1000. In fact, about 80% of applicants score between 0 and 600 points. The rule used to be that you needed a score of 600 points or greater to receive a site visit, but this is not a hard rule. In the last few years, there were several organizations that received site visits that scored less than 600. Receiving a site visit with less than 600 points is still not common, but it is possible—especially if you are a small business. The Baldrige Examiners are taught to be less stringent in their scoring of small companies. Examiners learn not to expect as much evidence of a systematic approach to everything. Informal approaches sometimes work very well in small companies.

WHAT IT TAKES TO WIN

People I talk to at workshops I teach on the Baldrige criteria generally believe that it takes a score of 900 or better to win a Baldrige. 1997's distribution of scores indicates that this is far from the truth. Many companies that have won Baldrige Awards received scores that were less than 750. None of the applicants received scores in the eight or nine hundreds, as might be expected. When deciding on a winner, the nine Baldrige Judges look less at the scores than they do the comments on strengths and areas for improvement, and how these factors relate to the business the applicant is in.

UNDERSTANDING THE SCORING SCALE

Scoring for the Baldrige is done using a scoring scale of 0–100%. Scores are generally done in multiples of 10, using guidelines provided by the Baldrige Award Office. The following chart shows a summary of the scoring scale that appears on page 45 of the 2000 Award Criteria Booklet.

RESULTS

SCORE	RESULTS
0%	■ no results or poor results in areas reported
10% to 20%	■ some improvements *and/or* early good performance levels in a few areas ■ results not reported for many to most areas of importance to the organization's key business requirements
30% to 40%	■ improvements *and/or* good performance levels in many areas of importance to the organization's key business requirements ■ early stages of developing trends and obtaining comparative information ■ results reported for many to most areas of importance to the organization's key business requirements
50% to 60%	■ improvement trends *and/or* good performance levels reported for most areas of importance to the organization's key business requirements ■ no pattern of adverse trends and no poor performance levels in areas of importance to the organization's key business requirements ■ some trends *and/or* current performance levels — evaluated against relevant comparisons *and/or* benchmarks — show areas of strength *and/or* good to very good relative performance levels ■ business results address most key customer, market, and process requirements
70% to 80%	■ current performance is good to excellent in areas of importance to the organization's key business requirements ■ most improvement trends *and/or* current performance levels are sustained ■ many to most trends *and/or* current performance levels — evaluated against relevant comparisons *and/or* benchmarks — show areas of leadership and very good relative performance levels ■ business results address most key customer, market, process, and action plan requirements
90% to 100%	■ current performance is excellent in most areas of importance to the organization's key business requirements ■ excellent improvement trends *and/or* sustained excellent performance levels in most areas ■ evidence of industry and benchmark leadership demonstrated in many areas ■ business results fully address key customer, market, process, and action plan requirements

APPROACH/DEPLOYMENT

SCORE	APPROACH/DEPLOYMENT
0%	■ no systematic approach evident; anecdotal information
10% to 20%	■ beginning of a systematic approach to the basic purposes of the Item ■ major gaps exist in deployment that would inhibit progress in achieving the basic purposes of the Item ■ early stages of a transition from reacting to problems to a general improvement orientation
30% to 40%	■ an effective, systematic approach, responsive to the basic purposes of the Item ■ approach is deployed, although some areas or work units are in early stages of deployment ■ beginning of a systematic approach to evaluation and improvement of basic Item processes
50% to 60%	■ an effective, systematic approach, responsive to the overall purposes of the Item ■ approach is well-deployed, although deployment may vary in some areas or work units ■ a fact-based, systematic evaluation and improvement process is in place for basic Item processes ■ approach is aligned with basic organizational needs identified in the other Criteria Categories
70% to 80%	■ an effective, systematic approach, responsive to the multiple requirements of the Item ■ approach is well-deployed, with no significant gaps ■ a fact-based, systematic evaluation and improvement process and organizational learning/sharing are key management tools; clear evidence of refinement and improved integration as a result of organizational-level analysis and sharing ■ approach is well-integrated with organizational needs identified in the other Criteria Categories
90% to 100%	■ an effective, systematic approach, fully responsive to all the requirements of the Item ■ approach is fully deployed without significant weaknesses or gaps in any areas or work units ■ a very strong, fact-based, systematic evaluation and improvement process and extensive organizational learning/sharing are key management tools; strong refinement and integration, backed by excellent organizational-level analysis and sharing ■ approach is fully integrated with organizational needs identified in the other Criteria Categories

Enough people have worked with the Baldrige criteria during the past 13 years that most organizations have a fairly good understanding of the scoring scale. In the early days of Baldrige, many self-assessment surveys misled companies into thinking they would score 500 to 600 points, and found out later they were closer to 300 points. I haven't heard this happening much recently. Most organizations who are serious about Baldrige assessment don't bother with a survey. They are all unreliable as a true measure of where you'd score on the Baldrige criteria.

The purpose of this chapter is to provide the reader with more guidance to use in assigning scores to an organization. This information is helpful for state or national award examiners, as well as for those in organizations who are simply doing a Baldrige assessment as part of their planning and improvement process.

IMPROVED 2000 SCORING SCALE

The Baldrige scoring scale has always been a little too subjective for my taste because they divided the scale into 30 point increments. For example, the 40 to 60% scoring band had the same descriptors, yet there is a huge difference between an organization at the 40% level that is a little better than off to a good start with systematic approaches and deployment of those approaches, compared to a 60% organization that is probably a Baldrige finalist and winner in many state award programs. These broad 30-point bands have been improved for 2000 by narrowing them to five 20-point bands and one set of descriptors for a zero score. I prefer to break the scoring scale down into 10 point bands because all scoring is done in multiples of 10. A 10% difference can have a big impact on overall points in some sections like those that ask for financial or customer results.

APPROACH/DEPLOYMENT ITEMS

Categories 1 to 6 are scored based upon an organization's approaches or systems, and implementation/deployment of the systems. What this means is that the examiners assess the way you run your organization. Over the years, the Baldrige criteria have become less prescriptive in the types of approaches they expect to see in a well run organization. In the early days of the criteria, many approaches were prescribed: use of terms, quality function deployment, strategic quality planning, benchmarking, empowerment of employees, and process modeling. You won't find any of these as a requirement in the 2000 Baldrige criteria. There are as many different successful approaches as there are types of organizations.

The difficult job for examiners with the current Baldrige criteria is scoring your approach when there is no one right answer. You don't get points for just having an approach—you need to have an effective approach. Judging your approaches can be a subjective process, which is why multiple examiners grade each application and must agree on the appropriate score during a consenus phone meeting. Because there is no one right approach, examiners evaluate your approaches by evaluating the extent to which they are:

- Appropriate for the size and type of organization being evaluated
- Planned and logical
- Based upon research and past experience
- Systematic
- Innovative or unique
- Regularly evaluated and improved

The same approach may receive very different scores in two organizations because it is appropriate for one and inappropriate for the other.

Deployment is the other dimension assessed in all of the items in Categories 1 to 6. Deployment essentially means:

- Have you answered all of the questions in the criteria?
- How widely have you implemented the approaches you discuss?

Both factors cause a lot of applicants to lose a lot of points. Ineffective approaches that are completely deployed will not earn any points. What the examiners like to see is a strong solid approach that answers all dimensions of the criteria, and has been implemented wherever it is appropriate in your organization. Deployment tends to be the downfall of many large organizations that may have implemented good approaches in a few units or facilities, not in all places where the approach is needed. When assessing the deployment dimension, the Baldrige scale looks at implementation of your approaches across:

- All transactions with customers, suppliers, and others.
- All operations, facilities, and business units.
- All products and services.
- All levels and functions of employees.

RESULT ITEMS

Category 7.0 is where all the results of an organization are evaluated. In this section, it is not important how anything is done. This section, which is worth about half the points, is where hard data needs to be presented. When evaluating your results, the Baldrige Examiners look at:

- Your overall level of performance.
- How your performance levels compare to industry averages, competitors and benchmarks (if appropriate).
- Rate of improvement or the slope of trends in your data over multiple years.
- Breadth of the results—whether improvements are shown on all key measures of performance.
- The degree to which results have been sustained and show continuous improvement over time.
- Absence of negative trends or flat performance at low levels.

IMPORTANCE AS A SCORING DIMENSION

Along with approach, deployment, and results, a fourth dimension used to assess your answers is the relative importance of the approach or result to your overall success. The Business Overview should highlight important success factors and challenges the company has faced. The points stressed in the overview, as well as your strategic plan, clue examiners to put more weight or less weight on particular items. While each of the 19 items has an assigned point value, examiners use their judgment and may upgrade or downgrade a score based on the importance of an approach to the company's overall success. For example, if a little-known company had a vision of being a major player in their market, brand recognition might be a key success factor for them to concentrate on. If the processes for achieving brand recognition were poorly thought-out and not well executed, this could have a big negative impact on the score. A company with 40% turnover that has an impressive and systematic new-hire training program might increase their score in item 5.2, which looks at training and development.

Scores of 0 on Approach/Deployment

Scores of zero are actually given out quite frequently by Baldrige Examiners when they evaluate each of the 19 Examination Items. Companies that assess themselves, however, rarely give zeros in any area. Part of this discrepancy stems from a lack of understanding of what constitutes a zero. The scoring scale uses the word "anecdotal" for the approach, deployment, and results factors when describing what a zero looks like. This means that the only evidence provided consists of stories, or anecdotes, illustrating how the company does in meeting the criteria. No matter how impressive, examples or stories are not worth anything on this scale.

Most of the items that ask about your approach are looking for a *system*. A score of zero would indicate that you probably have no system. Even a small business would be expected to have informal systems. You may also receive a score of zero if you have plans for a sound system, but you have not yet implemented it. This would indicate no deployment. Plans and intentions will not earn you points on the Baldrige scale until you have deployed the system. Most companies that do self-assessments tend to score themselves between 10% to 30% for good intentions in the future. A score of zero may indicate that the organization has some "pockets of excellence," but these pockets are tied to key individuals rather than the existence of a systematic approach. In general, the company's approach to getting good performance is to manage by the seat of their pants. I explain to the students in my workshops that a score of zero indicates that the organization is unconsciously incompetent in the area being evaluated. In other words, they don't even realize their shortcomings.

Scores of 0 on Results

A score of zero in an Area to Address or Examination Item that asks for results would indicate that one or more of the following conditions are present:

- There are no results other than anecdotes—no graphs or data.
- Data presented are irrelevant to the criteria/requirements of the item.
- Data show that performance on key measures has gotten worse, or has not improved at all.
- Performance is consistently below most competitors and industry averages.

Scores in the 10–20% Range on Approach/Deployment

If an examiner believes that an organization needs to go back and fix major structural problems in its approach before going any further, then a 10–20% is the appropriate score. This is the range in which a number of organizations beginning to do a Baldrige assessment fall. Although the words in the scoring scale are the same for both 10 and 20%, there is actually a great difference. A 10% score is a lot closer to zero than it is to 20%. In other words, a score of 10% should be considered to be a very bad score that shows you have almost no answer for the criteria. Hence, 10% is often called a "guilt score" by the examiners, usually given because they could find at least one minor positive comment. Many examiners will give a score of 10 if the organization talks about its good intentions for the future to create a system. In other words, the organization is consciously incompetent.

When scoring a 10% examiners must work hard to find anything positive to write, and the improvement comments indicate major problems or omissions. If one or two aspects of the approach are worth saving before the organization is told to go back to the drawing board, a 10% is the appropriate score. If three to five things are worth saving, but the organization needs to go back to the drawing board, a 20% is a more appropriate score. The scoring scale suggests that the beginnings of a systematic approach are present at the 10–20% scoring range. In reality, this means that the component parts of a systematic approach may be present, or that the blueprints of a good approach have been drawn, but no real construction has started. A 10–20% might mean that there are lumber and bags of cement at the site, but no construction has been started. It could also mean that the foundation has been poured and that it has some major flaws that need to be fixed before any further construction is done.

Deployment at the 10–20% range is limited; any foundation of an approach tends to be at the pilot test stage. Most of the organization will not have a systematic approach to the item implemented when the score is 10–20%. Whatever approach is used tends to be more reactive than proactive. In other words, if problems arise, they are dealt with and solved, as opposed to more proactive approach that anticipates and prevents problems.

Scores of 10–20% on Results

Results for scores in this range tend to show a mixed bag of slight improvements, flat performance, and slight declines in performance levels over the last couple of years. The 10–20% score on results might indicate a lack of data. It could be that data are not presented for several metrics identified in other sections of the application, or that only a couple of years worth of data are presented, making it impossible to identify trends. Levels of performance might be difficult to evaluate because of a lack of comparative data. In any event, a score in this range shows generally unimpressive results. A 10% score means that most graphs show poor performance on either level or trend, or both. Only because one or two data points on a couple of graphs show slight improvement is a score of 0 not given. A 10% score for results is also considered a "guilt score" that is closer to 0 than to 20%.

A score of 20% indicates that something positive might be happening. Up to half of the measures show at least some slight improvement, and the negative trends in others appear to be flattening out or possibly heading upward very slightly. Examiners give a score of 10% on results when they feel that this is really bad but at least a couple of graphs show some slight improvement. A 20% score, on the other hand, indicates that the company results might look impressive in four or five years if it continues its improvement efforts. A 20% shows that a company is on the road to improvement, but not very far down that road. Levels of performance in companies that score 20% on results tend to be below industry averages. Trends tend to show slight improvement, and often only over a couple of years. It is common to find some negative trends and levels with a score of 20%, but not in the majority of the graphs.

Scores of 30%–40% on Approach/Deployment

This is the level at which a great number of companies fall. In fact, the Baldrige office estimates that most well-run American companies fall at the 25% level in their overall score. There is a big difference between a score of 30% and that in the 10–20% range. To receive a 30% score you need to have the beginnings of the architecture in place of a solid system. At the 10–20% level there is no system, or it is fundamentally flawed. The feedback given to a company receiving a 10–20% score is to save a few good practices, but to start over, rethinking your entire approach. The feedback given to a company receiving a 30% score is to keep working, and what you have will eventually turn into a good system. An analogy that fits well here is to look at a 30% as the foundation being set, and the frame of the house being solidly built. Over time, this will mature into a fine structure, even though it is a long way from being a house. In other words, the structure of a systematic approach exists, and it is a good solid beginning. With a score of 10–20%, some material may be at the site, but the foundation isn't even poured yet, or it is flawed in some fundamental way.

Deployment at the 30% level tends to mean that a systematic approach or beginning has been implemented in at least one or two of the major functions or units in the organization. Implementation should be in a large enough component of the company to tell whether or not the system is working. The approach is beyond the testing or pilot phase at the 30% level, and is in the process of being gradually implemented.

A score of 40% or 400 points overall, will win a Silver Award in the state of California's award program. Not many Silver awards are given out each year, and 40% should be thought of as a fairly high score. One major difference between a 30% and 40% score is that you are a little beyond a good start at 40%. The approach is not yet mature, but it probably has gone through some minor improvements, or at least one evaluation/ improvement cycle. More components of the system are also built at the 40% level. To return to our house analogy, a 40% would show a sound framework, and some of the major systems in the house being installed (e.g., electrical, plumbing, etc.). At 40%, it should resemble a house, and more than half of the work has been completed, along with some minor improvements that were made along the way.

Deployment at the 40% level tends to be at least half of the organization. This might mean half of the business units, plants, or facilities. They all don't need to be at the same level of maturity, or have the exact same approach, but more than half need to show evidence of a systematic approach with some minor improvements. Companies that are at the 40% level tend to be beyond a bunch of programs or initiative such as TQM, re-engineering, process improvement, self-directed teams, etc. If there are any such initiatives in a 40% company, they tend to be well coordinated and knitted together as a comprehensive system. Disconnects and overlaps between programs and initiatives indicates a lack of overall architecture and may knock you back to 30% or below.

Scores of 30%–40% on Results

The difference between results at 20% and 30% is that a 30% company would show the beginnings of positive trends in *more* than half of the company's major indices of performance. Typically, most graphs will contain at least three data points, showing the beginnings of a trend, and the trends will be mostly positive. The level of results are not that impressive yet, and the company may not be doing better than most competitors, but they are getting better each year. You might still expect to see that some of the graphs show no improvement. You may also see inconsistencies in the data at this level. Even though more than half of the graphs show the start of an improving trend, other graphs show no trends, flat performance, and even that performance on a few indices has gotten worse. The bottom line is that more than half of the key indices show the start of positive trends for this level of scoring. At the 30% level there may be key data that are still missing from the application. Levels of performance tend to be at or slightly above competitors'.

The feeling one would have with a 30% score on results is that something is definitely happening in the company. Results in many areas show strong improvement, even though overall levels of performance may be average for the industry.

The differences between results at this level and at the 30% level are:

- Lack of significant adverse trends
- Consistency of results across all key performance indices
- Number of data points indicating trends
- Overall level of results compared with competitors
- Slope of trend lines or rate of improvement

We would not expect to see sustained world-class results to give a 40% score. Graphs in most or all of the areas of performance will show positive trends that are not yet conclusive. Statisticians generally believe that seven data points are needed to establish any kind of trend. We would not expect this yet. Three or four data points (typically, years versus weeks or months) that show the start of a good trend is more of what we would see at this level.

Scores of 50–60% on Approach/Deployment

In the Baldrige scoring scale, a 50% score is not considered average. Rather, a 50% is considered a fairly good score, indicating that a company has implemented effective systematic approaches in the majority of the organization, and has generally been through at least one major improvement cycle. In other words, you have systematically evaluated your systems or approaches, and made changes based upon the evaluation data. With a score of 50%, systems and approaches are not completely mature, but they are getting there.

One of the major differences between a score of 50% and a score of 40% is deployment of approaches to most major units or segments of the organization. At the 40% level, deployment tends to be to one or two major portions of the organization, whereas at 50% deployment should be to at least 75% of the company. It is OK that some segments of the organization have yet to implement the approaches, but they tend to be smaller units, or support functions.

Another major improvement found in an organization that reaches the 50% level is thorough integration across categories and items in the criteria. There are often many disjunctions, or a lack of integration, found at the 30–40% scoring level, but not when a company achieves a 50% or higher. The systems diagram of the Baldrige criteria from the previous chapter, and the information on links between various items, tend to check out with a score of 50%. A score of 50% also indicates that the company is probably a few years away from being a Baldrige winner. Usually it takes three or more years to go from 50% up to Baldrige winner level (70–80%), but not always. A few organizations I have worked with have gone from 500 points to winning a Baldrige in two years. In summary, a 50% score says that you have a well-integrated systematic approach that has been improved at least once in a fairly major way, and has been implemented in the majority of the organization's businesses or units.

To raise your score to 60%, the organization needs to show all of the characteristics I have described of the 50% company, as well as greater deployment, better integration with other items, and usually at least one more evaluation/improvement cycle. A 60% score is generally good enough to receive a site visit from Baldrige examiners, which means you made it to the finals and are a possible candidate for the award. A 60% score usually means that the examiners are having a hard time finding any negative comments. Comments regarding areas for improvement tend to be minor and focus on the need for additional refinement and implementation. In other words, there are no parts of the criteria that have not been addressed in a systematic manner. Companies that score in the 60% range tend to be only a year or two away from being good enough to win a Baldrige Award.

Some organizations that receive scores of 60% on their written application go on to win Baldrige Awards in the same year. When this happens the examiners find many more strengths in the site visit than were apparent in the written application. One of the 1998 winners received scores of mostly 60% on the written application and ended up winning the award after a positive site visit.

Applicants with scores of 60% on approach/deployment items show effective systems that have been deployed well, but they also tend to show a lack of innovation or creativity. In other words, you might find that their approach is fairly typical for their industry or type of organization. That is, there is not much to write about in a newspaper article regarding the organization's approaches. The company is not doing anything wrong, it is just that the approach does not have any elements that make it truly innovative.

Score of 50%–60% on Results

In addition to having no significant adverse trends, results at the 50% level should clearly show improvement trends in most of the major indices asked about in the Examination Item. Not all graphs will show clear trends, but many will. Another factor that differentiates results at this level is that the company's levels of performance on some graphs compare favorably to key competitors and possibly benchmarks. There is usually a lack of comparative data in results below 50%. Or the company's performance is below that of key competitors and benchmarks. At 50% there is not only comparative data, but the applicant's results are better than levels exhibited in the comparative data. We're certainly not expecting that the company show world-class results on all measures at the 50% level, only that some of the graphs of key measures have comparative data, and that the applicant's performance is at least slightly better than points of comparison. Again, not all graphs will show strong positive trends. Some graphs may still be flat or show slow steady improvements.

Results at the 60% level tend to be quite impressive. The majority of graphs depicting results will show either slow steady improvements over several years, or sustained high levels of performance over a number of years. Graphs at the 60% level also tend to show a lack of variability in the data, indicating that the company has these key measures in control as much as possible. Results at this level also tend to be superior to a number of different points of comparison. Most graphs will include two or three comparison points (e.g., industry average, largest competitor, and benchmark). Performance of the applicant will be better than industry averages, key competitors, and other comparison points on many graphs. Results may even approach or exceed benchmark levels on a few graphs.

Scores of 70–80% on Approach/Deployment

The descriptors in the official scoring scale for 50–60% and 70–80% are very close. Both call for effective approaches that have been deployed well to the majority of the organization, evidence of several cycles of evaluation and improvement, and links with other related Baldrige items. As I mentioned earlier, a score of 70–80% is good enough to win a Baldrige Award. Receiving a score in this range indicates that your approach is not only far above others in your own industry, but that other companies in other industries could benefit by studying your approach. In other words, you are the benchmark with a score of 70–80%. Some minor parts of the organization may have yet to implement the systematic approaches deployed to the majority of the company. There may also be some minor breaks identified between this item and other related Baldrige items.

Other characteristics of a 70–80% score are some creative or unique aspects of the approach. Companies that win the Baldrige Award tend to do several things that are worthy of a newspaper story, such as a creative way of partnering with suppliers, or a unique employee recognition program. One of the differences between a 70% and 80% is in the number of innovative aspects of the approach. A 70% score indicates that there may be one or two things that are creative, whereas an 80% score indicates that there are several creative aspects of the approach.

Organizations that score in this range tend to have approaches that have been evaluated and improved at least three times over 3–5 years. There is still room for further refinement and evaluation, but the approaches are clearly becoming mature and the nature of the changes in the last few years tend to be minor. The Baldrige criteria, for example have been through 13 evaluation and improvement cycles, and the changes made during the last two years have been very minor. Are the Baldrige criteria perfect? No. It is important that the system and its criteria are periodically evaluated and improved, but the Baldrige criteria have become a complete and mature system that would probably score at least 80% on its own scale.

An organization that scores in the 70–80% range is like a finely tuned machine. All of the systems and sub-systems work together in harmony to produce balanced results for shareholders, customers, employees, and any other stakeholders. An organization that scores at this level has internalized the Baldrige criteria to the point where it does not need separate programs or initiatives to integrate the criteria into its business systems. The criteria are second nature. Solectron and Solar Turbines, both Baldrige winners over the last couple of years, have achieved this level. They do not have separate Baldrige-based initiatives. The Baldrige criteria are the system by which these organizations perform day to day business. Neither of these organizations started out this way. It has taken many years to make the Baldrige criteria part of their culture. Another company that is making good progress on this front is Cargill, the parent company of 1999 winner Sunny Fresh Foods. I have worked with Cargill for seven years, and have seen huge progress in a number of its business units, including Sunny Fresh and the orange juice business in Frostproof Florida that won that state's Sterling Award a couple of years ago.

Scores of 70–80% on Results

Results in organizations at this level show either dramatic improvements in performance over many years, or sustained high levels of performance for five or more years. Most levels of performance show that the organization is ahead of its major competitors, and is often the industry leader on many metrics. Organizations that score 70–80% on Results tend to compare favorably to benchmark organizations on a number of measures. Companies scoring at this level are leaders in the industry, and are likely to remain so for the future. Results at this level of scoring tend to include graphs showing five or more years worth of data, and each graph typically contains a target or goal, industry average performance, and data on one or more major competitors. The graphs may show comparisons to world-class benchmarks outside of the applicant's industry, as well.

It is OK to have a dip in performance from time to time, but these dips need to be adequately explained, and performance must have recovered. Absent would be any flat or negative trends of several years' worth of data. An organization that lacks competitive information and other comparative data would not be able to score in this range for results even if trends were positive. To receive a score in this range trends and levels must be very strong. As I mention elsewhere in the book, it is impossible to evaluate levels of performance without appropriate comparative data.

Score of 90–100% on Approach/Deployment

While it is unlikely that an organization would score 900–1000 points overall on the Baldrige scale, some organizations receive scores of 90–100% on individual items. Realistically, scores of 100% are unlikely when a team of examiners must reach consensus on the appropriate score. When I train people to use the Baldrige scoring scale, I explain that a score of 100% should be given if you cannot think of even a minor comment that would be classified as an area for improvement. Organizations that score at this level have approaches that are incredibly innovative, completely mature, and deployed throughout the entire company. Examiners score an item at this level when it is the most impressive approach they have ever seen and is ideally suited to the organization and its culture.

If an examiner cannot tell the CEO of a single thing that could be done to improve this area, the score should be 100%. If the examiner can think of a couple of minor things that could be done to make the approach even better, then a 90% might be more appropriate. In either case, there are many things to write a newspaper article about, and the approach probably has been evaluated and improved five or six times over five to eight years. An organization that receives a score of 90–100% is the benchmark. In other words, other similar organizations could learn a lot by studying this organization's approaches, and it is likely to be significantly better than any other organization in its industry.

Scores of 90–100% on Results

In order to receive a score of 90–100% on Results items, a company pretty much has to walk on water. If you looked at the stock market performance of Solectron over the last eight years, those results would probably deserve a 90–100%. A $1000 investment in Solectron stock ten years ago would be worth over $100,000 today. Other financial measures in this Baldrige winner also show stellar performance over the same time period. Absent in a company that gets a score of 90–100% on results are graphs showing mediocre performance. All of the measures being assessed within an item would have to show outstanding trends, and levels of performance that identify the company as the clear market leader. These kind of results are very difficult to achieve in any business, but a few organizations have succeeded.

In order to give a score of 90–100% on Results, the examiner should feel like calling his broker to invest money in the company. The kind of results seen in a 90–100% company would be worthy of a feature story in the *Wall Street Journal* or similar periodical. Organizations that have done a major turnaround, like 1998 Baldrige winner Boeing

Airlift and Tanker Division, or earlier winner Cadillac, probably would not qualify for a score this high on Results. Even though the organizations have gone through impressive turnarounds, most Baldrige winners do not receive scores this high for all of the Results sections. This scoring range is reserved for the rare company that can show near flawless results over many years, and sustained performance demonstrating that it is the leader of its industry by a wide margin.

ADDITIONAL SCORING GUIDANCE

No amount of guidance in a publication can take the place of practice and feedback in learning the Baldrige scoring scale. I encourage you to obtain a copy of the 1998 or 1999 case study that was used to train current Baldrige Examiners. Score the case yourself, and then compare your score to the textbook answer to see how your scoring differs from a group of Senior Baldrige Examiners. By going through this exercise, you will gain a good understanding of what a 30% looks like, a 60%, an 80%, etc. A copy of the 1998 and 1999 case studies and textbook answers is available by calling the ASQ at 800-248-1946. The 2000 case studies will be available in late 2000.

Chapter 5

Interpreting the Criteria
for Leadership (1.0)

OVERVIEW OF THE LEADERSHIP CATEGORY

The 2000 Award Criteria define the Leadership category as follows:

> The **Leadership** Category examines how your organization's senior leaders address values and performance expectations, as well as a focus on customers and other stakeholders, empowerment, innovation, learning, and organizational directions. Also examined is how your organization addresses its responsibilities to the public and supports its key communities. (p. 10)

The 1.0 Leadership category is broken down into the following two Examination Items:

> 1.1 Organizational Leadership (85 points)
> 1.2 Public Responsibility and Citizenship (40 points)

As stated in the excerpt above, this category relates to the activities of the organization's senior executives as well as the management system as a whole. The term "senior executives" refers to the highest ranking official of the organization and the executives that report directly to the CEO or president. This would seem very clear, but applicants have been known to report on only the activities of their most senior executive, the CEO, with no information being provided on the activities of any of the other executives in the organization.

The sections that follow describe each of the Areas to Address, organized under each of the two Examination Items in the Leadership category. Each section begins with a double-ruled box containing the Examination Item, the point value, and any applicable Notes.* Areas to Address falling under that Item follow in a single-ruled box. In the upper right corner of each Area to Address box is an indication [brackets] of whether the Area pertains to approach, deployment, or results. All definitions and information appearing within these boxes are taken directly from the Baldrige criteria. Following each Area to Address is an explanation defining what the examiners are looking for in assessing your application for each of the individual questions under the Areas to Address. Next, I have supplied a list of indicators or evaluation factors that will assist you in interpreting the criteria and in preparing your application.

---

* Item Notes that apply to a specific Area to Address are appropriately listed in the box containing that Area.

1.1 ORGANIZATIONAL LEADERSHIP

Describe how senior leaders guide your organization and review organizational performance. (85 points)

Note: Organizational performance results should be reported in Items 7.1, 7.2, 7.3, 7.4, and 7.5.

AREA TO ADDRESS   **[APPROACH, DEPLOYMENT]**

1.1a. Senior Leadership Direction

(1) How do senior leaders set, communicate, and deploy organizational values, performance expectations, and a focus on creating and balancing value for customers and other stakeholders? Include communication and deployment through your leadership structure and to all employees.

What They're Looking for Here

Your response to this first question 1.1.a(1) should begin by explaining how you communicate the company's focus on the customer and your values. An important dimension of how the values are communicated is the methods used for communication. Some companies simply post the values on plaques that are posted on walls all over the company. It is important that you use a variety of methods and media to communicate the company's values and customer focus. Employees need reminders of the values to help keep their behavior aligned with those values. Because of this, the frequency of your communication is also important. Values need to be communicated in speeches, newsletters, training programs, meetings, reports, plans, and various other ways in which the company conveys information to its employees. It is also important to vary the media used. One company I worked with programmed every computer terminal so that the company values would appear on the screen when employees signed on in the morning. Because almost every employee worked with a computer terminal, they saw the values every day. Yet, not one of the approximately 50 employees I interviewed could recite those values for me off the top of their heads. The lesson to learn here is that it is important to vary the communication medium. People get used to seeing a plaque on the wall or words on a screen every morning, and don't really see it any more after a while.

The second part of this question in area to address, 1.1a, asks about how the senior leaders communicate expectations and set the future vision and mission of the company. Part of the job of senior executives is to review the market research described in section 3.1 of the criteria and decide what the mission and targeted markets should be for their own company. Part of what is assessed here is whether or not the leaders have completely defined the mission of the organization. The test of an effective mission statement is that it should not be able to fit any other company. It should define specific products/services, markets, and strategies that make the company unique when compared to its competitors. The mission defines what the company does and the customers it serves.

Executives also need to define a future vision for the company. The vision should be realistic, verifiable, and memorable. The best vision statements are short and sweet. According to television commercials, the vision of Snapple beverages is to be the number three soft drink manufacturer. They realize that they will never displace Coke and Pepsi from their number one and two positions in the market, and Snapple would be delighted if they could become number three. This is a good vision statement, because it might be achievable, and it is something that every employee can understand and remember. Many vision statements are several sentences in length and include vague words and phrases like: *world-class, leading edge, benchmark level, market-driven, and leading supplier.* The problem with these words and phrases in a vision statement is that they are vague, and their accomplishment is unverifiable. How could a company tell when it becomes "world-class," for example.

It is certainly not necessary that a company has a written mission and vision statement. In fact, some of the best companies I have seen don't bother posting written mission and vision statements on walls or publishing them on wallet cards. Good companies always have a clear definition of their mission and future vision, however. And the mission and vision need to be clear to all levels of employees. The Baldrige criteria assess whether or not the senior leaders have clearly defined the company's direction and communicated it to employees.

Your answer to question (1) in Item 1.1a should also explain how senior leaders communicate a balance of financial results with other factors such as employee and customer satisfaction. Early Baldrige winner FedEx does this by teaching employees that they will have three masters:

- Shareholders
- Customers
- Other Employees

Every FedEx employee learns not to trade off one for the other, but to achieve the appropriate balance between all three. FedEx communicates this balanced focus through new employee orientation, ongoing training, close-circuit television broadcasts, and perhaps most importantly, through their incentive compensation system. Incentives are based on achieving good performance for all three stakeholders. You obviously need not copy FedEx's approach, but describe your own methods for leaders to communicate their priorities and expectations to all employees. In a small organization, communication methods might be informal and face-to-face. Larger organizations, where executives cannot have personal contact with all employees, would need a more formal structure approach to communication. The use of multiple media and communication methods is also encouraged, because all employees learn differently.

Indicators for Question 1.1a(1)

- Executives have clearly defined the mission of the company.

- The mission is specific enough not to apply to any other company.

- Senior leaders have defined a future vision for the company, based upon a review of market, customers and their needs, and an assessment of the company's own capabilities.

- The future vision is realistic, verifiable, and understandable to all employees.

- The mission and vision have been clearly communicated to all employees.

- Employees understand how their jobs fit in and contribute to helping the company achieve its future vision.

- Senior leaders periodically review and revise the company's mission and vision as the business environment changes.

- Use of a wide variety of media and methods to communicate the values, expectations, and direction to employees.

- Evidence that the effectiveness of the communication methods has been evaluated and improved.

- Evidence that employees know and understand the values and expectations.

- Company establishes values and expectations that employees believe are realistic and achievable.

- Evidence of a systematic plan for teaching employees about behavior that is consistent with the values and expectations.

- A proactive approach is used throughout the organization to reward employee behavior that is consistent with the values.

- The values are integrated with leadership selection/training and with performance planning and assessment processes.

- There is evidence that the approaches used to reinforce behavior consistent with the values have been evaluated and improved.

- Executives communicate a balance in priorities for meeting the needs of shareholders, customers, and employees.

1.1a(2) How do senior leaders establish and reinforce an environment for empowerment and innovation, and encourage and support organizational and employee learning?

<u>What They're Looking for Here</u>

This question asks about how the senior leaders create a work environment that rewards risk taking and innovation and encourages employees to grow and learn. Here your answer should address how your organization purposely recruits people that are creative and risk-taking. A big part of the organizational culture is determined by the personalities of the people it hires. If you select people because they are "good soldiers" and fit in with a staid corporate culture, you're likely to have a company filled with people who have a hard time thinking outside of the box and taking risks. Companies such as 3M and Microsoft are known for hiring people that some might consider eccentric. Creativity and innovation are very much part of the culture of these two companies, so they look for people that may not fit the mold of the traditional employee.

Hiring the right people is only one dimension of having a risk-taking and learning culture. The other side of it is how the organization is structured and what it rewards. One organization that prides itself on innovation has a major banquet each year to celebrate the year's biggest failures. They give out trophies for major mistakes and failures in a variety of different categories. The idea is that if you punish failures, there will be no risk taking. This company believes that if they don't have a long list of failures each year, they are not exploring new avenues and taking risks.

The level of empowerment that exists in an organization is largely dependent upon the personalities of the senior executives. Many senior leaders I've encountered don't even trust their direct reports, let alone low-level employees. One major corporation I worked with had to have the president sign off on a purchase order because a new vice president wanted a table and waste basket that did not fall within the corporate guidelines for acceptable executive tables and waste baskets. That same president had to personally approve every new hire with a salary of over $30,000/year. With 40% annual turnover in some parts of the business, the president must have spent a lot of time each month reviewing hiring requisitions. Obviously, there was not a lot of trust and empowerment in that company.

The other part of this question focuses on how executives encourage employee learning. Remember, there is already an entire item (5.2) that asks about employee education, training, and development. This question asks specifically what do executives do to create a work environment that promotes learning. Two very concrete actions executives can take are to:

- Participate in training themselves rather than always sending staff members.
- Make training one of the last budget items that gets cut, rather than the first.

Former Baldrige winners AT&T and Motorola still invest a large percentage of their payroll costs in training compared to typical big corporations. Both companies have created cultures where continuous learning is an expectation for everyone, and the company provides significant resources to make the learning available.

Indicators for Question 1.1a(2)

- Employees are allowed to spend money and make decisions that were previously made by senior management.

- Decision making authority shows a high level of trust in employees and managers.

- Risk taking and thinking out of the box are rewarded rather than punished.

- Failures are acceptable as long as lessons are learned from them.

- Leaders try to hire people that are creative and different rather than always hiring people that look and think like them.

- Incentives are in place to encourage innovation and risk taking.

- The organization does not blame or fire people for a single failure.

- There is a great deal of trust in the organization.

- Evidence exists to suggest increased levels of empowerment of lower levels of employees.

- Executives spend less time today reviewing and approving expenditures than they did in the past.

- The company has created a culture that rewards and expects continuous learning for everyone.

- Executives participate in important training and development courses/events.

- The training/education budget is one of the last things that gets cut.

1.1a(3) How do senior leaders set directions and seek future opportunities for your organization?

What They're Looking for Here

A big part of the job of a senior executive team is to ensure that the organization will still be around and be successful over the next 10 or more years. Executives need to spend more time looking out the windshield, rather than watching the dashboard. While its important for executives to keep a handle on the daily operation of the organization, this is mostly the job of others. Part of ensuring future success is having a good vision, as I have discussed previously. What this question is about is how the leaders scan the business environment to find new opportunities for their organization. This might involve looking for new markets for your products/services that have never been tapped. Or, it might involve expanding your business by acquiring another company or forming a partnership with another organization. Part of the job of senior executives is also to "kill-off" parts of the business that no longer are viable. This was one of the first steps of Continental Airlines executives in their quest to go from "Worst to First." The company took a hard look at their flight schedules and routes and canceled the unprofitable ones.

Your answer to this question should not be vague and generic. Talk about the types of opportunities your executives look at, explain how these link into your vision, and provide some examples of new opportunities in the recent past that have helped the organization improve and grow. If possible, talk about current opportunities that are being explored, and how their achievement will help the organization.

Indicators for Question 1.1a(3)

- Executives spend a fairly large portion of time out of the company offices, exploring future opportunities.

- The organization has a proven track record of exploiting new opportunities.

- The organization's executives are aggressive in constantly looking for growth opportunities, or ways to make the company more successful.

- Senior leaders are quick to drop failing units or products/services when it is clear that it is necessary.

- New markets are constantly explored as a way of expanding market share.

- The organization has explored acquisitions or partnerships with other organizations when appropriate.

- The company shows a willingness to pay for new opportunities when they arise, and makes these decisions quickly, so as not to lose out to a competitor.

AREA TO ADDRESS   **[APPROACH, DEPLOYMENT]**

1.1b Organizational Performance Review

(1)   **How do senior leaders review organizational performance and capabilities to assess organizational health, competitive performance, and progress relative to performance goals and changing organizational needs? Include the key performance measures regularly reviewed by your senior leaders.**

What They're Looking for Here

Most senior executives get together once a month to review company performance. If this occurs in your company, you certainly want to describe this meeting in your answer to this question. Simply having a monthly meeting will not warrant many points unless the right people attend, and the right data are reviewed. It is important to have executives review performance on all the key metrics mentioned in the company scorecard (4.1) and the strategic plan (2.1). It is acceptable to refer to these other sections, rather than listing the metrics here. Along with reviewing how your own organization is doing, it is also important to review how and what competitors are doing. This should be done as part of the regular review meeting, rather than being a once-a-year process that is done in a planning meeting.

Reviewing performance data is also important outside of monthly executive meetings. Explain how executives receive feedback (on a daily basis) on key company statistics and how the data is reported or communicated to them. Having the performance data on-line or using other methods of communicating rather than paper reports will help improve your score in this area.

The answer to this question in the criteria might consist of a table that shows which executives review which data with what frequency. Another alternative is a matrix chart that shows daily measures, weekly measures, monthly measures, and quarterly metrics sorted according to the categories of metrics on the organization's scorecard (i.e., financial data, customer data, employee data, etc.)

Indicators for Question 1.1b(1)

- Executives meet on a regular basis to review and discuss company performance data.

- Data on all important metrics from the company scorecard (4.1) are reviewed on a regular basis by the appropriate executives.

- Performance is reviewed in relation to objectives or targets in the strategic plan.

- Performance is reviewed often enough to detect important changes so that problems can be quickly solved and opportunities may be exploited.

- Performance data are communicated using a variety of media and easy to read and understand formats.

> **1.1b(2) How do you translate organizational performance review findings into priorities for improvement and opportunities for innovation?**

What They're Looking for Here

The answer to this question should be fairly brief and straightforward. Explain how problems and opportunities are identified by reviewing data, and how you prioritize actions taken to fix problems and jump on the opportunities before it is too late. The point you want to get across is that you don't try to fix everything, or overreact when performance drops for a month or two. Your approach to prioritizing actions based on data analysis should sound logical, and careful. You might provide an example or two of recent improvement actions that were taken based upon trends identified in performance data, explain the result of those actions. For example, perhaps your review of competitor data indicated that they were copying your pricing strategy, so that prompted you to change your own pricing, or to focus on improving another aspect of your performance that would differentiate you from them.

Indicators for Question 1.1b(2)

- Answer presents a logical process for prioritizing actions based on data review.

- Process for prioritizing actions is integrated with overall planning process.

- Approach to data analysis shows thoroughness.

- Approach suggests that the organization is careful not to work on too many improvement actions/strategies at one time—continuous improvement of everything can lead to disaster.

1.1b(3) What are your recent performance review findings, priorities for improvement, and opportunities for innovation? How are they deployed throughout your organization and, as appropriate, to your suppliers/partners and key customers to ensure organizational alignment?

What They're Looking for Here

This question asks you to summarize what your recent performance reviews revealed as far as priorities. The answer to this question might work well in a chart with the following columns of information

Analysis Finding	Impact on Business	Action	Results

The first column would list the problems or opportunities you identified. Next, briefly describe how this could or did impact your organization. Describe the action taken and the results of this action. You need not present actual performance data here, but describe the result in words. Following this table or chart, include a paragraph or at least a couple of sentences explaining how action items or strategies are communicated internally and externally to the appropriate personnel.

Indicators for Question 1.1b(3)

- Scope of findings and action items is broader than simply financial issues.

- Actions are clearly linked back to prioritization method and data analysis.

- Analyses reveal that the organization is clever in detecting important trends inside and outside the company that may impact their future.

- Action items identified here are consistent with overall strategic and operational plans discussed in section 2.0 of the application.

- Adequate evidence is presented to suggest that actions are properly communicated to the right individuals both inside and outside the organization.

1.1b(4) How do senior leaders use organizational performance review findings and employee feedback to improve their leadership effectiveness and the effectiveness of management throughout the organization?

What They're Looking for Here

This final question pertains more to the entire Organizational Leadership (1.1) item, because it is not just about reviewing performance data and deciding on actions to improve performance. This section asks how senior leaders gather and use data to evaluate their own effectiveness as well as the effectiveness of the entire management team. Certainly the senior executives are judged on overall company performance, but this should not be the only type of data to assess their effectiveness. Some companies survey employees and ask them to rate management performance. Companies like Federal Express even link executive bonuses to ratings they receive from employees.

You should include a list of metrics or data that you use to evaluate the effectiveness of management, briefly explain how and how often the data are gathered and present some examples of how the leadership approach has been improved as a result of the evaluation data you have collected in the past. Your answer to this final question in 1.1 will have a direct bearing on whether or not your score is above 40%. Without evidence of proactive evaluation and improvement in your leadership approaches, 40% is probably the best you will get. Examiners tend to be impressed with details rather than generalities, so provide a bullet list of some of the changes and improvements that have been made in your leadership systems and approaches.

Indicators for Question 1.1b(4)

- Many different metrics and evaluation methods are used to assess the effectiveness of senior management.

- Evidence of a planned proactive approach to evaluating management systems and processes.

- Breadth and scope of data on management effectiveness.

- Evidence that data are actually used to make changes in leadership approaches and systems.

- Number and breadth of examples illustrating that refinements have occurred in the leadership approaches used in the organization.

- Number of evaluation and improvement cycles that have taken place.

1.2 PUBLIC RESPONSIBILITY AND CITIZENSHIP

Describe how your organization addresses its responsibilities to the public and how your organization practices good citizenship. (40 points)

Notes:

(1)   **Public responsibilities in areas critical to your business also should be addressed in Strategy Development (Item 2.1) and in Process Management (Category 6). Key results, such as results of regulatory/legal compliance, environmental improvements through use of "green" technology or other means, should be reported as Organizational Effectiveness Results (Item 7.5).**

(2)   **Areas of community support appropriate for inclusion in 1.2b might include efforts to strengthen local community services, education, the environment, and practices of trade, business, or professional associations.**

(3)   **Health and safety of employees are not addressed in Item 1.2; they are addressed in Item 5.3.**

AREA TO ADDRESS   **[APPROACH, DEPLOYMENT]**

1.2a Responsibilities to the Public

(1) How do you address the impacts on society of your products, services, and operations? Include your key practices, measures, and targets for regulatory and legal requirements and for risks associated with your products, services, and operations.

What They're Looking for Here

Being a Baldrige Award winning company takes more than having the right financial and customer satisfaction results and having the right systems in place. You also have to be a good corporate citizen. Examination Item 1.2 asks about how you develop plans and implement activities relating to corporate citizenship and public responsibility. What does this mean? It means factors such as environmental protection, legal, ethical, and regulatory responsibilities.

Begin your response for this area to address by describing how your company sets standards or goals relating to societal responsibility. Explain the process for setting these goals and/or standards and who is involved in the process. Your discussion should also mention the key legal and regulatory requirements that must be adhered to. Explain how the levels of performance in your own standards or targets relate to required levels. Obviously it will be more impressive if your approach is to do more than just satisfy the requirements—you have no choice in this. The examiners want to see evidence of going beyond meeting basic legal and regulatory requirements in how you set your goals and standards. Also, you should explain how you evaluate risks and possible consequences when setting these standards or requirements.

Indicators for Question 1.2a(1)

- Response includes delineation of key measures of corporate citizenship and public responsibility that are relevant and important to the company.

- A systematic process is used to define standards and goals relating to matters of corporate citizenship and public responsibility.

- Goals or standards specify levels of performance that will lead the company to a world-class level of performance on these factors.

- Evidence that risks and possible consequences are thoroughly assessed in the process of coming up with goals and standards in the area of public responsibility.

- Evidence provided to demonstrate how key goals and standards for public responsibility and corporate citizenship are translated into operational policies and procedures.

- Thorough communication of operational policies and procedures relating this item to all appropriate employees and locations within the company.

- Regularly scheduled review meetings are held to discuss progress in meeting goals and standards in the area of public responsibility and corporate citizenship.

- Plans are revised as necessary based upon changes in requirements, the business environment, or other factors.

1.2a(2) How do you anticipate public concerns with current and future products, services, and operations? How do you prepare for these concerns in a proactive manner?

<u>What They're Looking for Here</u>

The best companies are those that anticipate the future public concerns about their products or services and deal with those issues in a preventive fashion. Your response for this area should explain how you look into the future to identify trends that may impact your business, and how you plan for those trends.

An important aspect of judging your response to this area is the thoroughness and objectivity of your sources of information on future trends. Some companies rely on one or two sources of data. Others rely on a great many sources and devote a good deal of effort to predicting future trends that will impact their business. These tend to be the companies that are around for the long haul. Once you explain how and where you obtain data used to predict future trends, explain the process for using these data as inputs to your planning. An example or two will help to add credibility to your response, illustrating that you actually have used this data to change your plans.

Finally, 1.2a(2) asks how your company promotes legal and ethical conduct in all it does. Again, forget the general statements. Give us specifics of how you do this. For example, Northrop has an anonymous hotline number that employees can call to report unethical behavior or practices they have observed. This setup is combined with very thorough training for employees on what constitutes unethical behavior. These would be the types of activities that should be discussed here. Education and awareness are usually the first steps in the process, but there also needs to be measurement and control strategies in place to ensure that legal and ethical practices are followed on a continual basis.

Indicators for Question 1.2a(2)

- Number of different sources of data the company uses to predict future trends that may impact their products, services, or operations.

- Objectivity of sources of data on future trends.

- Evidence that the company acts to prevent possible problems with their products/ services in the future, rather than to cover them up.

- Amount and thoroughness of testing done on products/services sold by the company, and relevance of this testing to current and future public concerns.

- Evidence that information on future trends in public concerns are incorporated into the company's planning process.

- Existence of a specific process for integrating trends in public concerns into the planning process.

- Existence of a systematic approach to educating employees regarding legal and ethical behavior/practices.

- Extent to which employees at all levels and in all locations are provided with this education/training on legal/ethical issues.

- Existence of a system for monitoring extent to which employee behavior is consistent with legal/ethical guidelines.

- Control strategies are in place to ensure that legal/ethical practices are followed.

1.2a(3) How do you ensure ethical business practices in all stakeholder transactions and interactions?

What They're Looking for Here

Part of having good ethical practices is having a clear set of values that should have been presented in section 1.1. Solely communicating values to everyone does not do much to ensure they are followed if there is pressure to bend the rules to achieve results.

This portion of the criteria asks about how your organization encourages and promotes ethical behavior from employees. Part of this might involve screening potential new employees for ethics. Ethics are kind of difficult to teach if a person coming in the door doesn't have any. Employee orientation is also the proper place to do some ethics training. Most ethics training is dry and boring, but it doesn't need to be. Sandia Laboratories hired Dilbert creator Scott Adams to create an ethics training program built around a board game. Employees were not only entertained during the training, they remembered the lessons they learned. In spite of all of your good up-front efforts to encourage ethical behavior, there needs to be some monitoring and consequences in place. Ensure that your response to this question addresses both antecedents and consequences in your approach.

Indicators for Question 1.2a(3)

- Potential new employees are screened for possible ethics problems.

- Current and potential suppliers/partners are evaluated based upon their ethics.

- New employees are exposed to a clear set of organization ethics as part of their orientation program.

- All employees receive refresher training on ethics on a periodic basis.

- Ethics training is made interesting and relevant for employees.

- Systems are in place to monitor behavior of suppliers and employees for ethics.

- Consequences for unethical behavior are severe and consistently implemented.

AREA TO ADDRESS	[APPROACH, DEPLOYMENT]

1.2b Support of Key Communities

How do your organization, your senior leaders, and your employees actively support and strengthen your key communities? Include how you identify key communities and determine areas of emphasis for organizational involvement and support.

What They're Looking for Here

This area to address looks at two factors. First, it asks for information on what you are doing as a company to be a leader in demonstrating your corporate citizenship and involvement in the communities in which you operate. Second, it asks how you help other organizations in their quality improvement efforts. Sometimes these efforts overlap. For example, Baxter Healthcare, the world's largest manufacturer of medical supplies, held a workshop for area high school principals to teach them about the Baldrige criteria and how they may be applied in educational institutions. Because these principals are from the community surrounding Baxter's corporate offices, it is a community outreach effort. However, because it also involved helping promote total quality, it qualifies for the second half of this area to address as well. It is important that you are proactive and think strategically about the causes you choose to support. Many big companies are completely reactive, waiting for charities and community groups to ask for money and time. Writing a lot of checks will not get you a good score here. Think of Ronald McDonald House, the charity that McDonald's created to help parents with sick children. The money they spend helps parents and kids all over the world, but it also helps promote McDonald's' image.

A good way of responding to this area to address is to summarize in chart form the activities you engage in that make you a good corporate citizen. A sample of a portion of such a chart is shown in the example below.

ORGANIZATION	DESCRIPTION	NOTEWORTHY ACCOMPLISHMENTS
OPAR	Organization that funds and promotes AIDS research	• CFO is chairman • Company donated $50,000 in '99 • Meetings held at company facilities • Employees donated over 20,000 hours and $30,000 in '99
Portage Works Project	Workshop run by the mentally challenged	• All major mailings done by PWP • PWP one of our certified suppliers • Work from our company pays salaries of nine individuals from PWP
Juvenile Diabetes Foundation	Charitable organization for children with diabetes	• CEO is on the board • Company sponsors fundraising banquet each year, devoting many hours and dollars • Prepare all print advertising free for JDF • Company donates over $50,000 each year to JDF

In presenting information on the activities you engage in that make you a good corporate citizen, it may be helpful to provide some comparative data to help illustrate the importance of your accomplishments. For example, if your company donated $80,000 per quarter in 1999 to the United Fund, through employee contributions, and you have 18,000 employees, that works out to less than $5.00 per employee. The Baldrige Examiners may not know whether this is exceptional, average, or below par. Therefore, you might mention that for companies your size, it is typical for employees to average $3.20 per quarter in donations to the United Fund. This makes your performance look much better than the average company.

This area to address also asks about how you seek to enhance your leadership in corporate citizenship. Again, the worst thing to do is to present a general statement such as: "Our company continues to review and improve our approaches to corporate citizenship and promotion of community involvement, and hope to continually enhance our leadership position in these areas in the coming years." Most examiners would read a statement like this and write a comment such as: "It is not clear how the company plans to seek and exploit opportunities for improving its leadership in the areas of corporate citizenship." You need to get specific and explain how you intend to do this, and what your specific goals for leadership are in these areas.

Indicators for Question 1.2b

- Evidence of a planned systematic approach to charitable/community support.

- Breadth and scope of activities that indicate that the company is a good corporate citizen and concerned with the public welfare.

- Significance of the company's accomplishments in these areas.

- Evidence from news media and outside sources that the company is, in fact, a good corporate citizen.

- Comparison of the corporate citizenship and public responsibility activities of the applicant company to other companies that are similar in size.

- Evidence that the company has increased its efforts to be a good corporate citizen over the last few years.

- Awards and recognition received for efforts in this area.

- Lack of any "skeletons in the closet" that might prevent the company from being a good role model for the U.S. and the world. (If the issue is serious enough, it could completely disqualify an applicant.)

Chapter 6

___

Interpreting the Criteria for Strategic Planning (2.0)

OVERVIEW OF THE STRATEGIC PLANNING CATEGORY

Category 2.0 addresses the area of strategic business planning. The criteria in Category 2.0 focus on how the organization develops short- and longer-term business plans. Although it is only worth 85 points, your responses to this section can help or hurt your scores in other sections. Not having a good plan will probably dramatically impact your business results in section 7, which are worth 45% of the points.

The 2000 Award Criteria Booklet defines this category as follows:

> The **Strategic Planning** Category examines your organization's strategy development process, including how your organization develops strategic objectives, action plans, and related human resource plans. Also examined are how plans are deployed and how performance is tracked. (p.12)

This category is purposely vague about how a company needs to do strategic planning, because approaches may differ widely between a big corporation and a very small business. The small business is unlikely to have a formal strategic planning process and document, whereas the big corporation probably has many plan documents for its different businesses and has a much more structured approach to planning. As with any item that asks about your approach in Baldrige, what's important is that you tailor your approach to what's appropriate for your company or organization. A company with 25 employees that has a long and structured approach to planning with many levels of goals, objectives, and strategies may end up with a low score because their approach is overkill for a business their size.

This Category is divided into Examination Items:

    2.1 Strategy Development (40 points)
    2.2 Strategy Deployment (45 points)

Following are the descriptions of each of the two Examination Items and the Areas to Address that fall under them. As before, each section here begins with a double-ruled box containing the Examination Item, the point value, and any applicable Notes.[*] Areas to Address falling under that Item follow in a single-ruled box. In the upper right corner of each Area to Address box is an indication [brackets] of whether the Area pertains to

---

[*] Item Notes that apply to a specific Area to Address are appropriately listed in the box containing that Area.

approach, deployment, or results. All definitions and information appearing within these boxes are taken directly from the Baldrige criteria. Following each Area to Address is an explanation defining what the Examiners are looking for in assessing your application. Next, I have supplied a list of indicators or evaluation factors that will assist you in interpreting the criteria and in preparing your application.

2.1 STRATEGY DEVELOPMENT

Describe your organization's strategy development process to strengthen organizational performance and competitive position. Summarize your key strategic objectives. (40 points)

Notes:

(1) **Strategy development refers to your organization's approach (formal or informal) to a future-oriented basis for business decisions, resource allocations, and management. Such development might utilize various types of forecasts, projections, options, scenarios, and/or approaches to addressing the future.**

(2) **The word strategy should be interpreted broadly. It might be built around or lead to any or all of the following: new products, services and markets; revenue growth; cost reduction; business acquisitions; and new partnerships and alliances. Strategy might be directed toward becoming a preferred supplier, a low-cost producer, a market innovator, and/or a high-end or customized service provider. Strategy might depend upon or require you to develop different kinds of capabilities, such as rapid response, customization, market understanding, lean or virtual manufacturing, relationships, rapid innovation, technology management, leveraging assets, business process excellence, and information management. Responses to Item 2.1 should address the key factors from your point of view.**

(3) **Item 2.1 addresses overall organizational directions and strategy that might include changes in services, products, and/or product lines. However, the Item does not address product and service design; these are addressed in Item 6.1.**

AREA TO ADDRESS   **[APPROACH, DEPLOYMENT]**
2.1a Strategy Development Process

(1) What is your strategic planning process? Include key steps and key participants in the process.

What They're Looking for Here

It's amazing that this basic question was never asked in the 1998 version of the criteria. It was always assumed that one would describe the planning process in this section, and I have been instructing readers of this book to do so for years, but it was never explicitly asked for. How you answer this question should be fairly obvious. A graphic or flowchart that shows 4 to 6 major phases in your planning process is an effective first step. I've seen some with so many arrows, boxes, and feedback loops that it only conveys confusion. Make sure your diagram is simple and logical. Although there are certainly variations, most good planning models I've seen contain the following phases in the following sequence:

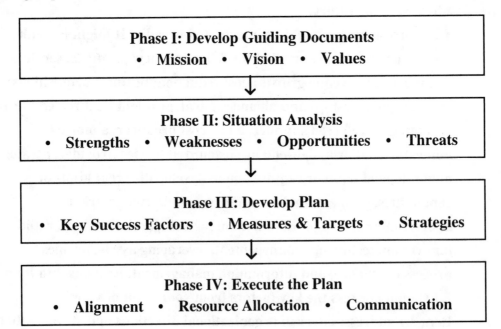

A simple and logical process like the one above will win more points than one that looks like an electrical diagram. Following the planning process graphic, you might want to describe each planning phase, in a few sentences. Keep in mind that there are other questions to be answered in this section, so don't spend four pages describing the planning process. The process is not nearly as important as the plan itself.

It is important that you show that you have a systematic approach, but also that your planning process is efficient. Many large corporations have systematic approaches to strategic and annual operating plan development. However, most of these same companies spend far too much time and money developing and rewriting plans, and far too little time using them for managing. Plans go through seven or eight drafts until they are finally approved by senior management and then they are put away in file drawers until it becomes time to begin writing next year's plans. I heard a story about the new CEO of Kodak who was horrified when he first took over the company, and found out that it took about 24 weeks each year to write the company's annual business plans. He set a goal that the plans had to be written and approved in 12 weeks the next year, and 4 weeks the following year. Four weeks is a reasonable amount of time to spend writing an annual business plan.

In your application, you need to get across the idea that your planning process is very thorough but also very efficient. I worked with a small shipping company in Long Beach, California, that won the California version of the Baldrige Award three years ago and received a site visit from Baldrige the following year. A couple of years ago they did not do strategic planning, even though they were an amazingly successful company. They had figured out a good market niche for themselves and did an outstanding job on all measures of performance, including both profits and customer satisfaction. They simply had never bothered writing a formal strategic plan. Even a small company like this needs to do some planning, which they did. However, you can bet they don't spend six months writing the plan, and they actually use it to manage with.

Indicators for Question 2.1a(1)

- Evidence of a planning process that is systematic and appropriate for the organization's size and complexity.

- Evidence that the planning process is efficient and done over several weeks rather than many months.

- Planning covers a wide variety of functions besides financials: customers/markets, products/services, human resources, research and development, etc.

- Goal or target setting is done in a scientific fashion.

- The planning process is flexible, allowing for changes to be made throughout the year as the business environment changes.

2.1a(2)   How do you consider the following key factors in your process? Include how relevant data and information are gathered and analyzed.

The factors are:

- **customer and market needs/expectations, including new product/service opportunities**
- **your competitive environment and capabilities, including use of new technology**
- **financial, societal, and other potential risks**
- **your human resource capabilities and needs**
- **your operational capabilities and needs, including resource availability**
- **your supplier and/or partner capabilities and needs**

What They're Looking for Here

Once you have defined your overall planning process, you need to go into some detail on the specific types of data that are collected in the situation analysis phase of the planning process, and talk about how these data are used to set goals and develop strategies.

The first bullet in 2.1a(2) asks about how information on current and projected customer requirements is used in the planning process. This is directly linked to section 3.1a , which asks about customer requirements now and in the future. The information you present in section 3.1 should define exactly what the most important requirements are for the different types of customers you serve. 3.1a also asks you to project who your customers might be in the future, and what you expect their requirements to be. Do not repeat this customer requirements information in this section. Rather, refer back to 3.1, and explain how customer requirements data are used to develop goals and improvement strategies. After briefly describing this in a couple of sentences, provide a couple of examples of how customer needs or requirements were used to initiate goals or strategies in your current plans. For example, you might talk about the fact that future customers are projected to want more ability to order small lots of product that are more customized to their specifications. This information has helped you to develop goals and strategies regarding small lot-size orders, and more flexibility in tailoring products to customer needs.

The next bullet in this area to address 2.1a(2) asks about how data on your competitors today and in the future are used in the planning process. You will see later that section 4.2 asks about data that you collect on your current and future competitors. Explain how information on competitor products/services and strategies is used to initiate goals and plans in your own organization. Again, examples will help lend credibility to your response. It is important that you illustrate a proactive approach rather than being a "me too" company that waits for competitors to come up with something new and then copies them. A recent example is United Airlines' Shuttle, which offers flights from cities in California and other locations. The United Shuttle, which was designed by a cross-functional team, spent a lot of time studying Southwest Airlines, the major competitor on the routes they were to serve. Rather than just copying Southwest's strategy, United tried to improve on their approach to take away some of their market share. United offers fares as low or even lower than Southwest's, but also offers what they hope customers will perceive as better service. For example, United has assigned seats; Southwest does not.

The third bullet in 2.1a(2) asks about how risks are identified and considered in the development of goals and plans. The types of risks asked about are financial, market, technological, and societal. As with the other sections, explain how data on risks are gathered and used in the development of strategies, and provide an example or two. Many companies don't do a realistic job of assessing their own capabilities when developing improvement strategies. We've all seen companies that are in one business that decide to diversify by buying another company that is in a totally different business. Business is business, right? Many of these companies fail with their new acquisitions because they don't know enough about the type of business they bought. Northrop was smart with their recent acquisition of Grumman, because the two companies are very similar. Both have similar technologies, products, people, and customers. This has helped make the transition go very smoothly, and the merging of the two company cultures very easy in comparison to what some companies have gone through. Analyzing supplier capabilities is also important in developing plans if you are heavily reliant on suppliers for your own performance. Just mentioning that you use supplier data in the planning process won't get you much credit. An example or two of how you gather and use supplier data to develop goal or strategies will help add credibility to your response.

One Baldrige applicant that received a very high score for this area presented a table that listed the various types of information used in the planning process, according to the five categories of data addressed in this area. A sample follows.

DATA USED IN PLANNING PROCESS				
Customer Requirements	Competitor Data	Risks	Company Capabilities	Supplier Data
• Focus group data	• Mascor Data	• Financial	• Telecommunication	• Northern Telecom
• Telephone survey	• Andress, Inc.	• Market	• Order processing	• NCR
• Mail survey	• J. Crew	• Societal	• Buying office	• Various

The fourth and fifth bullets ask about how you assess your own capabilities in developing plans or in seeking opportunities for future growth. The best companies today must be flexible enough to take their key competencies and move into new products, services, or markets as the business environment changes. Being able to do this well often makes the difference in whether or not a company succeeds. It is more important to realize and admit areas of improvement then to simply understand your strengths. According to some sources, Sony may have made a mistake by getting into the motion picture business. Perhaps making films is a different enough business from consumer electronics that the Sony executives' skills did not easily transfer to a different industry. Successful companies can become overconfident. This portion of the Baldrige criteria asks for information on how you identify your own strengths and weaknesses.

In discussing your approach to analyzing your capabilities, you might want to identify what you think your core competencies or strengths are. Your write-up might also benefit from an example or two that illustrates how understanding your own capabilities has helped you make the right decisions in deciding on business strategies or growth opportunities.

The sixth and final bullet of this area to address asks about how you consider supplier or partner capabilities as part of your planning process. Many organizations are heavily reliant on their suppliers, distributors, and other business partners for success. Section 6.3 of the criteria asks about how you select and manage suppliers. This portion of the criteria asks about how an assessment of supplier/partner strengths and weaknesses is integrated as part of the overall planning process. Again, you might want to present an example or two that illustrates how your knowledge of supplier/partner capabilities led you to developing the correct business strategy.

Indicators for Question 2.1a

- Degree to which quality and customer satisfaction goals, strategies, and issues are addressed in the long-term strategic business plan for the company/organization.

- Degree to which quality and customer satisfaction goals, strategies, and issues are addressed in the annual business plan for the company/organization.

- Degree to which short- and long-term employee and customer satisfaction goals are consistent with goals in other areas such as growth, profits, and markets/products.

- Planning and goal-setting processes are systematic, well organized, and include all functions in the organization.

- Evidence that customer requirements are thoroughly identified and that this information is used in developing goals and plans for the organization.

- Quality and customer satisfaction goals are based upon current and future quality requirements of customers in key markets, as well as projections of changes in customer requirements.

- Quality, customer satisfaction, and other performance improvement goals are set based upon performance of major competitors in target markets.

- Planning is done in a hierarchical fashion and at all levels in the organization, starting from the top.

- Feedback or "catchball" sessions are used to review and improve goals and plans.

- Availability of data on the capabilities of all important processes and technologies in the organization.

- Evidence that process and technology capabilities/limitations are taken into consideration when developing long- and short-term plans and goals.

- Extent to which supplier data are used as an input to the planning process.

- Degree to which the future competitive environment is addressed in the plan.

- Evidence that financial, market, and societal risks are considered in the development of goals and strategies.

- Evidence of systemic risk analysis being done as part of the planning process.

- Human resource capabilities and constraints are considered during the planning process.

AREA TO ADDRESS   **[APPROACH, DEPLOYMENT]**
2.1b Strategic Objectives

What are your key strategic objectives and your timetable for accomplishing them? In setting objectives, how do you evaluate your options to assess how well they respond to the factors in 2.1a(2) most important to your performance?

What They're Looking for Here

This portion of the criteria does not ask about how you do planning, it asks what your plans are. Last year, this was all in section 2.2, which made it clearer. This year, you describe your overall goals and objectives in this section, and present the details of your plan in section 2.2. If you have not identified your vision in the Leadership section (1.0), you definitely want to explain it here. Even if it was covered in section 1.0, you should refer to it here, so the reader remembers what you are trying to accomplish over the next three to five years. Following your vision, you might identify your key success factors, and explain how and why they were selected. Key success factors are specific areas of focus that will most help you achieve your vision. When Ericsson's Cellular Phones Division in the U.S. created a vision to become number three in market share, they focused on three key success factors: (1) brand recognition, (2) partnering with retailers and service providers, (3) new product development, with emphasis on digital technology. The company achieved its vision three years ahead of schedule, and is now on to a new vision and key success factors. When Continental Airlines wrote their vision, "Worst to First," they also identified some key success factors to get them to achieve the vision: (1) fly to win, (2) fund the future, (3) make reliability a reality, (4) working together. Each of these key success factors had specific definitions and metrics behind them, and focus on these factors has allowed Continental to dramatically improve revenue, net income, and customer satisfaction in a few short years. Ericsson and Continental Airlines are two great examples of companies with clear and explicit key success factors that got them to their vision.

In explaining your own key success factors or strategic objectives, or whatever you want to call them, make sure they do not sound too generic. I review a lot of strategic plans of big corporations and government agencies, and I see a lot of key success factors such as: provide valuable products and services to customers, become employer of choice, become supplier of choice, have a highly trained motivated workforce, growth in market share, innovation and risk taking, etc. All of these sound too generic and are fundamentals that apply to just about any organization. This is why you need to refer back to the information in 2.1a(2) to explain the rationale behind why you selected the strategic objectives or key success factors you discuss here.

Indicators for Question 2.1b

- The organization has a vision that is clear, inspirational, memorable, and realistic.

- There is evidence that a variety of information was considered in selecting key strategic objectives or success factors.

- Selected key objectives or success factors can be linked back to information on competitors, internal strengths/weaknesses, or other similar data.

- There are no more than five key strategic objectives or success factors.

- Key success factors are specific to the organization and not generic.

- Key strategic objectives or success factors are clearly defined.

- Selected strategic objectives logically sound like they will lead to accomplishment of the organization's overall vision.

- Key success factors or objectives have shown evidence of refinement or change as the business environment has changed in the last couple of years.

2.2 STRATEGY DEPLOYMENT

Describe your organization's strategy deployment process. Summarize your organization's action plans and related performance measures. Project the performance of these key measures into the future. (45 points)

Notes:

(1)   Action plan development and deployment are closely linked to other Items in the Criteria and to the performance excellence framework on page 5. Examples of key linkages are:

- Item 1.1 for how senior leaders set and communicate directions;
- Category 3 for gathering customer and market knowledge as input to strategy and action plans, and for deploying action plans;
- Category 4 for information and analysis to support development of strategy, to provide a sound performance basis for performance measurements, and to track progress relative to strategic objectives and action plans;
- Category 5 for work system needs, employee education, training, and development needs, and related human resource factors resulting from action plans;
- Category 6 for process requirements resulting from action plans; and
- Item 7.5 for accomplishments relative to organizational strategy.

(2)   Measures and/or indicators of projected performance (2.2b) might include changes resulting from new business ventures, business acquisitions, new value creation, market entry and/or shifts, and/or significant anticipated innovations in products, services, and/or technology.

AREA TO ADDRESS   **[APPROACH, DEPLOYMENT]**

2.2a Action Plan Development and Deployment

(1) How do you develop action plans that address your key strategic objectives? What are your key short and longer-term action plans? Include key changes, if any, in your products/services and/or your customers/markets.

(4) What are your key performance measures and/or indicators for tracking progress relative to your action plans?

What They're Looking for Here

Much information is required to answer question (1), which will make it hard to answer briefly. The first part of the question asks about **how** you develop strategies and action plans, linked to your key success factors or objectives described earlier. The process most organizations use to select their strategies is to brainstorm a long list of possible approaches for achieving an objective, and then evaluating each possibility based on a variety of factors such as cost, risk, likelihood of success, impact on other parts of the plan, etc. You should convey the idea that some sort of systematic decision making process is used to select the appropriate actions or strategies that are linked to your objectives. Your answer to this first part of the question need not be long—a paragraph or two should suffice.

The answer to the second part of this question will require some space. I've included question (4) in this box as well, because I think it makes sense to talk about measures, targets and action plans together in the application. An easy way to answer this first question and question (4) in this area to address that asks about performance measures is to prepare a chart or table that looks like the following.

Key Success Factor	Metrics	Strategies/Actions
International Market Growth	• $ in sales from int. customers • % international revenue • # of international proposals submitted	• Acquire new distributors • Sales offices • Targeted proposals to select prospects
Customized Products	• Increased loyalty from targeted customers • $ in revenue from customized products	• Small batches • Improved knowledge of cust. reqs. • Joint R&D with cust.

You would fill out the table or chart with all of your key objectives or success factors, and list the associated measures/metrics and strategies. You will not have the space to go into detail on the strategies, so simply listing them, and showing a good link back to the objectives is all that is necessary.

Another approach to creating a chart that summarizes your strategic plan is to also include specific short- and longer-term targets or goals for each of your performance metrics linked to your overall objectives. A chart like this might take up an entire page, and have the following headings:

Objective/KSF (Key Success Factor)	Metric	2000 Target	2003 Target	Strategies

How much detail you put into this section will depend upon the level of detail in your strategic plan, and the space limitations of a couple of pages for each Approach/Deployment Item.

Another approach to writing this section is to also include your overall performance metrics and appropriate long- and short-term targets and strategies in this section. In many organizations, there is not a separate set of organizational measures and targets. I realize that information on your organizational scorecard is asked for in Item 4.1, but it may be practical to put all of this information here because the planning and metrics sections are so closely linked. Somehow, you need to make the distinction between strategic metrics and targets, and those that cover business fundamentals like customer satisfaction, employee morale, or profits. One applicant simply used an asterisk and a number to code the metrics/targets that link back to specific key success factors or strategic objectives. An example of a portion of such a chart is shown below.

Example Strategic Plan Summary				
Metrics	**KSF (Key Success Factor) Link**	**'00 Target**	**'03 Target**	**Strategies**
<u>CUSTOMER</u> Cust. Sat. Index $ in Lost Accounts	No No	78/100 <6%	86/100 <4%	• Key account selling • Improved communication • Better selection of targeted customers
Loyalty Index	KSF # 3	56/100	72/100	• Customized products/standards
<u>FINANCIAL</u> Sales	No	$1.8 billion	$2.4 billion	• Market demand + Improved products
International $	KSF # 1	8%	21%	• Distributor partners • Acquisitions • Targeted proposals

As you can see from the example, some of the measures and targets are basic fundamentals that might be found in many companies. Others are linked to specific key success factors (KSF) such as building increased loyalty from key accounts (KSF # 3) and growth in international sales (KSF # 1). By including a chart with the information shown above, you will summarize on one page much of the information that is asked for in Items 2.2 and 4.1. Any time you can combine answers to multiple items like this is generally beneficial because it saves you space and it makes the job of the examiners easy by giving them some key charts that summarize a lot of information. You might notice that the **Strategies** column in the chart is a little vague in defining exactly how the organization will achieve its targets. You might use the text in section 2.2 to expand upon a few of the strategies. You will not have the space to go into much detail, but you want to provide the examiners with enough detail to let them know that you have a well thought-out strategic plan. They can see all the detail by reviewing your plan in the site visit. Your goal is to convince them that you warrant a site visit.

Indicators for Questions 2.2a(1) and (4)

- Use of a systematic decision making process to review and select appropriate strategies.

- Approach for deciding on action plans/strategies involves all the appropriate personnel.

- Strategy/action plan development process is done in a timely fashion.

- Strategies or action plans sound like they will help to achieve the overall vision and key objectives.

- Consistency between business strategies identified here and information on analysis of current and future customers' needs (3.1), leadership vision and direction of the company (1.1), and analysis of the competitive environment (2.1 and 4.1).

- Annual goals/targets have been developed for each major performance measure from section 4.1, and performance measures are linked back to key success factors or strategic objectives.

- Longer-term goals/targets are developed for each major performance measure from section 4.1, and performance measures are linked back to key success factors or strategic objectives.

- Goals/targets are measurable and are not confused with projects or activities— goals must be linked to result measures.

- Goals/targets will cause the company to stretch to achieve them, and help propel them to world-class levels of performance.

- Goals/targets are based on research of what is possible (i.e., through benchmarking and other means), rather than just being arbitrarily picked out of the air.

- Goals/targets and strategies are cascaded down throughout all units and levels of the company.

> **2.2a(2) What are your key human resource requirements and plans, based on your strategic objectives and action plans?**

What They're Looking for Here

This question asks about your human resource plans. The examiners want to see that your human resource goals are driven by the goals in your overall business plans. In some organizations the HR plan is developed by individuals who have no knowledge of the company's overall business goals. In order to receive a good score for this area, you need to demonstrate that there is a clear and logical relationship between your business plans and your HR plans. For example, if one of your business goals is to increase your market share in the telecommunications industry with more new products, this fact might lead to an HR goal that calls for increasing the levels of knowledge and skills among employees who design, manufacture, and market telecommunications-based products. You might also have a goal for recruiting more telecommunications experts into the company over the next few years. Examples will help the Baldrige Examiners see the relationship between human resources and overall business planning. Simply making a statement that "Our human resource planning is based upon our goals for quality and operational performance outlined in our business plan" is obviously vague and will not elicit favorable comments from the Examiners. In order to make your response more credible, you need to use illustrations and examples that are specific. Generalizing your response does not enable the Examiner to get a true picture of how well you really meet the criterion.

Up to this point, we have been discussing ways to explain how your HR planning process is integrated with your overall business planning process. Now, you need to present information in your response on the specific types of HR goals and plans asked for in the criteria. This Area to Address asks about four different types of HR goals and plans:

- Employee development (including education, training, and empowerment).

- Work design/organization, mobility, flexibility, and work scheduling.

- Compensation, recognition, and benefits.

- Recruitment and selection.

More information on these HR systems can be found in section 5.0 of the criteria. It is important to understand that HR goals are not projects or activities like: "Implement 360° appraisal process in all business by the end of the 3rd quarter." HR goals should be set for specific HR measures such as employee satisfaction ratings, safety, training hours per employee, etc.

For each of these four areas of human resources, you should list both your long-term and short-term plans or goals. If you use a chart, all of this information can be easily summarized on a page or less. Along with a summary of the goals for these four HR areas, the chart might also include information on which business goals or strategy each HR goal is tied into. If you present all of this information, you will have a very strong response to 2.2a(2).

Indicators for Question 2.2a(2)

- Demonstration that human resource plans and strategies are determined based upon long- and short-term quality and operational performance goals of the organization.
- Amount and credibility of evidence presented to suggest that business and HR planning are linked/integrated.
- Human resource plans are developed as part of the overall strategic business planning process, rather than as a separate planning activity.
- There are no arbitrary HR goals such as "Reduce head count by 10%," or "Every employee will receive 80 hours of training."
- Specific goals and plans exist for educating, training, and empowering employees.
- Specific goals and plans exist for improving mobility, flexibility, and workforce organization.
- Specific goals and plans exist for improving reward, recognition, compensation, and benefits.
- Specific goals and plans exist for improving recruiting and selection.
- Goals and objectives are measurable and specific.
- Both long- and short-term plans are presented for all of the four major HR areas asked about in the criterion.
- Clear relationship between long- and short-term plans for each of the four major HR areas asked about in the criterion.

2.2a(3)   How do you allocate resources to ensure accomplishment of your overall action plan?

What They're Looking for Here

I've worked with all kinds of large corporations and government organizations that develop very aggressive goals and objectives and fail to achieve them every year because they do not provide adequate resources. In many government and business organizations, the budgeting and planning processes are completely separate activities. Showing a flowchart that depicts how planning and resource allocation/budgeting are linked may not do much to convince examiners that you do a good job in this area. A more effective approach might be a brief narrative description of how you assign resources to achieve targets/goals in your plan, and then to provide several examples from the past.

It's important to keep in mind that resource allocation doesn't just refer to money. Resources include equipment, information technology (hardware and software), facilities, time, people, suppliers/vendors, and even data or information. You want to make two basic points in your answer to this section:

- You provide adequate resources for achievement of the goals/targets you set in your strategic plan.

- The planning and resource allocation processes are well integrated.

Simply making these two statements will not do much to convince examiners that it is true. Make sure to include an explanation of how the processes are linked, and how you ensure that adequate resources are provided for achievement of objectives and plans.

Indicators for Question 2.2a(3)

- Extent to which the budgeting and planing processes are integrated.

- Evidence that capital budgeting/planning is linked to strategic planning.

- Evidence that human resource plans and staff allocation is appropriate for targets/goals set in the strategic plan.

- Employee feedback on the adequacy of resources for achievement of plans.

2.2a(5)   How do you communicate and deploy your strategic objectives, action plans, and performance measures/indicators to achieve overall organizational alignment?

What They're Looking for Here

This question asks how plans are deployed. In other words, how do you take the overall goals for the company and cascade them down to different units, functions, and areas of the organization? Again, a graphic might help show this cascading process. The key is to illustrate that plans at all levels are linked, so that every employee is working toward the common goals of the entire organization. Every employee needs to understand how his or her job contributes to the company's vision and strategic plan.

If appropriate, you might also write about how plans and goals are communicated to suppliers, so they can help you achieve your own goals. Often this is an area where disconnects are found. Not only should you explain how goals are linked to the formation of supplier requirements, but you might want to provide a few examples.

It is also important that you explain how process reengineering or process improvement efforts are linked to the overall goals in the business plan. One way that former Baldrige winner AT&T Transmission Systems does this is by identifying what they call: "The 10 Most Wanted." These are the 10 process improvement efforts that are underway in the company at any one time. Each of the 10 most wanted is linked to strategic business goals, and only 10 projects are going at any one time, to help ensure that process improvement efforts are not too disjointed. Companies that tell every employee to go off and improve their processes frequently find that this leads to chaos, and the improvements in one area cause problems in others. Process improvement efforts need to be prioritized and channeled. Linking them to the strategic business plan is the way to do this.

Many organizations do a commendable job creating strategic business plans, but few do a good job translating those plans into actions throughout the year. The plans are written, reviewed, and often end up in a file drawer until the end of the year or until a periodic review meeting occurs. This section of the application should describe the mechanisms and systems you have in place to ensure that plans do not remain in file drawers but are actually implemented. Explain how plans are reviewed by various levels of employees and translated into individual performance plans. All levels of goals and objectives should be based upon and contribute to the overall plans of the organization.

Your response should explain how plans drive regular and ongoing work activities. Explain how major projects as well as recurring work tasks relate to major business and quality goals. Be as specific as possible, citing an example or two to illustrate that plans really do drive day-to-day activities in your company.

There should be regular review meetings that occur among various levels of employees to review plans, discuss progress toward meeting the goals outlined in the plans, and change/update the plans as necessary. Describe when these meetings occur and who attends. Explain how plans have been revised based upon changing business conditions, changing customer requirements, or other factors. Also, explain what you do when performance is not reaching projected goal levels. Be specific. The Examiners are looking for a positive approach rather than a punitive approach. One applicant who received a low score said, "Individuals who are not meeting their goals are talked to and reminded of the consequences to them of not meeting their goals." The mechanism for implementing strategies outlined in organizational plans may consist of projects, priority initiatives, task forces, teams, or other approaches. The specific approach you use is not important. What is important is that you have a clear and workable approach for translating your plans into actions and results. The leadership of the senior executives is critical to the success of implementing the plans.

Indicators for Question 2.2a(5)

- Existence of a well defined and workable process for deployment of long- and short-term plans in the organization to achieve quality and customer-satisfaction leadership.

- Scope of deployment includes all functions and levels of employees in the development of individual improvement plans that support overall plans for the company.

- Amount and objectivity of data to suggest that the plan implementation/ deployment process is successful in the organization.

- Manner of assigning and deploying resources is consistent with long- and short-term goals and priorities.

- Evidence that plans are used to direct and control day-to-day work activity in the organization, with management involvement to ensure implementation and follow-up.

- Plans are used to make decisions and control actions and priorities in the organization.

- Goals and plans are communicated to suppliers and linked to supplier/partner requirements, if appropriate.

- Productivity, cycle time, and other process improvement efforts are all linked to the goals and strategies outlined in the strategic plan.

> **AREA TO ADDRESS**   **[APPROACH, DEPLOYMENT]**
> **2.2b Performance Projections**
>
> **(1) What are your two-to-five year projections for key performance measures and/or indicators? Include key performance targets and/or goals, as appropriate.**
> **(2) How does your projected performance compare with competitors, key benchmarks, and past performance, as appropriate? What is the basis for these comparisons?**

What They're Looking for Here

This area to address asks for specific targets or goals for the next five years for key performance metrics. I recommend that you include this information in the charts I discussed for your answer to 2.2a(1) and (4). It simply does not make sense to have separate answers that relate to action plans [2.1a(1)], performance metrics or indicators [2.1a(4)], and targets or projections for desired levels of performance on each metric [2.2b(1)]. All of this information should be presented together in a single chart to show the relationships between the various factors.

As I mentioned earlier, when discussing targets or goals, it is important to convince the examiners that they are set on the basis of thorough research. The factors used to set good targets or goals include: past performance, customer requirements, resource constraints, competitor performance, and performance of benchmark organizations who may not be competitors.

The second question in this area to address requires more of a narrative answer. Your answer to this second question should read like an annual report to shareholders. Your task is to convince the Examiners that you know exactly where your business will be in the future, relative to your competitors. Avoid the term "world class" in your response. This is an overused, meaningless phrase that I often see in this section. It adds no value. "We're projecting that we will become the world-class supplier of . . ." does not say anything. Examiners are looking for specifics. Some examples of statements that are specific enough are as follows:

- By 2003, we will have at least 300 of the Fortune 500 companies as our clients.

- We will become the #4 supplier (in market share) of any company in our industry by the year 2002.

I saw a credit card company that has a projection to put American Express out of business by the end of the century. These statements are specific. It is in this section that you are allowed to write about what you want to do. In every other Baldrige category, you are only given credit for what you have already done. The key is to be realistic and specific. Explain where you think your company will be in the market, and how you will be performing on key measures. Talk about major factors such as the quality of your products and services, customer satisfaction, financial results, and operational measures.

You also need to explain where you think you will be relative to your major competitors. Keep in mind what the note to this area to address says. Your competition is getting better also, and they will be trying to take business away from you. Acknowledge the fact that competitors will not be standing still, and project what will happen to them as well. Will they be bigger, smaller, more profitable, etc.?

Along with projections of how your performance will compare to direct competitors, you need to explain how your organization will compare to benchmark companies that may not be in your same industry. Again, avoid empty statements like: "By the end of the century, companies will be benchmarking us, rather than us going to them." If you are projecting benchmark-level performance for your company, on what measures and on what processes or products? If you can get specific about areas where you are expecting to show benchmark-level performance, Examiners will be less likely to find fault with your response. Referring to the results sections of the application (7.2, 7.4, and 7.5) may also be appropriate to show the progress you have already made in achieving your longer-term projections.

Indicators for Question 2.2b(2) [Refer to Indicators under 2.1a(1) and (4) for assessing goals/targets asked for in 2.2b(1)]

- Breadth and scope of projections cover major business areas and products/services.

- Projections are specific and show that a thorough analysis has been done.

- Projections are consistent with long-term goals and strategies outlined in response to 2.2a.

- Level of specificity of projections.

- Comparisons are projected between applicant and major competitors.

- Information is presented on how key competitors are expected to improve and change over the next two-to-five years.

- Validity of sources of information used to make projections regarding company's position relative to competition in the future.

- How realistic projections are given current results and the business environment.

Chapter 7

_____

Interpreting the Criteria
for Customer and
Market Focus (3.0)

OVERVIEW OF THE CUSTOMER AND MARKET FOCUS CATEGORY

The third category in the Baldrige Award Criteria is Customer and Market Focus. In the model I outlined in Chapter 3, it indicates that Item 3.1 is the major input to the Baldrige system. Well-run organizations target specific groups of customers or markets, learn everything they can about what is important to those groups of customers, and measure their satisfaction. This section asks about all of these points. It also focuses on your approach to building loyalty through strong relationships with preferred customers. Increasing loyalty from select customers can have a dramatic effect on profits.

According to the 2000 Award Criteria, Category 3.0, Customer and Market Focus, is defined as follows:

> *Customer and Market Focus addresses how the organization seeks to understand the voices of customers and of the marketplace. The Category stresses relationships as an important part of an overall listening and learning strategy. Customer satisfaction results provide vital information for understanding customers and the marketplace. In many cases, such results and trends provide the most meaningful information, not only on customers' views but also on their marketplace behaviors—repeat business and positive referrals. (p. 33)*

Figure 7.1 is a macro process model of an organization that shows where customers and their satisfaction is assessed. Customer satisfaction is measured after the external customers have purchased the products or services produced by the organization. As you can see in the figure, this occurs at point 8, and this information is then fed back to the organization to aid them in producing better performing products and services.

The satisfaction level of internal customers is not addressed in Category 3.0. This category relates only to external customer satisfaction.

This chapter describes each of the two Examination Items in this category of the Award Criteria. As in previous chapters, each section begins with a double-ruled box containing

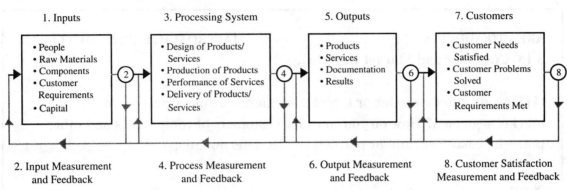

Figure 7.1: Macro Process Model of an Organization

the Examination Item, the point value, and any applicable Notes.* Areas to Address falling under that Item follow in a single-ruled box. In the upper right corner of each Area to Address box is an indication [brackets] of whether the Area pertains to approach, deployment, or results. All definitions and information appearing within these boxes are taken directly from the Baldrige criteria. Following each Area to Address is an explanation defining what the Examiners are looking for in assessing your application. Next, I have supplied a list of indicators or evaluation factors that will assist you in interpreting the criteria and in preparing your application.

3.1 CUSTOMER AND MARKET KNOWLEDGE

Describe how your organization determines short- and longer-term requirements, expectations, and preferences of customers and markets to ensure the relevance of current products/services and to develop new opportunities. (40 points)

---

* Item Notes that apply to a specific Area to Address are appropriately listed in the box containing that Area.

AREA TO ADDRESS   **[APPROACH, DEPLOYMENT]**
3.1a Customer and Market Knowledge

(1) How do you determine or target customers, customer groups, and/or market segments? How do you consider customers of competitors and other potential customers and/or markets in this determination?

Note:
(1)   If products and services are sold to end users via other businesses such as retail stores or dealers, customer groups [3.1a(1)] should include both the end users and these intermediate businesses.

<u>What They're Looking for Here</u>

Many organizations fall into their current marketplaces by accident. They don't proactively sit down and figure out who they should be selling to—they divide up their existing customers into groups. The problem with this approach is that you may end up with the wrong customers. Continental Airlines found out almost too late that they had too many low price customers that they describe as the sandals and knapsack market segment. AT&T Universal Card, a former Baldrige winner, does not exist as a company today because they did a poor job of deciding which customers they wanted to have their credit card. They made the mistake of selecting too many customers with great credit ratings who pay off their bills in full each month. Credit card companies make most of their money on customers they call "revolvers", those who pay only the minimum balance each month. AT&T Universal Card went out of business not long after winning the Baldrige Award, and their portfolio of customers now belongs to Citibank.

The lesson to be learned from both of these companies is that you need to be very careful about the types of customers from whom you solicit business. This question in the criteria asks about your market or customer segments, why you picked them, and what criteria you use to separate them. There is no right or wrong way to separate your customer into groups, but there needs to be some logic in your approach. For example, if half of your business comes from the automotive industry, it might make sense to segment your customers into two groups:

- Automotive
- Non-automotive

A manufacturer of printing equipment uses the following market segments to categorize its customers:

- Service companies.
- Educational institutions.
- Manufacturing companies.
- Government.
- Printers.

Along with a list of your various market segments, you need to explain the criteria for their selection. Certain characteristics of an industry might make them attractive or unattractive to your organization, so document what those characteristics are. There are two important points that you must convey in your answer to this first question:

- Customers are segmented logically according to common needs.
- Your organization has been deliberate in deciding what types of customers and market segments it wants to work with.

Indicators for Question 3.1a(1)

- Amount of evidence to suggest that the organization has been proactive in selecting particular markets or customer types.

- Customers are segmented into logical groups based upon common characteristics.

- New and potential market segments are evaluated periodically for growth opportunities.

- Customer segments are selected to reduce the organization's vulnerability to economic trends in a particular customer or industry.

3.1a(2) How do you listen and learn to determine key requirements and drivers of purchase decisions for current, former, and potential customers? If determination methods differ for different customers and/or customer groups, include the key differences.

What They're Looking for Here

Your response to this question should include an explanation of what the common requirements for all your customers are and what the requirements for customers in the different market segments you serve are. A common way to respond to this area is to make the following statement: "We have identified all of the requirements and expectations unique to each of the different market segments we serve." But as you have learned by now, using broad statements such as this will not earn many points. Listing the requirements and expectations of your different groups of customers will earn points in this area. A matrix with customer requirements and expectations listed along the left side, and market segments listed horizontally along the top is a great way to show common and unique customer requirements.

You also need to explain how you gather data on customer requirements. Your response will be evaluated according to the objectivity and reliability of your research methodologies and instruments. The examiners will also be looking at factors such as sample size, frequency of data collection, and use of a variety of different methods to gather data on customer requirements. Your own market research should be supplemented with data collected by outside firms to increase the objectivity of your data.

A great many customers may not be included in your efforts to gather data on customer requirements, and you may not hear from them when they have a service or product complaint. In fact, for every eight customers who are unhappy with a product or service, only one complains. Rather than complain, most unhappy customers simply take their business elsewhere. Two valuable sources of data on customers requirements are complaint data and an analysis of lost customers to determine why they leave. The examiners are looking for evidence that you gather data from customers who decide to buy their product/service elsewhere and that you use both this and customer complaint data to identify customer requirements that may not be apparent from the other market research you do.

Another good source of data is new customers. Surveying new customers to find out why they selected your product or service can provide valuable information. In your response, explain how data on lost and new customers is gathered and directed back through the appropriate channels to serve as input to the product/service design process.

Your response for this Area to Address should also explain how you use complaints and performance data as a way of identifying possible customer requirements. For example, a car company may look at the number of warranty repairs that customers have done on their cars during the first year as a set of performance data relevant to customer requirements for reliability.

The criteria in 3.1a(2) also suggest that companies need to focus on determining what customers are likely to want and expect in the future. This may seem a difficult task, but being able to predict future customer demands is what separates the leading companies from the followers. Many large manufacturing companies are designing products now that won't be on the market for several years. These companies need to be aware of how tastes and expectations of customers are likely to change in the future so that their new products will meet or exceed those expectations.

You should explain the time horizon for determination of future customer requirements. The time horizon should be based upon the trends and frequency of changes in your industry and a reasonable time frame within which you can predict trends. The amount of time you need to develop and test new products also should be considered in determining the time frame for your predictions. Some pharmaceutical companies are working on drugs that may not be on the market for more than five years. Clothing designers, on the other hand, come up with their product designs about a year or so before they hit the stores. In a fashion-oriented business, it is much more difficult to predict trends and customer tastes more than a couple of years in advance. Your response should explain the logic behind your selection of a particular time frame for predicting future customer expectations.

Your response should explain how needs of current and potential new customers are likely to change. You should also explain how you are in touch with the current and future expectations of competitors' customers. Explain how you predict your existing and potential customers' buying behavior. If you do market research, explain how you ensure that predictions made by this research have turned out to be valid.

Indicators for Question 3.1a(2)

- Data on requirements collected from your own and competitors' customers.

- Degree to which customer requirements have been identified for each market segment your company serves.

- Identification of the common and unique requirements and expectations for each market segment.

- Objectivity of data collection methods used to identify customer requirements and expectations.

- Frequency of data collection on each market segment.

- Sample sizes are large enough to be adequate representation of customer populations.

- How the company provides information to customers to help ensure that their expectations are realistic.

- Evidence of a proactive approach to identifying targeted customer markets.

- Use of multiple methodologies (e.g., telephone interviews, mail surveys, focus groups, etc.) to gather data on customer requirements.

- Use of comparative data for such areas as product/service performance, complaints, and gains/losses of customers to help determine customer requirements.

- Use of outside sources of data to supplement the applicant's own data on customer requirements.

- How the role of and logistical support for customer-contact personnel are determined.

- Use of a systematic process for gathering customer requirement data.

- Evidence that customer complaint data are summarized and used as input for design or enhancement of products/services.

- Lost customers are tracked and follow-ups are done to determine their reasons for buying products/services elsewhere and why they were dissatisfied with your products/services.

- Thoroughness of a system for following up with lost customers.

- Data gathered from new customers to determine why they selected the product/services offered by your company.

- Use of performance data on products/services to identify customer requirements.

- Evidence that data from new or lost customers are used to design, enhance, or change products and/or services.

- Extent to which requirements have been identified for all dealers or distributors if appropriate.

- Explanation of a time horizon for determination of how future customer requirements match applicant's business, products/services, and technology.

- Time frame for determination of future requirements is far enough in the future to allow the organization to capitalize on trends by designing and introducing products and services to meet future customer expectations.

- Extent to which projections are made about requirements of existing customers in the future and requirements of potential customers who currently do not buy the organization's products or services.

- Identification of important trends in technology, competition, society, economy, demographics, and other factors that may impact the business.

- Extent to which the company has identified how each of these trends will impact its business.

- Identification of specific strategies the company will use to capitalize on future trends in all areas listed above.

3.1a(3) How do you determine and/or project key product/service features, and their relative importance/value to customers for purposes of current and future marketing, product planning, and other business developments, as appropriate? How do you use relevant information from current and former customers, including marketing/sales information, customer retention, won/lost analysis, and complaints, in this determination?

Note:

(2)   Product and service features [3.1a(3)] refer to all important characteristics and to the performance of products and services throughout their full life cycle and the full "consumption chain." The focus should be on features that bear upon customer preference and repurchase loyalty—for example, those features that differentiate products and services from competing offerings. Those features might include factors such as price, value, delivery, customer or technical support, and the sales relationship.

<u>What They're Looking for Here</u>

This portion of the area to address asks about how you take the information on high-priority customer requirements (current and future) and use these data to design new products and services. Good companies not only spend a lot of time listening to customers, they find out what requirements or needs might really make a difference in customers' buying behavior. Understanding these priorities helps companies to make wise business decisions about how to invest their money. Often customers will express a desire for a particular feature or product/service characteristic, but be unwilling to pay for it when it is offered.

This section asks for information on how you determine the relative importance of current and future customer requirements, and get customers to assign a value to the things that they want to see in your products/services. The trick to doing this well is finding out information that allows you to predict customer buying behavior with a fair degree of certainty. Focus groups and surveys tend to produce unreliable results because customers are often not good predictors of their own buying behavior. They may tell you something is important, and that they would buy your product if it had a particular feature, and then not buy it for some reason. Explain the methodologies you employ to conduct research on customer priorities, and how this information serves as an input to the product/service design process you will discuss in more detail in 6.1a.

This portion of 3.1a also asks about how data on gains and losses of customers, and complaints are used to determine future product/service features. Customers cannot often articulate what they want until they don't get it. Therefore, complaints are a rich source of data for new product/service development. Customers might complain about how hard it is to find the on/off switch on a fax machine, but would never list the location of the on/off switch as one of their most important requirements.

Indicators for Question 3.1a(3)

- Evidence of a systematic approach being used to link high-priority customer requirements to the product/service design process.

- Use of a variety of different sources of data to identify customer priorities.

- Use of a systematic process to evaluate the importance of various future customer requirements.

- Demonstration that only the most important future customer requirements are translated into new product/service features.

- Clarity and completeness of explanation of how future trends are translated into customer requirements leading to design of new or enhanced products/services.

- Thoroughness of data collection process used to determine customer priorities.

- Deployment of customer requirements research to all customer market segments and product/services.

- Use of complaint data as input to the product/service design process.

- Use of gains and losses of customer referrals, and other similar data as input to the product/service design process.

- Use of data on future customer requirements to design new or enhanced products/services.

3.1a(4) How do you keep your listening and learning methods current with business needs and directions?

What They're Looking for Here

If you've come this far in this book, this portion of the Area to Address should look very familiar to you. The last question in a sequence typically calls for evidence that you systematically evaluate and improve a process. This is exactly what is being asked for here. The Baldrige Examiners are looking for evidence that you employ a systematic process to evaluate your market research and other investigations to determine future customer expectations. Begin your response with a list of the various types of research you do to determine customer requirements in the future. Along with a list of the various types of research, you might also mention who does the research, indicating whether you use outside firms or do it all using your own internal resources. For each type of research that is done, list the type of evaluation factors or measures used for assessment. Next, describe the methodology used to gather the evaluation data. Explain how the evaluation data are compiled and how conclusions are drawn.

Following your description of the methods used to evaluate your research approaches, you should explain how you use these evaluation data to improve your research methodology or expand the time horizon for your research. One area you should work on improving is the accuracy of your predictions and the length of your time horizons. The best companies in the future will be those that accurately predict long-range trends. You might end your response with an example or two of how you have used evaluation data to improve your research methodology, leading to improvements in the accuracy of your predictions or in the time horizons of your research.

Indicators for Question 3.1a(4)

- Evidence that a systematic process is used to evaluate the approaches used to determine future customer requirements.

- Extent to which evaluations are done on all methodologies employed to conduct research on future customer requirements.

- Degree to which evaluation methods are appropriate for the research methods used.

- Validity of measurement indices used for evaluation.

- Validity of evaluation approaches used.

- Clear description of a system to compile evaluation results and follow up on them.

- Evidence that evaluation results are acted upon and result in improvements in research approaches.

- Evidence to indicate that improvements have been made in the last few years in the accuracy and/or time frames of predictions about future customer requirements.

- Evidence of a number of improvements being made in approaches for determining customer needs and priorities.

3.2 CUSTOMER SATISFACTION AND RELATIONSHIPS

Describe how your organization determines the satisfaction of customers and builds relationships to retain current business and to develop new opportunities. (45 points)

AREA TO ADDRESS　　　　　　　　**[APPROACH, DEPLOYMENT]**
3.2a Customer Relationships

(1) How do you determine key access mechanisms to facilitate the ability of customers to conduct business, seek assistance and information, and make complaints? Include a summary of your key mechanisms.

Note:
  (1) **Customer relationships (3.2a) might include the development of partnerships or alliances.**

What They're Looking for Here

This is one area in which many otherwise well-run companies have difficulty. Probably the best way of ensuring easy access for customers to comment on an organization's products or services is to have a company representative visit each customer frequently. In some organizations this may not be feasible, so other methods must be used. The key here is to make it easy for the customer. Most organizations place the burden upon the customer to exert the effort and take the initiative to comment on service or product quality. If, however, you take the initiative to determine customer comments rather than waiting for them to complain, you will excel in this section.

Another aspect of your response for this area is that of how easy it is for the customer to take the initiative to comment or complain about your products or services. Many organizations have customer service 800 numbers or hotlines. Although this is a great idea, many of the companies I've dealt with don't adequately staff their customer service phone lines, so that the lines are either busy for hours or you're put on hold forever while waiting for the "next available customer service representative." If you have an 800 number or hotline for customer comments and questions, your response here should include data that indicate the prompt and efficient handling of incoming calls by your staff.

Comment cards are another common technique for allowing customers to voice their opinions. These are frequently used by hotels, restaurants, car dealers, and others. If you make use of these cards or a similar instrument, explain how customers receive or obtain the cards, how much time it takes to fill them out, and what the customers need to do to turn them in. If you simply leave the cards lying out in your place of business for the customer to choose to fill out—in their hotel room, on the seat of a new car, on the restaurant table—only people who are very upset about poor service will take the time to fill them out. If the customer needs to put a stamp on the card and mail it, even fewer of them will bother to fill out and send in the comment card. The same is true of product comment cards that are included with the owners manual of many consumer products. Only people who fill out the cards are part of the sample, so the sample is not representative of all customers.

To receive a high score for your response to this area, you must first have a well-designed and simple system for customers to comment on your products or services, and, second, a set of data from customer surveys and interviews that suggest how truly easy it is to comment, complain, or get a question answered. If 98 percent of your customers say that your customer service department answers the phones in three rings or less and is able to answer questions or resolve problems adequately almost every time, the Baldrige Examiners will take notice.

Indicators for Question 3.2a(1)

- Amount of effort and trouble customers must go through to comment or complain, or seek assistance.

- Use of frequent personal contact with customers where appropriate.

- Staffing levels and expertise of personnel manning toll-free lines designed to help customers are adequate to ensure minimal waiting and accurate answers to questions.

- How many times customers receive a busy signal when trying to call your toll-free lines (blocked calls) and how long they must wait on hold.

- Evidence of a proactive approach to get customers to comment and complain.

3.2a(2) How do you determine key customer contact requirements and deploy these requirements to all employees involved in the response chain?

What They're Looking for Here

In your response, define the major customer requirements or needs for each major point of interaction with customer-contact employees. Finally, explain how you track or measure whether or not you meet the requirements. What do you measure to determine your performance levels in meeting the customer requirements? Once again, this is a situation where a chart might be a good way of presenting all of the information called for. An example is shown below for an accounting firm that presents all three types of information asked for in this part of this Area to Address.

Major Interaction Points	Key Cust. Requirements	Indicators/Measures
Audit planning meeting	• All key players in attendance	Attendance log
	• Major milestones defined	Project plan
	• Labor budget established	Project plan
	• Efficiency of meeting	Customer satisfaction survey

As mentioned in other sections of this book, measures are meaningless without standards or goals. A customer service standard should always have two parts. The first part is the behavior or action the employee should perform, and the second is the standard or criterion that specifies how well the action must be done. Some examples are as follows:

"Approach customers *within three minutes* of the time they enter the department."

"End the transaction by *thanking the customer for using AT&T.*"

"Greet members *using their names* when they walk into the club."

The italicized parts of the statements are the criteria or standards that specify how a task should be done or how well it should be done.

Standards should always be stated in a manner that allows conformance to be reliably and objectively measured. Many applicants list standards that include words and phrases such as, "in a friendly manner," "showing empathy for the customer's situation," "promptly," or "in an efficient manner." Although these may all be good adjectives to describe service, they are neither precise nor objectively measurable. My definition of "promptness" may be quite different from yours. Standards need to be very specific and quantified whenever possible.

After listing your customer service standards, the second half of your response to this area should concentrate on how the standards are based upon customer requirements. Many organizations base their standards upon either past performance or industry standards. For example, a medical insurance company uses a standard of 30 days for the time that it should take to process a customer's claim. The 30 days is based upon industry standards. If, on the other hand, the company asked *customers* how long it should take (which it hasn't), customers would probably say one week or so. Your score in this area will be partially based upon how well you demonstrate that your major customer service standards are derived from customer requirements and expectations.

In almost all companies, it is impossible for customer-contact employees to meet customer service standards by themselves. In a restaurant, the waiter must rely upon the host/hostess, food buyer, restaurant manager, cooks, chef and others to help meet customer service standards. In a manufacturing plant, the sales representatives must rely upon production, quality assurance, procurement, accounting, production control, and other departments to help meet customer service standards. In any organization, the people who have the face-to-face contact with the customers must count on the cooperation of many others to help them deliver services and products that meet all of the customers' expectations and needs.

For this to happen, it is essential that all the employees who help the customer-contact people to achieve their goals are knowledgeable of the customer service standards and are held accountable for completing the tasks necessary to enable the customer-contact people to meet those standards. One applicant who received a high score in this area presented a list of customer service standards along the left side of a chart, and a list of the various functions in the organization horizontally along the top of the chart. Codes were used to indicate the degree of influence each support department had in helping to achieve the customer service standard. A portion of such a chart is shown as follows.

ACCOUNTABILITIES—CUSTOMER SERVICE STANDARDS					
STANDARDS	ACCOUNTING	PROCUREMENT	ENGINEERING	PRODUCTION	HRD
Deliver all orders by customer deadline	4	3	4	1	3
Provide appropriate prints and documentation with orders	4	4	1	3	3
Answer technical questions within 24 hours	4	4	1	2	3
Key: 1 = Primary Responsibility 3 = Support Responsibility 2 = Secondary Responsibility 4 = No Responsibility					

This chart is only one way of depicting the level of responsibility each function has in assisting customer-contact employees in meeting customer service standards. Your response needs to explain how support departments and others are made aware of the customer service standards and how they are held accountable for helping to achieve them.

Simply setting customer service standards and communicating them to all employees will not ensure that the standards are met. The expression "you get what you measure" is very true. If you do not track and measure the degree to which standards are met, you can almost guarantee that they will not be met on a consistent basis. Performance improvement is a matter of selecting measurement indices, setting standards, measuring performance against those standards, and sending performance feedback to employees who have influence or control over the indices.

Performance of customer-contact employees compared to established standards needs to be measured and the data fed back to employees in a timely and consistent manner. A great many service and manufacturing companies receive low scores for this area because they do not measure performance against the customer service standards, other than by surveying customers. Surveying customers is a very imprecise way to measure performance against standards. It is important to gather customer opinion about how well you meet satisfaction standards, but you should also have your own internal measurement that gets done.

As customers, the expectations and standards we have for the products and services we buy are constantly changing. Because of the poor on-time performance of airlines in recent years, many of us have lowered our expectations. Other standards have been raised. We expect our cars to be more trouble-free, to need less maintenance, and to run more efficiently than in the past.

Your response for this Area to Address should also briefly explain a process for periodically evaluating the validity of your customer service standards and your process for ensuring they are met. This should be done through ongoing research into customer requirements and expectations. The requirements and expectations should then be translated into new or revised customer service standards. After describing your approach to evaluating customer service standards, present information on how the standards have evolved or changed over the last several years. A trend indicating that the changes have resulted in more stringent standards will earn you points in this section of your application.

Indicators for Question 3.2a(2)

- Definition of key customer-contact points with customers, and most important requirements for each transaction.

- Identification of specific performance measures for each major interaction with customers.

- Extent to which measures have been identified for each customer interaction point.

- Evidence that measures are clearly related to customer requirements.

- Definition of standards for each measure associated with customer service levels.

- Standards exist for all measures.

- Standards are set based upon requirements and desires of customers and upon what competitors and benchmark organizations do.

- Evidence that data are collected on each major service measure.

- Data on extent to which standards are met is fed back to appropriate employees and used to improve performance.

- Processes for meeting or exceeding customer requirements are continually improved.

3.2a(3) What is your complaint management process? Include how you ensure that complaints are resolved effectively and promptly, and that all complaints received are aggregated and analyzed for use in overall organizational improvement.

What They're Looking for Here

Most companies have systems for filing and summarizing complaint letters and phone complaints made to customer service departments. However, the majority of customers who have comments on the services and products they buy don't bother writing a letter or calling a customer service department. Many organizations we buy from don't even have customer service departments. The Baldrige Examiners are looking for methods and procedures you have in place to capture the formal and informal customer comments or complaints. Most of the informal data get lost in many organizations, creating an unrealistic picture of actual levels of customer satisfaction. For example, the comments you make to the copier machine repair person or the field support representative from the computer company may never be recorded anywhere. Comments made to salespeople, or even customer-contact employees, are often heard and then forgotten.

In order to receive a high score for this area, you need to demonstrate that you have a comprehensive, yet simple, system for documenting all written and/or verbal comments made by customers about the quality of your products and services. You also need to have a system for summarizing and reporting all formal and informal complaints/ comments received from customers.

Your response should include a combination of process description and results. A flow chart, algorithm, or a list of steps should be included that depicts the process for responding to and correcting customer complaints. You should also explain the escalation process that occurs when a customer feels that his/her complaint has not been resolved satisfactorily. Your process will be assessed for its logic, thoroughness, and the degree to which it fits your type of business and the size of your company.

The second part of your response for this area should include data covering a variety of different indices that show you are timely in resolving customer complaints, and that complaints are resolved completely and with a minimum of inconvenience to the customer. Data on the number of complaints received is not really relevant to this Area to Address. The number of complaints received is a measure of the quality of services and/or products offered by the organization. This section should focus on how well you handle and resolve the complaints that do come in. Preventing complaints in the first place is addressed elsewhere.

One of the most common mistakes that applicants make in responding to these "process" items is to write a brief and very general description of how they deal with a particular issue or input. A typical response is as follows.

> *Each complaint received is analyzed by customer service representatives to determine its root cause. The cause of the complaint must be recorded on the Complaint Log form. Once a month, a summary report is prepared that lists the causes of complaints and provides statistics on the number of complaints tied to specific causes. Reports are sent to the department managers who have responsibility for correcting the causes of the complaints.*

The problem with a response such as this is that it is too vague and the process described does not explain:

- The steps a customer service representative follows to analyze the cause(s) of a problem.

- The knowledge customer service representatives have to analyze the cause(s) of customer complaints.

- How the organization follows up on corrective actions that need to be taken to correct problem situations.

- Evidence that the company has a system for recording all customer comments and complaints.

- Evidence that data on customer comments and complaints from all areas of the organization are aggregated and analyzed to identify trends that may help identify opportunities for improvement.

Sending a report to managers once a month is not an effective system for resolving problems.

The criteria also asks about how you summarize complaints and comments from throughout the company and use these data to better manage relationships with customers. Many companies do not do this. Complaints or comments are received by individual units or facilities, logged, and resolved. Many comments or minor complaints are never even logged, because they are resolved before they get worse. The only overall data on complaints that the company has are complaint letters or phone calls that made it to some corporate officer. These are few and far between in most companies. Baldrige is suggesting that companies have a tracking system to enable all complaint and comment data to be summarized. The key is to learn as much about customers and their needs as possible. Failure to aggregate these data and look at them across the entire company may handicap the company in making good decisions about how to improve relationships with customers.

Your response for this Area to Address should also explain how you use your analyses of the causes of customer complaints to improve processes, products, and services in the organization. Describe the process, and perhaps give an example or two of how you have used customer-complaint analyses to modify processes or a product/service.

Indicators for Question 3.2a(3)

- Comprehensiveness of system for tracking customer comments and complaints.
- Objectivity of the approach for gathering and documenting data on customer comments and/or complaints.

- All employees who have telephone or personal contact with customers have a simple but thorough way of documenting any incidental comments or complaints heard about the company's products or services.

- Data on customer comments/complaints from a variety of sources are aggregated for overall evaluation and comparison.

- Data on customer comments/complaints are fed back to appropriate personnel in a timely fashion.

- Customers believe that the comments/complaints they make to any of the organization's employees will get documented and reported.

- Existence of a formal and logical process for resolving customer complaints.

- Clearly defined escalation procedures for situations in which customers do not feel their complaint has been resolved by lower-level personnel.

- Trend showing reductions in the amount of time needed to resolve customer complaints over the past few years.

- Current performance on the amount of time needed to resolve complaints is exemplary.

- Objectivity and reliability of data on levels of customer satisfaction with the handling of complaints.

- Evidence is presented on the thoroughness with which complaints are handled.

- Organized and systematic process for analyzing the causes of customer complaints.

- Description of process clearly depicts inputs, process steps, and outputs.

- Level of clarity and amount of detail in description of process are appropriate.

- Those analyzing the causes of customer complaints have the knowledge and skills to do so.

- Information on the causes of customer complaints is fed back to employees who can correct the problems.

- Evidence that complaint data are used to initiate improvement projects that prevent future complaints and potential loss of customers.

- Evidence that analyses of causes of customer complaints are used to make changes in processes, products, and/or services.

> **3.2a(4) How do you build relationships with customers for repeat business and/or positive referral?**

What They're Looking for Here

3.1 asks how you select the most important customers for your company. 3.2a(4) asks how you build strong relationships with those important customers to ensure their future business, and hopefully generate positive referrals. In other words, how you get key customers to feel like they are married to your company for the long-run. Keeping targeted customers loyal generates a great deal of profit for some companies.

For example, United Airlines caters to its "100,000 miles a year" frequent flyers more than any other customers. In a year's time, these customers can easily spend up to $100,000 on plane tickets. These customers are also usually business travelers who pay full price for their tickets because they make reservations at the last minute and want to be able to change flights if necessary. United does many things to keep these customers loyal, and prevent them from developing allegiances with major competitors like American and Delta.

How does a company build customer loyalty? The formula is quite simple. Figure out what is most important to customers and do these things for them consistently. Also, find ways to delight and surprise them by offering extras that make them feel like they are getting more than their money's worth. For example, United sends free first class upgrades every additional 10,000 miles flown. They also give out 10,000 bonus frequent flyer miles at certain points throughout the year as mileage accrues. Little extras like this can make a big difference in loyalty. Ritz Carlton keeps a detailed data base on each guest, listing their preferences (e.g., non-allergenic pillow, non-fat milk with morning coffee, etc.). Every time a guest stays at a Ritz Carlton property, all of these little extras are automatically taken care of.

Another strategy for helping to ensure loyalty from customers is keeping the relationship hassle-free. Once a company develops a relationship with a supplier or vendor, it is often difficult and expensive to switch suppliers. Particularly if that supplier knows a lot about your company and its needs, and automatically gets you what you need without being inspected and managed. Banks have historically had a high degree of customer loyalty, and not always because of high performance. Although some customers are very unhappy with the service their bank provides, they stay because it is a complicated process to switch banks. One forward-thinking bank in California has built an advertising campaign around this concept, trying to lure customers who have been dissatisfied with other major California banks. This bank offers to switch over all of a customer's accounts with one phone call.

What the criteria look for in this area to address is evidence of a planned and logical approach to building loyalty from your most important customers. Loyalty from all customers is not critical. In fact, you might be better off having some of your customers buy from competitors. The key is to figure out which customers you want to be loyal, and then do whatever it takes to make them locked in to doing business with your company for the long haul.

Indicators for Question 3.2a(4)

- Evidence of a planned systematic approach to building loyalty from customers.

- Use of data on customer requirements to build loyalty strategy.

- Company is selective in deciding which customers are most important from which to build loyalty.

- Indication of a customized approach to building loyalty from different customers, rather than a "one size fits all" approach.

- Efforts made to make it difficult for key customers to switch suppliers.

- Measures of customer loyalty described in 3.2b are consistent with approaches to building loyalty described here.

- Deployment of loyalty-building activities to all target market or customer segments.

- Number or percentage of customers with whom partnerships or strategic alliances have been developed.

- Strength and length of time alliances or partnerships have been in effect.

3.2a(5) How do you keep your approaches to customer access and relationships current with business needs and directions?

Note:

(4)   **Customer satisfaction and dissatisfaction results and information on product/service measures that contribute to customer satisfaction or dissatisfaction should be reported in Item 7.1. These latter measures might include trends and levels in performance of customer-desired product features or customer complaint handling effectiveness (such as complaint response time, effective resolution, and percent of complaints resolved on first contact).**

What They're Looking for Here

This portion of the criteria asks about how you evaluate and improve your approaches for all of 3.2a. To receive a score of 40% or above on the Baldrige scale, you need to provide evidence that your approaches have been continually improved. Make sure that you address all of the variables covered in this broad item:

- Channels for customers to access information on products/services.

- Customer comment and complaint tracking.

- Complaint resolution process.

- Customer satisfaction measurement.

- Customer relationship building strategies/techniques.

A good way of answering this area to address is to list the variables on which you evaluate your approaches, describe the frequency and approach to evaluation in a sentence or two, and provide a laundry list of changes and improvements that have been made over the past few years. This will provide examiners with enough information to see that your approaches are mature and subject to continual evaluation and improvement. You won't have space to go into a lot of detail, but it might also be important to explain how some of the changes or improvements you've made are linked into key business strategies or plans, described in section 2.0.

Indicators for Question 3.2a(5)

- Evidence of a planned systematic approach to evaluating approaches outlined in this section.

- Identification of specific measurement indices for evaluating customer satisfaction and relationship-building approaches.

- Formal evaluation and improvement is done at least once a year.

- Mechanisms exist for ongoing continual refinement or improvement to approaches, along with more formal periodic evaluation and improvement.

- Major overhauls have been done to systems, along with minor tune-ups.

- Changes and improvements to approaches are consistent with business plans and strategies.

- Number and scope of changes and improvements that have been listed or described in the application.

- Evidence that approaches to customer satisfaction and relationship building are based upon the best practices of leading companies where appropriate.

AREA TO ADDRESS   **[APPROACH, DEPLOYMENT]**

3.2b Customer Satisfaction Determination

(1) What processes, measurement methods, and data do you use to determine customer satisfaction and dissatisfaction? Include how your measurements capture actionable information that reflects customers' future business and/or potential for positive referral. Also include any significant differences in processes or methods for different customer groups and/or market segments.

Notes:

(2)   Customer satisfaction and dissatisfaction determination (3.2b) might include any or all of the following: surveys, formal and informal feedback from customers, use of customer account data, and complaints.

(3)   Customer satisfaction measurements might include both a numerical rating scale and descriptors for each unit in the scale. Actionable customer satisfaction measurements provide reliable information about customer ratings of specific product, service, and relationship features, the linkage between those ratings, and the customer's likely future actions—repurchase and/or positive referral. Product and service features might include overall value and price.

What They're Looking for Here

Currently, it's rare to find an organization that does a great job of measuring customer satisfaction. While it's true that most organizations survey their customers to determine their satisfaction, most surveys miss the mark and often provide misleading data. For example, survey data show that about 90% of customers of one major car company are either satisfied or very satisfied with the car they purchased. Yet, only about 40% of those satisfied customers trade their car in for another one of the same make several years later. This suggests that there may be little correlation between customer satisfaction and buying behavior. Facts like this are causing many leading companies today to re-think their whole approach to customer satisfaction measurement. Most traditional surveys provide data that are not reflective of customers' true opinions and do little to predict their future buying behavior.

There are many ways to measure customer satisfaction. Most companies rely upon only two methods:

- Comment/feedback cards
- Annual mail survey sent to all or a sample of customers

Although these two approaches are certainly valid, if this is all you do, it is not likely that you are obtaining a clear view of the degree to which customers are satisfied with your products/services. The problem with comment cards and surveys is that most customers can't be bothered to take the time to fill them out. Or if they do fill them out, they do so quickly and carelessly, rating everything average or above average. As consumers of numerous goods and services, we are inundated with requests for our opinions and feedback. Most of us respond to a few of these requests and ignore the rest, unless we are extremely unhappy with the level of service or product quality. And when we are very unhappy, we usually don't bother with filling out a comment card or waiting for the annual survey—we write a letter or make a phone call right away.

The most objective way to measure customer satisfaction is by examining customers' behavior, not their opinions. The fact that Mr. Green traded in his 1995 Ford Taurus for a 2000 model from the same dealership says more about Mr. Green's level of satisfaction than any survey could. In fact, if you surveyed Mr. Green, you might find that there are a number of things he didn't like about his Taurus. The bottom line, though, is that he bought another one. The amount of repeat business an organization receives is one of the best indicators of customer satisfaction. (Unless you're the only game in town. If you live in Butte, Montana, for example, there may be only one car dealer who sells or services exclusively Mercedes.)

Market share can be an indicator of customer satisfaction, but it is not a good one. Market share is influenced by too many extraneous factors such as competition, advertising, and pricing. In this Area to Address, the Examiners are looking for an approach to measuring customer satisfaction that takes into account a variety of different sources of data. Opinion data should be gathered using several approaches and large representative samples of all the organization's customers. Other measures, such as repeat business, need to be used to supplement opinion data. The specific measures you utilize will depend upon the nature of your products/services. A single measure can be misleading, so the use of multiple indices and data gathering methodologies adds a great deal of objectivity and reliability to your approach.

If you are a large corporation with many products and/or services, chances are that you serve a variety of customers with differing needs and levels of satisfaction with your products/services. For example, a large service company might have hotels, restaurants, and amusement parks, each catering to different types of customers. A company that makes only personal computers may have many different types of customers for their single product. Customers may be segmented based upon how they will use their personal computers.

In this Area to Address, the Baldrige Examiners are also looking for evidence that you segment your customers in a logical manner and that your customer satisfaction efforts address the various segments. In some cases, it won't make sense to segment them at all. However, even if you are a small business you probably should be categorizing your customers somehow. If 60 percent of your business is conducted with AT&T, for example, and the rest is with miscellaneous small companies, you might segment your customers into two groups: (1) AT&T and (2) all others.

Indicators for Question 3.2b(1)

- Measures of loyalty of important customers are used as part of overall approach to customer satisfaction measurement.

- Company measures customer-perceived value as well as satisfaction.

- Number of different sources of data on customer satisfaction.

- Use of objective measures such as repeat business along with opinion data.

- Frequency with which customer satisfaction is measured.

- Adequate sample sizes used when measuring customer satisfaction.

- Extent to which customers in all segments/markets are included in customer satisfaction data.

- Validation done with customer satisfaction instruments prior to their use.

- Reliability of instruments used to measure customer satisfaction.

- Use of multiple approaches to gather customer opinion data, such as surveys, focus groups, etc.

- Logical approach for segmenting customers and customer satisfaction data.

- Use of measurement indices and instruments that are unique to each customer group's expectations and needs regarding your products/services.

- Separate sets of data collected on levels of customer satisfaction for each major market group or segment.

- Use of data collection instruments and methods that minimize the time customers must spend providing you with feedback.

- Evidence that approach to measuring customer satisfaction has been refined and improved.

- Evidence that soft measures of customer satisfaction (surveys, complaints, feedback) correlate with hard measures of customer buying behavior.

3.2b(2) How do you follow up with customers on products/services, and recent transactions to receive prompt and actionable feedback?

What They're Looking for Here

The frequency, thoroughness, and objectivity of the data you gather on how satisfied current customers are with your products and services are important in this Area to Address. A typical response for this Area is to explain, "We survey our customers once a year to determine their level of satisfaction with our products/services." Conducting a survey once a year represents a very weak follow-up approach. The Examiners look for frequent contact with customers (e.g., quarterly or monthly) to determine how satisfied they are with your products and services. They also want to see that you use a variety of different follow-up methods, such as phone calls, mail surveys, etc. Although the approach should be comprehensive, it is also very important that it minimizes the amount of time the customer must spend giving you feedback. Too much follow-up can be an aggravation to the customer and end up doing more to turn him/her off than anything else. Explain how your approach to follow-up is sensitive to these issues and back it up with any data that indicate customers' opinion of your follow-up system. It is also important that you do informal follow-up with customers—not to collect customer satisfaction data, but simply to build a more positive relationship.

Indicators for Question 3.2b(2)

- Percentage of customers surveyed during follow-up to determine their levels of satisfaction with your products and/or services.

- Frequent informal contact is done to build strong relationships with customers.

- Use of a variety of different data collection methods as follow-up on customer transactions.

- Follow-up approach demonstrates concern for minimizing customer time and hassle.

- Proactive follow-up is done for all types of customers and all of the organization's products and services.

3.2b(3) How do you obtain and use information on customer satisfaction relative to competitors and/or benchmarks, as appropriate?

<u>What They're Looking for Here</u>

This part refers to how you determine how your levels of customer satisfaction compare with those of your competitors. We are not looking for data here; the criteria ask *how* you determine comparative levels of customer satisfaction. Including a question or two on your customer surveys to ask your customers what they think of your competition is a common way of doing this. This is certainly not the most objective way, however. You are surveying your own customers and they may never have bought the competition's products/services, even though they may have an opinion about them. A more complete approach is to use an outside research firm to measure customer satisfaction among your own and your competitors' customers. J. D. Power, the market research firm used by the automotive industry, uses the same instruments to measure customer satisfaction among customers of all car companies. This way, the data are objective and can be easily compared. Your approach need not be as comprehensive as that used by the automotive industry, but you need to demonstrate that you gather reliable data on the levels of customer satisfaction your competitors achieve relative to your own levels.

<u>Indicators for Question 3.2b(3)</u>

- Use of a variety of sources of data on competitors' levels of customer satisfaction.

- Objectivity of data gathered on how your customer satisfaction levels compare with competitors.

- Amount of data collected on comparison of customer satisfaction levels to those of competitors.

- Reliability of data gathering methods used to assess competitors' levels of customer satisfaction.

3.2b(4) How do you keep your approaches to satisfaction determination current with business needs and directions?

What They're Looking for Here

You should begin your response here by listing the indices you use to measure and evaluate the organization's approach to determining customer satisfaction. Explain why these indices have been selected as the best measures of the effectiveness of your customer satisfaction measurement system. Next, list the steps or phases involved in your evaluation process, along with the outputs of each phase. Describe how evaluation data are summarized and reported, and explain who receives the reports. Finally, explain the process you use to review the evaluation results and develop an action plan for improving your approach to measuring customer satisfaction. A description of some of the changes you've made over the years to the customer satisfaction measurement system will help demonstrate that you do, in fact, take action based upon the evaluation data. The Baldrige Examiners are looking for a trend of continuous improvements.

Indicators for Question 3.2b(4)

- Explanation of a well-defined and systematic approach to evaluate a customer satisfaction measurement system.

- Objectivity and reliability of methodology and instruments used to evaluate customer satisfaction measurement system.

- Evaluation data are summarized and sent to appropriate managers and other employees.

- Action plans based upon evaluation data are created to identify improvements needed in customer satisfaction measurement system.

- Evidence that actions plans are actually implemented and that changes have been made in measurement instruments and/or methodologies based upon evaluation data.

- Trends showing continual improvements/enhancements in the approach to measuring customer satisfaction over the last several years.

- Evidence that improvements have been made in measurement of customer dissatisfaction indicators.

Chapter 8

Interpreting the Criteria for
Information and Analysis (4.0)

OVERVIEW OF THE INFORMATION AND ANALYSIS CATEGORY

The 2000 Baldrige Award Criteria define the Information and Analysis category as follows:

> The **Information and Analysis** Category examines your organization's performance measurement system and how your organization analyzes performance data and information. (p. 16)

The 4.0 Information and Analysis category is worth a total of 85 points and is broken down into the following three Examination Items:

- 4.1 Measurement of Organizational Performance (40 points)
- 4.2 Analysis of Organizational Performance (45 points)

The purpose of this category is to assess the types of data you collect relating to company performance and to examine the process by which you analyze those data in order to make decisions. This chapter describes the two Examination Items and two Areas to Address that fall under this category. Again, each section begins with a double-ruled box containing the Examination Item, the point value, and any applicable Notes.* Areas to Address falling under that Item follow in a single-ruled box. In the upper right corner of each Area to Address box is an indication [brackets] of whether the Area pertains to approach, deployment, or results. All definitions and information appearing within these boxes are taken directly from the Baldrige criteria. Following each Area to Address is an explanation defining what the Examiners are looking for in assessing your application. Next, I have supplied a list of indicators or evaluation factors that will assist you in interpreting the criteria and in preparing your application.

This category forms the foundation of a sound performance system. If you have a poor information and analysis system, this will lead to a low score in the sections that deal with planning (2.0), human resource focus (5.0), management of processes (6.0), and business results (7.0). If you select the wrong indices to measure, this will lead to low scores in a number of different areas that ask for results. Even if your graphs look great, you won't end up with a good score for results if the performance indices on the graphs are inappropriate.

---

* Item Notes that apply to a specific Area to Address are appropriately listed in the box containing that Area.

Category 4.0 in the 2000 Baldrige criteria is a central part of a company's strategy, outlined in section 2.1, and its results, presented in section 7.0 of the application. Even though this category is only worth a possible 85 points out of 1000, it is critical to high scores in other sections. In fact, if you do a poor job on this section, it will have a negative impact on section 7.0 that asks for results. Thus, section 4.0 actually impacts 85 points on its own, and another 450 points relating to results in section 7.0.

Some of the metrics that a company selects to measure their performance are directly related to the strategy and goals outlined in section 2.1 of the application. The measures that are discussed in section 4.0 will also be those on which results data are presented later in the application.

4.1 MEASUREMENT OF ORGANIZATIONAL PERFORMANCE

Describe how your organization provides effective performance measurement systems for understanding, aligning, and improving performance at all levels and in all parts of your organization. (40 points)

Notes:

(1) **The term information and analysis refers to the key metrics used by your organization to measure and analyze performance. Performance measurement is used in fact-based decision making for setting and aligning organizational directions and resource use at the work unit, key process, departmental, and whole organization levels.**

(2) **Deployment of data and information might be via electronic or other means. Reliability [4.1a(1)] includes reliability of software and delivery systems.**

AREA TO ADDRESS   **[APPROACH, DEPLOYMENT]**

4.1a Measurement of Organizational Performance

(1) How do you address the major components of an effective performance measurement system, including the following key factors?

- **Selection of measures/indicators, and extent and effectiveness of their use in daily operations**
- **Selection and integration of measures/indicators and completeness of data to track your overall organizational performance.**

What They're Looking for Here

- How do you measure performance in your organization?

- Why were these measures selected?

- Which metrics do you look at to evaluate daily operational performance and which metrics look at overall organizational performance?

Question 4.1a(1) asks you to list the performance measures on your organization's scorecard, and to explain how each relates to the operation of your organization, or to your overall business strategy. What is important here is that you collect data on a reasonable number of performance measures, and that you have good balance in your metrics. If your CEO or President regularly looks at more than 20 performance measures, you may receive a lower score. Leading organizations such as three-time Baldrige winner AT&T focus on a few key measures: Economic Value-Added, People Value-Added, and Customer Value-Added. Many companies have scorecards that include 10 to 15 measures, which is also reasonable. The problem with recording too many measures is that it clouds your focus and ends up distracting you from the vital few performance metrics. The best indicator of a balanced scorecard approach to measurement is a relatively equal number of measures in each of the categories in your data base. This is an area where many organizations have problems. Seventy to ninety percent of the data they collect and review on a regular basis are financial and operational. They prepare 50 pounds of financial reports each month, and maybe 1 pound of customer-related or employee satisfaction data. Financial performance is measured a hundred different ways every single day, and employee satisfaction is measured once a year with a single survey.

It is this imbalance of data that often causes applicants to receive low scores in this section.

Along with a reasonable number of performance measures, the concept of balancing the time perspective of your data is also important. Performance measures in many organizations focus almost exclusively on measuring the past. A good balanced scorecard includes measures from three perspectives: past, present, and future. Another aspect of balance that is important is that measures focus on the needs of more than just your shareholders or owners. Measures should focus on how well you satisfy customers, employees, and stakeholders, such as the community in which you operate.

The second part of this question asks about how your performance measures relate to your priorities, key success factors, or goals. Key success factors are not generic things like quality, productivity, or being customer-focused. Key success factors, which are discussed in more detail in section 2.1, are those things that you need to concentrate on to differentiate your business from major competitors. Key business drivers or success factors should be specific to your business, and may relate to strengths that need to continue to be exploited, or weaknesses that need to be corrected. For example, a company that provides cellular phone service identified competitive pricing, wide variety of rate plans, and transmission sound quality as its three key business drivers. If they are better than their competitors on all three of these measures, they will continue to grow market share at a faster rate than their competitors. For additional information on linking performance measures to key business drivers, consult my book: *Keeping Score: Using the Right Metrics to Drive World-Class Performance* (Quality Resources, 1996).

In responding to this question, an effective format might be to list your performance measures down the left side of a table, grouped by category of data. For example, a common set of categories that correspond to the Baldrige criteria include:

- Customer focused measures

- Financial and market measures

- Human resource measures

- Supplier and partner measures

- Organizational effectiveness measures.

Along the top of your table, you could list key goals or key success factors, and an additional column labeled "Business Fundamentals." Business fundamentals are used to indicate the measures that may not relate specifically to your key success factors or business drivers, but are important for running the business. For example, you will probably want to have some measure of profit, and perhaps safety in your scorecard, even though these might not be key business drivers for the organization right now. Using X's in the boxes in your matrix, indicate which of the performance measures relate to which of the key business drivers or to business fundamentals. Assigning a percentage weight to each of the measures based on its importance in your overall business strategy is another good way of showing the linkage between your measures and your strategy.

Indicators for Question 4.1a(1), bullets 1 and 2

- Organization has developed a specific set of criteria for screening out unnecessary measures from their data base.

- Evidence that the data base was built with a plan, rather than being something that just evolved over time.

- CEO or President looks at not more than 20 measures every month to evaluate the overall organization's performance.

- Degree to which macro measures have been derived from key business drivers/goals or analysis of future success factors for the company.

- Extent to which measures have been developed for all business drivers or goals.

- Consistency of performance measures with mission, vision, and values.

- Consistency of measures across business units and/or locations.

- Evidence that the organization has a well-balanced set of metrics, with approximately equal amounts of data in each of the following categories: financial performance, operational/process measures, customer satisfaction, employee satisfaction, product/service quality, supplier performance, and safety/environmental performance.

- Inclusion of both hard (customer buying behavior) and soft measures (customer opinions) of customer satisfaction in overall measures.

- Use of multiple measures of employee satisfaction.

- Selection of 3 to 6 key financial metrics that are a good mix of short- and long-term indicators of success.

- Operational/process measures are related to customer or stakeholder requirements.

- Company data base includes measures of cycle time and productivity or efficiency.

- Several overall measures of safety and environmental performance are included in the overall data base.

- Metrics include a good mix of measures of past, present, and future performance.

4.1a(1) How do you address the major components of an effective performance measurement system, including the following key factors?

- **selection, and extent and effectiveness of use of key comparative data and information**

<u>What They're Looking for Here</u>

This portion of the criteria asks about how you identify the types of competitor and comparative data needed to evaluate your own performance, and to develop appropriate strategies. You might begin your response to this section by identifying your major competitors, explaining the data you have to indicate that these organizations are, in fact, your most important competitors. For example, you might cite some industry data that outline the major players in your business or marketplace. Next, you should explain how you identify the types of data you need on your competitors. There will obviously be many sources of data on many competitors that you could gather. What the Baldrige Examiners want to see is that you are very selective in deciding what data to gather on which competitors.

Following a description of how needs for competitor data are determined, present the same sorts of information regarding comparative data. Comparative data might consist of information on other locations or business units within your own company. Comparative data might also consist of industry performance, or information on similar companies that are in a related business. For example, a hotel might compare its reservations function to the reservations function in an airline or car rental company.

What the Examiners also want to hear about in your response for this Area to Address is how you select those organizations to which you compare your own performance and practices. It is important to do both competitive comparisons and benchmarks. You might select your direct competitors as the companies you use for benchmarking purposes, or you might select companies that are totally outside your industry. A good approach employed by many exemplary organizations is to collect comparison data on all major competitors and to benchmark yourself against a variety of different functions in a variety of different organizations. In this section, you need to explain the process by which you select comparative organizations or "benchmarking partners."

One factor on which your response for this item will be evaluated is the number of different functions or indices used to compare yourself to competitors and benchmark organizations. If you compare your company with one other competitor who is also one you benchmark yourself against, you won't receive a very high score for this Area to Address. Many organizations select one or two past Baldrige winners and compare every function in their organization to them. This approach will not necessarily be effective because being a Baldrige winner does not mean that every function in the company is world-class. If, on the other hand, you have identified a dozen or more functions and compare yourself to world-class benchmarks on each function, you might end up with a perfect score in this Area to Address.

What is also considered important here is that the functions or processes you select as benchmarking and comparison targets must relate to your own goals and priorities for performance improvement, as outlined in the company's strategic and annual plans. Benchmarking is often done independently of the organization's performance improvement goals and plans. You should explain how the benchmarking and competitive comparison activities you engaged in during the past few years have supported your long-term and annual performance goals and priorities.

Within your response to this Area to Address, you should also explain how you determined which organizations were the best at performing a particular function. Some organizations do a much better job of self-promotion than others. It may be that the best organizations get overlooked in benchmarking studies because no one knows that they are the best. Explain what type and how thorough a job you did in identifying the world-class organizations used for benchmarking purposes. The more thorough your research the better. Use of benchmarking data bases has received mixed reviews, so don't use this as your only source of data.

What the Baldrige people want to see in this section is that you actually use the competitive and benchmark data as stimuli to encourage improvements. Many companies conduct benchmarking studies, review the findings, and go about business as usual. You need to have some sort of process in place for using the benchmarking studies and competitive comparisons as a way to improve processes in your company. Your response for this section should begin with an explanation of what happens to benchmarking studies and competitive analyses. Explain how studies are reviewed, who reviews them, and how action plans are developed to use the data to capitalize on improvement opportunities.

Indicators for Question 4.1a(1), Third Bullet

- A systematic process is used to identify the needs and types of competitor data that are collected.

- Needs for competitor data are consistent with the company's chosen mission, vision, and goals for the future.

- Various types of competitor data are prioritized so that those gathering and reporting the data understand which information is most critical to the business.

- A systematic approach is used to review and decide on the types of comparative data that might be most useful to the organization.

- The company has a systematic process for deciding which processes to benchmark or compare to others.

- Evidence of a systematic process for selecting competitive organizations for comparison purposes.

- Scope and breadth of data collected on competitors.

- Strong relationship between process/functions selected for competitive comparisons and benchmarking and quality goals and plans for the organization.

- Thoroughness of research done to identify organizations that are the best at particular functions or processes.

- Use of comparisons to both competitors and benchmarks for setting improvement goals.

- Number and appropriateness of criteria used for selecting competitors with which to compare your organization.

- Number and appropriateness of criteria used for selecting benchmark organizations with which to compare your organization.

- Objectivity and clarity of the criteria for selecting competitors and benchmarks for comparison purposes.

- Linkage of competitor/benchmark data with key business drivers.

- Number of different sources of data on competitors.

- Objectivity and reliability of sources of data on competitors.

4.1a(1) How do you address the major components of an effective performance measurement system, including the following key factors?

- **data and information reliability**

What They're Looking for Here

This bullet asks about how you ensure the integrity and reliability of your data. One common way of doing this is using an outside party to collect the data for you. This is often done to obtain data on customer or employee satisfaction, because comparative data is available for assessing levels of performance. Use of an outside firm does not guarantee reliability, but a good mix of inside and outside data is probably preferable to all internally-collected data. Another topic that might be discussed here is data collection techniques. Sample size selection, item analyses on surveys, survey design methodology, and topics such as these are good subjects to discuss in this section. You don't need to go overboard here and list the methods used to ensure reliability and data integrity for each metric on your corporate scorecard. Nor, do you just want to make a blanket statement like: "We use a variety of techniques to test and ensure the reliability of our data." Something in between is appropriate.

Indicators for Question 4.1a(1), Fourth Bullet

- A variety of methods are used to ensure reliability of performance data.

- Automated measurement devices are used where possible to increase reliability.

- Regularly scheduled reliability checks are done of measurement and data collection instruments.

- Automated data collection instruments are calibrated regularly according to established standards and methods.

- Use of outside data where appropriate to ensure objectivity of data.

- Evidence that appropriate sampling techniques are used.

- Consistency of metrics and data collection methods across units and facilities, if appropriate.

4.1a(1) How do you address the major components of an effective performance measurement system, including the following key factors?

- **a cost/financial understanding of improvement options**
- **correlations/projections of data to support planning**

What They're Looking for Here

These last two bullets actually fit better in the next item that asks about analysis of performance data, but the authors of the 2000 criteria elected to ask for analyses and correlations in this item. I would not go into detail in your answer to these two bullets about specific analyses or correlational studies that you have done—save this for 4.2. What I would explain in this section is how your overall collection of metrics allows you to assess the financial impact of various courses of action, and how your "scorecard metrics" link to the planning process. For example, you might discuss the strategic or key success factor metrics that we talked about in section 2.0 and how when combined with your business fundamental metrics, you are provided with a good overall picture of the state of health of your organization.

Indicators for Question 4.1a(1), Fifth and Sixth Bullets

- The organization makes a distinction between leading and lagging indicators and has a mix of both on their scorecard.

- Evidence that performance data are used to determine the financial risks and benefits of different strategies or scenarios.

- Strategic metrics, or those linked to key success factors are differentiated from business fundamental or operational metrics.

- There is a good mix of metrics that address past, present, and future time perspectives.

4.1a(2) How do you keep your performance management system current with business needs and directions?

What They're Looking for Here

Your response for this Area to Address should explain how you systematically evaluate your metrics, data collection systems, and instruments. Describe how the evaluation is done, the procedures used, instruments, etc. Don't respond with a statement such as: "We regularly evaluate and improve the scope and accuracy of our measures and data collection." Be specific. Explain exactly how you evaluate the data collection system. Your approach will be assessed based upon its thoroughness, objectivity, validity, and use of accepted evaluation methodologies. You should begin by listing the specific indices you use to measure the effectiveness of your data base. The measurement indices should include internal customer satisfaction, process, and output measures. Follow this list with a flow chart or list of steps involved in the evaluation process.

In this section you might also write about any actions you have taken to get business units and/or facilities to work together to develop common measures. If you have employed any objectives or incentives to encourage sharing of data it would also be appropriate to mention this here.

The Baldrige Examiners are also looking for evidence that you have taken actions to streamline the information processing cycle and to implement countermeasures to improve quality. Even more important is an explanation of how your performance metrics have been evaluated and improved. Measures are often added and deleted as problems arise and go away and strategy changes. For example, one company measured how well it handled phone calls from customers until performance exceeded standards for several years. The metric is still tracked but it is not given the importance rating it was when this area was a problem for the company.

Indicators for Question 4.1a(2)

- Evidence that measures or metrics have been improved to be more closely linked to business drivers or goals.

- Existence of a systematic approach for evaluating data collection systems.

- Evaluation measurement indices include measures of internal customer satisfaction, process, and output quality.

- Evidence that company has increased employees' access to data and information.

- Validity and objectivity of evaluation instruments and methodologies.

- Number of years during which evaluation has been done.

- Evidence of improvements in data collection system based upon evaluation.

- Evidence that data gathering, analysis, and reporting process has been streamlined over the last several years.

- Amount of data indicating that cycle time of data collection and dissemination has been reduced.

- Description of specific strategies and tactics that have been employed to reduce cycle time of collecting, summarizing, and disseminating data.

- Evidence of steps taken to closely align the company's performance measures with process improvement efforts.

4.2 ANALYSIS OF ORGANIZATIONAL PERFORMANCE

Describe how your organization analyzes performance data and information to assess and understand overall organizational performance. (45 points)

Notes:

(1)   **Analysis includes trends, projections, comparisons, and cause-effect correlations intended to support performance reviews and the setting of priorities for resource use. Accordingly, analysis draws upon all types of data: customer-related, financial and market, operational, and competitive.**

(2)   **Performance results should be reported in Items 7.1, 7.2, 7.3, 7.4, and 7.5.**

AREA TO ADDRESS   **[APPROACH, DEPLOYMENT]**

4.2a Analysis of Organizational Performance

(1) How do you perform analyses to support your senior executives' performance review and your organizational planning? How do you ensure that the analyses address the overall health of your organization, including your key business results and strategic objectives?

What They're Looking for Here

This section asks about what you do with all the data you collect that is described in section 2.0, 4.1, 5.0, and 6.0. Many organizations collect a great deal of data that they do not actually use. An important point to remember about answering this question is that you should have already talked about how executives and managers review performance in your organization. This information is asked for in the new 1.1b. Information on review of performance data was in this item in 1998. This is one of the most difficult items of all those in Baldrige for most organizations.

As I have mentioned several times already, the key to success in the new Baldrige criteria is **balance.** Quality has to be balanced with financial results, process improvements and improvements in productivity need to be balanced with employee satisfaction, and so forth. To receive a high score, 2000 Baldrige applicants will need to show world-class levels of both financial and quality-related results. One way of achieving good results in all areas is to understand the relationships between individual measures on the company's scorecard. For example, how much will a 5-point improvement in customer satisfaction impact profits or repeat business? Some leading companies today have conducted the research to identify and understand these correlations. For example, IBM recently completed research that shows the correlation between their Net Satisfaction Index (NSI), which is an overall measure of customer satisfaction, and future revenue for the corporation. IBM has found that even a 1-point improvement on the overall NSI translates into several million dollars in future revenue. Satisfied customers not only stay with IBM, but they are more likely to spend more on IBM products and services in the future. By understanding the relationships between these measures, IBM can make intelligent business decisions regarding investments and are supposed to increase their NSI score.

Another organization that has attempted to analyze their performance data and find links is Sears. In 1992, Sears had the worst year in its long history—the company lost almost $4 billion on $52 billion in sales. Part of the turnaround strategy was to sell-off all non retail businesses such as Budget Rental Car, Allstate Insurance, Coldwell Banker Real Estate and Discover Card. By 1995, the company had a new vision, a new strategy, and what looked like a balanced scorecard of performance metrics. Sears began collecting regular data on employee morale, customer satisfaction, and other variables besides traditional financial measures. They sought the help of Dr. Thomas Buzas to assist them in analyzing their data to find links or correlations between leading and lagging indicators. Sears hypothesis was that there should be a strong link between employee satisfaction and customer satisfaction, and between customer satisfaction and future revenue. Based on the analyses that were done, Sears found that the links were so weak, that it did not make a lot of sense to invest huge sums of money to drive either employee satisfaction or customer satisfaction. The correlations found were:

| 5 point increase→ | **DRIVES→** | 1.3 point increase→ | **DRIVES→** | 0.05% increase in |
| employee morale | | customer satisfaction | | revenue growth |

Dr. Buzas suggested that Sears take a look at the metrics and data collection instruments used to collect data on customer and employee satisfaction, because most companies find that there is a stronger link. Having this analysis told Sears that it would not be wise to invest millions of dollars to improve employee morale, because the data shows that there is a weak link between morale and other results like revenue. It appeared Sears was going to turn the corner to financial success again early in 1998, but the end of the year's results are quite disappointing. If Sears were to apply for a Baldrige Award, they would get points in this item for doing the analyses, and hopefully showing that their strategic plan is consistent with these analyses.

I would begin my answer to this first question with an overall description of how various types of data are analyzed and compared in your organization. You might want to indicate which measures you believe are leading indicators of success and which ones are lagging indicators. For example, customer satisfaction survey date might be a leading indicator that is linked to and predicts customer buying behavior or loyalty, which links to future revenue. After explaining your overall approach to analyzing performance data, list some of the correlations or links you have found, and summarize the actions or plans you have implemented based upon that knowledge. Summarizing these correlations in a table or chart might be a good idea. The headings on such a chart might be as follows:

Leading Indicators	Lagging Indicators	Correlation	Action Plans

The metrics or indicators listed in this chart might come from your overall scorecard (4.1), from your strategic plan (2.2), or from sections of the application that look at processes such as 5.0 Human Resource Focus or 6.0 Process Management.

The reason that the relationships between different performance measures are so important to understand is that you can then make scientific business decisions. This removes much of the guesswork of running a business. When decisions are made with data, and those data are well understood, there are no, or at least few, surprises. For example, when McDonald's took a risk and became the first fast-food chain to ban smoking, do you think they wondered how it would impact their business? I doubt it. McDonald's does not make a move without research and data to tell them that it is the right move. McDonald's took the risk, whereas their competitors waited and watched to see what happened. When it turned out to be a smart move that did not hurt business, and further enhanced McDonald's' image as a clean, family-oriented place, their competitors followed suit. If you want to be a leader rather than a follower, it is imperative that you measure the right things, and understand how those measures impact each other. This is the essence of what 4.2 is all about, and why it is so important in Baldrige.

This Area to Address asks about how you translate improvements in customer satisfaction or the quality of products or services into financial measures. What the Examiners want to see here is an explanation of how you measure the return on investment in your quality efforts. Let's say, for example, that you reduced the percentage of defects in your products from 2% down to .03%. The Examiners will want to know how improvements in defect rates translate into financial benefits for the company. You also need to explain the relationship between key operational measures and key financial measures. A good way of presenting this data would be a matrix that lists your key financial measures along the top and the key quality and operational measures along the left side. The matrix should indicate which quality and operational measures have a strong degree of impact upon the key financial measures. An example of such a matrix chart is shown below.

KEY MEASURES	PROFITS	MARKET SHARE	SALES	ROA
Customer Satisfaction Index	M	H	H	M
Product Defects	H	M	M	H
Design Cycle Time	L	M	M	L

A chart such as this should be supplemented with an explanation of how and why key measures of quality and operational indices lead to financial measures. You need to explain, for example, how your customer satisfaction index has a high degree of impact on both market share and sales.

Following the explanation of the review and data-analysis processes, you need to provide some examples of how analysis of financial information has led to decisions or the initiation of changes that resulted in improved levels of operational results or improvements in customer satisfaction. The examples will add credibility to your process description. One of the major factors that the Baldrige Examiners look for once they have determined that you have a sound systematic approach is deployment. A good way of giving them information on deployment is through a series of examples that include various functions and levels of employees in your organization. Space limitations will prevent you from listing as many examples as you might like, but matrices and charts are a good way of presenting a number of examples in a limited amount of space. You might create a four-column chart that looks like the following.

EXAMPLES—FINANCIAL ANALYSIS AND ACTION PLANS

FINANCIAL DATA	ANALYSIS	DECISION/ACTION	RESULTS
Loss of market share in Midwest region	11 new Wal-Mart stores open in 1994	Increased newspaper and direct mail advertising More competitive pricing Increased staffing Additional service training	1st quarter results show improvements

Indicators for Question 4.2a(1)

- Evidence that the company has conducted research to identify correlations between customer satisfaction measures and financial performance.

- Evidence of research being conducted to identify correlations between measures of product/service quality and customer satisfaction.

- Evidence of research being conducted to identify correlations between measures of supplier performance, product/service, quality, and other performance measures.

- Analysis of relationships between individual performance measures is used to make key business decisions.

- Understanding of relationships between different performance measures has been documented for all key areas of the business.

- Continued monitoring of trends and correlations is done to identify changes in correlations and possible new ones.

- Validity/rigor of research done to demonstrate correlations between measures.

- Deployment of correlations across all key performance measures identified in 4.1a and 2.1.

- How well understanding of correlations between measures have been communicated throughout the organizations.

- Evidence that major business decisions are based upon analysis of data and an understanding of how each measure relates to others.

4.2a(2) How do you ensure that the results of organization-level analyses are linked to work group and/or functional-level operations to enable effective support for decision making?

What They're Looking for Here

This was a new question for 2000 and it is a very good one. In plain English, what this question asks is how do you communicate the analyses you discussed in 4.2a(1), and how do you ensure that actions and plans throughout the organization are in concert with these analyses? This tends to be very difficult in large diverse organizations that might be spread across numerous locations. This is one area where Sears has done a fine job. Sears uses a mural to depict their vision, and shows employees how their jobs can impact the company vision, and how they can avoid Sears falling into the "retail graveyard" wherein lies W. T. Grant, Woolworth, and many other former retail giants. Every new and existing Sears employee is taken through a several hour training session to teach them about their role in helping the company make the right decisions and achieve the right results.

On site visits, examiners often find a number of projects, programs, and initiatives in a large organization that overlap, contradict each other, and often are directly contrary to the company's overall strategic plan. For example, one company had a large quality organization consisting of teams, team leaders, quality improvement projects, meetings, etc. Hundreds of thousands of dollars were being spent to improve product and service quality, with literally hundreds of "continuous improvement" projects going on at any one time. The problem was that company-level analyses had revealed that both product and service quality were fine, and that previous improvements had not led to increases in either customer satisfaction, or more importantly, increased revenue. Yet, the company had not communicated this message to employees and it let them continue their quality improvement projects. This sort of disconnect between actions of lower-level employees and analysis done by executives is actually quite typical.

A good way of impressing the examiners in this section is to first explain how you communicate the results of your analyses to employees. Stress how you make this information understandable to all, and how you make it relevant for all levels of employees and job functions. For example, why would a systems analyst in the I.T. department care about the link you have found between external customer satisfaction and future loyalty? After describing what you communicate and the methods used for communication, you need to explain how you ensure that organizational initiatives are consistent with your analyses. This is another situation where a table or chart might be appropriate. Such a chart might include the information outlined in the example below.

Initiative/Program	Desired Results	Link to Analyses
Process Reengineering	Improved efficiency Decreased costs	• Low cost provider study • Growth in operating expenses/revenue • Western Region Pilot Studies
New Hire Assessment Center	Reduced 1st year turn-over of new hires	• HR study by WMJ Associates • Analysis of cost of turn-over in 1st year
Customer Intimacy Program	Increased loyalty Increased profits	• Arthur Andersen study '98 • Internal data on sources of profitability

The format of your chart need not follow the one above exactly but you want to convey the idea that your current initiative or programs are based upon thorough analyses that show that each one will lead to the overall success of your organization.

Indicators for Question 4.2a(2)

- Evidence that organizational analyses are well communicated to all appropriate employees and stakeholders.

- Percentage of employees who can correctly explain impact of analyses of their jobs/functions.

- Evidence that the organization cancels initiatives or programs when they are inconsistent with current plans and analyses.

- No disconnects exist between initiatives/programs and analyses of data discussed in 4.2a(1).

- Company vision, key success factors, and strategic plans are consistent with analyses discussed in this section.

- Deployment of organization-level analyses to business units, facilities, and other portions of the organization.

- Evidence that key analysis data are used to guide decision making in the organization at all levels that are appropriate.

4.2a(3) How does analysis support daily operations throughout your organization? Include how this analysis ensures that measures align with action plans.

What They're Looking for Here

This question is fairly close to the previous one in that it asks about how you use data analyses to guide operations and to do planning. Whereas the previous question asks about linking organizational initiatives and higher-level programs to analyses, this question asks about how your analyses link to managing key work processes. There is a close link between this section and section 6.0 that focuses on Process Management. The setting of performance standards or control limits for process metrics should be based upon analysis of data, for example.

A good way to answer this question is to begin with a couple of sentences, explaining how data analysis forms the basis for operational planning and decision making. Your response will be much more credible if you can provide a series of examples of decisions that were made, standards that were set, or strategies/action plans that were developed that are linked to the analyses you have done. For example, after finding a link between reduced hold time in their call center and fewer abandoned calls (hang-ups), the company adjusted its standard for hold time to 45 seconds, which required additional resources. Analysis of actual hang-ups told them they typically occur only after the customer has waited at least 45 seconds. Changing the standard from 90 seconds to 45 seconds dramatically reduced the number of abandoned calls, which, in turn, led to an increase in customer satisfaction. Providing examples like this illustrates that you use data analyses to help improve your work processes.

Indicators for Question 4.2a(3)

- The organization has provided a description of how analyses and correlational studies have been used to support performance of key work processes.

- Evidence is presented to suggest that performance standards and control limits are based upon thorough analyses.

- A number of credible examples are presented to suggest that data analyses are actually linked to daily operations and decision making.

- Depth and breadth of examples illustrating links between analyses and process management and operational planning.

Chapter 9

Interpreting the Criteria for
Human Resource Focus (5.0)

OVERVIEW OF THE HUMAN RESOURCE DEVELOPMENT AND MANAGEMENT CATEGORY

The fifth category of the Baldrige criteria is defined as follows in the 2000 criteria:

> The **Human Resource Focus** Category examines how your organization enables employees to develop and utilize their full potential, aligned with the organization's objectives. Also examined are your organization's efforts to build and maintain a work environment and an employee support climate conducive to performance excellence, full participation, and personal and organizational growth. (p.18)

This category is divided into three Examination Items:

5.1 Work Systems (35 points)
5.2 Employee Education, Training, and Development (25 points)
5.3 Employee Well-Being and Satisfaction (25 points)

This category examines the processes used to select, develop, and motivate the employees in your organization, to achieve high performance. As with other Baldrige categories that ask about your approaches and deployment of those approaches, there is not a single preferred approach. Rather, the Examiners, are expecting that your human resource (HR) processes match your business, culture, and size of company. What is important here is that your HR systems are based upon logic and analysis of real needs, rather than tradition. It is important in all three items that you demonstrate how your HR processes have been designed based on an analysis of the best way to get employees and managers to consistently perform their jobs above standards.

Innovation may help improve your score, if you demonstrate novel approaches to job design, feedback, or training, but is certainly not necessary. An organization with very traditional HR processes may end up with a high score, it can show the logic behind the approach, and that the HR processes have been evaluated and improved many times over the last few years. Evidence of teams, empowerment, and other trappings of TQM programs of the past is certainly no longer a requirement, but may still be a plus if an organization finds these approaches effective.

The pages that follow include detailed explanations of how to interpret the four individual Areas to Address in this Category. As before, the information on the overall item is found in a double-ruled box and the explanation of the Areas to Address appears in a single-ruled box. In some cases, there is a separate explanation of individual subpoints [e.g., 5.2a(1)] when this is the best way of presenting the material. Following each explanation of the Areas to Address and subpoints, there is a list of indicators of what the Examiners might expect to see when evaluating your response to this Area to Address. As in the previous chapter, these indicators are not requirements, or a checklist, but simply suggestions of the type of performance an Examiner might see in a company that received a high score.

5.1 WORK SYSTEMS

Describe how your organization's work and job design, compensation, career progression, and related work force practices enable employees to achieve high performance in your operations. (35 points)

AREA TO ADDRESS   **[APPROACH, DEPLOYMENT]**

5.1a Work Systems

(1) How do you design, organize, and manage work and jobs to promote cooperation and collaboration, individual initiative, innovation, and flexibility, and to keep current with business needs?

Notes:

(1)   The term employees refers to the organization's permanent, temporary, and part-time personnel, as well as any contract employees supervised by the organization. Employees include managers and supervisors at all levels. Contract employees supervised by a contractor should be addressed in Item 6.3.

(2)   The term work design refers to how employees are organized and/or organize themselves in formal and informal, temporary, or longer-term units. This might include work teams, process teams, customer action teams, problem-solving teams, centers of excellence, functional units, cross-functional teams, and departments—self-managed or managed by supervisors. The term job design refers to responsibilities, authorities, and tasks of individuals. In some work systems, jobs might be shared by a team, based upon cross-training.

What They're Looking for Here

Business Week and other national magazines have presented feature or cover stories recently on the changing nature of jobs and work. In case you haven't noticed, the traditional job, office, and organization structures are disappearing. IBM eliminated several floors of offices in its 590 Madison Avenue building in New York City by eliminating offices for salespeople and others. IBMers are given laptop computers, cellular phones, and told to spend work time at customer locations, or at home. If they need an office, they can rent one for the day at IBM's facilities, plug in a phone and computer, and go to work. When employees complained that they missed the personal touches of their own office, IBM scanned pictures of their husbands, wives, kids, and even dogs into their laptop computers to take with them wherever they go. Desert Hospital in Palm Springs, California, has practically eliminated separate departments such as radiology. Employees work on cross-functional teams to provide a variety of different services to patients. Examples like these can be found all over America in all different industries. These are exactly the types of things that will earn you a good score in 5.1.

The first part of your answer to this Area to Address should explain how you have designed jobs and work flow. This explanation should refer back to and build upon the explanation of your organization structure that appeared in section 1.1. Begin by explaining your approach to job and work design. Expand upon this explanation with examples of how jobs and work have changed over the years. This information will help Examiners assess the degree of deployment. Keep in mind that if you have an innovative approach to design of jobs for your salespeople, but salespeople only make up 7 percent of your workforce, you may still end up with a fairly low score because of a lack of deployment.

It is important that you explain how job designs make it easier for employees to contribute to improving the organization. Empowerment is not specifically asked for in the criteria this year, but it is still hidden in there. Self-directed work teams that are given authority to monitor their own performance are not a requirement, but are an approach that would likely earn you some positive comments from the Examiners. If you still form teams to work on problems or projects, this is not necessarily a negative. Problem solving teams and cross-functional teams do serve a purpose. Baldrige is asking that you go beyond simply adding some teams to traditional jobs and work methods. Although the Baldrige criteria for 2000 are much less prescriptive than they used to be, they still promote concepts like:

- Teamwork
- Empowerment

- Flexibility
- Employee involvement

You will not find the word "team" in the criteria for this item, but you will see it all through Note (2) that accompanies 5.1. Because many will read the notes as part of the requirements rather than suggestions on how you might respond to the Item, teams are still likely to be talked about in Baldrige applications.

5.1a(1) asks about how your approach to jobs and work design encourages employees to contribute ideas for improving the company, and how you have empowered employees or given them more authority than they had in the past. With traditional departments and jobs, employees are often more concerned with their own department's needs than the needs of their customers. Departments that should work together and talk to each other often don't. Hopefully, your approach to jobs, departments, and the assignment of tasks eliminates these barriers and makes it easy and necessary for employees to talk and work together. Organizing work around key processes is one way some companies I've seen help encourage this communication and teamwork.

In order to get a high score for this Area to Address, you also need to show how your approaches to job and work design have been evaluated and improved over the last few years. Explain the factors that are used to measure effectiveness, describe your evaluation methodology, and tell the Examiners what you have changed or improved over the last few years based on this analysis. If the measures that you use to evaluate job designs and organization structure are not tied back to overall performance measures, this will end up hurting your score. Having a lot of empowerment or teamwork is not how to get a good score. You need to show the link between approaches like self-directed teams and flexible job designs and business results like profits, productivity, and customer satisfaction.

Indicators for Question 5.1a(1)

- Significance of changes to work and job design compared to traditional approaches.

- Use of self-directed work teams to complete day-to-day work in the company.

- Evidence that jobs are more flexible than they used to be.

- Extent to which the organization structure and job designs allow employees many different opportunities to suggest and implement ideas for improving the company's practices and performance.

- Innovation in creativity in job/work design.

- Evidence that employees in various positions have more authority than they did in the past—empowerment.

- Employee opinions on the effectiveness of new approaches to job and work design.

- Deployment of new approaches to job and work design across all functions, levels, and locations in the company.

- Evidence that new approaches to job and work design promote more open communication and more cooperation between department units and locations that need to work together.

- Evidence that all employees are evaluated on how well they satisfy their internal and/or external customers.

- Job performance measures are consistent with overall performance measures defined in section 4.1 of the application.

- Evidence of the effectiveness of new approaches to job and work design.

- Employee opinions on empowerment or levels of authority that exist today versus the past.

- Evidence that company management listens to employees and adopts their suggestions, or allows employees to implement their own ideas/suggestions.

- Evidence that motivation for redesign of jobs and work flow goes beyond saving money and getting more work out of employees.

- Identification of specific measurement indices for evaluating the effectiveness of new approaches to job and work design.

- Evidence of continuous improvement in job and work design approaches.

- Systems exist for promoting teamwork and sharing across units, levels, and locations.

5.1a(2) How do your managers and supervisors encourage and motivate employees to develop and utilize their full potential? Include formal and/or informal mechanisms you use to encourage and support employees in job- and career-related development/learning objectives.

What They're Looking for Here

This was a new question in the 2000 Baldrige criteria for 5.1, and it is a good addition. It asks how managers and supervisors reinforce good performance from their people, and encourage them to grow. Keep in mind that there is a question later in this area to address that asks about recognition and compensation programs. This question focuses more on informal, daily acts managers are encouraged to do to reward and motivate good performance. For example, an engineering organization I worked with had weekly department meetings where one team got to present their project to the others, for the purpose of sharing good ideas, and getting those who worked on the project some recognition from their peers. The engineers were proud of their projects and seemed to thrive on the peer and supervisor recognition received in these meetings. A plant manager I worked with made it a point to spend a couple of hours a week walking around the plant talking to people about their jobs and accomplishments. Positive attention from the plant manager was important to most of the workers, and they learned to look forward to his visits because he never criticized or challenged them on their decisions or approaches.

The point you must get across in the answer to this question is that you have mechanisms in place to encourage managers and supervisors to use effective approaches for motivating and rewarding employees. A three-day management training program often does little to change behavior of the attendees once they return to the work environment. Describing the good practices of a few key managers will not earn a lot of credit here. You need to convince the Examiners that motivation techniques are being used by each individual in a management or supervisory role.

Another topic that you might discuss in this section is how you work with employees on career development. This might be a formal developmental planning process, or a less formal counseling session managers have with employees periodically. If your approach is informal, you will need to explain how you ensure that all managers have these discussions with employees. Another topic that might be discussed here is your criteria and process for selecting managers and supervisors. Many organizations select managers and supervisors based on their technical knowledge and skills and later find that they do not have the interpersonal skills to be effective in a supervisory role.

Indicators for Question 5.1a(2)

- Evidence that the organization understands what motivates its employees.

- Systematic approaches are used by managers and supervisors to reinforce high performance from employees.

- Evidence that motivational approaches are deployed across all managers and levels in the organization.

- Approaches for motivating employees are tailored to different work groups as appropriate.

- Career development discussions are held at least once a year between manager and employee across the organization.

5.1a(3) How does your employee performance management system, including feedback to employees, support high performance?

What They're Looking for Here

This question is fairly straightforward in asking about your employee performance planning and assessment program. Having a formal system is certainly not a requirement. In fact, if you follow Dr. Deming's philosophies, you would not have a performance appraisal system because it wastes a great deal of time and only makes most people feel bad. What would impress Baldrige Examiners is that you have designed a performance management system that actually promotes better performance, and requires a minimum of meetings and forms to fill out. In my 20 years of consulting experience, I have never seen an impressive performance management system. I've seen some good features and creative approaches, but each program also had its share of flaws.

One innovative approach that has been developed in the federal government is the system being used today at the Department of Energy's Savannah River facility. Terry Frizzell and Brent Armstrong have convinced the office of personnel management to let them pilot a system that does not have numerical ratings or grades. Inflation had caused almost everyone at the site to receive the highest ratings over the years, so the ratings had become fairly meaningless. The new system is a pass/fail rating. The emphasis in the new program is on feedback and development, rather than on assigning a rating. The forms associated with the new approach are also much simplified, so managers and supervisors at the site are providing positive feedback.

An approach that has become popular in human resource circles over the last few years is 360 degree appraisals. In other words, an employee gets his performance assessed by his peers, customers, boss, and perhaps suppliers. Most systems that I've reviewed have three to five times more meetings and forms to fill out than traditional appraisal systems, and the ratings are no more valid. As one employee I talked to explained: "It was inaccurate when only my boss subjectively graded my performance based on her memory. Now I have five people who get to make a subjective judgment about me and my performance and give me a rating."

The point here is that newer approaches are not necessarily better. You need to describe your performance planning and appraisal system, and stress why and how your approach is effective, and better than what the Examiners might find in a typical company. You would probably get more points from some Examiners for not having a performance management system, than keeping one that adds no value. If you use different approaches for different levels of employees and managers, you need to point out those distinctions in your answer.

Indicators for Question 5.1a(3)

- Amount of creativity shown in performance management system.

- Consistent implementation of the performance management system across levels and units in the organization.

- Evidence that managers and employees think that the performance management system is valuable and worth the time investment.

- Methods are in place to ensure reliability/consistency in ratings if any are used.

- Emphasis is one development and performance improvement rather than giving a rating to past performance.

- The performance management system requires minimal time and hassle to administer for managers and employees.

- The performance management system is not designed to take the place of good supervisory practices.

> **5.1a(4) How do your compensation, recognition, and related reward/incentive practices reinforce high performance?**
>
> **Notes:**
> **(3)** **Compensation and recognition include promotions and bonuses that might be based upon performance, skills acquired, and other factors. Recognition includes monetary and nonmonetary, formal and informal, and individual and group recognition.**

What They're Looking for Here

A high performance work system includes mechanisms for rewarding the desired behavior and results from employees. One of the big disconnects in many companies is their compensation systems don't reward anything except sticking around for another year, or they exclusively reward short-term financial results.

Many organizations claim to be committed to quality and customer satisfaction, but they compensate employees based upon seniority, level, or job function. Few of the companies that have performance-based pay plans base the pay that employees receive upon quality. Performance-based pay is most often based upon sales, profits, and other financial measures. Some past Baldrige applicants have explained that they've implemented a gainsharing plan as a way of promoting improved quality. However, gainsharing in many cases is nothing more than profit sharing.

Based upon my own experience consulting with large companies, the ideal situation is that a large percentage of all employees' compensation is based upon their individual and group performance against quality goals and standards. Many organizations have bonus programs for executives and upper management, but not for other levels of employees. Three criteria are important in assessing the compensation systems in a company. First, a portion of employees' compensation should be based upon the degree to which individual and group performance goals have been met. The second criterion is that all levels and categories of employees should participate in performance-based compensation programs. Third and last, a large enough percentage of income should be based upon quality results to make a difference in motivating employees. Allowing employees who earn an average of $30,000 to earn an annual bonus of up to $500 for exceeding their goals is not going to do much to motivate them.

Your task in this section is to convince the Examiners that your compensation plan drives performance excellence from teams and individual employees. Many former Baldrige winners have very traditional compensation systems. The new criteria ask for evidence of a compensation program that rewards performance that is critical to organization performance. For example, the key business drivers and performance measures and goals that you discussed in sections 2.0 and 4.0 might be the foundation of your compensation or bonus plan. In some leading edge companies, all employees earn a bonus, and that bonus is based upon achieving a balance between all of their measures on their own scorecards. For example, at Federal Express, employee bonuses are based on how well you satisfy internal and/or external customers (Service), how well you satisfy your employees or teammates/peers (People), and how well you achieve or control financial results (Profit). All employees from the CEO to the package sorter are on this bonus plan, and it keeps everyone focused on their three priorities.

Another aspect of your high performance work system that is evaluated here is how you recognize employees in nonfinancial ways. Everyone likes money, but motivating employees and influencing their behavior through compensation alone is very limiting. Nonfinancial recognition is probably more important and more powerful if it is done right. Some of the important factors that will be assessed regarding your approach to recognition are:

- How much of it do you do?

- How well have you analyzed the needs and preferences of employees in designing recognition programs?

- How much creativity has been put into recognition programs to make them interesting and fun for employees?

- To what extent are the behaviors and accomplishments that are recognized consistent with organizational values, goals, and key performance measures?

Most companies and organizations pay very little attention to employee recognition, other than a few unimaginative mostly useless programs like "Employee of the Month." No imagination is put into the effort, very few employees receive any kind of recognition, and the items and privileges that are given out for recognition are often perceived by employees as insulting or at best small "thank yous." Certificates, hats, t-shirts, and coffee cups may not be too rewarding if you and your team just saved the company $15,000. Future Baldrige winners will need to put a great deal of emphasis on the approaches they use to motivate and recognize individuals and teams of employees. Companies like 1997 winner 3M Dental Products and 1998 winner Solar Turbines put a great deal of effort into recognizing employees.

The most important factor in a successful recognition program is to have senior management that believes in the importance of recognition and positive reinforcement, and is willing to make this a priority that does not get delegated down to an HR clerk who updates the employee of the month bulletin board once a month. Your approach to recognition should also be consistent with your organization structure and job design. If you have organized your organization around teams, for example, you wouldn't want all of your recognition to be based on individual performance.

Noncontingent recognition, such as periodic parties or celebrations that everyone attends regardless of their performance, may help build morale, but it is not relevant here. Write about things you do to boost overall morale in section 5.3, not here.

Indicators for Question 5.1a(4)

- Percentage of employees who have pay at risk, and percentage of overall compensation that is at risk—percentage is large enough to properly motivate desired performance.

- At-risk compensation is tied to overall performance measures over which employees have strong influence or control.

- Compensation system is consistent with organization structure, job, and work design.

- Compensation system is considered fair by employees.

- Compensation system rewards exceptional levels of performance from individuals and groups of employees.

- Evidence of creativity and use of leading edge approaches to compensation.

- Percentage of employees who receive recognition of some sort each year.

- Involvement of employees in the design of recognition programs.

- Recognition is based upon performance on key measures from 2.1, rather than separate factors.

- Creativity in approaches to recognition.

- Good mix of team and individual recognition efforts.

- Items and/or privileges used for recognition of employees promote peer reinforcement.

- Evidence of constant evaluation and improvement of approaches to compensation and recognition.

5.1a(5) How do you ensure effective communication, cooperation, and knowledge/skill sharing across work units, functions, and locations, as appropriate?

What They're Looking for Here

This was another good, new question for 2000. Effective communication is a problem for just about every organization. This area is so important, that one company that used the Baldrige assessment to evaluate its business units each year felt the need to create a "Category 8.0" in Baldrige called "Teamwork and Sharing," which looked at communication and cooperation. I don't think this warrants an entire section though, because communication is generally asked for in most approach/deployment sections.

What is asked for in this question is how you communicate information to employees and others that might help them perform their jobs better. For example, if a group in one business unit develops a new market research approach that works very well, how do they communicate this to other units that might also benefit from such an approach. An important issue to discuss in this section is how you avoid locations or business units looking at each other as competitors from whom they should hide all their secrets to success. This is actually very common in big business and government organizations. Some organizations actually encourage this competition, feeling that it will motivate better performance. Motorola, a former Baldrige winner that has fallen on hard times recently, even has a name for this approach: "warring tribes." Making a statement that units and locations in your organizations are encouraged to share and work together for the common good will not earn much credibility without evidence to support this assertion.

Another point that you want to make in this section is that you make use of a variety of different communication methods and media. People learn and communicate differently. Some are more visual, others need to read to understand, and still others need to experience something to understand it. Preparing a brief table that summarizes the types of communication methods you use and the types of information communicated might be appropriate if it does not require a lot of space.

Indicators for Question 5.1a(5)

- Use of multiple communication media and methods.

- Evidence that communication methods used are based on research on what will be most effective in the organization.

- Strength of evidence to suggest that units and locations are encouraged to share successes with one another rather than look at each other as competitors.

- Breadth and depth of approaches used for ensuring communication of best practices across the organization.

- Evidence on the effectiveness of sharing of best practices.

5.1a(6) How do you identify characteristics and skills needed by potential employees; how do you recruit and hire new employees? How do you take into account key performance requirements, diversity of your community, and fair work force practices?

What They're Looking for Here

This crucial question should have been included in this section years ago, but never was. The caliber of people an organization hires is one of the most important determinants of their success. In fact, Ritz Carlton Hotels, a former Baldrige winner, regards their recruitment and selection process to be their most closely guarded corporate secret. Competing hotel chains swear that Ritz has a machine that creates new employees! They can't understand how Ritz finds so many employees that are all perfectly groomed, with impeccable appearance and manners. You need to start out your answer to this question by listing the generic traits or competencies that you look for in employees. Maintaining a consistent corporate culture depends on your ability to hire people with the same sets of values and personalities. Characteristics such as values or work ethic are not trainable.

Some organizations have some unique requirements and unique ways of assessing potential new employees. Southwest Airlines believes that employees in their company must have a good sense of humor if they are to fit into the corporate culture. This is especially true of customer contact employees. They assess for this dimension by having each candidate get up in front of the selection committee and tell three jokes. While they don't have an applause meter, they do grade candidates on their sense of humor. A standard list of employee competencies that you assess in potential new hires will not earn you a lot of points.

Another important point to make in this section is the different approaches you use to evaluate potential new employees. Some organizations test to see if the candidate is breathing and that's about it, whereas others put candidates through rigorous tests and assessments before they hire them. I worked for a small consulting firm that put me through a grueling assessment process before I was hired. After being interviewed individually by everyone in the office as well as a few group interviews, spending a day being tested by a psychologist, I had to work a week for them for free to see how I would perform with clients in actual work situations.

Another point that needs to be addressed here is your approach for ensuring the diversity of your communities is reflected in your selection practices. In a desire to maintain a unified culture, many organizations hire people that all look and think like them. The key is to balance diversity with a need for common values and personality traits. One company that does this better than any I've seen is agricultural giant Cargill of Minneapolis. I have worked with Cargill employees all over the world and from all different cultures. Yet, they all have the same values and ethics. Cargill is often benchmarked for its ethics and corporate culture and its wonderful job of balancing diversity with common values.

Indicators for Question 5.1a(6)

- Use of creative/innovative approaches for recruiting and selecting new employees.

- Identification of specific competencies and/or traits needed for all new employees.

- Thoroughness of reliability of assessment methods used.

- Evidence of an approach to selection that balances the need for diversity with the need for a consistent corporate culture.

- Evidence that characteristics that are assessed in potential new hires are actually correlated with success.

5.2 EMPLOYEE EDUCATION, TRAINING, AND DEVELOPMENT

Describe how your organization's education and training support the achievement of your business objectives, build employee knowledge, skills, and capabilities, and contribute to improved employee performance. (25 points)

Note:

Education and training delivery [5.2a(4)] might occur inside or outside the organization and involve on-the-job, classroom, computer-based, distance learning and/or other types of delivery (formal or informal).

AREA TO ADDRESS   **[APPROACH, DEPLOYMENT]**
5.2a Employee Education, Training, and Development

(1) How does your education and training approach balance short- and longer-term organizational and employee needs, including development, learning, and career progression?

<u>What They're Looking for Here</u>

This first question asks about how well-balanced your training is. Like your organizational scorecard, training needs to be balanced to include hard and soft skills, current and future skills, and knowledge needs. An effective way of showing how balanced your training resources are is to present a pie chart or graphic of some sort that shows how your total training resources are divided. You might separate education and training into the following categories:

- Technical.
- Developmental.
- Regulatory/required.
- Safety.
- Non-technical.
- Job-specific.
- Leadership.
- New employee.

The idea is to show that you balance your training resources appropriately for your type of organization. If you are a telemarketing firm with 50% turnover per year, new hire training might be a large percentage of your budget. A nuclear fuel facility might spend 65% of their training budget on training mandated by the Nuclear Regulatory Commission or other regulatory groups. There is no single, correct way to allocate your training resources. You only need to convince the examiners that you have done so in a logical fashion for your type of organization.

Indicators for Question 5.2a(1)

- Breadth and depth of types of training identified are appropriate for the organization.

- An effective balance exists in allocating resources to short-term needs such as new hire training and longer-term training needs such as development of employees or leadership training.

- Training addresses both organizational and personal needs of employees.

5.2a(2) How do you design education and training to keep current with business and individual needs? Include how job and organizational performance are used in education and training design and evaluation.

5.2a(3) How do you seek and use input from employees and their supervisors/managers on education and training needs, expectations and design?

What They're Looking for Here

I've addressed these questions together because they both ask about how you evaluate training needs. It is important that you derive some of your training needs by looking at the organization's strategic plan and other similar documents. And, it is also important that you listen to employee's views on their own training needs as well as those of subordinates. Again, what the Examiners want to see is balance in your training curriculums. Some courses might be more geared toward personal development or generic skills, whereas others are more specific to the organizations' needs.

Employee knowledge and skills are becoming increasingly important determinants of a company's success. Even formerly low-tech jobs and industries have become high-tech. Today's auto mechanic needs to understand computer hardware, software, on-board diagnostics, as well as all the old mechanical and electrical skills. Successful companies have found that their employees need to continuously upgrade their knowledge and skills to remain competitive. This section of the Baldrige criteria is all about what you do to maintain and continually develop employee knowledge and skills. Because training is so important, and also so expensive, it is crucial that the company link its education and training to the key success factors and overall strategic objectives of the company. One way of doing this is by developing a strategic training plan. A strategic training plan is a method for identifying needed competencies and skills based upon the long-term goals of the business. This approach begins with the business goals and works backward until specific training needs have been identified. Knowledge and skills identified in this manner are those that will help the company to meet its long-term goals.

5.2a(2) asks for evidence that training is linked to the overall goals of the business. It is not necessary that you develop a strategic training plan. It is important that you have a mechanism for ensuring that education and training are one of the stones in your foundation for improving organizational performance. Refer back to previous sections of the application where you discuss your key success factors, and longer-term goals and strategies. Next, explain how training needs are identified and linked to these goals and plans. A clear way of presenting this is a chart that lists long-term business goals along the left side, major training initiatives or curriculums along the top, creating a matrix. Using this format, you can show which types of education and training are linked to which business goals, or key business drivers.

The criteria in this Area to Address also ask about how your education and training help lead to the development of employees. 5.2a(2) asks for evidence that you do not just concentrate on knowledge and skills needed to perform today's jobs. One way of responding to this item is to discuss your approach to succession planning or individual career development of all employees. Indicate how education and training needs for future jobs are identified, and how these requirements are met. To show deployment on this area to address, make sure you provide a number of different examples that show that your development approaches are not just limited to a few select groups of employees.

Many organizations approach training and education by buying a series of packaged programs from vendors who tell them what their employees need. What the Baldrige Examiners are looking for in this area is that you conduct a systematic needs assessment to determine the specific knowledge, skills, and competencies needed by different categories of employees in your organization. A systematic needs analysis does not mean conducting a survey to ask employees which courses they would like to take. A training/education needs analysis is a process that involves an initial analysis of the functions and jobs, and then a determination of the knowledge and skills needed to do the jobs and functions correctly. Group or individual interviews are conducted to identify the specific tasks employees must perform in their jobs, as well the knowledge and skills needed to perform well.

The key to this process is that the knowledge and skills are derived from analyzing job tasks. From this, relationships are identified between particular job tasks and specific skills and knowledge.

It is also important that training needs are derived from an analysis of the company's business goals. Identification of key competencies that are needed to meet business goals is the first step. Current employee skills and competencies then need to be assessed. The gap between existing and needed competencies form the foundation for a needs analysis.

Some organizations adopt the one-size-fits-all approach to training/education. Giving all of the same courses to all employees only produces the result that:

- Training is not tailored to individual needs
- Time and money are wasted on training that is irrelevant
- There will be no discussion of job/function-specific applications of the quality tools and techniques
- Skills and knowledge learned in the classroom will not translate into changed behavior on the job

Needs analysis for education and training should also be based upon individual performance appraisals and developmental plans created for each type of employee. Succession plans also can provide key data to be used for training needs analysis. Area to Address 5.2a(3) asks about how employees' input is sought for the needs analysis process. This does not mean, as I mentioned earlier, that you should do a survey to find out which courses employees want to take. Instead, employees are involved in needs analysis through the techniques called job and task analyses, which were discussed earlier. It is impossible to conduct a thorough training needs analysis without involving employees.

This Area to Address also asks for information on how employee input is sought in determining training needs. For example, some companies form training committees of managers and employees from different parts of the organization. These committees help the training department to define training needs and actually design courses. It is certainly not necessary to form training committees, but you do need to have some method of obtaining employee input in identifying training needs and developing materials to be used for education and development.

<u>Indicators for Question 5.2a(2) and (3)</u>

- Development of a strategic training plan or similar approach for linking training and education to business goals.

- Evidence that all training and education can be directly linked to one or more key business drivers or long-term business goals.

- An ongoing process exists for ensuring that training and education are closely tied to business goals and success factors.

- Linkage between training/education activities and HR goals outlined in Item 2.2.

- Evidence of a systematic approach to identifying future training needs of employees to promote their development and growth.

- Existence of a career development plan for each employee, with an identification of education and training needs for potential future assignments.

- Depth and breadth of developmental plans and related training/education needs.

- The organization has conducted systematic needs analysis to identify the knowledge and skills needed by employees to function in the work systems and organization structures used in the company.

- Training on generic topics like leadership and safety has been designed based upon a thorough needs analysis.

- Curriculums have been designed that organize courses into logical sequences.

- Curriculums have been defined for most key positions in the organization.

- Leadership training is well integrated with the company's approach to job and work design.

- Employees at various levels and from various functions provide input to aid in designing and developing training.

> **5.2a(4) How do you deliver and evaluate education and training? Include both formal and informal education, training, and learning, as appropriate.**

What They're Looking for Here

This question actually asks for two pieces of information that are fairly complex:

- Methods and media used to deliver education and training
- Approaches used to evaluate the effectiveness of training.

Let's start by explaining how to answer the first question. The point you want to get across is that you use a variety of training media and methods that are tailored to practical considerations such as the size of the training audience, scheduling logistics, and content and audience characteristics. You want to ensure that the media matches to content of the training. For example, you would not want to have a lecture class that is supposed to improve the diagnostic skills of technicians, or a video to teach salespeople how to overcome objections better. It is also important to show how you have considered the capabilities and preferences of your employees in designing training. For example, if many new employees have trouble reading, you might design a video or use another delivery method than a book that trainees have to read.

A good way of presenting how you link training delivery methods to content types and audience characteristics is to prepare a chart that lists all the major types of education and training you deliver along with left side, and the training media/delivery methods along the top, indicating which methods are used with which types of training.

This question also asks about how you evaluate the effectiveness of your education and training. This education and training should be evaluated on four dimensions:

- Reaction

- Learning

- Behavior Change

- Results

Reaction data are the most common, and are collected via questionnaires or surveys filled out by participants at the end of a class. The typical questionnaire asks the participants to rate the course, the instructor, the content, and the relevancy of the material on a five-point scale, along with a few open-ended questions.

The second education/training evaluation dimension is *learning*. This is another index that provides data on the effectiveness of the training delivery. This set of data should not simply report what the trainees/participants thought of the courses, but rather should indicate whether or not employees have mastered the material covered. Testing is the only appropriate means of measuring learning in an education/training program. Many large organizations do no testing in any of their courses, and hence have no data to demonstrate that participants learned any of the material. Testing does not have to consist of a paper-and-pencil, multiple-choice test. In any course in which skills are taught, performance tests are much better than written tests. A performance test might be a case study, a simulation, a role play, a demonstration, or any other situation where the trainee must demonstrate that he/she has mastered the skills taught in the course. Tests should be developed based upon the objectives of the courses, and should simulate how the trainees will use the skills in the job environment.

The third dimension of training/education evaluation is *behavior change*. This dimension considers whether trainees' behavior on the job has changed as a result of the training/ education they received. Many large and small organizations do not have data on behavior change. This type of data, however, is even more important than data on what was learned. If skills learned in training are not used on the job, performance will not improve, and the money and time spent on the training will have been wasted. The degree to which employees apply and use the knowledge and skills they have learned in training is usually a direct result of the strategies employed in doing follow-up coaching and reinforcement. Data on behavior change are often collected via follow-up surveys of the trainees, their bosses, and their peers. An even more objective way of gathering such data is a measurement or audit of the actual products of people's behaviors and/or behavior changes. For example, an auditor might count the number of correctly prepared control charts posted in offices and work areas, or the number of quality improvement project reports that have been completed according to the criteria outlined in the training. A combination of process (behavior) and output (accomplishments/products) measures will earn high marks from the Baldrige Examiners in this area.

The final type of evaluation data that should be collected on training/education programs and courses is data on quality *results*. Employees might like the course, master the tests, and apply the skills on the job, but results may not improve. The major reason an organization invests in training and education is to produce better results from its employees' performance. If courses on quality improvement tools and techniques don't result in improved quality, something is wrong. The examiners want to see that you identify and measure key dimensions of performance that will be impacted by each course in your education/training curriculum. You should compare performance results data both before and after the training to see whether the training has made any difference. Of course, various other activities occurring in the organization will also impact performance, so it is important that you use a sound, applied research/experimental design in your evaluation effort to rule out alternative explanations for the improvements seen in quality results. Results might also relate to costs. If you can show how improved training saved the company money or allowed it to grow or be more profitable, these types of findings would be important to discuss here.

In summary, the examiners are looking for several types or dimensions of evaluation data here. They are also looking to see that you can demonstrate clear cause–effect relationships between the education/training and improvements in both employee performance and overall company/work unit performance.

Indicators for Question 5.2a(4)

- Use of a variety of methods (if appropriate) for delivery of training/education. For example, video, self-study, case studies, simulations, etc.

- Training delivery methods match the types of content and skills covered in individual courses or modules.

- There is evidence that audience characteristics are considered as part of the criteria when deciding on training delivery methods.

- The company uses the most cost-effective training delivery methods.

- Deployment of evaluation methods across all types of education and training.

- Collection of data on trainee reactions or satisfaction levels with courses.

- Learning or mastery of material is tested in courses designed to teach specific knowledge and skills.

- Where appropriate, employee use of skills learned in training on the job is measured.

- Training process measures such as the quality of instruction or delivery are measured as part of the education/training evaluation approach.

- The company measures the impact of certain courses on performance results such as customer satisfaction, financial results, productivity, or product/service quality.

- Evidence of continuous improvement in training and education as a result of evaluation data.

5.2a(5) How do you address key developmental and training needs, including diversity training, management/leadership development, new employee orientation, and safety, as appropriate?

<u>What They're Looking for Here</u>

This fifth question was new for 2000, or at least sort of new! The criteria asked about new employee orientation last year, but not about diversity, leadership, or safety training specifically. The problem with this question is a lack of space to provide much detail on any of the topics asked about here. Given that this section 5.2 is about 3 pages in length in total, and that there are 7 questions to answer, there is not much space for each answer—less than half a page for each question. As before, I recommend summarizing your response in a table or chart that might include the following categories of information, as shown in the example below.

Training Type	Methods/Media	Audience	Length	2000 Participation
Orientation Program	Classroom, multi-media	new employees	2 days	2800
Leadership Course	Classroom, exercises	new managers	3 days	460
Diversity Course	Game	all employees	1/2 day	4200

A chart like this one summarizes the scope and breadth of your training on the topics asked about in this question without taking up a lot of space. If there are any unique features to your approaches to training on any of these topics you might want to mention them, and encourage Examiners to get more information during the site visit. Remember, the overall goal of the application is to provide enough information to make the Examiners want to come on a site visit.

Indicators for Question 5.2a(5)

- Comprehensiveness of employee orientation program, and extent to which all new employees are consistently exposed to it.

- Evidence that leadership training actually improves skills of managers and supervisors.

- Deployment of leadership training to all appropriate personnel.

- Use of innovative approaches to diversity training.

- Safety training is based on thorough analysis of needs, and training is evaluated for its effectiveness.

- Overall deployment of types of training asked about in this question.

- Evidence of customization, if appropriate to the types of education/training asked for in this question.

5.2a(6) How do you address performance excellence in your education and training? Include how employees learn to use performance measurements, performance standards, skill standards, performance improvement, quality control methods, and benchmarking, as appropriate.

What They're Looking for Here

This item sounds like a "throwback" to the old TQM or quality training that used to be asked in early versions of the Baldrige criteria. Notice how the criteria today are careful to avoid overusing the word "quality," but use other TQM buzz-words like benchmarking. I'm surprised to see the term "quality control" has made it back into the criteria as well. Anyway, what this item asks for is similar to what the previous item asked for. Specific information on specific types of training. This section asks what types of training you give your people to help them make your organization the best in its field. As in the previous question, it is probably a good idea to list the types of training you do relating to performance improvement, and provide a brief description of each course. A couple of examples are shown below in narrative fashion, but the information could also be put into a table.

Example Performance Improvement Training Descriptions

Strategic Benchmarking and Comparisons—This two-day course is designed to teach participants about the importance of gathering comparative and benchmarking data in a systematic fashion. The course is designed to provide attendees with a specific methodology for selecting comparative organizations, gathering data on processes and results, and documenting the information in a consistent data base and report. Approximately 600 employees and managers have attended this course in 1998 and 2000 to date, and about 200 more will attend in 2000.

Baldrige Assessment and Improvement Planning—This two-day course is designed to teach managers and employees about how to complete a Baldrige assessment and use the information for strategic planning. Attendees learn about the criteria, scoring scale, and how to document strengths and areas for improvement. They also learn how to prioritize areas for improvement, and develop metrics, targets, and action plans that become part of their overall strategic plan. The top 180 executives and managers in the company have all been through this course, and plans are to take it down to the next level of management in 2000/2000 fiscal year.

You may not have room to go into as much detail as I have done in these examples, but keep in mind what the Examiners will look for in your answer is a good systematic (and perhaps unique) approach and good implementation to the right people. Information that you choose to highlight should be in these two areas. Listing a bunch of off-the-shelf training packages you have purchased will not earn a high score. In addition, Examiners will look that your curriculum in this area has remained current with business direction. For example, one company I worked with has had the same TQM curriculum for 12 years, and the courses have not changed at all. They are still teaching concepts such as Deming's theories, basic quality tools, and computing the price of non-conformance. The company has stopped using all of these ideas and approaches at least 4 years ago, yet continue teaching these concepts to new employees.

Indicators for Question 5.2a(6)

- Linkage between performance improvement training and key success factors/strategies outlined in strategic plan.

- Evidence that thorough analyses have revealed a real need for the courses outlined in this answer.

- Use of innovative training techniques or media.

- Deployment of performance improvement training to all the right employees and/or stakeholders.

- Evidence that training in this area has evolved based on evaluation data and changes in organizational direction and strategy.

- Employee feedback on the usefulness of these courses in actually improving performance.

5.2a(7) How do you reinforce knowledge and skills on the job?

What They're Looking for Here

When discussing on-the-job reinforcement of training, a typical response is to explain that "employees at all levels are encouraged to use the skills they learn in performance training throughout various aspects of their jobs." What the Examiners are looking for here is that you have planned and implemented a systematic process for ensuring that skills learned in training are reinforced in the work environment. Most organizations have no such plan, and end up with a low score. I consult with many large organizations that spend millions of dollars on quality and related training and nothing on following up the training with coaching and reinforcement to make sure that the trainees apply the skills on the job. Consequently, the training fails to change job behavior or produce any improvements in performance. What usually follows is that the training itself is blamed, and the organization buys a different program, hires a different consultant, or develops a new program of their own. They usually find that the second or third training program works no better than the first one. All that a good training or education program can do is provide people with knowledge and skills. It cannot ensure that those knowledge and skills are applied and used on the job.

A lack of systematic and planned follow-up is the number one reason why training of any sort fails in organizations. As much—or more—time and money need to be spent on what happens after the classes as is spent preparing and conducting the classes.

Another effective approach is to teach employees job-specific applications for the tools and techniques they learn. This will help in bridging the gap between the classroom and the job environment. A more formalized reinforcement program would result in an even higher score in this area. One award applicant describes a program whereby supervisors and managers hand out coupons and "thank you" notes to employees when they see them going beyond quality standards or making use of the quality improvement techniques learned in training courses. Coupons are posted on sheets, and completed sheets are used to earn symbolic recognition or a small monetary/privilege award. The existence of a program such as this, along with data on its effectiveness, would help to earn a high score in this area.

Indicators for Question 5.2a(7)

- Supervisors and managers have been trained to provide on-the-job reinforcement of employees' use of quality improvement tools and concepts.

- Employee opinion about the degree to which supervisors/managers reinforce/encourage their use of quality tools and techniques.

- Executives and upper management reinforce managers' use of quality tools and techniques.

- Existence of a systematic plan to ensure that training/education courses on quality are followed up with appropriate coaching and reinforcement.

- Training is scheduled in a "just-in-time" fashion so that skills and knowledge have immediate application on the job.

- Degree to which employees receive follow-up coaching on the use of quality and performance improvement tools and techniques.

- Employees are given adequate time to practice and master quality improvement tools/techniques on the job after formal training is completed.

- Evidence that the company has a systematic approach to evaluating its education and training.

5.3 EMPLOYEE WELL-BEING AND SATISFACTION

Describe how your organization maintains a work environment and an employee support climate that contribute to the well-being, satisfaction, and motivation of all employees. (25 points)

AREA TO ADDRESS   **[APPROACH, DEPLOYMENT]**

5.3a Work Environment

How do you address and improve workplace health, safety, and ergonomic factors? How do employees take part in identifying these factors and in improving workplace safety? Include performance measures and/or targets for each key environmental factor. Also include significant differences, if any, based on different work environments for employee groups and/or work units.

What They're Looking for Here

Companies that are known for their efforts to delight employees are rare today. Many have words in their vision and value statements about the importance of employees to their success, but few really operate that way. Downsizing, right-sizing, or simply laying off employees has become the favored approach to get a short-term boost in lagging profits for American companies. One former Baldrige winner waited until a week after they received the award to announce that they were laying off ten percent of the workforce. Sometimes cutting staff is unavoidable, even in a very well-run organization. Most of the time it is avoidable, though, through careful planning, prudent hiring, and other methods. This Examination Item is about what you do to make your organization a safe and enjoyable place to work.

Something that Examiners will look for in your response to this Area to Address is that you approach safety and employee health with the same systematic prevention-based approach as you employ for ensuring the production and delivery of high quality products and services. Most organizations and virtually all manufacturing companies have some type of safety program. Having a decent safety program may not earn you many points, but you will certainly lose some if you don't have one. What Examiners will need to see to give you a good score is a preventive approach to safety. Most safety programs are not preventive. Companies approach safety in much the same manner that fire departments approach fire prevention. Fire departments spend about 10 percent of their time on prevention-oriented activities, and the rest of the time fighting fires. One key indicator of a detection approach to safety is in how the organization measures safety. Most companies measure safety in lost time accidents or incident rates. This is like measuring quality by counting the number of defects found in products after they are made. Once an accident has occurred, it's too late to do anything about it. We can learn from the accident and correct the situation that allowed it to occur, but this is a detection approach to safety.

One organization I worked with measures employee behavior and inspects the work environment on a regular basis as their major safety measures. Safety boils down to employee behavior. If you can get employees to always follow safety rules and practices, you will not have safety problems. This company that I worked with monitors employee behavior for safe practices on almost a daily basis. They still measure defects such as incidents, near misses, and lost time related to accidents, and their safety record is near benchmark level for their industry.

Having a proactive approach to preventing safety problems would tend to earn you a very good score from Examiners. If your approach is characterized by safety audits conducted a few times a year, some safety training, and a few posters placed throughout the facility, you will probably end up with a very low score. Meeting OSHA or other regulatory requirements will also not earn you many points. You have no choice but to do this. Baldrige is looking for organizations that go way beyond minimum requirements.

The criteria in 5.3a asks about how health, safety, and ergonomics (human factors engineering) are improved. The approach you use to achieve good performance in these areas is the same as the approach you employ to achieve good results in other areas, such as quality or customer satisfaction. You need to identify good measures of health, safety, and ergonomics, benchmark other organizations to identify world-class levels of performance, set stretch goals or targets based on benchmarks, assign resources, and improve processes to achieve excellent levels of performance on these measures.

5.3a also asks for specific information on your safety/health measures and goals or targets. This information is probably best presented in a chart that lists measures along the left side, followed by annual targets and longer-term targets or goals. As I mentioned earlier, what is important is that all of your measures are not defect-detection oriented. You need to have a good mix of prevention-based measures and detection-based measures. A good prevention-based measure is not the number of safety training programs conducted or posters put up on the wall, either. The frequency with which you collect data on safety, health, and ergonomic factors is also important. To have a prevention-based approach, you need to collect data more often than once every few months.

Measures of employee health need to be preventive as well. Tracking employee health problems or sickness and absenteeism/sick leave by themselves are detection-oriented measures. You need to be careful with preventive measures to ensure that you drive the right behavior. One organization that had an on-site gym/health club used to measure the percentage of employees who used the gym, and the average amount of time spent in the gym per employee. Many used the gym as a social activity, however. They'd go to the gym, do 10 minutes on the Stairmaster, do a couple of sit-ups, and spend 45 minutes talking with co-workers, or sitting at the juice bar reading the newspaper. After realizing that hours spent in the gym was not a good measure, the company started measuring cardiovascular fitness, body fat percentage, blood pressure, and other health-related factors that were really important in maintaining employee health.

The last part of 5.3a asks you to note any significant differences in approaches based on different facilities or work groups. Often the company corporate headquarters will have a health club, medical clinic, smoking cessation, weight loss, and any number of other programs to promote employee health. However, only 20 percent of the company's employees might work at headquarters. The rest are in plants or offices in remote locations that have none of these facilities or services. In assessing deployment on this Area to Address, Examiners are interested in what you are doing for all of your employees in all of your facilities. This last sentence in the criteria also asks about different approaches you might have for different employee groups—read diversity. If you have locations in different locations including international facilities, you may need to use different approaches to employee health safety and ergonomics. Examiners will look for evidence that you do not adopt a one-size-fits-all approach, but that you tailor your approaches to the culture and demographics of the employees in different locations if appropriate.

Indicators for Question 5.3a

- Absence of citations from health/safety regulatory agencies, or lawsuits relating to health/safety issues.
- Identification of a good set of measures for employee safety that is a combination of prevention and detection types of metrics.
- Benchmarking and other comparative information are used to set stretch goals for safety performance.
- Specific goals and targets have been set for all measures of employee safety.

- How employees feel about the degree to which the company promotes health and safety.
- Evidence of process changes and improvements that will promote better employee safety performance.
- Evidence of a preventive approach to employee health, safety, and ergonomics.
- Level of attention given to safety and employee well-being by senior management.
- Evidence that the company goes way beyond regulatory requirements in this area and strives to be a role model for others.
- Frequency with which data are collected on health and safety issues.
- Levels of resources devoted to health and safety efforts compared to companies of similar size in the same industry.
- Scope and breadth of improvements made in ergonomics.
- Programs the company has in place to promote the health of their employees (e.g., weight loss, stop smoking, health club, smoke-free environment, etc.).
- Existence of a systematic process for analyzing the causes of accidents when they do occur.
- Evidence that employee health and safety initiatives are tailored to different cultures, locations, and employee groups if appropriate.

AREA TO ADDRESS   **[APPROACH, DEPLOYMENT]**

5.3b Employee Support Climate

(1) How do you enhance your employees' work climate via services, benefits, and policies? How are these enhancements selected and tailored to the needs of different categories and types of employees, and to individuals, as appropriate?

Notes:

(1) Approaches for enhancing employees' work climate [5.3b(1)] might include: counseling; career development and employability services; recreational or cultural activities; non-work-related education; day care; job rotation and/or sharing; special leave for family responsibilities and/or for community service; home safety training; flexible work hours; outplacement; and retiree benefits (including extended health care).

(2) Specific factors that might affect employee well-being, satisfaction, and motivation [5.3c(1)] include: effective employee problem or grievance resolution; safety factors; employee views of management; employee training, development, and career opportunities; employee preparation for changes in technology or the work organization; work environment and other work conditions; workload; cooperation and teamwork; recognition; benefits; communications; job security; compensation; and equal opportunity.

What They're Looking for Here

Almost all companies do something in this area. What the Examiners are looking for is the breadth and depth of the special services you provide to employees, and the degree to which these services have been tailored to the special needs of the organization's employees. For example, in an organization populated largely by women, child care might be an appropriate and appreciated special service. In a situation in which an organization's surrounding community education system is poor, remedial reading or other similar programs may be needed. If you have done a thorough analysis of your employees and have identified their special needs, and have tailored your employee assistance programs to those needs, you will do well in this area.

Most organizations approach this area either by offering what other companies offer in the way of employee services, or waiting until a problem occurs and then developing a program to deal with the problem (e.g., drugs or alcohol). If, however, you take a proactive/preventive approach to employee assistance, this will be noticed more by the examiners. If you can demonstrate that you offer more than your competitors do in the area of employee services, this too will be of interest to examiners. Your response might consist of a table that lists all employee assistance programs on the left side of the page, and the name of your organization and a few of its competitors along the top. A matrix like the one that follows then could be created to illustrate which employee assistance programs you offer, as compared to your competition.

EMPLOYEE ASSISTANCE PROGRAMS			
	Your Organization	Competitor A	Competitor B
Child Care	X	X	
Home Financing Assistance	X		X
Health Club Membership	X		
Weight Control Program	X		
Stop Smoking Program	X		
Drug/Alcohol Program	X		
Discount Symphony Tickets	X		
Annual Family Picnic	X	X	X
Counseling	X	X	
Outplacement Assistance	X	X	

What is important in this section is that you get creative in offering programs and services that meet the real needs of your workforce. These serve to attract potential employees to your organization. For example, a software development firm offers free coffee for employees. Another firm has an on-site dry cleaner and hair salon that both offer discounted prices. MBNA, the credit card giant, has a separate department that plans for funerals for relatives of employees. MBNA's bereavement department does all the arrangements and pays most of the bills associated with the funeral so as to relieve employee stress. This program does a lot to build loyalty from employees because the company helped them through a very difficult time. MBNA also has a department that plans marriages and honeymoons for employees. If two employees get married to each other (which happens a lot when most of your workforce is under 30), they receive additional time off for the honeymoon.

Indicators for Question 5.3b(1)

- Whether or not a needs analysis has been completed to determine the employee assistance programs that may be needed in the organization.

- Number of different employee assistance programs offered.

- Breadth/variety of employee assistance and special services offered.

- How the organization's employee assistance programs compare to major competitors'.

- Employee opinion on the assistance programs offered.

- Evidence that services and programs are offered to all employees in all locations.

5.3b(2) How does your work climate consider and support the needs of a diverse work force?

What They're Looking for Here

This was a new addition for 2000, and could actually be answered as part of your response to the previous question in 5.2b. Essentially what the Examiners want to see is that your initiatives and employee support programs are tailored to the diversity of your workforce. What we often see is a traditional list of benefits and service that might have made sense 25 years ago. As the employee population has changed, we want to see that the programs and services have changed to meet the needs of the population. Government organizations I've worked with actually tend to do a better job in this area than many big corporations.

I would answer this question by presenting a list of programs and initiatives that have been designed or tailored to different groups of employees in your organization. You might want to refer the reader back to the overview, wherein you describe the composition of your employee population. The Examiner might have forgotten that your workforce is 32% Asian, for example. If there are unique features about your efforts in this area, or if your programs have been benchmarked by other organizations, you should definitely discuss this. What will impress the examiners is the creativity of your approaches, and how far they go in making employees feel comfortable in the work environment. Gestures that look like a token effort could be viewed as a cop-out.

Indicators for Question 5.3b(2)

- Evidence that the organization understands the cultural issues that might impact the success of its employee support programs.

- Number of different employee support programs that have been designed for specific groups of employees, based on their unique needs and preferences.

- Appropriate allocation of resources toward unique employee support programs tailored to different groups.

- Deployment of good approaches to employee support programs across all locations and facilities.

- Evidence that employee support programs are different and tailored to the employee bas in each facility, where appropriate.

- Number of organizations that have benchmarked your diversity and/or employee support programs.

- Evidence that employee support programs have evolved and changed as the work force make-up has changed.

AREA TO ADDRESS   **[APPROACH, DEPLOYMENT]**
5.3c Employee Satisfaction
(1) How do you determine the key factors that affect employee well-being, satisfaction, and motivation?

What They're Looking for Here

This excellent new question was added to the 1999 criteria. It is similar to the logic in section 3.0 wherein 3.1 asks how you segment customers and determine their requirements and needs. This question asks you to do the same for employees. You might start out your answer by explaining how and why you segment employees into different groups. Be careful how you do this, so as not to be implicitly offensive. Although there are some cultural differences, it might not be a good idea to explain that you have two types of employees: white and non-white. Separating employees into professionals and workers might also be offensive. The employee segments you define should be based upon important differences in what they want from the job and work environment, and not necessarily their ethnic background, or level in the company.

After listing the different segments or groups of employees, proceed by explaining how you determine what's important to them. Remember the discussion from 3.1 about how traditional market research methods like surveys and focus groups tend to be very unreliable. Examiners will be impressed if you come up with some creative ways of determining what's really important to your employees. Part of your answer might be data you have collected on the success of things you have tried to make the work place more enjoyable. For example, one company found out that employees did not like to have after work social events because they were boring, and they felt obligated to attend for fear of not being seen as a "team player". Often employees never think to analyze what they like and don't like at the place they work, so it is hard to get them to articulate in a survey.

After describing the approaches you employ to determine the needs and preferences of your employees, you must explain what your research revealed. These factors might be listed in priority order from most to least important. The list of employee needs and desires should be consistent with the services and programs you described in 5.3b, and the human resources you describe in sections 5.1 and 5.2.

Indicators for Question 5.3c(1)

- Employees are segmented into logical groups based on common characteristics or priorities.

- Research is conducted to determine what is most important to each group of employees about their jobs and work environment.

- Use of creative approaches to find out what motivates employees and makes them like or dislike their job and work place.

- Employee needs and priorities are researched often to determine if preferences and priorities have changed.

- Extent to which employee needs and priorities are generic or very specific to the organization and its people.

- Evidence that the organization learns from its mistakes by not continuing or repeating initiatives to improve employee satisfaction that have had the opposite result.

- Deployment of employee "market research" methods across all locations and levels of employees.

- Evidence of planned evaluation and refinement of methods used to gather data on employee needs and priorities.

5.3c(2) What formal and/or informal assessment methods and measures do you use to determine employee well-being, satisfaction, and motivation? How do you tailor these methods and measures to a diverse work force and to different categories and types of employees? How do you use other indicators such as employee turnover, absenteeism, grievances, and productivity to assess and improve employee well-being, satisfaction, and motivation?

Note:

(3)   **Measures and/or indicators of well-being, satisfaction, and motivation [5.3c(2)] might include: safety; absenteeism; turnover; turnover rate for customer-contact employees; grievances; strikes; other job actions; insurance costs; worker's compensation claims; and results of surveys. Results relative to such measures and/or indicators should be reported in Item 7.3.**

What They're Looking for Here

What they are looking for in this question is that you use a thorough and objective approach to measuring employee satisfaction, and that you do so with reasonable frequency. An annual 10-item morale survey that has been completed by only a portion of employees will not earn you many points in this area. An annual morale survey is a good start, but the Baldrige Examiners will be looking at how thorough and how frequent your survey is, and at the percentage of employees who actually complete it.

Surveys are only one means of measuring employee satisfaction. Other types of data are much better indicators of the level of employee satisfaction in an organization. You should include statistics on:

- Average hours worked per week
- Turnover

- Reasons why employees leave the company (obtained via exit interviews or follow-up surveys)
- Absenteeism
- Incidence of stress-related illnesses or disorders
- Requests for lateral transfers in and out of locations or functions

The extent to which your data on employee satisfaction are based upon multiple measures will have a large impact on the score you receive in this area. What your organization does with the data on employee satisfaction is also examined in this area. Many organizations conduct morale surveys that end up being reviewed and thrown away, with the issues never being dealt with. The Baldrige people are looking for evidence that you have a process for reviewing these data and for developing action plans to improve the issues uncovered in the survey. Examples of situations where you uncovered problems relating to employee satisfaction and have corrected them will help make your response more credible.

Indicators for Question 5.3c(2)

- Use of thorough employee morale/satisfaction surveys on a regular basis.

- Objectivity of survey methodology and instruments.

- Frequency with which employee satisfaction is measured.

- Good mix of hard (e.g., turnover) and soft (e.g., morale survey) measures of employee satisfaction.

- Percentage of employees at all levels and in all functions who complete surveys (return rate and sample).

- Use of multiple measures/indices over and above surveys to measure employee satisfaction.

- Objectivity of employee satisfaction data.

- Evidence that a systematic process is used to review employee satisfaction data and develop corrective action plans for dealing with problems or situations with which employees are dissatisfied.

- Evidence that approach to measuring employee satisfaction is evaluated and continuously improved.

- Extent to which safety issues are addressed as part of employee satisfaction measures.

5.3c(3) How do you relate assessment findings to key business results to identify work environment and employee support climate improvement priorities?

What They're Looking for Here

This portion of the area to address asks about how the company establishes links between employee satisfaction and other measures of performance. One link that many companies have found is a link between employee satisfaction and customer satisfaction. Companies such as IBM have determined that improvements in employee satisfaction are a prerequisite to improvements in customer satisfaction. You might also report that there is a link between individual measures of employee satisfaction. For example, turnover might be impacted or related to employee morale levels. You might also report on correlations between measures of employee health and safety and costs, such as benefits or healthcare. Relating employee satisfaction measures to operational and financial metrics might also be done here.

You might begin your response to this portion of the criteria with a general description of your findings regarding the correlation between employee satisfaction and other performance measures in the company. Then, proceed to describe the specific relationships or correlations that have been defined. For example, "we have found that there is a 2/1 correlation between improvements in our Employee Satisfaction Index, and our Customer Satisfaction Index." Although this section does not call for results, you might show a graph that depicts the correlation's between some measure of employee satisfaction and another measure of company performance.

Indicators for Question 5.3c(3)

- Evidence that the company has conducted research to identify correlations between individual metrics relating to employee satisfaction (e.g., morale and turnover or absenteeism).

- Development of an employee satisfaction index that combines several individual metrics into a single number.

- Research has been conducted to identify correlations between measures of employee satisfaction and operational/financial performance.

- Correlations have been defined between safety performance and cost.

- Correlations have been defined between employee health and healthcare or benefits costs.

- Evidence is presented to suggest that employee well-being and satisfaction factors are considered when making investments and business decisions.

- The company can provide evidence of the return on investment for expenditures relating to the improvement of employee morale and/or well-being.

Chapter 10

Interpreting the Criteria for Process Management (6.0)

OVERVIEW OF THE PROCESS MANAGEMENT CATEGORY

Category 6.0 covers Process Management. The category addresses how you assure and improve the quality and reliability of the products and services you offer to customers through process management strategies. Emphasis should be placed on the word *how*. This category deals with *processes*, not results. Results are assessed in Category 7.0, Business Results. The Award Criteria define Category 6.0 as follows:

> ***Process Management*** *is the focal point within the Criteria for all key work processes. Built into the Category are the central requirements for efficient and effective process management—effective design, a prevention orientation, linkage to suppliers and partners, operational performance, cycle time, evaluation and continuous improvement, and organizational learning.*
>
> *Flexibility, cost reduction, and cycle time reduction are increasingly important in all aspects of process management and organizational design. In simplest terms, flexibility refers to the ability to adapt quickly and effectively to changing requirements. Depending on the nature of the organization's strategy and markets, flexibility might mean rapid changeover from one product to another, rapid response to changing demands, or the ability to produce a wide range of customized services. Flexibility might demand special strategies such as implementing modular designs, sharing components, sharing manufacturing lines, and providing specialized training. Flexibility also increasingly involves outsourcing decisions, agreements with key suppliers, and novel partnering arrangements.*
>
> *Cost and cycle time reduction often involve many of the same process management strategies as achieving flexibility. Thus, it is crucial to utilize key measures for these requirements in overall process management. (pp 38–39).*

In this chapter we'll discuss the three Examination Items and the four different Areas to Address that fall within this category. As in previous chapters, each section begins with a double-ruled box containing the Examination Item, the point value, and any applicable Notes.* Areas to Address falling under that Item follow in a single-ruled box. In the upper right corner of each Area to Address box is an indication [brackets] of whether the Area

---

* Item Notes that apply to a specific Area to Address are appropriately listed in the box containing that Area.

pertains to approach, deployment, or results. All definitions and information appearing within these boxes is taken directly from the Baldrige criteria. Following each Area to Address is an explanation defining what the examiners are looking for in assessing your application. Next, I have supplied a list of indicators or evaluation factors that will assist you in interpreting the criteria in preparing your application.

6.1 PRODUCT AND SERVICE PROCESSES

Describe how your organization manages key product and service design and delivery processes. (55 points)

Notes:

(1) **Product and service design, production, and delivery differ greatly among organizations, depending upon many factors. These factors include the nature of the products and services, technology requirements, issues of modularity and parts commonality, customer and supplier relationships and involvement, and product and service customization. Responses to Item 6.1 should address the most critical requirements for your business.**

(2) **Responses to Item 6.1 should include how customers and key suppliers and partners are involved in design processes, as appropriate.**

(3) **Results of operational improvements in product and service design and delivery processes should be reported in Item 7.5. Results of improvements in product and service performance should be reported in Item 7.1.**

AREA TO ADDRESS   **[APPROACH, DEPLOYMENT]**
6.1a Design Process

(1) What are your design processes for products/services and their related production/delivery processes?

What They're Looking for Here

This is another one of those obvious questions that was never asked for in earlier versions of the Baldrige criteria. Your answer should simply be a description or graphic depicting the overall phases in your product/service development process. As with any process diagram, it is important that the process be logical, and that the diagram not be too confusing with many boxes and arrows. I've seen some process models of product development approaches that fill an entire wall. You can show the Examiners your detailed version later in a site visit. Keep the diagram you put in your application simple.

While there is not preferred product/service design process Examiners look for (as they might have in the past), factors such as:

- Involvement of the right people in the process.
- Feedback loops built into each phase.
- Link to customer requirements and capabilities research.
- Link to organizational strategic plans.
- Simplicity and efficiency.

Indicators for Question 6.1a(1)

- A logical product/service development process is presented.

- The process appears to balance the need for rigor and thoroughness with the need for short cycle time.

- The product/service design process is documented in a format that is easy to understand.

- The overall process includes appropriate feedback loops.

- The process is adapted to different product/service areas and business conditions when appropriate.

6.1a(2) How do you incorporate changing customer/market requirements into product/service designs and production/delivery systems and processes?

What They're Looking for Here

This section of the criteria asks about how you use the information you discussed in section 3.1 on customers and their requirements to design new products and services. Customer requirements and priorities change all the time, and it is important to keep abreast of those changes and integrate them into your products and services. For example, a current fad today is cigar smoking. Both New York and Los Angeles have opened exclusive private cigar smoking clubs where members can relax, talk, and smoke their cigars without fear of offending anyone. A number of Sheraton Hotels have followed suit by opening cigar lounges in some of their major hotels. With all the backlash against cigarette smokers today, who would have predicted that cigar smoking would become a fad?

There is a direct link between the customer requirements you identify in section 3.1 of the application, and the new products and services you discuss in this section. The better job you do in researching customer requirements, the more likely that your new products/services will be successful. The key is in designing features into your products and services that differentiate you from your competitors in the customer's eyes. McDonald's listened to a lot of customers who told them they would buy a low-fat hamburger if McDonald's introduced it. They tested the new sandwich with consumers and they reported that it tasted quite good, and that they would buy it. In 1996, McDonald's removed the "McLean" from their menu, admitting that the product was a failure. Even though customers reported a desire for lower-fat choices on the menu, their buying behavior indicated otherwise. When faced with a choice, it seemed that more consumers chose the Big Mac and other higher-fat items than the McLean. McDonald's, certainly did its market research, and employed a systematic process to design and test market this new product, and it still failed. The lesson that might be learned from this is that customer desires are often better assessed by watching behavior, rather than by asking people what they want.

This question also asks about how changes in technology might initiate the design of new or enhanced products/services. Customers probably never thought about or asked for photocopiers or fax machines before these machines existed, and now can't imagine how to do without them. Your response should explain the process you employ to review technology and evaluate potential applications to your business. A proactive approach is what is desired, rather than waiting for salespeople to come to you with ideas on how their technologies could be applied to your business.

Along with describing the overall process you use for reviewing customer requirements and technology and designing new product and services, you should present some examples. The examples should be a mix of products/services that were designed based on changing customer requirements and technology.

This portion of the area to address also asks for evidence of a systematic approach for designing processes for production of new products/services and for their distribution. As with other approach/deployment criteria, there is no one right way of doing this. The Baldrige Examiners simply want to see that you have a systematic approach that is appropriate for your business. Having a flow chart or process model is not what is important, in any case. What is important is that you actually use a systematic approach that involves the right people in the design process.

The best way of responding to this portion of the criteria is to present an overall description of the approach or process used to design production/distribution processes. Next, present several examples of operational and quality requirements, and how these have been translated into features of production and distribution processes. The examples are used to provide evidence of deployment, illustrating that you actually use the systematic approach described earlier.

Indicators for Question 6.1a(2)

- Evidence of a systematic process such as quality function deployment being used to prioritize customer requirements and identify those that are most critical to integrate into designs.

- Use of a variety of sources of data on customer requirements in the product design process.

- Use of sound statistical methods to analyze market research data on customers and their requirements.

- Evidence that customer requirements have been translated into engineering specifications and characteristics during the design phase of the new product development cycle.

- Evidence of a proactive approach for reviewing technology for possible application to the company's products/services.

- Evidence of a systematic process for designing new products and services that is both thorough and efficient.

- Evidence that new products/services have been designed around customer requirements and/or new technology.

- Deployment of a systematic product/service development process to all the company's units, products, and services.

- Clear definition of quality and operational requirements has been done for all major products and services.

- A systematic approach exists for designing production/distribution processes for new products/services.

- Evidence that the production/distribution design processes match the company's business and product/services.

- New products have been effectively launched in the last few years that are free from major defects.

- Production and distribution personnel are involved in the design process early enough to have input at a point in time where change is the least costly and disruptive.

6.1a(3) How do you incorporate new technology into products/services and into production/delivery systems and processes, as appropriate?

What They're Looking for Here

Just about any organization could answer this question by saying that they have a systematic process for viewing technology and assessing its applicability to their business. Consequently, making a statement like that will not get much credit. Some organizations are very good at this because they are faster than their competitors, and they bring in technologies that others may have never thought of. Barnes and Noble book sellers did not get serious about sales on the internet until Amazon.com started increasing its market share in retail book sales.

Your response to this question should start with a paragraph that describes your overall approach to surveying technology for possible application to your business. Make sure to highlight some of the more obscure and unexpected places you look. Then I would provide some examples of new technologies that you have introduced in either products/services or in production/delivery processes that have worked out well. Baldrige winners tend to be pioneers rather than followers. If you jump into a new technology only after all your competitors have proven its applicability, you won't get a lot of credit in this section.

Indicators for Question 6.1a(3)

- Number of different places/sources reviewed to look for technology that might be applicable to the organization.

- Use of a systematic approach for evaluating technologies for their applicability.

- Evidence that the organization has pioneered the use of new technologies in its products/services or processes.

- Breadth and scope of technology applications to products/services and production/delivery processes.

6.1a(4) How do your design processes address design quality and cycle time, transfer of learning from past projects and other parts of the organization, cost control, new design technology, productivity, and other efficiency/effectiveness factors?

6.1a(5) How do you ensure that your production/delivery process design accommodates all key operational performance requirements?

What They're Looking for Here

This question was not explicitly asked in the 1998 criteria, but was part of the question that asked about your overall design process. What they're asking here is how information from various parts of the organization gets fed into the product/service design process. This is often very difficult in large organizations that do not have the mechanisms in place to communicate relevant information to the appropriate personnel in the design processes. I've seen a few Baldrige applications that attempt to convey this transfer of information in a complicated graphic, with too many boxes and arrows. I think this is a situation where a table or even a list might be better. The examiners will look for evidence of both simplicity and thoroughness. It is important that it be easy for employees and managers from different functions to communicate data to the design folks or it will probably never happen.

One way of bringing in lessons learned and other appropriate data to the design process is to ensure that the design team is made up of a diverse group of people. Many years ago, R&D was responsible for new product designs. In today's organizations, most new product/service design teams include folks from marketing, production, operations, finance, HR, IT, and R&D. A cross-functional design team helps ensure that different view points and data are considered. Another approach to making sure the design process teams have considered all appropriate data is to involve a wide variety of people in the review process. These individuals may not be members of the design teams, but play an important role in ensuring the success of new products/services.

Question number 4 is similar to the previous one, but is more specific in asking how you involve operational or production folks in the design process for new products/services. One obvious way of ensuring this is to make sure that production/operational people are on the design teams. Alternatively, they could at least be involved in reviewing major outputs of each phase in the design process. Whatever your approach, the point you want to make in your answer is that all important operational variables and capabilities are considered before you get too far along in the design process. Your answer to this question might want to refer back to research you've done on customer requirements (3.1) and on competitors products/services (4.2) and how this information is used to derive appropriate process measures and standards for production/delivery processes associated with new products/services.

Indicators for Question 6.1a(4) and (5)

- Evidence of systems for communicating relevant information to product/service design personnel.

- Extent to which such systems are actually used and have helped improve the design process on specific products/services.

- Use of cross-functional product/service design and review teams.

- Evidence that input is sought from diverse sources in the organization early in the design process when the input will be most valuable.

- Involvement of operations/production personnel on design teams.

- Thoroughness of design reviews so as to include all appropriate production/operational variables.

- Link between customer requirements, process metrics and standards for production/delivery processes associated with new products/services.

6.1a(6) How do you coordinate and test design and production/delivery processes to ensure capability for trouble-free and timely introduction of products/services?

What They're Looking for Here

This section of your application should describe the overall process you use to introduce and test new products and services. You should include a graphic that shows the phases and steps in your product/service development cycle. Most applicants that are manufacturing companies do a pretty good job on this section of their applications. Most organizations have a process defined for developing new products and services. Simply having a systematic product/service development process won't earn you many points by itself. What the Examiners are looking for in this Area to Address is the extent to which quality is built into the development process. Moreover, they are looking for evidence of a preventive approach to quality, rather than a production spot-check and correction cycle.

One important criterion for the design phase of a new product or service is that all the important functions that will be involved with the product/service participate in the design process. A major problem in many large companies is the number of changes made to designs, drawings, and specifications due to input from manufacturing, field service, marketing, legal, etc. Every department responsible for some detail of the product or service will offer its input. The problem is that the input is usually too late, causing numerous revisions to the product/service designs. A preventive approach involves getting representatives from each of these functions involved early in the design phase of the product/service and obtaining their input at key points, before all the drawings are done and the specifications finalized.

Another aspect of your development process examined in this area is the number and thoroughness of tests you perform on the product/service. Explain the types of tests you conduct, when they are conducted, and what the test is used to determine. Remember that the Baldrige Examiners may not understand your business or technology well, so make sure you avoid industry jargon and technical terms if at all possible.

In reviewing your process for designing new products or services, the Baldrige Examiners will be looking for evidence that key factors such as product and service performance, and process and supplier capabilities, are taken into consideration. Capabilities need to be considered in reviewing the feasibility of product and service designs. Involving suppliers in the design review process is critical when outside parts, materials, and/or services are required in order to meet key product/service requirements.

Indicators for Question 6.1a(6)

- Novel ways of improving product design and introduction.

- Systematic process for designing and coordinating new products and/or services across functions.

- Suppliers are involved in reviewing product/service designs and production/delivery processes associated with new designs.

- Evidence of a participative approach to the design phase of a new product/service, involving all of the functions/departments that will work with the product/service.

- Reviews take into account product/service performance data.

- Use of a preventive approach to assuring quality in the design and manufacture of new products/services.

- Reviews involve an assessment of process capabilities when appropriate.

- Thorough testing of new products and/or services before they are introduced.

- Use of techniques such as Alpha Tests, Beta Tests, and controlled market introductions, if appropriate.

- Objectivity and reliability of methods used for testing new products/services.

- Number and frequency of changes that occur in product/service designs (changes should be minimized).

- Thoroughness of design reviews.

- Continued deployment of the voice of the customer through concurrent engineering or similar process through the production/distribution processes.

AREA TO ADDRESS   [APPROACH, DEPLOYMENT]
6.1b Production/Delivery Processes

(1) What are your key production/delivery processes and their key performance requirements?
(2) How does your day-to-day operation of key production/delivery processes ensure meeting key performance requirements?
(3) What are your key performance measures and/or indicators used for the control and improvement of these processes? Include how real-time customer input is sought, as appropriate.

What They're Looking for Here

Once you have identified your key products and services, and identified the three to six major processes associated with the production and delivery of each one, you need to prepare a second matrix that indicates how you measure and control your processes. This matrix chart might look like the one below.

KEY PROCESSES	REQUIREMENTS	MEASURES	STANDARDS	CONTROL STRATEGIES

The key processes are taken from the first chart in this section, where you indicated which processes are associated with which products and services. Chances are there will be a number of generic processes that cut across all products and/or services, like delivery or distribution. Make sure that processes have verbs in them, and that you don't go too deeply into subprocesses. Requirements are important dimensions of the process that directly relate to important customer requirements. For example, at Alcoa plants that manufacture aluminum that is used for beverage cans, one of the customers' key requirements is the thickness of the aluminum. In a hotel, if we were looking at delivery of room service as a process, one of the key customer requirements is how long it takes to get the meal delivered. Requirements sometimes translate directly into measures; sometimes they do not. In the room service example, a good measure obviously would be cycle time from the time the customer calls in the order until it is delivered to her room. In the Alcoa example, some of the measures are not so obvious. One of Alcoa's key manufacturing processes is rolling. They start off with a big hunk of aluminum called an ingot that is about two feet thick and ten feet long. This ingot is rolled until it becomes longer and thinner. One of Alcoa's key process measures is the temperature of the aluminum as it is being rolled. Do customers care about the temperature of the finished product? No. If it is cold outside when it is delivered, the aluminum is cold. Customers do care about thickness and strength though, which are two product dimensions that are influenced by the temperature of the aluminum as it is being rolled.

After identifying several key measures for process that are tied back to requirements, you need to identify the targets, standards, or control limits for each measure. Measures are meaningless without standards or goals. You might have a band consisting of an upper and lower control limit, or simply one standard. In the hotel example, the standard for the delivery of room service might be 45 minutes or less. If the meal is delivered in 30 minutes that is not a problem, so we don't need an upper and lower standard or control limit. Standards or targets for process measures should tie back to customer requirements that are identified in section 3.1 of your application. As you will come to learn, almost everything ties back to 3.1 eventually. This is why I advise applicants to write 3.1 first to help ensure that everything else is consistent with it.

The final column in your matrix chart is used to identify the control strategies that are used to keep the process performance within the standards or levels that have been set. In the Alcoa example, the control strategy is easy. Everything is automated. If you go into an Alcoa plant, there are almost no people. The place almost runs by remote control. In most service businesses, and many manufacturing businesses such as aerospace, most processes have human behavior as a major component. If this is the case, the Baldrige Examiners want to know what control strategies you have in place to ensure that employee behavior stays within acceptable limits or standards. Procedures are not a control technique because they are usually not looked at. McDonald's is a company that is a master at controlling processes dependent upon human behavior. They have automated where they can, but some things just can't be automated yet. McDonald's' control strategies consist of thorough training, clear and precise procedures and work rules, constant monitoring, feedback, and consequences. Employees are rewarded for desired behavior and following process rules, and punished for failure to conform to standards.

Your response to this item should explain the various methods you employ to ensure that your product and/or services meet the standards outlined in the design specifications. These approaches might include in-process inspection of components, products, or services as they are delivered, as well as an inspection of the final products or accomplishments. An accomplishment produced by a service might be a repaired car, a served meal, or a completed set of architectural drawings. The examiners will also assess the degree to which your approach is prevention-based. In other words, do you have systems in place for preventing the occurrence of defects, or are your systems focused on the detection and correction of defects?

Within this Area to Address you also need to explain how process deviations are corrected and the corrections verified. Once single or multiple causes have been identified, there are usually several different alternatives for countermeasures. Your response to this area should explain how you decide on the most appropriate countermeasure, how you implement it, and how you verify that the change produced the desired result. As in most other areas, the examiners are looking for evidence of a systematic process.

This area should address your follow-up after the implementation of countermeasures designed to improve quality. Many organizations do not do follow up. For example, a large bank conducted an experiment that showed that if clerks in the operations area were put on incentive pay, their productivity and quality would improve. Upon implementation of the pay system, they found that the incentive pay worked well only for about three months. After that time, productivity stayed up but quality began to deteriorate. If the bank had not conducted a thorough follow-up evaluation, it might have left the incentive system intact for quite some time before realizing that it was no longer producing the desired results.

One important criterion regarding your follow-up approach is the scope of your follow-up activities. Do you conduct follow-up of *all* changes implemented to improve quality, or only the major ones that impact the whole organization? Do you conduct follow-up assessments in the support organizations as well as in the line organization? Another important criterion is the objectivity of the approach and instruments you use to conduct follow-up evaluations. Conducting a survey of employees' bosses six months after the employees have been through quality training is a poor way of evaluating the impact of training, for example. It's analogous to "the emperor's new clothes." People expect to see a change after the training, so that's how they respond to the survey. Surveys should never be used when it is possible to obtain "hard" data on quality measures.

The duration of your follow-up is also considered important. Some side effects don't appear immediately. If your evaluation occurs only a couple of months following implementation of a countermeasure, you won't know what happens after six months or a year. The effectiveness of countermeasures may deteriorate significantly after the first few months.

Indicators for Questions 6.1b(1), (2), and (3)

- Clear identification of all important processes relating to the production and delivery of products and/or services.
- Use of statistical process control where appropriate.

- Relationships identified between individual products/services and processes.

- Approach to process control is preventive in nature.

- Process owners and/or accountabilities identified, if appropriate.

- Degree to which process control is automated where appropriate and possible.

- Frequency of measurement of key process variables.

- Thoroughness of control mechanisms used to ensure that processes stay within specified tolerances or guidelines.

- Control mechanisms for ensuring that processes based upon employee behavior are systematic and thorough.

- Adequate sample sizes used to collect data on end-of-process measures.

- Adequacy of in-process measures.

- Use of valid statistical procedures for analyzing process data.

- Number of different process measures for which data are collected.

- Use of established and acceptable model for cause analysis.

- Use of different processes for analyzing common-cause and special-cause problems.

- Thoroughness and rigor of cause-analysis process.

- Examples or evidence to suggest that the analysis process is successful for discerning the root causes of process upsets and other quality-related problems.

- Clear linkages between customer requirements, process measures, and standards.

AREA TO ADDRESS   **[APPROACH, DEPLOYMENT]**

6.1b(4) How do you improve your production/delivery processes to achieve better process performance and improvements to products/services, as appropriate? How are improvements shared with other organizational units and processes, as appropriate?

What They're Looking for Here

This section asks for just about the same information as 6.1a(4). The previous section asks about how you evaluate and improve the design process, whereas this section asks about improvement of the production delivery process. You should include evaluation indices and describe the evaluation methodology.

Modeling all processes in an organization is a great way to identify opportunities for improvement. Many processes have never been documented. The act of documenting a process forces employees to question whether all of the steps are really necessary and to see ways in which the processes may be streamlined. Many large and small companies are currently working on modeling all of their processes, which number in the thousands, and are finding that it is a great deal of work. The activity, however, has already produced numerous improvements.

Evaluation of new or updated technology is another way to identify opportunities for improvement. Acquiring new technology may give you the ability to significantly reduce customer processing time in a service business, for example. Hyatt Hotels have applied the technology from ATM machines to test self-service check-in in some of their hotels. The customer inserts his credit card and a room key is dispensed. This technology has greatly reduced check-in time for guests who just want to get to their rooms.

Opportunities for continuous improvement are also identified by reviewing competitive and benchmark data. A competitor or company you have benchmarked yourself against may exhibit performance superior to yours on a particular measure. Their level of performance should then become the goal for your company to achieve or surpass.

Your approach to continuous improvement should be well rounded. In other words, do not base all your opportunities for continuous improvement around what the competition is doing. You will never rise to the top using such an approach because you will be too busy playing catch-up. Include data from a variety of sources in your approach, and make your approach proactive as well as reactive. Employees from all levels and functions within the organization should be involved in the continuous improvement process.

Your response for this Area to Address should also explain how you evaluate various process improvement alternatives to decide on the best approach. The Baldrige Examiners are looking for evidence of a systematic approach to deciding on the best way to improve processes. A typical response to this area is to explain that "We use a participative group process to brainstorm possible process improvements and decide upon the most appropriate approach." This may sound good, but the Examiners want more information.

As with many of the Areas to Address relating to evaluation and improvement processes, a good way to respond here is to include a flow chart or similar graphic that depicts the steps in your decision-making process. Describe who uses the process and how and when it is used. If every employee has been trained in the process, state this in your response.

Your approach should have certain characteristics. First, it should be participative; the process should allow for input from several employees who have knowledge of any problems. Second, it should involve brainstorming or a similar approach for generating alternative actions. Finally, it should include a process for evaluating alternative actions or countermeasures against specific criteria and constraints found in the work environment. For example, a particular action may be very effective, but if there is not enough time to implement it, or if it costs too much money, it is not a good choice.

This Area to Address asks for information on a variety of stimuli, which may be used to initiate process improvement. The first segment (1) asks about how simply analyzing a process and conducting research can serve as a stimulus for improving it. Sometimes all it takes is to draw a flow chart of a process to realize how inefficient it is, and to spot key steps that can be eliminated. Benchmarking or comparative data, which are asked about in 4.2, often stimulates process improvement because one sees how another company performs the same or a similar process. It may be that you never considered it possible to perform a process the way the benchmarked company does. Process improvements are also sometimes generated based upon research.

Examining alternative technology may allow you to make improvements in a process. The hand-held computers that I described earlier in the Hyatt Hotel example are a great illustration of how a new technology was used to greatly improve and simplify the process of checking into a hotel.

Sometimes internal and external customers provide inputs that lead to process improvements. Customers can sometimes see a lack of logic in processes, or opportunities for improvement that those performing the processes can't discern. I recently was a passenger on a foreign airline and was amazed at the approach it used to count the number of passengers on the plane. There were no assigned seats, so everyone rushed into the plane at once, fighting for the best seats. Even when everyone had found a seat, we realized that there was still almost an hour before takeoff time. It was a big plane, holding at least a couple of hundred people. Upon looking around, the plane appeared almost completely full—there were only about six to eight empty seats in the entire plane. While we waited, a flight attendant walked slowly down the aisle with a hand counter, counting the passengers on the left side of the airplane. Once she got to the back, she walked back toward the front, clicking off the number of passengers on the right side of the plane. The entire process took about ten minutes because she was being very careful. The man next to me was extremely annoyed at the apparent lack of sense to this procedure. He said, "They know how many seats are in this plane. Why don't they just count the number of empty seats—wouldn't that be a lot easier?" While we were all laughing about this silly procedure, another flight attendant started down the aisle, with a hand counter. The man next to me stopped the attendant and said, "What are you doing? Someone already counted the passengers. Why don't you just count the number of empty seats? The plane is almost full." You can just guess the answer: "Our procedure is that we need to do a count of all passengers twice to ensure accuracy. We would not be following the procedure if we did it any other way." With this, he proceeded to walk through the entire plane again, repeating the counting procedure that was performed by the other flight attendant ten minutes before. You may think this is a funny story that would never happen in another airline, or certainly not in your company. But every company I've ever seen has some processes like this one—processes that may have made sense at one time but are laughable under changed circumstances. Listen to your internal and external customers when they ask: "Why do you have to do it this way?"

Using challenge goals based on benchmarks is a good way of stimulating process improvement. Once a process has been mapped and data are collected on current levels of performance for key process variables, a stretch goal is set to force people to do the process differently. I once heard the chief financial officer of Motorola talk about how they do this in his function. A process that had always caused them a great deal of grief and overtime was completing the month-end close of the books. Everyone in the department ended up working late at the end of every month, and the antacids flowed freely because of the high stress. After mapping and measuring this process, the CFO set a stretch goal for the process improvement team. They had to figure out how to do the month-end close in half the usual time (labor hours) and without any overtime. They were told that they could change anything they wanted, as long as they didn't violate any regulations or generally accepted accounting practices. Big surprise—they did what they all thought was impossible at first. They did a major overhaul of the process, cutting out many unnecessary steps. Closing the books at the end of the month is no longer a nightmare for those who work in the finance department of Motorola. This is the type of example the Examiners want to see in your use of stretch or challenge goals to stimulate process improvements.

Indicators for Question 6.1b(4)

- Use of process modeling as a means for identifying opportunities for improvement in processes and resulting products/services.

- Objectivity and methodological rigor of process modeling approach.

- Scope of process modeling to include all functions in the organization.

- Use of field data, when appropriate, as a way of identifying opportunities for continuous improvement.

- Systematic analysis of new and changing technology as a means for identifying quality improvement opportunities.

- Number of different stimuli used as impetus for continuous improvement efforts.

- Use of competitor or benchmark data as stimuli for identifying opportunities for quality improvement.

- Scope of continuous improvement efforts includes all departments/functions and all levels of employees.

- Existence of a systematic process for making decisions regarding countermeasures designed to correct quality-related problems or process upsets.

- Approach to deciding on process improvement strategy is participative and adaptable for use with groups, as well as with individuals.

- Approach to process improvement is based upon one or more established models for systematic decision making.

- Use of brainstorming or similar technique to generate a variety of alternative actions to consider for improving processes.

- Evidence that process analysis is used as a stimulus for process improvement.

- Breadth and scope of process improvements initiated via process analysis.

6.2 SUPPORT PROCESSES

Describe how your organization manages its key support processes. (15 points)

Note:

(1)   Support processes are those that support the organization's products/services design and delivery processes, and business operations. For many organizations, this might include information and knowledge management, finance and accounting, facilities management, research and development (R&D), administration, and sales/marketing. The key support processes to be included in Item 6.2 are unique to each organization and how it operates. Focus should be on the most important processes not addressed in Items 6.1 and 6.3.

(2)   Results of improvements in key support processes and key support process performance results should be reported in Item 7.5.

AREA TO ADDRESS   **[APPROACH, DEPLOYMENT]**
6.2(a) Support Processes

(1) What are your key support processes?

What They're Looking for Here

This first question is straightforward and requires little explanation. You simply need to list your major support functions. Remember that processes are verbs and not necessarily departments. So, don't list Information Technology or Finance; list key processes within those functions, such as maintaining the company hardware and software, new software development/acquisition, or auditing financial results.

You might want to prepare a list of key processes that is sorted by function or department like the example below:

EXAMPLE SUPPORT FUNCTIONS & PROCESSES		
Finance	Human Resources	Facilities
• Data collection	• Recruiting/hiring	• Building maintenance
• Data analysis	• Training/development	• Construction
• Auditing	• Performance management	• Groundskeeping
	• Labor relations mgmt.	• Maintaining security

As you can see from the example, you want to keep the list of support processes down to 3 to 5 per function or department.

Indicators for Question 6.2a(1)

- A complete list of support processes is provided.

- Processes are listed as activities or at least have verbs in them.

6.2a(2) How do you determine key support process requirements, incorporating input from internal and/or external customers as appropriate? What are the key operational requirements (such as productivity and cycle time) for the processes?

6.2a(3) How do you design these processes to meet all the key requirements?

6.2a(4) How does your day-to-day operation of key support processes ensure meeting key performance requirements? How do you determine and use in-process measures and/or customer feedback in your support processes?

What They're Looking for Here

I've lumped these three questions together in the same box because I don't think your response needs to be separate for each one. Given that this entire item (6.2) is worth a possible 15 points, it should be given about three quarters of a page to one page maximum. Part of this area to address asks about how you determine customer requirements and use that information to design support processes and set standards for performance. I would recommend a paragraph that explains the systematic approach you employ to research the needs of the internal and external (if appropriate) customers of support functions. Acknowledge the fact that most support functions have multiple customers with sometimes conflicting requirements. For example, customers who are waiting for approval of ad copy from the law department might be most concerned with cycle time. The law departments other customer is the corporation though, who is most concerned with managing risk and thoroughness. Question (3) asks about the approach you use to design new and/or improved support processes. You might refer back to the new product/service design process you presented in 6.1a if the approach is similar, or describe your support product/service design process here. You should also provide a couple of examples of new or innovative support processes that have been designed based on customer input to give the Examiner the idea that your support functions are very customer focused.

Next, I would prepare a chart that summarizes how you manage and control the major support function processes on a daily basis. A chart like this would look similar to the one in 6.1b. The chart might look like the example below:

Support Processes	Requirements	Measures	Standards	Control Strategies
HR Recruiting/selection	speed	cycle time	15 days	Feedback SLAs
	right person	30-day review	95% pass	SLAs

You obviously won't have enough room to list all of your support functions so you should list a good cross-section. The Examiners will want to see information on how all support processes are managed during the site visit, but you need to give them enough information to make them want to come see your organization.

Indicators for Questions 6.2a(2), (3), and (4)

- Support departments conduct research to identify the most important requirements of their internal and external customers for key support processes.

- Deployment of customer requirements research across all major support processes and functions.

- Information is presented that explains how conflicting customer requirements are resolved (e.g., corporate customer wants low cost, employee customer wants good service).

- A systematic process is in place for designing new support processes based on customer needs.

- Requirements have been defined for support processes based upon customer requirements and other factors.

- All internal and external customers' input is sought in defining performance requirements.

- Evidence is presented that support processes are designed based on customer requirements.

- Performance standards and process metrics are linked back to customer requirements.

- Metrics for support processes are a good mix of process and output measures and targets or standards have been identified for each metric.

- Support department managers and employees are evaluated on how well they satisfy their customers.

6.2a(5) How do you improve your support processes to achieve better performance and to keep them current with business needs and directions, as appropriate? How are improvements shared with other organizational units and processes as appropriate?

<u>What They're Looking for Here</u>

This fifth and final question in 6.2 asks for evidence that your organization improves support processes and changes them as business needs change. Support functions in organizations are often steeped in tradition and many have not changed their HR or accounting processes since the 1950s. Even information technology processes that you would think would be more current, are often not in sync with current organizational needs. I wouldn't waste space with a generic explanation of how you employ a systematic process of listening to customers, and reviewing technology to drive process improvements in support function. I would give a paragraph explanation of the specific steps used to analyze and improve support processes. Refer back to 6.1, if appropriate. To address the deployment portion of this question, I would present a short list of some of the innovative new or improved processes you have implemented over the last few years in support functions. This will tend to impress examiners more than another generic process improvement flowchart.

Indicators for Question 6.2a(5)

- Customer input is considered in reviewing and improving existing support processes and designing new ones.

- New technologies are reviewed and appropriately used in support processes where possible.

- The organization has pioneered many innovative approaches to support processes.

- Depth and breadth of example support process improvements shows good deployment.

- Support functions have been benchmarked by others inside and outside of the organization for some of their unique approaches/processes.

6.3 SUPPLIER AND PARTNERING PROCESSES

Describe how your organization manages its key supplier and/or partnering interactions and processes. (15 points)

Note:

(1) **Supplier and partnering processes might include processes for supply chain improvement and optimization, beyond direct suppliers and partners.**

> **AREA TO ADDRESS**   **[APPROACH, DEPLOYMENT]**
> **6.3a Supplier and Partnering Processes**
>
> **(1) What key products/services do you purchase from suppliers/partners?**

What They're Looking for Here

This is another basic question that should have been asked, but was not in earlier versions of the Baldrige criteria. Usually the Overview section includes this information, but it bears repeating here as a reminder. What you need to list is the organizations that you spend 75 to 80% of your supplier/partner dollars on. Organizations often have literally hundreds of suppliers, but often spend most of their money with a handful. These are the ones that should be listed here. It is not necessary to list specific companies. Rather, present a list of the types of suppliers, that are sorted by category or type. For example, a chemical company listed raw materials suppliers, equipment suppliers, and distributors as their three major categories. Another Baldrige applicant simply grouped them as upstream and downstream suppliers. Upstream suppliers were those that sold goods and services that helped them design and produce products, and downstream suppliers were those that helped deliver, sell, and maintain the products.

Indicators for Question 6.3a(1)

- List of major supplier/partner types is consistent with those listed or discussed in Business Overview.

- List of key suppliers/partners is consistent with key success factors and strategic objectives defined in section 2.0.

- Suppliers/partners are grouped logically.

- Products and services purchased from major suppliers are listed.

6.3a(2) How do you incorporate performance requirements into supplier and/or process management? What key performance requirements must your suppliers and/or partners meet to fulfill your overall requirements?

6.3a(3) How do you ensure that your performance requirements are met? How do you provide timely and actionable feedback to suppliers and/or partners? Include the key performance measures and/or indicators and any targets you use for supplier and/or partner assessment.

Note:

(2)   **If your organization selects preferred suppliers and/or partners based upon volume of business or criticality of their supplied products and/or services, include selection criteria in the response.**

What They're Looking for Here

I've combined these two questions together in one discussion because of the limited space you have in 6.3 for your answer. As with the previous area, you have about a page for your entire answer to the six questions in 6.3, so you need to summarize the information very concisely.

6.3a(2) begins by asking about how you design processes to work with suppliers and partners. Part of this should be an explanation of the strategy and logic you employ in deciding what to buy from suppliers and partners, and what to do yourself. Many companies today outsource all those functions that they do not view as key competencies. Regardless of whether you farm out a lot or little of the work that gets done by your organization, you need a defined process or several processes for working with these outside organizations. Suppliers or partners can consist of "upstream suppliers" that you buy raw materials, parts, or services from, as well as "downstream" suppliers who might be dealers, delivery personnel, or companies that repair your products.

Part of a good supplier management system is a thorough set of criteria for selecting good companies to do business with. Several organizations such as Shea Homes, Pacific Bell, and American Express select their suppliers based on how they perform against the Baldrige criteria. They want to buy from well managed companies and believe that the Baldrige criteria are a good yardstick to use. While this approach is not a requirement, the Examiners look for evidence that you employ a thorough process for reviewing and selecting the suppliers and partners with whom you will do business.

6.3a(2) also asks about your approach to determining performance requirements for goods and services you receive from key suppliers. Many large organizations use hundreds or even thousands of suppliers. If this is true of your company, you may want to identify who your most critical 10 to 50 suppliers are, and discuss your efforts with them rather than trying to include all of them. Once you've identified your key or critical suppliers, list the critical quality requirements for perhaps the top 10 or so. One way of doing this might be by means of a table or chart. Next, list the critical measures or indicators you use to monitor and evaluate supplier performance. All of this information could be neatly summarized in a chart like the one shown in Figure 10.3.

Make sure that your response also includes a clear explanation of how you communicate quality indicators and requirements to suppliers. You should also have mechanisms in place to provide regular feedback to key suppliers on how they do in meeting performance requirements. This means that you need to have a thorough approach in place for measuring supplier quality.

TOP 10 SUPPLIERS

SUPPLIER COMPANY	PERFORMANCE INDICATORS	REQUIREMENTS
(1) Southern International	• Number of defective generators • Delivery when promised	< 0.05/1000 < 5% late deliveries
(2) Federal Manders	• Number of defective switches	

Figure 10.3: Example of Chart Summarizing Key Suppliers, Performance Indicators, and Performance Requirements

It is important that you have a well-defined and successful approach for ensuring that your suppliers meet your performance standards. All organizations have suppliers, but in some they play a more important role than in others. For instance, a manufacturing company may buy all of the components for the products it produces from outside suppliers. Hence, supplier performance is critical to the quality of the final products. A service business such as a bank may have relatively few suppliers who perform non-critical services or sell supplies to the bank. The effort your organization puts into ensuring quality from its suppliers should be directly proportional to the degree to which you rely on suppliers for your success.

6.3a(3) asks about how you make sure that suppliers and partners meet your requirements.

Begin your response for this area with a general description of the approach you use to assure performance excellence. Explain how you determine your requirements for the goods and services provided by suppliers, and how you communicate these to suppliers. Next, explain how you monitor supplier performance and feed back the data to them so that they may correct existing problems and/or prevent future ones. If you use an audit or periodic assessment, describe how it is conducted, how often it is done, etc.

As in many of the other areas, using a chart or table is a good way to summarize the information. Rather than listing each supply company, you might group them according to the type of products or services you buy from them. Using a matrix, indicate which quality assurance strategies you employ with each group of suppliers. It doesn't matter whether you use certification, testing, audits, or another approach. What matters is that your approach is effective for your organization and suppliers, and is multifaceted. In other words, it should include more than just one strategy/approach.

Indicators for Questions 6.3a(2) and (3)

- Evidence of a systematic and thorough approach for selecting suppliers and partners.

- Deployment of the supplier/partner selection process to all critical suppliers.

- Criteria for selection of suppliers go beyond price and quality and assess how supplier/partner companies are managed.

- Identification of critical suppliers, if appropriate.

- Extent to which measurable performance indices and requirements/standards have been identified for suppliers.

- Percentage of suppliers/partners for which performance indices and requirements/standards have been identified.

- Degree to which suppliers/partners are involved in the formulation of indices and standards/requirements.

- Existence of an effective system for communicating standards/requirements to suppliers/partners.

- Feedback system is in place for keeping key suppliers informed on a regular basis of their performance on key quality indicators.

- Amount of effort devoted to assurance of supplier performance is appropriately geared to the degree to which organization relies on suppliers/partners.

- Use of a multifaceted approach to assure supplier performance.

- Organization's requirements have been defined and clearly communicated to suppliers.

- Systems exist for measuring supplier performance on a regular basis and for feeding back the data to suppliers to help them improve their performance.

- Objectivity and reliability of measures of supplier/partner performance.

- Procedures are in place for periodically auditing or assessing supplier processes, products, and services.

6.3a(4) How do you minimize overall costs associated with inspection, tests, and process and/or performance audits?

6.3a(5) How do you provide business assistance and/or incentives to suppliers and/or partners to help them improve their overall performance and to improve their abilities to contribute to your current and longer-term performance?

Note:

(3)   **Results of improvements in supplier and partnering processes and supplier/partner performance results should be reported in Item 7.4.**

What They're Looking for Here

I've combined these two questions into one discussion because a complete answer to both separately would use more space than allotted on your application. In addition, they both address efforts in your organization to help suppliers improve, and make them more responsible for their own results. Question 4 is about what you have done to minimize your role in inspecting and overseeing suppliers and their results, and question 5 is about what you are doing to make them more independent and improve their own performance. The best company I have ever worked with in this area is Shea Homes, that I've mentioned in other sections. Shea builds thousands of homes each year in California, Arizona, and Colorado, using a workforce that consists of almost entirely outside suppliers. These trade partners as they are called, are painters, framers, pool installers, tile companies, and all the various building trades necessary to build a house. Shea has managed to reduce its number of contractors more than 400% in some divisions by partnering with the suppliers that have proven that they can consistently meet Shea's requirements. As a result of these partnerships, Shea has dramatically reduced the time they used to spend inspecting workmanship of each contractor. This has also resulted in reducing the time it takes to build the houses. To help suppliers improve their business, Shea provides contractors with all sorts of free training.

A major initiative started in the Arizona division of Shea Homes is to evaluate contractors each year against all the items in the Baldrige criteria. Suppliers prepare an abbreviated Baldrige application that is graded by Shea Homes "Examiners." Several of the more advanced contractors actually prepared full applications for the Arizona State Quality Award. Several have gone on to win these awards in the last year. Shea Homes is using the Baldrige assessment and improvement process as a way to teach contractors how to run a better business. Both the contractors and Shea Homes have seen huge benefits of this process because they have improved financial results, dramatically improved workmanship/customer satisfaction, and become better places to work.

In preparing your answer to 6.3a(4) and (5), you should start with a sentence or two explaining how you have pushed more responsibility for good performance and self-inspection on your major suppliers. This was probably a gradual process that occurred over several years, so you might tell the story of how and when you started this effort, and how it has progressed to what you do today. Next, you need to describe your efforts to partner with suppliers/contractors to help them get better. This might involve supplier training and assessment like Shea Homes does, or simply asking for different types of data. When Coca Cola buys fructose from Cargill, they do not inspect the quality and purity of the product—Rather, they monitor key process variables in Cargill's plants. The use of process metrics and standards has helped Cargill improve the consistency of its products and lessens the work for customers such as Coca Cola.

Indicators for Questions 6.3.a(4) and (5)

- Depth and breadth of efforts to reduce time and costs associated with supplier/partner inspection and oversight.

- Evidence that the organization trusts suppliers/partners more than in the past.

- Empowerment of suppliers/partners to do self-inspection.

- Use of process data, where appropriate rather than inspecting outputs.

- Number and breadth of innovative approaches to help suppliers/partners improve their business and performance.

- Evidence of partnering with suppliers that have proven they can consistently meet organizational requirements.

- Deployment of supplier/partner performance improvement approaches across all key types of suppliers/partners.

- Evidence of innovative approaches to help suppliers improve performance.

6.3a(6) How do you improve your supplier and/or partner processes, including your role as supportive customer/partner, to keep current with your business needs and directions? How are improvements shared throughout your organization, as appropriate?

<u>What They're Looking for Here</u>

This last question asks about the approaches used to evaluate and improve the way you select and interact with suppliers. One applicant answered this very concisely by listing the performance measures they look at to evaluate the supplier management process. Metrics include:

- Total number of suppliers.
- Percentage of suppliers on multi-year contracts.
- Money and time spent doing inspections/audits.
- Internal customer satisfaction with procurement function.
- Percentage of preferred suppliers.
- Reduced costs of supplier goods/services.
- Percentage of suppliers who give company high satisfaction ratings.

After listing the metrics by which you evaluate your supplier management process, you might want to provide a short list of initiatives you have recently begun or improvements you have made to the process. Make sure these are the impressive initiatives; not little things like "simplified P.O. requisition form." The point that you want to make in this answer is that your supplier management system is highly evolved and has been subjected to continuous improvement and refinement over the years.

Indicators for Question 6.3a(6)

- Evidence of a proactive approach to assessing supplier/partner management processes and approaches.

- Identification of specific performance measures for evaluating supplier/partner management process.

- Metrics/measures include both process (leading) and output (lagging) measures.

- Deployment of evaluation and improvement approaches across all major types of suppliers.

- Number and scope of changes and improvements that have been made to the supplier/partner management process over the last few years.

Chapter 11

Interpreting the Criteria for Business Results (7.0)

OVERVIEW OF THE BUSINESS RESULTS CATEGORY

This seventh category, Business Results, is one where organizations are really put to the test. The previous six categories concentrate on processes and activities. A good writer may even make your approach and processes seem like they meet all the criteria in the first six categories, but this section (7.0) tells the true tale of the success (or lack thereof) of your performance improvement efforts. In this section, you must provide evidence that all of the processes and programs you employ have really worked to improve quality and overall performance in your organization.

The Baldrige Award Criteria define this category as follows:

> The **Business Results** Category examines your organization's performance and improvement in key business areas—customer satisfaction, product and service performance, financial and marketplace performance, human resource results, supplier and partner results, and operational performance. Also examined are performance levels relative to competitors. (p. 24)

This category is worth more points than any of the others (450 points) because it separates good organizations from mediocre ones. You might be able to talk about all the wonderful approaches you deploy in the previous sections, but this section is where you must prove their effectiveness. To receive a high score in this category, you need to show that your levels and trends in performance results separate you from your competitors and other comparative companies. Effective proposal writing will help get a higher score in other sections, but not here. The Examiners are looking for data, not words.

The seventh and final category in the Baldrige criteria consists of five items:

7.1 Customer Focused Results (115 points)
7.2 Financial and Market Results (115 points)
7.3 Human Resource Results (80 points)
7.4 Supplier and Partner Results (25 points)
7.5 Organizational Effectiveness Results (115 points).

As in the previous chapters, the information on the Examination Item appears in a double-ruled box, and the Areas to Address appear in single-ruled boxes. The indicators for this chapter are a little different, because the criteria do not ask about your approaches or practices. The indicators in this chapter relate to the types of measures, levels, and trends on which positive results should be presented.

7.1 CUSTOMER FOCUSED RESULTS

Summarize your organization's customer focused results, including customer satisfaction and product and service performance results. Segment your results by customer groups and market segments, as appropriate. Include appropriate comparative data. (115 points)

Notes:

(1)   **Customer satisfaction and dissatisfaction results reported in this Item should relate to determination methods and data described in Item 3.2.**

(2)   **Measures and/or indicators of customer satisfaction relative to competitors might include objective information and data from customers and independent organizations.**

(3)   **Comparative performance of products and services and product/service performance measures that serve as indicators of customer satisfaction should be included in Item 7.1a(3).**

AREA TO ADDRESS   **[RESULTS]**
7.1a Customer Focused Results

(1) **What are your current levels and trends in key measures and/or indicators of customer satisfaction, dissatisfaction, and satisfaction relative to competitors?**

<u>What They're Looking for Here</u>

As with any result item, levels and trends are the two most important dimensions of your performance. This is the area for which data should be reported that demonstrates how levels of customer satisfaction have improved over the last several years due to performance improvement efforts. This section should include graphs of customer satisfaction data for the different groups of customers you serve. Refer back to the guidelines included in Chapter 2 of this book for a discussion of how to prepare graphs and tables. Don't make the mistake some applicants have made and respond with a single graph of customer satisfaction data. Present several different graphs of customer satisfaction data from at least the past three years. Three data points do not establish much of a trend, so the more historical data you can present, the better.

In evaluating this section, the Baldrige Examiners will be looking for several things. The first is the amount of data you present on customer satisfaction. While you are constrained by the maximum of 50 pages for your entire application, some applicants devote only a couple of pages to this important Area to Address. Include as much data as you can, and don't be afraid to use several pages for this area. It is possible to fit as many as eight separate graphs on one page. Tables or charts also allow you to fit a great deal of data in a small space. (Make sure that your graphs and charts are readable, however.)

Two other related factors examined are the level of customer satisfaction you have achieved and the current level of performance in relation to past levels. If 80 percent of your customers are satisfied or very satisfied with your quality, a large number (20 percent) still remain unsatisfied. If only 50 percent were satisfied three years ago, you will receive some credit for a big improvement, but your overall levels of satisfaction are still low. Improvement is much more difficult when you are already doing well. It may take more effort and thus be more significant if you have raised customer satisfaction levels from 94 to 98 percent in three years. A trend showing steady improvement over the last three to five years is considered very positive.

The final factor examined in this Area to Address is the number of different indices and types of data you present on customer satisfaction. Different measures of customer satisfaction (or the same indices among different segments or groups of customers) should be presented. For example, you might present data on overall levels of satisfaction among new customers, existing customers, large company customers, small company customers, government customers, private sector customers, etc. Choose the breakdowns that make the most sense for your products/services and markets.

Obviously, not all of the indices mentioned regarding dissatisfaction will be relevant to your organization. You should respond to this section by presenting data you have for any indicators that are a good gauge of customers' dissatisfaction with your products and/or services. Present the data graphically and include at least three years of statistics. The number of different indices for which data are presented and the degree to which the data show a steadily decreasing trend are the factors that will be evaluated in your response to this section.

It is likely that not all of the results and trends will be entirely positive. Performance on one or more indicators of customer dissatisfaction may not show a consistent downward trend. It is important that you thoroughly explain each of these anomalies or adverse trends. A thorough explanation does not mean that blame should be placed elsewhere for the occurrence of the anomaly. It simply means that you can describe exactly why these phenomena occurred and explain the steps taken to prevent future lapses in performance.

In this section of your application, you should also present data demonstrating that your customers are more satisfied with your products and/or services than any of your competitors' customers are with their products/services. Your performance relative to that of your competitors is the most important factor evaluated in your response to this area. This is an Area to Address on which many applicants lose points because they have little comparison data, or their results are not significant when compared to competitors' levels of customer satisfaction. You can earn a high score on Item 7.1 for your customer satisfaction results and still earn a very low score for this Item if your levels of customer satisfaction are not better than most of your competitors'.

It is important in your response for this Area that you compare your performance on several dimensions of customer satisfaction to several key competitors. The organizations you compare yourself to are also important. Comparing yourself to a world-class leader instead of local competitors obviously will earn you more points.

Indicators for Question 7.1a(1)

- Presentation of a wide variety of customer satisfaction data.

- Number of different indices of customer satisfaction for which data are presented.

- Presentation of customer satisfaction data by customer or market group.

- Trend showing continual improvements over the last several years in all measures of customer satisfaction.

- Amount of historical data presented on levels of customer satisfaction.

- Overall levels of customer satisfaction (percent of customers satisfied with service, etc.).

- Clarity of graphs and explanations of customer satisfaction data.

- Number and types of different breakdowns of customer satisfaction data.

- Number of different indices for which data are presented.

- Data are presented for all important adverse indices or measures of dissatisfaction in industry.

- All adverse indicators show a steady downward trend over the past three or more years.

- Minimum number of anomalies or positive trends in satisfaction/dissatisfaction indicators.

- Clear and complete explanations provided for all anomalies in data or positive trends in satisfaction/dissatisfaction indicators.

- Overall levels of performance on indicators of dissatisfaction.

- Number of different competitors to which comparisons are made.

- Number of different indices of customer satisfaction on which comparisons are made to the competition.

- Status/level of competitors (e.g., world-class leader in field) to which comparisons are made.

- Percentage of customer satisfaction indices on which applicant is superior to the competition.

- Applicant's superiority to competition in measures of customer satisfaction.

- Objectivity of data on how the applicant compares to competition.

- Extent to which competitors in all major markets and with all major products/services are used for comparison.

7.1a(2) What are your current levels and trends in key measures and/or indicators of customer loyalty, positive referral, customer-perceived value, and/or customer relationship building, as appropriate?

What They're Looking for Here

This was a new question in 2000, and it reflects the fact that this item has been broadened to include more than just customer satisfaction results. As I mentioned in section 3.2, a number of companies have found that improved customer satisfaction scores don't necessarily increase loyalty or predict future buying behavior. This new section asks for data on hard measures that should link directly to financial results. The types of measures for which you provide data in this section should be consistent with those mentioned in sections 3.2b and 4.1. Some examples of important metrics that might be included here are:

- Growth in business from preferred customers.
- Reduction in defecting or lost customers.
- Increased loyalty to your products/services.
- Customers giving your organization more business and giving less to competitors.
- Number and percentage of partnerships formed with key customers.
- Number and/or percent of customers who will provide a positive referral.
- Percentage or money amount in new business that is based upon referrals from existing customers.
- Customer-perceived value data collected through surveys, focus groups, or other similar methods.

Aside from the value-perception data, most of the metrics in this section are what I would call "hard" measures because they are measures of actual customer behavior, not just their thoughts or opinions. The data you present in 7.1a(1) should correlate with the data presented in this section. If you can show increased customer satisfaction and value linked to future loyalty and increased spending, this will really impress the Examiners. In fact, any sort of links between the soft and hard measures in this section will be impressive.

As with the previous section, it is important to show multiple years worth of data and to present as many sources of comparative data as you can. The data in this section tends to be weighted more heavily by Examiners because hard measures of customer buying behavior are a much stronger indicator of their overall satisfaction than any survey or complaint metric.

Indicators for Question 7.1a(2)

- Many different indicators of customer loyalty for which data are presented.

- Data on customer loyalty are presented according to market segments identified in 3.1.

- Trends in loyalty data show impressive improvements over several years.

- Levels of customer loyalty and value-perception are clearly superior to industry averages and major competitors.

- Adverse indicators such as losses of customers/defections show a decreasing trend and levels that are better than all major competitors.

- Breadth and integrity of comparative data that are presented.

- Extent to which correlations or links are shown between leading indicators of customer satisfaction shown in 7.1a(1) and lagging indicators of loyalty shown in this question [7.1a(2)]

- Number of different indices in this section for which correlations are shown to other metrics that relate to customer satisfaction or even other lagging indicators such as sales or profits.

- Data suggest that the organization has been careful to build loyalty from the "right" customers.

7.1a(3) What are your current levels and trends in key measures and/or indicators of product and service performance?

Note:

(4)   The combination of direct customer measures/indicators in 7.1a(1) and 7.1a(2) with product and service performance measures/indicators in 7.1a(3) provides an opportunity to determine cause and effect relationships between product/service attributes and evidence of customer satisfaction, loyalty, positive referral, etc.

What They're Looking for Here

This was a new question in 1999, that used to be asked a long time ago when Baldrige was about quality. There used to be a separate item that asked about product/service quality results. In the last few years, these data were asked for in the last item in this section. I think it is a positive change that hard internal measures of product and service are now in this section because they are often predictors of customer satisfaction levels and their future loyalty. You will notice that the word "quality" is not used in the criteria here. The question asks about data on any product/service performance dimension that might be important to customer satisfaction. The types of metrics for which you provide data in this section should be consistent with your customer requirements research you described in 3.1.

The key here is to present data on metrics that are strongly linked to customer satisfaction. For example, FedEx tracks a metric each day called the Service Quality Index. It is a measure of the frequency and severity of the mistakes they make each day that impact how customers feel about the service. For example, losing a package completely might be weighted as a 10 because it is the worst mistake that could occur. Delivering a package an hour late might be weighted as a 1 because it is only a minor inconvenience to most customers. Another good example is a metric tracked by a major rental car company. They figured out through research that if customers see the competitors' shuttle busses pass by twice while waiting at the airport before their bus shows up, the customer gets quite angry. Consequently, they keep track of how many times their customers see competitors busses drive by before theirs shows up at the airport pick-up locations.

These are great examples of the types of internal performance metrics that an organization might report in this section. Along with the usual graphs of your own and competitor performance, this section calls for some explanation. It may not be obvious to the Examiner why you are tracking the measures for specific data presented in this section. You need to explain how and why these metrics were selected, and how they link both to customer satisfaction measures [7.1a(1)] and customer loyalty measures [7.1a(2)]. In fact, if you can show graphs that depict correlations or links between these and other measures, that will be sure to impress the Examiners.

Indicators for Question 7.1a(3)

- Number and breadth of metrics for which product/service performance data are provided in this section.

- Trends in product/service performance measures show excellent improvement over multiple years.

- Levels of performance are superior to industry averages and all major competitors.

- Product/service performance metrics selected are based upon thorough research, linking them to customer satisfaction and other important performance dimensions.

- Adverse indicators show both decreasing trends and levels that are better than relevant comparative data.

- Integrity of data on internal measures of product/service performance.

- Number of metrics in this section that can be linked to other metrics of customer satisfaction, loyalty, or even financial results.

- Strength of correlations shown will help improve the accuracy of business decision making.

- Breadth of data presented covers all major products/services and is segmented appropriately.

7.2 FINANCIAL AND MARKET RESULTS

Summarize your organization's key financial and marketplace performance results, segmented by market segments, as appropriate. Include appropriate comparative data. (115 points)

Note: Aggregate measures such as return on investment (ROI), asset utilization, operating margins, profitability, profitability by market/customer segment, liquidity, debt to equity ratio, value added per employee, and financial activity measures are appropriate for responding to 7.2a(1).

AREA TO ADDRESS   **[RESULTS]**
7.2a Financial and Market Results

(1) What are your current levels and trends in key measures and/or indicators of financial performance, including aggregate measures of financial return and/or economic value, as appropriate?
(2) What are your current levels and trends in key measures and/or indicators of marketplace performance, including market share/position, business growth, and new markets entered, as appropriate?

What They're Looking for Here

This important section asks you to present your financial and marketplace results. Most organizations have no shortage of these types of data. The problem may lie in selecting the most important graphs to present, given the limited space you have in the application. You should present overall financial indicators that are listed in your response to Item 4.1, which asks about the performance metrics in your company. If you mention that Economic Value Added (EVA) is your primary financial statistic, you better present some data on EVA here. It is a good idea to present a mix of financial performance data that represent the past (profit, EVA, ROI, etc.), the present (cash flow, money in booked orders, assets/liabilities), and the future (growth, money in outstanding proposals, money invested in R&D or new products/services). By presenting data on your financial performance from all three time perspectives, you give the Examiners a good overall picture of your financial health.

It is important to keep in mind that the Examiners are looking for evidence that your results are better than your competitors, and that you show a long history of good performance. Therefore, it is important to present data over multiple years. Getting comparative financial performance data on your competitors may be difficult, but this will help your score, if your results show that you are clearly the industry leader.

This section is also used to present marketplace data, which might include market share, gains and losses of business, or other similar data. Again, comparative data are very important. One Baldrige applicant showed that their marketshare had been steadily increasing over the last five years, in a flat market. Which meant that their competitors' share of the market was being lost to the applicant's company. These kinds of data will be very impressive to the Examiners. Make sure when you present data on marketplace results you indicate the source of any comparative data on your graphs. Using market data from an outside impartial source such as an industry trade association will give the presentation more credibility than if they are data you collected yourself.

Some marketplace data may actually belong better in section 7.1. For example, gains and losses of key customers, might be a very good hard measure of customer satisfaction. Another one, used by IBM that could go either in 7.1 or 7.2 is increases or decreases in revenue from existing customers from year to year. You decide in which item to present the data, keeping in mind that both sections should include about equal amounts of data, and that these first two Areas to Address in Category 7.0 are worth 23 percent of the points.

Indicators for Question 7.2a

- Presentation of financial results shows levels that are clearly superior to major competitors and industry averages.

- Data are presented on all major financial indices listed in section 4.1 of the application.

- Financial performance data include a good mix of indicators of past, present, and future financial health.

- Trends show continuous improvement over three or more years.

- Trends show better improvement rates than industry averages and/or competitors.

- Competitor data presented are actually the companies against which the applicant most often competes.

- Financial results represent the entire company's performance rather than a single unit or division.

- Financial results compare favorable to benchmark or world-class organizations in similar business.

- Credibility of sources of comparative data.

- Market data show applicant's performance is clearly superior to all major competitors.

- Trends in market share and other similar metrics shows excellent trends over time.

- Trends in market share growth are superior to industry averages and competitors.

- Length of time during which levels and trends in financial and market performance are superior to industry averages and major competitors.

7.3 HUMAN RESOURCE RESULTS

Summarize your organization's human resource results, including employee well-being, satisfaction, development, and work system performance. Segment your results by types and categories of employees, as appropriate. Include appropriate comparative data. (80 points)

Notes:

(1) Results reported in this Item should relate to activities described in Category 5. The results should be responsive to key process needs described in Category 6, and the company action plans and related human resource plans described in Item 2.2.

(2) For appropriate measures of employee well-being and satisfaction, see Notes to Item 5.3. Appropriate measures and/or indicators of employee development might include innovation and suggestion rates, courses completed, learning, on-the-job performance improvements, and cross-training.

(3) Appropriate measures and/or indicators of work system performance and effectiveness might include job and job classification simplification, job rotation, work layout, and changing supervisory ratios.

AREAS TO ADDRESS   **[RESULTS]**
7.3a Human Resource Results

(1) What are your current levels and trends in key measures and/or indicators of employee well-being, satisfaction and dissatisfaction, and development?

What They're Looking for Here

This first question in 7.3 calls for data associated with the metrics you defined in 4.1 and 5.3, relating to employee satisfaction. As in the Customer Focus Results section, it is important to present data on both leading and lagging indicators of employee satisfaction. Obvious metrics like employee survey data would be included here, as would metrics like turnover, absenteeism, and grievances or employee complaints. Other data might be included here that one wouldn't normally think of as employee satisfaction.

Safety is a big deal in most manufacturing companies, and even many service organizations. If that is the case in your organization, make sure to include a good mix of preventive and outcome metrics in your results. For example, you might present data on safety audit scores, near misses, minor mishaps, test scores, in safety training, and so forth as preventive data. You also need to include the typical outcome measures of number of lost-time accidents, severity ratings, worker compensation costs, etc. The same sort of data might be presented for employee health and well-being. Preventive metrics might include vital signs like weight, percentage of smokers/non-smokers, blood pressure, and heart rate. These might be compared to the general population or the past to show that efforts have been made to improve the health of your work force.

As note 3 mentions, data included here might be measures of employee development, cross training, suggestions, and so forth. Essentially, the data on employee education and training from the metrics defined in section 5.2 would also go in this section. This is a little confusing, and you have to read the fine print to realize that training results go here, and not in 7.3a(2). It does not really matter to your score, but there tends to be more data relating to work systems [7.3a(2)], so it is probably wise to include education/training results here.

Indicators for Question 7.3a(1)

- Number and breadth of metrics for which employee satisfaction, development, and well-being data are presented.

- Safety results show dramatic improvements and levels of performance that are better than both industry averages and key competitors.

- Employee well-being results show that the organization has improved the overall health of its work force over the last few years.

- Programs and initiatives relating to employee well-being and safety show impressive results in both process and outcome measures.

- Employee satisfaction levels and trends are markedly better in both level and trend when compared to industry averages and other comparable organizations.

- Education and training data show that the organization is a leader in providing its employees with effective developmental opportunities.

- Number and breadth of results relating to employee education, training, and development.

- Decreasing trends are shown and healthy levels of performance are demonstrated in indicators of employee dissatisfaction.

- Organization-specific employee-related metrics show good trends and levels of performance.

7.3a(2) What are your current levels and trends in key measures and/or indicators of work system performance and effectiveness?

<u>What They're Looking for Here</u>

This second question in 7.3a asks for results relating to item 5.1 Work Systems. Some of the most important results to include in this section are those that show the success of your recruitment efforts. Common measures reported here might include:

- Number or applicants for each open position.
- Percentage of jobs filled with internal/external candidates.
- Offer/acceptance ratio.
- Initial 30- 60- and 90-day ratings of new hires.
- First year turnover.

The key to presenting those results is to demonstrate that your results are better than relevant comparative organizations. Other types of data to report in this section might relate to job design, use of alternative work methods, reduction in organizational layers or supervision, empowerment of employees, career development/promotion metrics, recognition data, and effectiveness of compensation and other reward programs.

The key is to present data on all the metrics identified as important in either item 5.1, or another portion of the application such as 4.1 or the Business Overview. The challenge with many of these metrics is getting relevant comparisons with other organizations. As with any of these sections that ask for results, it is important to include comparative data so that levels of performance can be evaluated.

<u>Indicators for Question 7.3a(2)</u>

- Data are presented for all important metrics identified in 5.1, relating to work systems.

- Trends show dramatic improvements over the last few years, or high levels of performance that have been maintained.

- Levels of performance on important metrics are superior to industry averages, competitors, and other relevant comparisons.

- Breadth and scope of data on work systems.

- Results presented are a good mix of process or activity measures and output/outcome metrics.

- Correlations have been demonstrated between results in this section and those in other sections such as Customer Focus Results, (7.1), Financial and Market Results (7.2), and Organizational Effectiveness Results (7.5).

- Strength of correlations can be used for practical business planning and decision making.

- Negative trends or anomalies in the data are adequately explained.

- Results show that performance system changes like job redesign, teams, suggestion systems, compensation, recognition, and other approaches actually lead to improvements in financial and operational performance, or have positive impact on important measures on the company's performance metrics.

- Measures of HR process focus more on effectiveness than on activity measures like hours of training or percentage of employee on teams.

7.4 SUPPLIER AND PARTNER RESULTS

Summarize your organization's key supplier and partner results. Include appropriate comparative data. (25 points)

Note:

Results reported in this Item should relate directly to processes and performance requirements described in Item 6.3.

AREA TO ADDRESS   **[RESULTS]**

7.4a Supplier and Partner Results

What are your current levels and trends in key measures and/or indicators of supplier and partner performance? Include your performance and/or cost improvements resulting from supplier and partner performance, and performance management.

What They're Looking for Here

Once again the word "trends" appears in the criteria statement. This should tell you that they want graphs and statistics, not just words. Often, applicants formulate a written response to this area by simply explaining how suppliers' performance has improved due to the applicant's efforts. Without supportive data, however, they end up with a very low score in this area—regardless of how well written the description may be.

The Examiners want to see evidence that key measures of supplier performance have improved over the last few years. If you have over 500 suppliers, obviously you don't have room to present data on every one of them. What you might do is select the two or three that you conduct the most business with, and present graphs on their performance trends. You could then summarize results for other suppliers in a table or chart similar to the one that follows.

SUPPLIER QUALITY DATA					
Company	Measure	1997	1998	1999	2000
Canon	Photocopiers Uptime	82%	78%	88%	94%
Cleansweeps Janitorial	Cleanliness Ratings	3.4/5	3.7/5	4.3/5	4.6/5
ABC Office Supplies	On-time Deliveries	82%	88%	90%	90%

Your response for this area will be evaluated both on the amount of supplier data you present and the degree to which supplier performance shows a trend of continuous improvement. Where there have been drops in supplier results, you will be expected to provide explanations.

You also need to explain how your suppliers' performance compares to that of your competitors' suppliers, and/or to benchmark organizations. Begin your response for this section by explaining the bases for your comparisons. You should address such questions as:

- How are competitors selected for comparison?
- How are suppliers for which comparative data are presented selected?
- How are benchmark organizations selected for examining supplier performance?

After explaining how you select supplier data from competitors and benchmark organizations, you should present the comparative data. As in the other sections, it is a good idea to present supplier data using graphs. Your response will be judged according to the amount of data you present and the level of quality your suppliers achieve in relation to competitors' suppliers.

The criteria in this Area to Address also ask you to present data on how you have reduced costs or improved other measures of performance, working with suppliers or partners. For example, going with a single source supplier may have reduced your raw material costs by 5 percent over the last few years. Or, outsourcing your Information Technology function may have improved system uptime and saved hundreds of thousands of dollars. These types of data are important to present here, rather than in 7.2, which asks for financial results.

Indicators for Question 7.4a

- Percentage of suppliers/partners for which performance data are presented.

- Trend showing continual improvement in supplier/partner performance over the last several years.

- Overall levels of supplier/partner performance are high.

- Percentage of suppliers/partners showing trend toward improved quality.

- Evidence to suggest that actions by applicant to help suppliers/partners improve their performance have resulted in improved performance.

- Objectivity and reliability of data presented on suppliers/partners.

- Percentage of suppliers/partners for which comparative data are presented.

- Importance of suppliers/partners for which comparative data are presented.

- Presentation of benchmark data on suppliers/partners.

- Degree of difference between quality performance of applicant's suppliers/ partners and that of competitors' suppliers/partners.

- Number or percentage of suppliers/partners for which the applicant's supplier performance is superior to competitors' suppliers.

- Trend of performance improvement in applicant's suppliers/partners as compared to competitor's suppliers.

- Levels and trends in company performance results attributed to supplier/partner performance.

- Number of different areas for which data are presented illustrating supplier/partner contribution to good company performance.

7.5 ORGANIZATIONAL EFFECTIVENESS RESULTS

Summarize your organization's key operational performance results that contribute to the achievement of organizational effectiveness. Include appropriate comparative data. (115 points)

Notes:

(1)   Results reported in Item 7.5 should address key organizational requirements and progress toward accomplishment of key organizational performance goals as presented in the Business Overview, and in Items 1.1, 2.2, 6.1, and 6.2. Include results not reported in Items 7.1, 7.2, 7.3, and 7.4.

(2)   Results reported in Item 7.5 should provide key information for analysis (Item 4.2) and review (Item 1.1) of organizational operational performance and should provide the operational basis for customer results (Item 7.1) and financial and market results (Item 7.2).

(3)   Regulatory/legal compliance results reported in Item 7.5 should address requirements described in Item 1.2.

AREA TO ADDRESS   **[RESULTS]**
7.5a Organizational Effectiveness Results

(1) What are your current levels and trends in key measures and/or indicators of key design, production, delivery, and support process performance? Include productivity, cycle time, and other appropriate measures of effectiveness and efficiency.

(2) What are your results for key measures and/or indicators of regulatory/legal compliance and citizenship? What are your results for key measures and/or indicators of accomplishment of organizational strategy?

What They're Looking for Here

This Area to Address is the same as last year, except that internal product/service quality and performance now go in 7.1. As you can surmise from the description, this is a broad and important category. This section gives the applicant the opportunity to present results that are important to their particular business and industry. For example, in a nuclear facility, the Examiners would expect to see a great deal of regulatory and compliance data presented here. As with any of the previous sections in this category, the results presented should be consistent with the measures listed in previous sections of the application.

The types of data to include in this section are as follows:

- Operational results like cycle time, productivity, or efficiency

- Regulatory/compliance results (e.g., environmental or public safety data)

- Public responsibility results

- Process results

- New product/service performance results

- Results from support functions

At first glance, it seems that this Area to Address duplicates others in this category by asking for customer satisfaction and financial results. These types of data are not asked for here. What is asked for is operational or internal measures whose performance impacts customer satisfaction or financial performance. For example, a key measure of service quality might be on-time delivery, for which you would present data here, even though performance on this measure clearly impacts overall customer satisfaction. You might also present data in this section of productivity (e.g., sales per employee). Performance on this metric would clearly have an impact on company profits or return on investment.

One effective method of presenting the data in this section is to begin with a matrix chart that lists the performance metrics for which you will present data in this section along the left side of the matrix and the overall measures of customer and shareholder/owner satisfaction along the top of the chart. Use the matrix to indicate the level of impact of the internal (7.5) metrics on the customer (7.1) and financial/marketplace (7.2) metrics.

The results you present in this section of your application should correspond to the operational indices that you stated you measure in section 4.1, and the measures on which you set goals as described in section 2.2. What is considered important about your response to this Item is the scope and breadth of the data you present. You should present data for a variety of operational and financial measures. The key here is to select and present data for those measures that reflect *overall company performance*. An error that Baldrige applicants could make in this section (judging from errors made in similar sections in the past) is to present graphs showing only those indices that signal an improving trend. When Examiners see this they tend to wonder what performance looks like on the other indices for which there are no graphs. When the criteria refer to "operational results," they are not asking about quality data. Operational measures typically fall into three categories:

- Productivity
- Timeliness
- Quantity

Keep in mind that Examination Item 7.5 is a catchall category where you would report a wide variety of results. Along with product/service quality and operational results, some of the major types of data that might be presented in this section are:

- Ethics measures
- Environmental performance
- Public health/safety results
- Corporate responsibility results

Read over the example indices listed in the criteria for types of indices that should be taken into account. A study that was done by the U.S. General Accounting Office in 1991

on the impact of using the Baldrige criteria to improve organizational performance lists
eight operating indices used to evaluate past Baldrige finalists:

- Reliability
- Order processing time
- Product lead time
- Costs of quality

- Timeliness of delivery
- Errors or defects
- Inventory turnover
- Cost savings

Data on all of these metrics could go in section 7.5. Data on product/service errors or
defects are reported in 7.1. The other seven indices are all appropriate, however. I am not
suggesting that you need to present data on these indices, only that these should be
considered in determining what is appropriate for your company.

Another type of data that should be presented in this section is data on measures that are
unique to your industry or your organization. These should be indices by which the
company measures itself.

In order to determine how significant or insignificant your results are, you need to present
data on competitors and industry averages. What is important about your response to this
Area to Address is the extent to which several different comparative statistics are
presented for each of the indices presented in 6.2a. A good way of presenting these data
is to prepare a chart that lists the various performance indices along the left and
performance of your company and several others in the remainder of the chart. A portion
of an example of such a chart is shown below.

Comparison of Operational Results					
Measures	Our Company	Competitor A	Competitor B	Industry Best	Benchmark
Order Processing Time	8 days	14 days	11 days	6 days	3 days
Sales per Employee	$140,000 per employee	$113,000 per employee	$110,000 per employee	$150,000 per employee	N/A
% On-Time Delivery	96%	95%	88%	98%	N/A

Another way of presenting these data is to present graphs showing trends over the last
three to five years in your performance as compared with competitors and others. The
problem with using a matrix like the one shown above is that only one year's worth of

data is presented. The Examiners are interested in how your overall levels of results compare with competitors', but they are also interested in how your *trends* compare with others. If other companies have improved at about the same rate as you have, your positive trends will not be nearly as impressive. The sources of your data on competitors and other companies will also be questioned, so make sure that you explain where these data come from.

Obviously, what is important for this Area to Address is that your levels of performance are better than your major competitors', and, in the best-case scenario, than industry leaders' and other benchmarks you use for improvement planning.

Indicators for Questions 7.5a(1) and (2)

- Number of different performance metrics for which data are presented.

- Data are presented for all important performance measures, not just a few.

- Number of years' worth of historical data presented to show trends.

- Degree to which all indices show continuous and steady improvement.

- Clarity of graphs included in this section.

- Amount of variability in performance.

- Clarity of explanations of quality results.

- Measures include inputs, processes, and outputs (the scope should not be limited to outputs alone).

- Number of adverse trends or anomalies noted in performance data.

- Credibility and clarity of explanations for anomalies or adverse trends.

- Evidence that when adverse trends are the fault of the organization, the situations causing the problems have been thoroughly investigated and corrected (this should be indicated by level of performance following the adverse trend).

- Use of outside sources of data on competitors.

- Use of reliable and appropriate sources to gather data on competitors.

- Use of ethical and fair methods of gathering data on competitors.

- Number of different sources of competitor data.

- Number of different aspects of the business that are compared to competitors.

- How much better the applicant's quality results are than those of major competitors.

- How applicant's product/service quality results compare to competitors and world-class leaders in the field.

- Number of different quality indices on which comparisons are made with competitors.

- Linkage of product/service quality and operational results to customer satisfaction and overall financial performance.

- Scope and breadth of indices for which operational and process data are presented.

- Correspondence between measures identified in 4.1 and data presented in 7.5.

- Extent to which positive trends are demonstrated in productivity, waste, cycle time, and other key operational measures.

- Presentation of enough data to establish trends (typically three to five years).

- Amount of improvement occurring over the last three to five years for key indices of operational performance.

- Extent to which indices are appropriate measures of overall company performance.

- Presentation of data on key process performance measures (see Items 6.1 and 6.2).

- Levels and trends in measures of environmental performance and other measures of public responsibility.

- Levels and trends in regulatory/compliance results with no significant adverse findings.

- Levels and trends of company/industry-specific performance measures.

- Levels of financial performance have significantly improved over the last three to five years.

- Consistency of trends across all different financial indices for which data are presented.

- Percentage of indices for which competitor and industry-leader results data are presented.

- Competitors are the companies against which the applicant most often competes.

- Credibility of sources for competitor data and benchmark data.

- Extent to which data are presented for major competitors, industry leaders, and benchmarks.

- Extent to which current levels of performance by the applicant are better than all major competitors, industry leaders, and benchmarks.

- Extent to which positive trends exhibited by the applicant are significantly better than trends in competitor data.

- Length of time (number of years) during which the applicant's performance on company-specific measures is superior to the competition.

Chapter 12

Preparing for a Site Visit

Many organizations have done a fine job writing Baldrige or state award applications, and had many of their strengths turn to areas for improvement after the site visit. Organizations that receive a site visit should be congratulated because it signifies that the written application warranted more data collection by examiners. In the Baldrige process, you generally need about 600 points out of 1000 to receive a site visit. Some states such as Minneapolis perform site visits on all applicants; therefore, it is not an indication of "finalist" status as it is with the Baldrige. The purpose of this chapter is to let you know how to prepare for a site visit if you are an applicant for an award, as well as how to prepare and conduct a site visit if you are an examiner. The first portion of the chapter explains how to prepare for the examination, and the second section of this chapter presents tips for examiners on conducting a site visit.

PURPOSE OF THE SITE VISIT

In spite of what it might seem, Baldrige is not an essay contest. An effective proposal or application certainly helps, but does not ensure winning an award. Review of the written application is the first step in the assessment process. If the application includes enough strengths to convince a team of examiners that yours is a well-run organization, they will probably request a site visit. Unlike an audit, the purpose of a site visit is not to look for problems that weren't uncovered in the written application. Examiners are not trained to strictly look for negatives. The purpose of a site visit is to look for positive aspects that may not have been addressed in the application, as well as for weaknesses or parts of the company's systems that may not be as effective as they appeared in the written application. Many factors are difficult to assess by reading an application. For example, employee morale is something a team can assess after spending a few hours talking to a cross-section of employees. The extent to which systematic processes have been implemented or deployed is also a major purpose of the site visit. With only 50 pages to tell your story, it is hard to provide enough detail on where your systems and approaches have been deployed.

The overall purpose of a site visit is to reveal the truth about the organization, and provide a thorough assessment by spending a few days talking to its people and examining its systems and approaches. While it may be possible to "snow" a team of examiners by writing a great application, it is impossible to fake a good site visit. The world-class companies stand out right away, and identifying companies that don't meet the Baldrige ideals becomes very easy after a few days at the company.

WITH WHOM WILL EXAMINERS WANT TO TALK?

Anyone they want to. Keep in mind that you don't control the agenda during the site visit, the examiners do. They tell you what sites they want to visit, which people they want to interview, and what documents they want to see. They know that your agenda is to receive a good report, or win an award, so they are leery of any suggestions about whom they should talk to, or which facilities ought to be visited. In general, you can count on the examiners surely talking to most if not all senior executives. The CEO or president typically knows more about the overall systems in the company then anybody, and is often the only one who truly sees the "big picture." Other members of the senior management team are also interviewed by examiners. Examiners will not only ask questions about the 1.0 Leadership category, but tend to ask executives about issues that cut across all seven categories.

Examiners also like to talk with individual contributors or hourly employees. In particular, those that have a great deal of customer contact are often asked a lot of questions by examiners. When examiners talk to employees individually or in groups, they are often probing for deployment issues, testing how well the company has communicated its vision, values, and plans. They also talk to employees about how they feel about the company, workload, pay, and whether or not employees feel like valuable members of a team. Beginning below is a list of questions that examiners usually ask of executives, middle management, and individual contributors.

QUESTIONS TYPICALLY ASKED OF EXECUTIVES

- What is your role in the company?

- What is the vision of the company for the next 5 or more years, and how do you communicate that vision to your people?

- How much time do you personally spend each month with customers, suppliers, and employees?

- How would you characterize your management style?

- Why is the company organized the way it is, and what data do you look at to tell you this is the ideal structure?

- What methods do you use to stay in touch with your business?

- How do you seek out growth or expansion opportunities for the company to ensure its future survival and success? Can you give some examples?

- How do you select members of your executive team, and what sort of traits do you look for in a good executive?

- How will you ensure that your company will continue to be successful once you have retired or moved on to other opportunities?

- Describe your leadership system.

- What are your most important key success factors?

- How will you maintain excellence as your organization grows and perhaps becomes more diverse?

- How do you know that the leadership system and your individual behavior is effective? What metrics do you look at?

- Give me some examples illustrating how your leadership approach/system has changed or improved over the past few years.

QUESTIONS TYPICALLY ASKED OF MIDDLE MANAGERS

- Who are the customers of your organization/department?

- What is the mission or purpose of your organization/department?

- What are the most important requirements of each of your customers?

- What is the most important priority of senior management in the company?

- What are the key processes in your organization?

- What are the performance measures for your organization/department?

- How do these performance metrics relate to those of senior management?

- What targets have you set for each of the performance metrics?

- What are the strategies for reaching your goals/targets?

- Can you give some examples of new products or services that you have introduced in the past few years? Explain how successful they have been.

- How do you communicate your vision, mission, and plans to your staff?

- What methods do you use to stay in touch with the daily operation in your organization?

- How do you ensure that work is done consistently in your organization, and that your outputs are defect-free?

- How do you know that you are cost-competitive?

- How do you get promoted? What are the most important criteria?

- What is this company's biggest problem?

- Can you think of any reason why this company would not be a good role model for other companies around the world?

QUESTIONS TYPICALLY ASKED OF EMPLOYEES

- Who are your customers?

- What are the most important requirements of each of your customers?

- What are the major work processes in your area?

- How do you measure your performance?

- What your individual goals or objectives?

- How do these relate to the department and company goals and objectives?

- What are the values of the company? Do they really live by these values or are they just words?

- What is the company's vision for the future?

- What can you do in your area to help the company achieve its vision?

- What kind of training do you receive?

- What are the most important priorities of management?

- How are you involved in helping the company improve performance? Can you give me some examples?

- How much authority do you have to make decisions and spend company money?

- Do you currently have more authority than in the past?

- Is this a good place to work? Why or why not?

- What gets rewarded or recognized in this company?

- How important is safety and employee well-being in the company?

TYPICAL APPROACH/DEPLOYMENT
SITE-VISIT ISSUES BY CATEGORY

Along with the questions I have just outlined that are often asked of senior executives, middle managers, and employees, it is important to understand what examiners typically ask about in each of the six Baldrige categories concerned with approach/deployment issues. Following is a list of typical site-visit issues by category. Of course, some of these issues may not apply to a given application. However, in my experience, most teams of examiners tend to look for many of the same site-visit issues in most organizations. Those listed here are variables that are hard to evaluate strictly from the written application. Those that begin with the word "clarify" mean that the examiners need additional information on an approach or its deployment. When the word "verify" is used, the examiners are looking for evidence to substantiate a claim made in the written application. This generally means that they need more proof before they agree that it is a strength.

<u>1.0 Leadership Site-Visit Issues</u>

- Clarify what the company's leadership system is, and how it works to direct and control performance.

- Verify that senior executives are in-touch with the business by spending adequate time with customers, suppliers/distributors, and employees.

- Clarify why the company is organized a certain way.

- Verify claims made about open communication and accessibility of senior management.

- Clarify roles and responsibilities of various layers of management in the company.

- Clarify the actions senior executives take to look for future opportunities for the company and ask for examples of how this has been done in the past.

- Verify that the behavior of senior executives is consistent with the company values.

- Verify that all senior executives engaging activities to keep them in touch with employees, customers, and key suppliers/partners.

- Clarify the metrics and methods used to evaluate the leadership system.

- Verify that improvements have been made over the years in the company's leadership system.

- Clarify any inconsistencies between executive compensation and the importance of nonfinancial factors such as employee satisfaction, customer satisfaction, and innovation/growth.

- Verify that all senior executives actually review the performance metrics outlined in section 4.1 on a regular basis, and use this data to assess company performance.

- Clarify the company's criteria for selecting charitable/community organizations to support.

- Verify that the company stands out as better than other companies their size for their support of community/charitable activities.

- Clarify what the company does to encourage employees at all levels to give back to the community or support charitable organizations.

- Verify the company's environmental record and look for evidence of any unethical behavior.

- Verify that there are no ethical, human relations environmental, or other similar problems that might not make the company a good role model for the U.S.

2.0 Strategic Planning Site-Visit Issues

- Verify that the planning process described in the application is actually the one used.

- Clarify the specific data gathered during the situation analysis phase of the planning process.

- Clarify the difference between strategic planning and annual planning.

- Verify that plans address more than just financial and operational issues.

- Verify that the Baldrige assessment is a major input to the planning process and not a separate and distinct activity.

- Verify that the planning process is logical, efficient, and that plans are finalized in a short time frame each year.

- Clarify the company vision and the key success factors it will use to differentiate itself from major competitors.

- Clarify that the company has completely articulated its strategies.

- Verify that strategic planning is an integral part of running the business, as opposed to a separate activity done once a year to satisfy some corporate requirement.

- Verify that plans have been well communicated to all levels of employees, and that unit, department, or functional plans are well integrated with overall company plans.

- Verify that performance against targets or goals in the plan is reviewed on a regular basis.

- Verify that the strategic plan is a living document that is revised as company strategy might change.

- Clarify the metrics used to evaluate the planning process, and obtain specifics on how the process has improved over the past 3 to 5 years.

- Clarify the company's mission and vision if they are vague.

- Clarify the link between the performance measures outlined in section 4.1 and the targets or goals appearing in the strategic plan.

- Clarify the data that were used to set targets/goals.

- Clarify how the plans are communicated to all levels of employees.

- Clarify the HR plans and ask for an explanation of links between HR goals/strategies and overall company goals and strategies.

- Verify that the company has collected adequate data on the market, competitors, and other factors to prepare valid projections/forecasts of position in 3 to 5 years.

3.0 Customer and Market Focus Site-Visit Issues

- Clarify what percentage of business comes from each major group of customers.

- Verify that market research methods described in the application are actually used.

- Clarify the thoroughness of methods used to gather data on customer requirements.

- Verify that important requirements have been defined for all major market segments.

- Verify that all major groups of customers and potential customers' needs have been researched.

- Verify that research on customer requirements is a major input to the new product/service development process. Ask for examples to illustrate how customer requirements are integrated into new product/service designs.

- Clarify how new or enhanced products/services have led to greater market share or customer loyalty.

- Clarify the metrics and methods used to evaluate market research techniques.

- Verify that improvements have been made in the methods for market research.

- Clarify the major points of interactions between customers and the organization.

- Verify that customer contact employees are selected with care, trained well, paid well, and given the authority to quickly resolve customer concerns.

- Verify how easy it is to access the company by testing 800 numbers or other methods used for customers to contact the organization.

- Clarify standards for customer service.

- Clarify efforts to build loyalty from the most important customers and ask about the effectiveness of these efforts.

- Verify that complaint management process works as described in the application.

- Clarify how customer satisfaction is measured by reviewing instruments, data collection plans, and looking at reports.

- Verify that customer satisfaction is measured for all types of customers.

- Verify that reliable data are collected on customer satisfaction levels of competitors and other comparative organizations.

- Clarify how customer satisfaction data are reviewed and analyzed on a regular basis.

4.0 Information and Analysis Site-Visit Issues

- Clarify the criteria used to select the metrics that appear on the company scorecard.

- Clarify the data collection methods and frequencies with which data are collected on each performance metric.

- Verify that the metrics listed in the application are actually reviewed by management on a regular basis and used to assess business performance.

- Verify link between key success factors and vision and performance metrics.

- Verify that performance data are easily accessible, clearly presented, and understood by employees.

- Clarify how performance metrics have been evaluated and improved over the past 3 to 5 years.

- Clarify how promotions and compensation are linked to the company performance metrics.

- Verify that business unit, facility, department, and functional performance metrics are well linked to overall company performance metrics.

- Clarify the criteria used to select competitors and other organizations against which to compare.

- Verify that data bases on competitors are complete and up-to-date.

- Verify that data on competitors is used for goal setting and planning.

- Clarify the scope of any benchmarking efforts and ask about changes that have been implemented based upon benchmarking.

- Verify that comparative data are used to improve processes if claimed in the application.

- Verify that performance data are actually analyzed as opposed to simply reviewed once a month in meetings.

- Verify that correlations have actually been defined for key metrics such as customer satisfaction and employee satisfaction and/or customer satisfaction and financial results. Ask for copies of correlation studies or data.

- Verify that analysis approach described in written application is actually used at all levels of the organization.

- Verify that performance against targets or goals is reviewed on a regular basis, and that actions are taken or diagnoses performed when performance is not up to par.

- Verify that the company makes all major management and investment decisions by analyzing appropriate performance data. Ask for examples to illustrate deployment of this practice.

5.0 Human Resource Focus Site-Visit Issues

- Clarify the company approach to recruiting and selection and look for links between selection criteria and values and the company vision for the future.

- Clarify the logic behind the company approach to designing jobs, and get them to explain how their approach is the most effective way of dividing work tasks.

- Clarify any inconsistencies with the companies values, stated direction/vision and their approach to work systems.

- Verify deployment of innovative work system practices such as self-directed teams, cross functional work groups, etc.

- Clarify the amount of authority employees at each level have and verify claims by talking to employees.

- Verify deployment of recognition programs and ask employees about the fairness of the programs.

- Verify that the items/privileges given to recognize employees are, in fact rewarding to them.

- Clarify the criteria for receiving various reward/recognition items.

- Clarify the link between performance and compensation.

- Verify deployment of performance-based pay across levels and functions in the organization.

- Clarify the link between performance measures identified in section 4.1 and reward/compensation to look for any disconnects.

- Verify that there no inconsistencies between the company's desire for teamwork/cooperation and their performance appraisal, promotion, recognition, and compensation programs.

- Verify the effectiveness of any innovative work system approaches such as 360 appraisal, self-directed work teams, knowledge-based pay, etc.

- Verify link between company strategic plans, and training needs analysis approaches. Ask for examples that illustrate how key competencies are identified that will help the company achieve its vision.

- Verify deployment of systematic training needs analysis to all types of training.

- Verify that training is not used as a "band-aid" solution to all performance problems.

- Clarify the delivery methods used for various types of training.

- Verify that training evaluation data show its effectiveness.

- Verify that training content and delivery methods are integrated with overall approach to work systems.

- Verify that appropriate input is sought from various sources in doing training needs analysis.

- Clarify methods used to ensure transfer of training and for rewarding use of skills learned in training back on the job.

- Verify that training is continuously evaluated and improved.

- Clarify the company approaches to ensuring a safe work environment.

- Verify that there is as much emphasis on safety as is claimed in the application. Talk to hourly employees about this.

- Clarify the company efforts to ensure employee wellness and check on deployment of programs, such as health club memberships or participation in weight loss or "stop smoking" programs.

- Verify that special services offered to employees are actually the ones they want, and that these services are used by the majority of employees.

- Verify that team building activities are a positive/fun experience rather than a dull obligation that must be met to avoid appearing like one is not a team player. Talk to employees about how they feel about picnics, parties, and other similar events.

- Verify that the company really tries to delight employees.

- Verify data collection methods for measuring employee satisfaction by reviewing instruments and data collection procedures.

- Verify that executives review data on safety and employee satisfaction as often and with as much emphasis as they do financial and operational results.

- Verify that the company can demonstrate how changes in employee well-being and satisfaction are correlated to other key results such as customer satisfaction and financial performance.

6.0 Process Management Site-Visit Issues

- Verify that market research data on customer requirements is suited to drive development of new products/services.

- Verify deployment of product/service development process to all new products/services.

- Verify that the development process actually works efficiently, and involves all functions identified in written application.

- Clarify how production processes are designed and how parameters are set to ensure that new products/services meet or exceed customer requirements.

- Verify market success of new/enhanced products and services.

- Clarify key processes, metrics, standards, and control strategies.

- Verify that process metrics are correlated to important output metrics.

- Verify that standards or targets for process metrics are linked to research on customer requirements and correlations with output performance.

- Verify effectiveness of control strategies in eliminating or minimizing variability in processes.

- Clarify scope of process improvement efforts.

- Verify use of benchmarking, technology review, market research, competitor analysis and other data in process improvement efforts.

- Verify deployment of process improvement methodology across all projects.

- Verify deployment of process improvements across all locations, units, and functions as appropriate.

- Verify employee understanding of process analysis and improvement methodologies.

- Verify link between process improvement activities and company strategic plan.

- Verify that each support function has defined its customers and their most important priorities.

- Clarify how support functions deal with conflicts between various internal customers such as the corporation versus users of their services.

- Verify that each support process has done research to identify what services and products their internal/external customers really want them to produce/deliver.

- Clarify the key processes, metrics, standards, and control strategies for each major support department/function.

- Verify deployment of process improvements across all functions/locations as appropriate.

- Verify success of any innovations found in support areas.

- Verify effectiveness of approaches to control variability in support processes.

- Verify that support functions collect and use data on internal customer satisfaction.

- Clarify how the company identifies its key suppliers/partners.

- Clarify the criteria used to select various types of suppliers/partners and ask for examples illustrating deployment of these criteria in the selection process.

- Clarify the company approaches to partnering with proven suppliers/partners.

- Verify that the company has selected the right partners/suppliers by talking with employees who use the services/products provided by these firms.

- Verify that true partnerships exist with suppliers by reviewing contracts and partnership agreements and looking at the frequency with which proposals/bids are asked for.

- Verify evidence of a cooperative approach of working with suppliers versus an adversarial relationship.

- Verify use of supplier report cards or evaluation systems with all key suppliers.

- Clarify how the criteria for evaluating suppliers are linked to customer and internal performance requirements.

- Verify efforts to reduce internal inspection of supplier goods and services.

- Clarify approaches that have been used to simplify the procurement process.

TYPICAL SITE-VISIT ISSUES REGARDING RESULTS

Compared with approach/deployment items, results are fairly easy to evaluate by looking at the written application. Examiners do ask about results in the site visit, but they are mainly looking for data to support the validity and completeness of the graphs presented in section 7.0 of the application. For each major graph or summary of performance data appearing in section 7.0, examiners usually ask the following questions:

- Can I see the raw data that were used to calculate this graphs?

- What is the process/methodology used to collect these data?

- Can I see graphs of the subsidiary data that make up this index or overall performance data?

- How do ensure that these data are reliable and consistently measured?

- What is the source of these data on industry averages, competitors, and benchmarks, and may I see those source documents?

- Can I see any missing years worth of data that are not included on the graph in your application?

- Can I see the graphs of performance data you said you collected in section 4.0, 5.0, or 6.0, but you did not provide in the application?

- What happened on this graph that shows a performance spike (could be positive or negative), and what was learned from the analysis?

Although almost 50% of the points in a Baldrige application focus on results, you will find that most time in the site visit is spent concentrating on the approach/deployment issues.

PREPARING FOR THE SITE VISIT

One of the keys to receiving an award is impressing the examiners during the site visit. Most winners have managed to "blow away" the examiners in the site visit, convincing them that the company is even better in reality than it is on paper. One of the most impressive factors for an examiner is consistency of deployment. I've heard a number of examiners exclaim how impressed they are when every employee they talked to knew the company vision, key success factors, customers, processes, and so forth. A number of companies have actually run through a few dress rehearsals for the site visit, grilling employees on the key questions I've listed.

Drilling Employees

Knowing what the examiners are going to ask up front doesn't really help unless employees know the appropriate answers. If you are really interested in winning, it might be worth the time to teach these questions and answers to all employees, and run them through practice drills to make sure they understand their answers? Pulling out a wallet card or crib sheet in a site visit interview kind of destroys your credibility. Therefore, it is important the employees learn to memorize the right answers? Is this ethical? Sure it is. Hopefully it will be more benefit to the organization for every employee to know this information than simply to impress the Baldrige Examiners. Many companies spend a lot of time and money teaching employees to understand their customers, and how their job fits in with the company's plans.

Training Executives and Managers

It is also important that executive and managers present consistent information to the examiners' questions. I've known a number of companies who fell down in this area because the executives used their own judgment on how to answer questions, all giving different answers to the same questions. This led the examiners to conclude that the executive team lack a unified focus and did not really work well as a team. Training executives and managers is more of a challenge because they tend not to think that they need it. An approach I've seen that works well for them is to hire an outside consultant that is a trained examiner and have him or her grill the executives for practice. A debriefing session after this mock site visit can go a long way toward coaching them in the right responses. An outsider is often preferred for this task because of his or her ability to give honest and sometimes critical feedback to executives without fear of repercussion.

Preparing Documents for the Examiners

One organization at which I performed a site visit did a great job preparing materials for the examiners. They prepared seven "bankers boxes" of file folders, each labeled with the appropriate Baldrige category and item. In the folders were documents that answered many of our questions about site visit issues. In some cases, they went a little overboard since we only had time to review about 25% of what they put in the boxes. However, it saved the examiner team a great deal of time by having most the documentation we would have requested already there for us. I would highly recommend this practice. It shows the examiners that you understand the type of information they will be requesting, and that you are considerate of maximizing their productivity while on site. Most site visits for state awards or internal company awards do not last 4 to 5 days. In the state of California, for example, we do many site visits in one day. Because of this limited time, it makes it even more important to make it easy for examiners to find the information they need without hunting for it.

I can't really tell you what should go into each of the seven boxes or 20 file folders, but I can give you a list of the typical documents that examiners ask to see in most site visits. You can almost guarantee that these will be requested and reviewed:

- Market research data/reports.

- Strategic and annual plans.

- Monthly performance reports reviewed by executives.

- Process models/maps.

- Benchmarking studies.

- Reports on key competitors.

- Safety plans.

- Human resource plans.

- New product/service development process and related documentation.

- Supplier report cards.

- Surveys and other data collection instruments.

- Organization charts and job descriptions.

- Supplemental performance data not included in the application.

GENERAL TIPS FOR DEALING WITH EXAMINERS DURING SITE VISITS

As I mentioned earlier, I've talked to many examiners who believe applicants have performed poorly in the site visit on the basis of how they appear to examiners. These tips are based on discussions with both examiners and applicants I've met with during the past 10 years of my experience.

- Don't over explain anything—answer questions with brief responses.

- Listen to the question and make sure you know what is being asked before you answer it.

- Do not attempt to be too friendly with examiners—they want to maintain a certain distance to ensure objectivity.

- Do not try to control the discussion.

- Do not offer gifts, privileges, or anything else that might be seen as attempted bribery.

- Do not ramble and tell war stories.

- Find out the time for the interview and stay within the designated time frame.

- Do not constantly change the schedule for interviews on examiners.

- Make sure that all of your key people are in town and accessible when the examiners visit.

- Be honest about skeletons in your closet that may be discovered later by reviewing records from regulatory agencies.

- Do not prepare a dog and pony show at the beginning of the site visit. This will be viewed negatively by most examiners.

- Find out the background and experience of each examiner so you know their experience base.

- Do not attempt to argue or defend your approach.

- Do not ask the examiner for feedback during the site visit (e.g., "Is that what you are looking for?").

THE EXAMINER'S POINT OF VIEW

Up to this point, I've been discussing how to prepare for a site visit if you are an applicant. Much of this information is also relevant to examiners, such as the typical site visit issues, but it is more aimed at the applicant. In this section, I'll discuss tips for an effective site visit for the examiner team.

Preparing the Site-Visit Plan

Most teams of examiners who are new to the experience often over plan for the site visit. Site-visit issues ("verifies and clarifies") are listed during the course of the application review. This often results in a list of 100 or more issues per examiner. Considering that there are usually at least 5 examiners on a team, this can mean many site-visit issues to check out during the visit. Most teams of examiners prioritize their site visit issues prior to arrival, making sure that they spend time on the most important issues. It will be impossible to check out 100 or more site visit issues in 3 to 4 days on site at an organization. Most teams narrow down to about 25 to 40 critical site visit issues.

The criteria you should use in selecting the most important site-visit issues are as follows:

Answers given by applicants should addresses the overall purpose of the item, rather than a sub-issue.

- The answers given at the site visit could make a major difference in the applicant's score.

- Focus on information that is difficult to assess from reading the application.

- Focus on issues that cut across more than one category.

- Verify something that is a major theme in the organization's strategy for differentiating itself from competitors.

- Verify the deployment of innovative or impressive approaches.

The process for narrowing down site-visit issues is to use team consensus, or voting by examiners. This is usually done without much argument. Arguments often arise from individual examiners that insert their own biases. For example, the engineers on the team always want to spend a lot of time on the Process Management and new product design issues. Or, the information technology examiners want to spend most of the time looking at the company's information systems. A good senior examiner will help to ensure that the site-visit issues that make the short list are balanced. Figure 12.1 shows a sample format for prioritizing the site visit issues.

Figure 12.1: Prioritization of Site-Visit Issues—Sample Worksheet

Item/ Area	**Issue:** What to clarify. What to verify.	Priority
1.1	Verify Senior Executives spend an average of 1 day a month with customers	Low
1.1	Clarify roles and responsibilities of various levels of management	Low
1.2	Clarify how the company decides which charitable causes it supports	Low
2.1	Verify claims that planning process follows systematic model	Moderate
2.1	Verify thoroughness of SWOT analysis done as part of planning process	Low
2.1	Clarify difference between annual and strategic planning	Low
2.2	Verify that targets are set based on data	Moderate
2.2/ 4.1	Clarify company vision and key success factors and explain link to performance metrics	High
3.1	Verify that customer requirements have been defined for other 3 market segments not defined in application	Moderate
3.1/ 6.1	Verify that high priority customer requirements are integrated into new product designs	High

Once you have identified the most critical site visit issues, the team needs to prepare a plan, outlining where they will go to gather the information, and who on the time will gather it. An example format of a data collection worksheet shown in Figure 13.2. Each examiner would have a different set of data collection worksheets. It is common practice to divide site visit issues among the examiners and often to pair-up examiners on critical interviews.

Figure 12.2: Sample Data Collection Worksheet

Examiner: <u>John Example</u>

Item/ Area	Issue: What to clarify. What to verify.	Data Collection Method: What to Ask. What to Review. Who to Ask.	Schedule	Notes
2.1	Verify claims made that planning is done using systematic model	Interview Planning vice president	10:00–11:30	Evidence supports full use of process.
		Review Strategic Plan, Business Unit Plans and Operating Plans	11:30–1:00	Some questions about use of process in business unit plans.
		Interview Planning Committee	1:30–2:25	Approach sounds less structured than vice president suggests; keep original score of 40%.

Site-Visit Data Collection Strategies

There are many different ways to collect data in a site visit, including:

- Individual interviews.

- Group interviews.

- Review of documents.

- Review of performance data.

- Demonstrations.

- Walking around.

It is important that you don't spend all of your time in individual interviews. In fact, these are probably the least efficient means of gathering data in a site visit. This is particularly true of executive interviews. Executives generally know the right answers and are very articulate and convincing in an interview. I have found that one of the best ways of gathering data in a site visit is wandering around and watching people as they work. You can tell a lot about an organization by just observing employees as they do their work. Demonstrations or work-throughs are also an effective technique for evaluating things like how user-friendly a system is. Make sure that your site-visit time includes an hour or two of free time each day for each examiner. This free time might be spent doing walk arounds or making last minute decisions to interview someone who wasn't on the original schedule.

Generic Site-Visit Questions

Although it is important to come up with specific site-visit issues, I find that a logical series of questions can be used to evaluate approach/deployment in any of the first six sections of the Baldrige criteria. I keep these questions on my clipboard during each site visit interview, and tend to ask them over and over for each category. The questions are:

- How do you do this? What is the process?

- Why do you do it this way?

- Where is it done this way and where isn't it?

- How do you measure this process?

- What has been done to improve this process?

These five questions address approach, deployment, and continuous improvement, which are the major issues addressed in Categories 1 through 6. They can be used when asking about leadership, planning, training, or process management.

When looking at results, questions always center around levels, trends, and variability in the data. When spikes or anomalies occur in performance data, it is important to understand why these occur and what has been done to reduce the variability of the performance.

Reaching Final Consensus After the Site Visit

One of the most challenging parts of the site visit is reaching final consensus on the findings. This tends to be much easier when everyone has reviewed the same written application. In the site visit, everyone has seen or heard different things. Consequently, you often get some very diverse opinions about whether or not to raise or lower the applicant's score on a given item. In the Baldrige process, your scores are not actually changed, but most state awards do involve modification of the scores based on site visit findings. I've participated on some site-visit teams where each team member is responsible for one or two of the seven categories. These individuals are primarily responsible for gathering data on the category, and make the final decision in the consensus meeting if agreement cannot be reached in a reasonable period of time.

Chapter 13

_____

Using a Baldrige Assessment as a Strategic Planning Tool

ASSESSMENT ALTERNATIVES

The previous chapter presented details on how to audit your organization against the Baldrige criteria. This approach is very thorough, but many organizations don't have the resources to use it to the best effect. Most of the companies I've worked with in conducting Baldrige assessments over the past few years don't use the full-scale audit approach. Rather, a number of other basic methods are used. These are listed below in order of least to most objective and thorough, and of least to most expensive.

1. Survey based on the Baldrige criteria

2. Armchair assessment

3. Mock Baldrige application

4. Formal Baldrige or state-level application

5. Audit against the Baldrige criteria

1. Baldrige Survey—The simplest and least expensive method of establishing some baseline data on where you stand in your implementation of the Baldrige standards is to send out a survey to all or a sample of employees, having them rate the organization on how well it has implemented each of the items making up the Baldrige criteria. A large variety of surveys exist that may be used for this purpose. One that has been written by the author was published for the last few years in the *Journal for Quality and Participation.*

Using such a survey, or similar ones available through management consulting firms, is the least expensive way of evaluating your own status. However, it is also the least reliable, regardless of which survey instrument you are using. The problem with any survey is that it is subjective. People responding to the survey don't usually have the "big picture" of what is happening in the company, and they often mark their responses to the survey items based upon limited and most recent experiences. I've administered Baldrige surveys to 100 or so people in a single organization and gotten scores that ranged from 250 to 800 out of a possible 1,000 points. Does this mean that the survey instrument is poor? Perhaps, but I believe that all Baldrige surveys are at best a very rough and rudimentary indicator. Considering the low cost of the survey, however, this tool does provide you with a basic idea of where you stand, without spending much money or time.

2. Armchair Assessment—The second approach is a good deal more thorough and more useful than a survey, without much added expense. I have used this approach with a number of large organizations and have talked to a number of others that use a variation on it. Here's how it works. A team of senior executives from the business unit or organization being assessed attend a two-day workshop to learn the Baldrige criteria and gain an understanding of how an assessment is done. Next, the executive team attends a one-day meeting where they begin to assess their own organization. During the meeting, a facilitator begins by reviewing the first Baldrige Examination Item, explaining what it means. Next, the participants brainstorm a list of the organization's strengths and areas for improvement relating to that Item. The pluses and minuses are listed by the facilitator on a flip chart. After listing a page or so of strengths and areas for improvements, the facilitator asks the group to suggest a percentage score in multiples of 10. The group discusses and reaches consensus on a percentage score, the facilitator writes it on the flip chart, and together they move on to the next Item. This process continues until all 19 Items have been completed. A time limit of 15 minutes is observed for discussing each Item, so the meeting is very fast-moving. After listing comments and scoring each of the 19 Baldrige Items, percentage scores are multiplied by the official point value of each Item to compute the final score. The 19 flip chart pages are typed and become the complete assessment report. Total time commitment for the approach is three days.

While this approach is quick and relatively inexpensive, it does have some problems. First, the objectivity of the senior executives is not always what it should be. The executives sometimes find it easier to list the good things than to spend time thinking of areas for improvement. They also tend to give more credit for partial deployment of systems or approaches than a Baldrige Examiner would. Executives also tend to score a little higher than a Baldrige Examiner might. The personality of the CEO or the most senior executive in the meeting also can make this approach problematic. I've observed a few assessment meetings where the participants simply deferred to what the senior executives said and what he/she said the score was.

Even with its problems, this approach is much better than using any kind of survey. The assessment is more thorough; you end up with a page of strengths, areas for improvement, and a score on each of the 19 items; and executives buy in to the results of the assessment more readily because they did it. This approach will only work, however, if the senior executives are willing to devote three days for training and assessment. Executives in many organizations don't feel they need to be involved in such training or assessment and prefer to delegate this task to others. The Armchair Assessment will only work if you can get the senior executives to commit to it. The Armchair Assessment is appropriate for organizations whose overall score is 300 or less.

3. Mock Baldrige Application—This is by far the most commonly used approach for assessment against the Baldrige criteria. This approach has been or is currently being used by, among others, AT&T, Baxter Healthcare, Northrop, McDonnell Douglas, Roadway Express, Whirlpool, Cargill, Ericsson, Westinghouse, Johnson & Johnson, Appleton Papers, and Boise Cascade. The approach involves having business units, facilities, or even departments in a company prepare their own application using the same format as the Baldrige application. Generally, all 19 Items are required to be addressed and the applications are often about the same size (50 pages) as an official application. Applications are reviewed and individually scored by a team of examiners from other departments or units, who then get together to reach consensus on the final scores. Examiners are usually company employees who have been trained in a 2–4-day workshop. Some companies use outsiders to supplement their team of internal examiners, adding Baldrige consultants, customers, and suppliers, for example.

In some companies, such as Cargill, the examiners score the written applications and do site visits on the best (usually the top 25%–50%). Most organizations also have their own awards that they give out to the best performers. The major difference between the Armchair Assessment and the Mock Baldrige Application is that one always uses examiners from one business unit or department to evaluate another business unit or department. Some organizations have gotten senior executives involved as part of their team of examiners. Cargill, a major agricultural firm with 70,000 employees, has a team of about 120 examiners that includes many senior executives. Many executives and high level managers in Ericsson also have spent at least one year serving as an examiner for their assessment. A side benefit of getting executives to be examiners is that they almost always come away from the experience as staunch believers in the value of the Baldrige criteria as a tool for running a better organization.

The advantage of this approach over the previous two, then, is the objectivity and thoroughness of the assessment and feedback. The approach can give you the same level of analysis and feedback that a company would get by applying for the Baldrige Award. The approach also does a great deal to help move the organization toward being an excellent company. Examiners become internal experts on the Baldrige criteria, and can help others to work toward satisfying the criteria. Another advantage is that you can get near immediate feedback on your application and probe the examiners for details if the feedback is unclear. Examiners can provide recommendations about what the organization should do to improve the areas for improvement that were uncovered in the assessment.

The only real disadvantage of this approach is that it is much more expensive than the other two. You will recall from Chapter 3 that it takes a great deal of time to write an application. In this case, time will also need to be spent in training examiners, having them review and score the applications, and possibly go on site visits. Examiners in many companies that use this approach can be expected to spend the following amount of time on the activities listed:

- Attend examiner training   3 days
- Score written applications   2 days × 3 applications = 6 days
- Reach consensus on scores   .5 day × 3 applications = 1.5 days
- Prepare and conduct site visit   5 days
- Prepare and present feedback report   2 days
                                           17.5 days

When you consider that some large companies such as AT&T have over 100 examiners, this can add up to a major investment. If you supplement your team of internal examiners with consultants or other outsiders, the cost can become even greater. However, this is a great developmental opportunity for potential future senior managers and executives. This approach is appropriate for organizations above 300 points that would benefit from some outside objective feedback.

4. Formal Baldrige or State Application—A fourth and less commonly used approach for assessment is to formally apply for the Baldrige or State Award to see where you stand. This strategy was used by a number of organizations that later went on to win the award. (They applied and failed to win at least once before finally winning the award.) Miliken, Federal Express, Cadillac, and others all used the initial feedback they received to then go on to win. The $4,500 it costs to apply for the award for a large organization is minimal compared to the value of the feedback received. For $4,500 ($1,500 for small companies) you get a team of six to eight official examiners who will individually score your application, reach consensus on your scores, and present you with a feedback report that gives you a page of strengths, areas for improvement, and scores for each of the 19 Baldrige Items. If you are lucky enough to receive a site visit, a team of examiners will spend up to a week in your organization doing a further assessment. If you were to pay an outside consulting firm to conduct such an assessment, you would probably pay $30,000–$50,000 or more. Applying for the Baldrige Award to receive feedback is perhaps one of the government's biggest bargains. State award programs offer most of the benefits of applying for Baldrige, and are even less expensive (usually $500–$2,000).

If formally applying for the award offers such advantages, why don't more companies do it? Besides the initial cost (relatively small though it may be), the disadvantages are as follows. First, there is the delay between the time you send in the application (June 1st) and the time you receive feedback (November or December). This means that you can't use the feedback for planning purposes until the following year. A second disadvantage is that the approach forces you to apply as an entire company, or at least its major business units; units or facilities that have fewer than 500 employees are not allowed to apply for the Baldrige Award. A third disadvantage is that you do not receive your final score—only ranges are provided. This makes it difficult to gauge the level of improvement each year. Another problem is that you are not allowed to talk to anyone about your feedback. I know of one Baldrige applicant that received a feedback report that was extremely vague. One page had three positive comments, an area for improvement, and a score of 20 percent. When the organization called the Baldrige office and asked to speak to the examiners or someone who could explain their feedback and scores, they were informed that no one was allowed to talk to them about these matters. One final reason why applying for the award as an assessment method may not be a good idea is that a low score might have a negative impact on employee morale. Imagine how the results would play if you received a score of 175 out of 1,000 (when you may have been expecting around 600). Such results will be used as ammunition by those employees who believe total quality management is just another passing fad. Baldrige also does not provide you with an overall score, or scores for each of the 19 items.

A better alternative to actually applying for a Baldrige Award is to apply for one of the state-level Baldrige-based awards. Most states have their own award programs that follow the Baldrige criteria and application process. While the national award has received fewer applicants over the last few years, applicants for state awards have risen dramatically. We had over 50 applicants for the California Award this year, as did North Carolina. State-level awards are typically easier to win and many (California, Arizona, and others) offer a three-level award program (gold, silver, bronze) like the Olympics that ensures that most applicants receive some type of recognition. Contact the Baldrige office at NIST for information on Baldrige-based awards in your state.

5. *Audit Against the Baldrige Criteria*—The most thorough and most expensive way of evaluating your implementation of total quality management is to prepare and conduct an audit of the organization's practices and results based upon the Baldrige criteria. This involves developing a detailed audit plan, creating audit instruments, and spending many hours interviewing various levels of employees, reviewing quality data, and observing processes and practices. The advantages of this approach over the other four are its objectivity and the level of detailed feedback provided. The scope of the audit can vary considerably and can be tailored to the organization's resource constraints. Some large organizations devote thousands of hours to such audits and assign 10 to 20 employees to work full time for several months on the audit. Another organization I know of assigned a task force of seven people, and each spent a total of about 10 person-days on the audit.

The audit is very similar to the approach taken by the Baldrige Examiners when they do a site visit. However, you don't need to prepare a mock or real Baldrige application to conduct a Baldrige audit. The audit instruments are developed using the Baldrige criteria and the assessments are done based upon interviews, observations, and reviews of data rather than by reading a 50-page summary of the organization's approach and results.

USING THE BALDRIGE ASSESSMENT TO DRIVE IMPROVEMENT

Getting assessed against the Baldrige criteria is the organizational equivalent of getting a three-day physical. The problem, however, is that many organizations have not figured out how to take the information from a Baldrige-style assessment and use it for improvement planning. An organization I'm familiar with has been doing Baldrige assessments of each of its business units for the last six years; each year teams of examiners spend a great deal of time on site visits to evaluate the organization's approaches, deployment, and results. Findings of the assessment are presented to senior management, and the examiners are thanked for doing such an honest and thorough evaluation. In 1991, when this was first done, each of the business units received a score of around 300 points out of a possible 1,000. In 1992, the same type of assessment was done on the same business units, and, once again, the organizations all received scores of around 300 points. Some areas were slightly better; some had gotten worse. In 1993, a team of examiners did the third Baldrige assessment, and the scores once again ended up being around 300. In 1997, the company has simply told its business units to do their own assessments using whatever process they think works best. In late 1997 the company was purchased by a bigger firm and no longer does Baldrige assessments.

The problem is that this company, like many others, has not figured out how to put *teeth* into the assessment and assure that areas for improvement end up getting addressed in the overall business plan of the organization. This is what I will attempt to provide guidance on here.

<u>Trying to Fix Everything at the Same Time</u>

One commonly used approach in trying to make improvements is to take each area identified in the Baldrige assessment as lacking and developing an action plan for addressing the problem. Committees and task forces are formed and hundreds of people are involved in trying to improve the organization's performance in, often, more than 100 different areas. A year is spent and thousands of dollars in labor are expended working on the various improvement projects. The assessment is done again the following year, and, to everyone's surprise, the overall score does not improve much. The reason for the failure is that such an approach is too diluted, too uncoordinated, too lacking tie-in to the company's strategic business plan. Teams end up stepping on each others' toes, perhaps improving performance in one area only to make it worse in another.

<u>A Smarter Approach—Selecting a Few Major Areas to Work on Improving</u>

A better improvement planning approach is to prioritize the areas for improvement before proceeding to develop action plans. With this approach, you take the 120 or so areas for improvement from the Baldrige assessment and select the most important 10–20 to work on over the next year. Senior executives may assign a score to each area for improvement, using the following variables and scale:

- IMPACT—to what extent will fixing this weakness impact our performance on key measures of quality, customer satisfaction, or financial performance? (1 = no impact; 10 = great impact on a number of performance measures.)

- URGENCY—to what extent do we have to address this weakness immediately? (1 = can be postponed for several years; 10 = this needs to be fixed *now*.)

- TREND—is performance in this area currently getting worse, stable, or better? (1 = performance is improving rapidly; 10 = performance is getting worse all the time.)

By adding the scores for each area for improvement as given by each member of the senior executive team, you should be able to list the 100 or so areas in order of their priority. You then take the top ten and develop action plans for improving performance in these areas. A project manager is assigned to each action plan, and specific tasks and deadlines are developed for each improvement project.

Linking a Baldrige Assessment With Your Strategic Business Plans

Back in Category 2 of the Baldrige criteria, I explained that an important part of strategic planning is doing a thorough situation analysis, where you assess strengths, weaknesses, opportunities, and threats. A Baldrige assessment is a large part of this SWOT analysis that a company should do each year. The Baldrige assessment focuses both on the internal and external environment, incorporating data from customers, suppliers, and key competitors. There are other factors that should be examined in detail as part of the SWOT analysis, however. Knowledge of the strategies and strengths and weaknesses of key competitors is crucial information for planning. The same is true of knowledge of changes in regulatory conditions or requirements.

At best, the Baldrige assessment is one of several inputs to the planning process. **An organization should never develop a specific plan to address the weaknesses uncovered in a Baldrige assessment.** While this is a practice I have often seen, I have never seen it work well. The Baldrige criteria are a set of generic guidelines that are important for all organizations to address. However, every weakness found in an assessment does not necessarily need to be corrected. Organizations always have constraints on their resources, and those resources should be put to use improving the aspects of their performance that are most needed at the current time. This might mean ignoring a number of the negative findings from a Baldrige assessment and putting them on the back burner to be addressed later.

Strategic Planning Model

An overall strategic planning model shown below is followed by a number of major companies and government organizations:

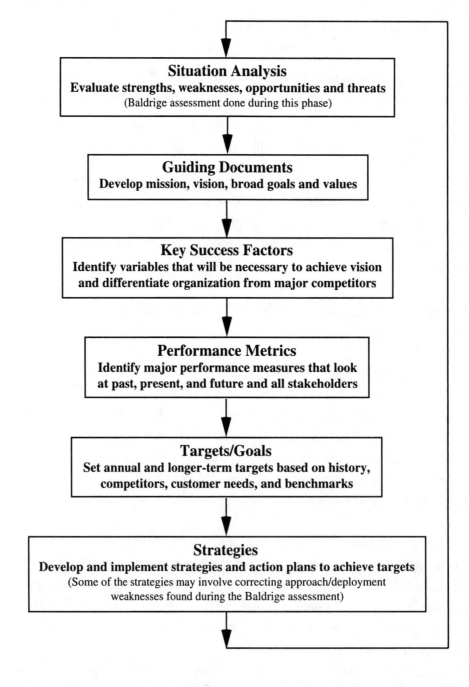

Situation Analysis
Evaluate strengths, weaknesses, opportunities and threats
(Baldrige assessment done during this phase)

Guiding Documents
Develop mission, vision, broad goals and values

Key Success Factors
Identify variables that will be necessary to achieve vision
and differentiate organization from major competitors

Performance Metrics
Identify major performance measures that look
at past, present, and future and all stakeholders

Targets/Goals
Set annual and longer-term targets based on history,
competitors, customer needs, and benchmarks

Strategies
Develop and implement strategies and action plans to achieve targets
(Some of the strategies may involve correcting approach/deployment
weaknesses found during the Baldrige assessment)

Achieving the targets set in the plan obviously requires a great deal of work, and plans are often revised as performance improves, priorities change and new problems arise. The Baldrige assessment is useful at two points in the planning process. First, it is an important part of your situation analysis that occurs before you even begin developing a vision of where you want to go. The Baldrige assessment also becomes useful at the end of the planning process when you develop action plans or strategies to achieve your goals and targets. Weaknesses found in your approaches or deployment of those approaches from categories 1 to 6 in Baldrige may become improvement projects that are part of your strategic plan. The key is to make sure that the improvement projects or strategies selected will help the business get healthier. Forget focusing on improving your Baldrige score. If you make your company healthier, your Baldrige score will improve all on its own. Because almost half of the points in Baldrige focus on your business results, a higher Baldrige score will obviously be correlated with better company performance.

Breaking Out of the 400 to 500 Point Range

Just like most people who get annual physicals don't get much healthier the next year, most organizations don't get healthier as a result of Baldrige assessments. Once in a while you'll run across a company that is in so much trouble, and Baldrige looks like it might save them. These companies are certainly motivated to change because they sense that the end is near unless they do something dramatically different. The problem for these companies is that it is usually too late. They are so far in the hole, that a long-term approach like Baldrige is too late.

In the 11 years I have been teaching organizations about the Baldrige criteria and how to use them for improvement, I have seen a few success stories. One such organization is the cellular phones division of Ericsson, Inc. Ericsson is one of the largest telecommunication companies in the world, with about 80,000 employees world-wide. About five years ago, their U.S. cellular phones division that manufactures cellular phones was in trouble. The parent company had been supporting them for years, and they had not made any money, or become a big player in the cellular phone business. They began looking at the Baldrige criteria due to urging from the corporate office in Sweden that required all Ericsson business units to evaluate themselves against their country's quality award criteria. Their initial score was quite low, as is typical of a business first being assessed. Many of the basic framework items were not even in place such as market research (3.1), a clear vision and strategic plan (2.2), and a balanced set of performance metrics (4.1). Based upon their initial assessment, their general manager worked with others in the business to develop a clear vision, key success factors, and a strategic plan that was communicated to each employee. Part of the longer-term vision was to achieve a Baldrige Award someday. In 1997, the division received the highest score of all Ericsson divisions in the U.S. on an internal Baldrige assessment, and is applying for the North Carolina State Quality Award in 1998. Their overall Baldrige score went from the low 200s to around 600 in about four years.

Another organization I worked with went on to be a Baldrige finalist in three years after receiving an initial score of around 250/1000. How did these two organizations improve so much when most others did not? Focus. As a result of the Baldrige assessment, both companies came to the realization that they lacked focus. They were working on a variety of improvement initiatives, but lacked the fundamentals of a good business such as sound performance measures and an effective strategic plan. Another important characteristic of both companies is that their CEOs realized how Baldrige looks at all aspects of running a business, and made sure that necessary changes were made to improve the company's performance in areas where they were weak.

The Key to Success With Baldrige

The Baldrige criteria provide a set of general guidelines on how to cook, but you must design the menu, create the recipes, and develop the concept for your restaurant. Just as their is no one formula for a successful restaurant, there are many ways to achieve a good score from Baldrige. Employing planned systematic approaches throughout the organization and focusing on continuous improvement are the building blocks to the success of any organization. This book does not give you a formula for success. It helps you interpret the Baldrige criteria so that you can assess yourself and develop your own unique formula for success.

FURTHER READING

Alexander, Keith L. "Company Commitment Pays Off." *USA Today,* November 18, 1998, p. 5B.

Bemoski, Karen. "A Pat on the Back is Worth a Thousand Words." *Quality Progress,* March, 1994, pp. 51–54.

Brennen, Niall. *Lessons Taught by Baldrige Winners.* New York: The Conference Board, 1994.

Brewer, Bill. "Boeing Flies High." *News for a Change*, November 1999, 1–12.

Brewer, Bill. "Xerox Documents Success." *News For a Change,* November, 1998, 1–4.

Brown, Mark Graham. "Measuring Your Company Against the 1997 Baldrige Criteria." *Journal for Quality and Participation*, September, 1997.

————— *Keeping Score: Using the Right Metrics to Drive World-Class Performance.* New York: Quality Resources, 1996.

————— *The Pocket Guide to the Baldrige Award Criteria,* 5th ed. New York: Quality Resources, 1998.

————— *The Small Business Pocket Guide to the Baldrige Award Criteria.* New York: Quality Resources, 1997.

————— *Winning Score: How to Design and Implement Organizational Scorecards*. Portland, OR: Productivity, Inc., 2000.

Brown, Mark Graham, Darcy Hitchcock, and Marsha Willard. *Why TQM Fails and What to Do About It.* Burr Ridge, IL: Irwin Professional Publishing, 1994.

Castañeda-Méndez, Kicab. *The Baldrige Assessor's Workbook.* New York: Quality Resources, 1997.

DeCarlo, Nell J., and Kent J. Sterett. "History of the Malcolm Baldrige National Quality Award." *Quality Progress*, March, 1990, pp. 41–50.

Fisher, Donald. *The Simplified Baldrige Award Organization Assessment.* New York: Lincoln-Bradley, 1993.

Garvin, David A. "How the Baldrige Award Really Works." *Harvard Business Review*, November/December, 1991, pp. 80–95.

Hardy, Quentin. "Motorola Broadsided by the Digital Era, Struggles for a Footing." *Wall Street Journal*, April 22, 1998, A-1, A-12.

Hart, Christopher W.L., and Christopher E. Bogan. *The Baldrige: What It Is, How It's Won, How to Use It to Improve Quality in Your Company*. New York: McGraw-Hill, 1992.

Hertz, Harry S. "The Criteria: A Looking Glass to Americans' Understanding of Quality." *Quality Progress*, June 1997, p. 46–48.

Jones, Del. "Teamwork Speeds Boeing Along." *USA Today*, November 18, 1998, p. 5B.

Moore, Martha T. "Is TQM Dead?" *USA Today*, October 17, 1995, p. B-1.

Reichheld, Frederick F. *The Loyalty Effect—The Hidden Force Behind Growth, Profits, and Value*. Cambridge, MA: Harvard Business School Press, 1996.

Rohan, Thomas M. "Do You Really Want a Baldrige?" *Industry Week*, April, 1991.

Rucci, Anthony J., Kirn, Steven P., and Quinn, Richard. "The Employee Service Profit Chain at Sears." *Harvard Business Review*, January/February, 1998, pp. 83–97.

Schaffer, Robert H., and Harvey A. Thomson. "Successful Change Programs Begin with Results." *Harvard Business Review*, January/February, 1992, pp. 80–89.

Stratton, Brad. "Goodbye ISO 9000: Welcome Back Baldrige Award." *Quality Progress*, August, 1994, p. 5.

U.S. General Accounting Office. *Management Practices—U.S. Companies Improve Performance Through Quality Efforts*, Publication GAO/NSIAD–91–190. Washington, D.C.: U.S. General Accounting Office, 1991.

Wolff, Michael. "Pushing to Improve Quality." *Research and Technology Management*, May/June, 1990, pp. 19–22.

Woodyard, Chris. "Engine Maker Never Stands Still." *USA Today*, November 18, 1998, 5B.

Appendix A

State Awards Based on the Baldrige Criteria

ALABAMA

<u>State Award Program</u>

State Award Name: Alabama Quality Award
Award Office Address:
Alabama Productivity Center
Associate Director
Box 870318
Tuscaloosa, Al 35487
Tel: 205-348-8956
Fax: 205-348-9391
E-mail: Linda@proctr.cba.ua.edu
Web: http://proctr.cba.ua.edu/index.html
Award Categories:
 1) Small Business; 2) Manufacturing; 3) Service (includes government); 4) Health Care; and 5) Education

ALASKA

No State Award Program in Place

ARIZONA

<u>State Award Program</u>

State Award Name: Arizona's Pioneer and Governor's Award for Quality
Award Office Address:
Arizona Quality Alliance
7510 E. Main St., Ste.3
Scottsdale, AZ 85251-4523
Tel: 888-346-7768 or 480-481-3454
Fax: 480-481-3097
E-mail: aqa@arizona-excellence.com
Web: http://www.aqa@arizona-excellence.com
Award Categories: 1) Small (1–99); 2) Medium (100–499); 3) Large (500+) All sectors compete in the same categories. Sectors include private, public non-profit (including education and health care), state and federal government.

ARKANSAS

State Award Program

State Award Name: Arkansas Quality Award
Award Office Address:
1111 West Capitol Ave.
Room 1013
Little Rock Arkansas, 72201-3005
Tel: 800-447-9330 or 501-373-1300
Fax: 501-373-1976
E-mail: arkansasquality@compuserve.com
Web: http://www.arkansas-quality.org
Award Categories: Any company or organization — for profit or not-for-profit

CALIFORNIA

State Award Program

State Award Name: California Governor's Quality Awards
Award Office Address:
CalQED
P.O. Box 1929
Danville, CA 94526-6929
Tel: 925-944-1835
Fax: 925-944-3455
E-mail: calqed@calqed.org
Web: http://www.calqed.org/index.html
Award Categories: 1) Business: Manufacturing, Service, Small Business Gov't & Nonprofit;
2) Education: Small and Large; and 3) Health: Small and Large

State and Senate Productivity Award

State Award Name: California Quality Awards
Award Office Address:
California Council for Quality & Service
P.O. Box 1235
Poway, CA 92074-1235
Tel: 858-486-0400
Fax: 858-486-8595
E-mail: ccqs@ccqs.org
Web: http://www.ccqs.org
Award Categories: 3 Level Awards in Manufacturing, Service, Government, Education,
Military, Health Care, Non-Profit.

COLORADO

No State Award Program in Place

Local Award Program

Local Award Name: Excellence in Customer Service
Award Office Address:
Better Business Bureau
3022 N. El Paso
Colorado Springs, CO 80907
Tel: 719-636-5076 x 101
Fax: 719-636-5078
E-mail: ppbbb@bbbnet.org
Web: (None)
Award Categories: 1) Small (1–20 employees); 2) Mid-size (21–50 employees) and 3) Large (251 employees or more.)

CONNECTICUT

State Award Programs

State Award Name: Connecticut Award for Excellence
Award Office Address:
P.O. Box 67
Rocky Hill, CT 06067
Tel: (800) 392-2122
Fax: (860) 721-8511
E-mail: Michael.Rose@po.state.ct.us
Web: (None)
Award Categories: 1) Business (Service and Manufacturing); 2) Education (K–12 and Colleges); 3) Government (State and Local); and 4) Health Care. Within each sector, the Award categories are subdivided into small/medium (300 or less) and large (300+) organizations.
State Award Name: Connecticut Quality Improvement Award
Award Office Address:
P.O. Box 1396
Stamford, CT 06904-1396
Tel: 203-322-9534
Fax: 203-329-2465
E-mail: Cqia@aol.com
Web: http://www.ctqualityaward.org
Award Categories: Small (1–100), Medium (101–500), Large (500+)

DELAWARE

State Award Program

State Award Name: Delaware Quality Award
Award Office Address:
Delaware Economic Development Office
99 Kings Highway
Dover, DE 19901
Tel: 302-739-4271
Fax: 302-739-5749
E-mail: ztucker@state.de.us
Web: http://www.state.de.us/dedo/initiatives/Quality/index.htm

Award Categories: 1) Manufacturing (large, small — 2 awards each); 2) Non-manufacturing (large, small — 2 awards each); 3) Not-for-profit (one size category — 2 possible awards)

FLORIDA

State Award Program

State Award Name: Governor's Sterling Award
Award Office Address:
Florida Sterling Council
Post Office Box 13907
Tallahassee, Florida 32317-3907
Tel: 850-922-5316
Fax: 850-488-7579
E-mail: dlowman@floridasterling.com
Web: http://www.floridasterling.com
Award Categories: (None)

GEORGIA

State Award Program

State Award Name: Georgia Oglethorpe Award
Award Office Address:
148 International Blvd., Suite 525
Atlanta, GA 30303-1751
Tel: 404-651-8405
Fax: 404-651-9377
E-mail: goap@bellsouth.net
Web: (None)
Award Categories: Large Business — more than 200 employees; Small/Medium Business — up to 200 total employees; Large Industry — more than 200 employees; Small/Medium Industry — up to 200 employees; Government; Education; Healthcare; Not-for-Profit

HAWAII

State Award Program

State Award Name: The Hawaii State Award of Excellence
Award Office Address:
Pacific Region Institute for Service Excellence (PRISE)
Chamber of Commerce of Hawaii
1132 Bishop Street, Suite 200
Honolulu, HI 96813
Tel: 808-545-4394
Fax: 808-545-4309
E-mail: chamber@hula.net
Web: (None)
Award Categories: Business; Government; Military; Health; Education; Not-for-Profit

IDAHO

<u>State Award Program</u>

State Award Name: Idaho Quality Award
Award Office Address:
Idaho Quality Award
800 Park Blvd., Suite 200
Boise, ID 83712
Tel: (208) 334-2999
Fax: (208) 364-4035
E-mail: rolands@uidaho.edu
Web: http://www.idoc.state.id.us/iqa/iqa.html
Award Categories: Marketplace, Workplace, or Community, Quality Management System

ILLINOIS

<u>State Award Program</u>

State Award Name: Lincoln Awards for Business Excellence (ABE)
Award Office Address:
Lincoln Foundation for Business Excellence
820 W Jackson Blvd., 5th Floor
Chicago, IL 60607
Tel: 312-258-5301
Fax: 312-258-1066
E-mail: info@lincolnaward.org
Web: http://www.lfbe.org/
Award Categories: 1) Education, 2) Government, 3) Health Care, 4) Industry, 5) Service

INDIANA

<u>State Award Program</u>

State Award Name: State of Indiana Quality Improvement Award
Award Office Address:
Indiana Business Modernization and Technology Corporation
One North Capitol Avenue
Suite 925
Indianapolis, IN 46204-2242
Tel: 317-635-3058 x 246
Fax: 317-231-7095
E-mail: qualityaward@bmtadvantage.org
Web: http://www.bmtadvantage.org/hottopics/quality_award.htm
Award Categories: One category includes all for-profit and not-for-profit organizations

IOWA

<u>State Award Program</u>

State Award Name: Iowa Award for Competitive Excellence
Award Office Address:
Woods Quality Center
Gary Nesteby — Program Director
4401 6th St SW
Cedar Rapids, Iowa 52404
Tel: 319-399-6583
Fax: 319-399-6457
E-mail: gnesteby@wqc.org
Web: (None)
Award Categories: 1) Small business manufacturer; Small business service; 3) Manufacturer; and 4) Service

KANSAS

<u>State Award Program</u>

State Award Name: Kansas Award for Excellence
Award Office Address:
151 N. Volutsia
Wichita, KS 67214
Tel: 316-978-3376
Fax: 316-978-3175
E-mail: (None)
Web: (None)
Award Categories: (None)

KENTUCKY

<u>State Award Program</u>

State Award Name: Commonwealth of Kentucky Quality Award
Award Office Address:
Kentucky Quality Council
167 West Main Street, Suite #500
Lexington, KY 40507
Tel: 800-453-0798 or 606-255-9458
Fax: 606-252-7900
E-mail: contact@kqc.org
Web: http://www.kqc.org/awards.htm
Award Categories: Manufacturing Companies (large and small), Service Organizations, Educational Institutions, and in 1998, Health Care and Government Organizations.

LOUISIANA

State Award Program

State Award Name: Louisiana Quality Award
Award Office Address:
Louisiana Quality Foundation
Louisiana Productivity Center
PO Box 44172
Lafayette, LA 70504-4172
Tel: 318-482-6422
Fax: 318-262-5472
E-mail: cad8292@usl.edu
Web: http://www.laqualityaward.com/
Award Categories: 1) For Profit - Manufacturing and Service; 2) Non-Profit; 3) Government;
4) Education

MAINE

State Award Program

State Award Name: Margaret Chase Smith Maine State Quality Award
Award Office Address:
Margaret Chase Smith Quality Association
7 University Drive
Augusta, ME 04330-9412
ATTN: Andrea Jandebeur, Program Administrator
Tel: 207-621-1988
Fax: 207-282-6081
E-mail: mcs@Maine-Quality.org
Web: http://www.maine-quality.org/awards_program.html
Award Categories: 1 and 2) Large Manufacturing and Large Service (100 or more employees),
3 and 4) Small Manufacturing and Small Service (fewer than 100 employees), and 5) Non-Profit
(no size qualifications)

MARYLAND

State Award Programs

State Award Name: Maryland Quality Award and the Maryland Senate Productivity Award
Award Office Address:
The Maryland Center for Quality and Productivity
4511 Knox Road, Suite 102
University of Maryland
College Park, Maryland 20740
Tel: 301-403-4413
Fax: 301-403-4478
E-mail: pleedham@rhsmith.umd.edu
Web: http://www.bsos.umd.edu/mcqp/spa98.html
Award Categories:
1) Manufacturing, 2) Service, and 3) Public Sector/Non-Profit

State Award Name: Governor's Quality Awards
Award Office Address: Baltimore
Tel: 410-767-4751
Fax: 410-333-7456
E-mail: cromanow@dbm.state.md.us
Web: (None)
Award Categories: LARGE ORGANIZATIONS: Public Sector organizations of 1,500 employees or more. Either the entire entity or an organizational unit can apply. MEDIUM ORGANIZATIONS: Between 500–1,500 employees. Either the entire entity or an organization unit can apply. SMALL ORGANIZATIONS: Less than 500 employees. The entire entity must apply.

MASSACHUSETTS

State Award Program

State Award Name: Massachusetts Quality Award
Award Office Address:
Massachusetts Council for Quality, Inc.
Center for Industrial Competitiveness
600 Suffolk St. (5th Floor)
Lowell, MA 01854
Tel: 978-934-2403
Fax: 978-934-4035
E-mail: mcq@massquality.org
Web: http://www.massquality.org
Award Categories: Manufacturing, Service, Small Business (<200 employees), Non-Profit

MICHIGAN

State Award Program

State Award Name: Michigan Quality Leadership Award
Award Office Address:
Michigan Quality Council
523 O'Dowd Hall
Oakland University
Rochester MI 48309-4401
Tel: 248-370-4552
Fax: 248-370-4628
E-mail: kalmar@oakland.edu
Web: http://www.michiganquality.org/recog/Brochure/index.html
Award Categories: Manufacturing; Service; Health Care; Education; Public Sector; Small Enterprise

MINNESOTA

State Award Program

State Award Name: Minnesota Quality Award
Award Office Address:

Minnesota Council for Quality
2850 Metro Drive, Suite 300
Bloomington, MN 55425
Tel: 612-851-3181
Fax: 612-851-3183
E-mail: MC4quality@aol.com
Web: (None)
Award Categories: Education; Government; Health Care; Manufacturing; and Service. A Non-Profit category was piloted in 1996. There are small, medium, and large segmentations in each of these categories.

MISSISSIPPI

State Award Program

State Award Name: Mississippi Quality Award
Award Office Address:
State Board for Community and Junior Colleges
3825 Ridgewood Road
Jackson, MS 39211
Tel: 601-982-6518
Fax: 601-982-6363
E-mail: dhamill@sbcjc.cc.ms.us
Web: http://www.sbcjc.cc.ms.us
Award Categories: (None)

MISSOURI

State Award Program

State Award Name: Missouri Quality Award
Award Office Address:
Excellence in Missouri Foundation
205 Jefferson St., 14th Floor
P.O. Box 1085
Jefferson City, MO 65101
Tel: 573-526-1725
Fax: 573-526-1729
E-mail: crackawa@mail.state.mo.us
Web: http://www.mqa.org
Award Categories: Manufacturing; Service; Education; Health Care; Public Sector; (non-profit in all of above categories.) Awards may be presented in the following size classes by number of employees: Small = 0–99, Medium = 100–499, Large = 500+ employees.

MONTANA

No State Award Program in Place

NEBRASKA

State Award Program

State Award Name: The Edgerton Quality Award
Award Office Address:
301 Centennial Mall South
P.O. Box 94666
Lincoln, NE 68509-4666
Tel: (402) 471-6513 or (800) 426-6505
Fax: (402) 471-4374
E-mail: dmichael@ded1.ded.state.ne.us
Web: http://assist.neded.org/edge2/eqa/home.htm
Award Categories: 1) MANUFACTURING; 2) SERVICE. In Manufacturing, a separate award will be presented to a manufacturer that has done an outstanding job in adapting technology to increase quality. In Service, too, a separate award will be provided to a company that has done an exceptional job of adapting technology.

NEVADA

No State Award Program in Place

NEW HAMPSHIRE

State Award Program

State Award Name: Granite State Quality Award
Award Office Address:
Granite State Quality Council
PO Box 29
Manchester NH, 03105-0029
Tel: 603-223-1312
Fax: 603-223-1299
E-mail: QUALITY@GSQC.COM
Web: http://www.gsqc.com
Award Categories: 1) Service: Small (<200 employees) and Large (200 employees); and 2) Manufacturing (Small and Large). Health, education, not-for-profit, and small businesses are eligible under either of the two categories.

NEW JERSEY

<u>State Award Program</u>

State Award Name: New Jersey Quality Achievement Award
Award Office Address:
Mary G. Roebling Building
20 West State Street
P.O. Box 827
Trenton, NJ 08625-0827
Tel: 609-777-0940
Fax: 609-777-2798
E-mail: qnj@qnj.com
Web: http://www.qnj.org
Award Categories: Manufacturing, Service, Small Business, Government, Education and
Health Care.

NEW MEXICO

<u>State Award Program</u>

State Award Name: New Mexico Quality Awards
Award Office Address:
Quality New Mexico
P.O. Box 25005
Albuquerque, New Mexico 87125
Tel: 505-944-2001
Fax: 505-944-2002
E-mail: qnm@quality-newmexico.org
Web: http://www.quality-newmexico.org
Award Categories: None. All organizations of any type eligible with a minimum of 5 full time
employees.

NEW YORK

<u>State Award Program</u>

State Award Name: The Governor's Award for Excellence
Award Office Address:
The Empire State Advantage: Excellence at Work
11 Computer Drive West, Suite 212
Albany, NY 12205
Tel: 518-482-1747
Fax: 518-482-2231
E-mail: info@esaprograms.org
Web: http://www.esaprograms.org
Award Categories: For-profit and Not-for-profit Sectors; Private; Government; Education; and
Health Care

NORTH CAROLINA

State Award Program

State Award Name: North Carolina Quality Leadership Award
Award Office Address:
North Carolina Quality Leadership
4904 Professional Court, Suite 100
Raleigh, NC 27609
Tel: 919-872-8198 or 800-207-5485
Fax: 919-872-8199
E-mail: ncqlf@aol.com
Web: http://www.rtpnet.org/~ncqlf
Award Categories: 1) Manufacturing; 2) Service; 3) Education: Public school systems (K–12) or private educational institutions (K–12), Community Colleges and Public or Private Colleges and Universities; 4) Public Sector: (state, county, city, and federal government located in North Carolina and agencies of any other government entity or special district.)

NORTH DAKOTA

No State Award Program in Place

OHIO

State Award Program

State Award Name: Ohio Award for Excellence
Award Office Address:
Ohio Award for Excellence
PO Box 206
Perrysburg, Ohio 43552
Tel: 330-672-3586
Fax: 330-672-9495
E-mail: (None)
Web: http://www.oae.org
Award Categories: Business, Education, Government, Health Care, and Not-for-Profit. The award program is new in 1999.

OKLAHOMA

State Award Program

State Award Name: Oklahoma Quality Award
Award Office Address:
P.O. Box 26980
Oklahoma City, OK 73126-0980
Tel: 405-815-5295
Fax: 405-815-5142
E-mail: Mike_Strong@odoc.state.ok.us
Web: (None)

Award Categories: Manufacturing, Service, Health Care, Education, Government: 1) Small (<50), 2) Medium (51–250), and 3) Large (251+)

OREGON

State Award Program

State Award Name: Oregon Quality Award
Award Office Address:
18640 NW Walker Road
Suite 1066
Beaverton, OR 97006
Tel: 503-725-2800, 2805, or 2806
Fax: 503-725-2801
E-mail: information@performancecenter.org
Web: http://www.performancecenter.org/oqa/oqa.html
Award Categories: (None)

PENNSYLVANIA

No State Award Program in Place

Local Award Programs

Local Award Name: Lehigh Valley Community Quality Award
Award Office Address:
Manufacturers' Resource Center
125 Goodman Drive
Bethlehem, PA 18015-3715
Tel: 610-758-4596 or 800-343-6732
Fax: 610-758-4716
E-mail: tony@net.bfp.org
Web: (None)
Award Categories: Manufacturing, Service, Non-Profit, Health Care, Education, Finance, Government, Retail, and Other
Local Award Name: Lancaster Chamber of Commerce Business Excellence Award
Award Office Address:
100 South Queen Street
P.O. Box 1558
Lancaster, PA 17608-1558
Tel: 717-397-3531
Fax: 717-293-3159
E-mail: cwagner@lcci.com
Web: http://www.lcci.com
Award Categories: (None)

RHODE ISLAND

State Award Program

State Award Name: RACE Award for Performance Excellence
Award Office Address:
Brian Knight
P O Box 6766
Providence, RI 02940
Tel: 401-454-3030
Fax: 401-454-0056
E-mail: labmk@ids.net
Web: (None)
Award Categories: Manufacturing; Service; Health Care; Government (state); Not-for-Profit.
U.S. government and trade associations are not eligible.

SOUTH CAROLINA

State Award Program

State Award Name: South Carolina's Governor's Quality Award
Award Office Address:
Quality Institute
University of South Carolina at Spartanburg
800 University Way
Spartanburg, SC 29303
Tel: 864-503-5990/888-231-0578
Fax: 864-503-5995
E-mail: (None)
Web: (None)
Award Categories: (None)

SOUTH DAKOTA

State Award Program

State Award Name: South Dakota Business Excellence Awards
Award Office Address:
South Dakota Chamber of Commerce and Industry
P.O. Box 190
Pierre, SD 57501-0190
Tel: 605-224-6161
Fax: 605-224-7198
E-mail: (None)
Web: (None)
Award Categories: Any private-sector, non-government, for-profit business

TENNESSEE

State Award Program

State Award Name: Tennessee Quality Award
Award Office Address:
Tennessee Quality Award
Tennessee Economic Development Center
333 Commerce St.
Nashville, TN 37201-3300
Tel: 800-453-6474 or 615-214-3106
Fax: 615-214-8933
E-mail: tqa@bellsouth.net
Web: http://www.tqa.org
Award Categories: Any public or private organization

TEXAS

State Award Program

State Award Name: Texas Quality Award
Award Office Address:
Quality Texas
P.O. Box 684157
Austin, TX 78768-4157
Tel: 512-477-8137
Fax: 512-477-8168
E-mail: Qualtex@swbell.net
Web: http://www.texas-quality.org
Award Categories: 1) Manufacturing; 2) Service; 3) Small Business (less than 100 employees); 4) Public Sector; 5) Education; and Health Care

UTAH

State Award Program

State Award Name: Utah Quality Awards
Award Office Address:
Utah Quality Council
2120 State Office Building
Salt Lake City, UT 84114
Tel: 801-773-6632
Fax: 801-538-3081
E-mail: pedhrm.cwhipple@state.ut.us
Web: (None)
Award Categories: 1) Manufacturing (organizations that produce, process, or assemble products); 2) Service/Non-Profit (for profit or non-profit organizations that provide services); 3) Education (institutions that are degree granting or credit giving according to Utah law); and 4) Government (federal, state or local.) Each of these categories has these groupings: a) Large, b) Medium, and c) Small.

VERMONT

State Award Program

State Award Name: Vermont Performance Excellence Awards
Award Office Address:
Vermont Council for Quality
Champlain Mill
1 Main Street
Winooski, VT 05404
Tel: 802-655-1910
Fax: 802-655-1932
E-mail: vcqual@aol.com
Web: (None)
Award Categories: (None)

VIRGINIA

State Award Program

State Award Name: U.S. Senate Productivity and Quality Award for VA
Award Office Address:
PO Box 6099
Suffolk VA 23433
Tel: 757-523-6762
Fax: 757-523-6030
E-mail: spqa@spqa.org
Web: http://www.spqa.org
Award Categories: Private Sector Manufacturing; Private Sector Service; Public Sector State and Federal Agencies; Public Sector Local Agencies

WASHINGTON

State Award Program

State Award Name: Washington State Quality Award
Award Office Address:
Washington State Quality Award Program
Administrative Office
P.O. Box 11669
Olympia WA 98508-1669
Tel: 800-517-8264 or 360-664-2189
Fax: 360-664-4250
E-mail: tamarag@secstate.wa.gov
Web: http://www.wa.gov/wsqa
Award Categories: 1) Government, 2) Private, 3) Not for Profit, 4) Education (all categories are further divided by large (201+ employees) and small (less than 201 employees)

WEST VIRGINIA

No State Award Program in Place

WISCONSIN

<u>State Award Program</u>

State Award Name: Wisconsin Forward Award
Award Office Address:
Wisconsin Department of Workforce Development
P O Box 7972
Madison WI 53707-7972
Tel: 608-261-4422 or 888-933-9475
Fax: 608-267-0330
E-mail: langema@dwd.state.wi.us
Web: http://www.forwardaward.org
Award Categories: All eligible

WYOMING

<u>No State Award Program in Place</u>

Criteria for Performance Excellence

integrity

accomplishment

competitiveness

Malcolm Baldrige
National
Quality
Award

A Public-Private Partnership

Building active partnerships in the private sector, and between the private sector and all levels of government, is fundamental to the success of the Baldrige National Quality Program in improving national competitiveness. Support by the private sector for the Program in the form of funds, volunteer efforts, and participation in information transfer continues to grow.

To ensure the continued growth and success of these partnerships, each of the following organizations plays an important role:

The Foundation for the Malcolm Baldrige National Quality Award

The Foundation for the Malcolm Baldrige National Quality Award was created to foster the success of the Program. The Foundation's main objective is to raise funds to permanently endow the Award Program.

Prominent leaders from U.S. organizations serve as Foundation Trustees to ensure that the Foundation's objectives are accomplished. A broad cross-section of organizations from throughout the United States provide financial support to the Foundation.

National Institute of Standards and Technology (NIST)

The Department of Commerce is responsible for the Baldrige National Quality Program and the Award. NIST, an agency of the Department's Technology Administration, manages the Baldrige Program. NIST promotes U.S. economic growth by working with industry to develop and deliver the high-quality measurement tools, data, and services necessary for the nation's technology infrastructure. NIST also participates in a unique, government-private partnership to accelerate the development of high-risk technologies that promise significant commercial and economic benefits, and — through a network of technology extension centers and field offices located in all 50 states and Puerto Rico — helps small- and medium-size businesses access the information and expertise they need to improve their competitiveness in the global marketplace.

American Society for Quality (ASQ)

ASQ assists in administering the Award Program under contract to NIST. ASQ is dedicated to the ongoing development, advancement, and promotion of quality concepts, principles, and techniques. ASQ strives to be the world's recognized champion and leading authority on all issues related to quality. ASQ recognizes that continuous quality improvement will help the favorable positioning of American goods and services in the international marketplace.

Board of Overseers

The Board of Overseers is the advisory organization on the Baldrige National Quality Program to the Department of Commerce. The Board is appointed by the Secretary of Commerce and consists of distinguished leaders from all sectors of the U.S. economy.

The Board of Overseers evaluates all aspects of the Program, including the adequacy of the Criteria and processes for determining Award recipients. An important part of the Board's responsibility is to assess how well the Program is serving the national interest. Accordingly, the Board makes recommendations to the Secretary of Commerce and to the Director of NIST regarding changes and improvements in the Program.

Board of Examiners

The Board of Examiners evaluates Award applications and prepares feedback reports. The Panel of Judges, part of the Board of Examiners, makes Award recommendations to the Director of NIST. The Board consists of leading U.S. business, health care, and education experts. NIST selects members through a competitive application process. For 2000, the Board consists of about 400 members. Of these, nine (who are appointed by the Secretary of Commerce) serve as Judges, and approximately 70 serve as Senior Examiners. The remainder serve as Examiners. All members of the Board must take part in an Examiner preparation course.

In addition to their application review responsibilities, Board members contribute significantly to information sharing activities. Many of these activities involve the hundreds of professional, trade, community, and state organizations to which Board members belong.

Award Recipients

Award recipients are required to share information on their successful performance and quality strategies with other U.S. organizations. However, recipients are not required to share proprietary information, even if such information was part of their Award application. The principal mechanism for sharing information is the annual Quest for Excellence Conference.

Award recipients in the 12 years of the Award have been very generous in their commitment to improving U.S. competitiveness and the U.S. pursuit of performance excellence. They have shared information with hundreds of thousands of companies, education institutions, health care organizations, government agencies, and others. This sharing far exceeds expectations and Program requirements. Award recipients' efforts have encouraged many other organizations in all sectors of the U.S. economy to undertake their own performance improvement efforts.

Malcolm Baldrige
National Quality Award

Baldrige National Quality Program
Department of Commerce • Technology Administration • National Institute of Standards and Technology

To:　U.S. Business Community

From:　Harry S. Hertz, Director
　　　　　Baldrige National Quality Program

Subject:　The Baldrige Challenge

Whether you are a CEO, a business executive, a mid-level manager, an employee committed to improving your organization, or a student of business practices, the Baldrige Criteria for Performance Excellence can help you prepare for the changes occurring in today's global marketplace. Study them and you will learn; use them and your organization will improve. With ever-increasing competition in today's business environment, your organization is seeking every opportunity to improve its business results. For more than a decade, the Baldrige Criteria for Performance Excellence have been a significant tool used by thousands of U.S. organizations to assess and then improve performance on the critical factors that drive their business success.

Whether your business is small or large, involved in service or manufacturing, or located down the street or across the globe, the Criteria provide a valuable framework and can help you assess and measure performance on a wide range of key business indicators: customer, product and service, operational, human resource, and financial. The Criteria are built upon a foundation of Core Values and Concepts vital to your business: visionary leadership, customer driven, organizational and personal learning, valuing employees and partners, agility, focus on the future, managing for innovation, management by fact, public responsibility and citizenship, focus on results and creating value, and a systems perspective. Also, the Criteria can help you align resources; improve communication, productivity, and effectiveness; and achieve strategic goals. Baldrige Award recipients report outstanding results; as a group, those who report productivity as income per employee have reported an average compounded annual growth rate of over 9 percent.

If you are ready to take the Baldrige challenge, you must decide whether to perform a self-assessment only or also to submit an Award application. Self-assessment allows you to identify strengths and to target opportunities for improvement on processes and results affecting all key stakeholders — including customers, employees, owners, suppliers, and the public. In the most competitive business sectors, organizations with world-class business results are able to achieve a score above 700 on the 1,000-point Baldrige scale. Even if you don't expect to win the Malcolm Baldrige National Quality Award, submitting an application has valuable benefits. Every applicant receives a detailed feedback report — based on an independent, external assessment conducted by a panel of specially trained and recognized experts.

Ultimately, your application may lead to a site visit. It also may lead to a Baldrige Award. It will most certainly identify high priority opportunities for performance improvement. Many Award recipients tell us their greatest rate of improvement occurs the year after receiving the Award. While we make no promises for the future, on average, publicly-traded, Baldrige Award recipient companies have outperformed the Standard & Poor's 500 by 3 to 1. If you receive the Baldrige Award, you may publicize and advertise your organization's winning status.

We make only one requirement of recipients: that you share non-proprietary information from your application summary and participate in the Quest for Excellence Conference in April 2001, so that others might learn from your success.

The Criteria are in your hands ... so is an incredible opportunity. Why not take the challenge? Turn these pages, and turn the corner toward performance excellence.

Quest for Excellence XII Conference

Each year, Quest for Excellence, the official conference of the Malcolm Baldrige National Quality Award, provides a forum for Baldrige Award recipients to share their exceptional performance practices with worldwide leaders in business, education, health care, and not-for-profit organizations. Quest for Excellence XII will showcase the 1999 recipients.

For the last 11 years, executives, managers, and quality leaders have come to this conference to learn how these role model organizations have achieved performance excellence. CEOs and other leaders from the Award recipients who are transforming their organizations give presentations covering all seven Categories of the Baldrige Criteria, their journey to performance excellence, and their lessons learned. Conference attendees will have the opportunity to ask questions of the Award recipients. This three-day conference is designed to maximize learning and networking opportunities.

The Quest for Excellence XII Conference will be held March 12-15, 2000, at the Marriott Wardman Park Hotel in Washington, DC. For further information, contact NIST, Baldrige National Quality Program, Administration Building, Room A635, 100 Bureau Drive, Stop 1020, Gaithersburg, MD 20899-1020; telephone: (301) 975-2036; fax: (301) 948-3716; or E-mail: nqp@nist.gov.

The Malcolm Baldrige National Quality Award

The Award, composed of two solid crystal prismatic forms, stands 14 inches tall. The crystal is held in a base of black anodized aluminum with the Award recipient's name engraved on the base. A 22-karat, gold-plated medallion is captured in the front section of the crystal. The medal bears the inscriptions: "Malcolm Baldrige National Quality Award" and "The Quest for Excellence" on one side and the Presidential Seal on the other.

The President of the United States traditionally presents the Awards at a special ceremony in Washington, DC.

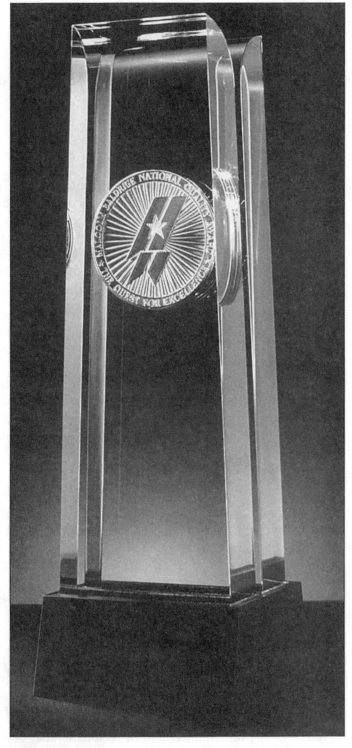

Crystal by Steuben

The Malcolm Baldrige National Quality Award logo and the phrases "Quest for Excellence" and "Performance Excellence" are trademarks and service marks of the National Institute of Standards and Technology.

CONTENTS

Education and health care organizations should use the appropriate Criteria booklets for their respective sectors. See page 53 for ordering information.

If you plan to apply for the Award in 2000, you will also need the booklet entitled *2000 Application Forms & Instructions for Business, Education, and Health Care.* Ordering instructions are given on page 53.
Eligibility Forms due — April 6, 2000   Award Applications due — May 31, 2000
We are easy to reach. Our web address is http://www.quality.nist.gov.

Criteria Purposes

The Malcolm Baldrige Criteria for Performance Excellence are the basis for organizational self-assessments, for making Awards, and for giving feedback to applicants. In addition, the Criteria have three other important roles in strengthening U.S. competitiveness:

- to help improve organizational performance practices and capabilities;

- to facilitate communication and sharing of best practices information among U.S. organizations of all types; and

- to serve as a working tool for understanding and managing performance, and guiding planning and training.

Criteria for Performance Excellence Goals

The Criteria are designed to help organizations enhance their performance through focus on dual, results-oriented goals:

- delivery of ever-improving value to customers, resulting in marketplace success; and

- improvement of overall organizational effectiveness and capabilities.

Core Values and Concepts

The Criteria are built upon a set of Core Values and Concepts. These values and concepts are the foundation for integrating key business requirements within a results-oriented framework. These values and concepts are the embedded behaviors found in high performing organizations. The Core Values and Concepts are:

Visionary Leadership

An organization's senior leaders need to set directions and create a customer focus, clear and visible values, and high expectations. The directions, values, and expectations should balance the needs of all your stakeholders. Your leaders need to ensure the creation of strategies, systems, and methods for achieving excellence, stimulating innovation, and building knowledge and capabilities. The values and strategies should help guide all activities and decisions of your organization. Senior leaders should inspire and motivate your entire work force and should encourage involvement, development and learning, innovation, and creativity by all employees.

Through their ethical behavior and personal roles in planning, communications, coaching, developing future leaders, review of organizational performance, and employee recognition, your senior leaders should serve as role models, reinforcing values and expectations and building leadership, commitment, and initiative throughout your organization.

Customer Driven

Quality and performance are judged by an organization's customers. Thus, your organization must take into account all product and service features and characteristics that contribute value to your customers and lead to customer satisfaction, preference, referral, and loyalty. Being customer driven has both current and future components — understanding today's customer desires and anticipating future customer desires and marketplace offerings.

Value and satisfaction may be influenced by many factors throughout your customer's overall purchase, ownership, and service experiences. These factors include your organization's relationship with customers that helps build trust, confidence, and loyalty.

Being customer driven means much more than defect and error reduction, merely meeting specifications, or reducing complaints. Nevertheless, defect and error reduction and elimination of causes of dissatisfaction contribute to your customers' view of your organization and are thus also important parts of being customer driven. In addition, your organization's success in recovering from defects and mistakes ("making things right for your customer") is crucial to retaining customers and building customer relationships.

Customer-driven organizations address not only the product and service characteristics that meet basic customer requirements, but also address those features and characteristics that differentiate products and services from competing offerings. Such differentiation may be based upon new or modified offerings, combinations of product and service offerings, customization of offerings, rapid response, or special relationships.

Being customer driven is thus a strategic concept. It is directed toward customer retention, market share gain, and growth. It demands constant sensitivity to changing and emerging customer and market requirements, and the factors that drive customer satisfaction and retention. It demands anticipating changes in the marketplace. Being customer driven thus demands awareness of developments in technology and competitors' offerings, and rapid and flexible response to customer and market requirements.

Organizational and Personal Learning

Achieving the highest levels of performance requires a well-executed approach to organizational and personal learning. Organizational and personal learning is a goal of visionary leaders. The term organizational learning refers to continuous improvement of existing approaches and processes and adaptation to change, leading to new goals and/or approaches. Learning needs to be embedded in the way your organization operates. The term embedded means that learning: (1) is a regular part of daily work; (2) is practiced at personal, work unit, and organizational levels; (3) results in solving problems at their source; (4) is focused on sharing knowledge throughout your organization; and (5) is driven by opportunities to affect significant change and do better. Sources for learning include employee ideas, research and development (R&D), customer input, best practice sharing, and benchmarking.

Organizational learning can result in: (1) enhancing value to customers through new and improved products and services; (2) developing new business opportunities; (3) reducing errors, defects, waste, and related costs; (4) improving responsiveness and cycle time performance; (5) increasing productivity and effectiveness in the use of all resources throughout your organization; and (6) enhancing your organization's performance in fulfilling its public responsibilities and service as a good citizen.

Employee success depends increasingly on having opportunities for personal learning and practicing new skills. Organizations invest in employee personal learning through education, training, and opportunities for continuing growth. Opportunities might include job rotation and increased pay for demonstrated knowledge and skills. On-the-job training offers a cost-effective way to train and to better link training to your organizational needs. Education and training programs may benefit from advanced technologies, such as computer-based learning and satellite broadcasts.

Personal learning can result in: (1) more satisfied and versatile employees; (2) greater opportunity for organizational cross-functional learning; and (3) an improved environment for innovation.

Thus, learning is directed not only toward better products and services but also toward being more responsive, adaptive, and efficient — giving the organization and your employees marketplace sustainability and performance advantages.

Valuing Employees and Partners

An organization's success depends increasingly on the knowledge, skills, innovative creativity, and motivation of its employees and partners.

Valuing employees means committing to their satisfaction, development, and well-being. Increasingly, this involves more flexible, high performance work practices tailored to employees with diverse workplace and home life needs. Major challenges in the area of valuing employees include: (1) demonstrating your leaders' commitment to your employees; (2) providing recognition opportunities that go beyond the normal compensation system; (3) providing opportunities for development and growth within your organization; (4) sharing your organization's knowledge so your employees can better serve your customers and

contribute to achieving your strategic objectives; and (5) creating an environment that encourages risk taking.

Organizations need to build internal and external partnerships to better accomplish overall goals.

Internal partnerships might include labor-management cooperation, such as agreements with your unions. Partnerships with employees might entail employee development, cross-training, or new work organizations, such as high performance work teams. Internal partnerships also might involve creating network relationships among your work units to improve flexibility, responsiveness, and knowledge sharing.

External partnerships might be with customers, suppliers, and education organizations. Strategic partnerships or alliances are increasingly important kinds of external partnerships. Such partnerships might offer entry into new markets or a basis for new products or services. Also, partnerships might permit the blending of your organization's core competencies or leadership capabilities with the complementary strengths and capabilities of partners, thereby enhancing overall capability, including speed and flexibility.

Successful internal and external partnerships develop longer-term objectives, thereby creating a basis for mutual investments and respect. Partners should address the key requirements for success, means of regular communication, approaches to evaluating progress, and means for adapting to changing conditions. In some cases, joint education and training could offer a cost-effective method of developing employees.

Agility

Success in globally competitive markets demands creating a capacity for rapid change and flexibility. All aspects of electronic commerce require more rapid, flexible, and customized responses. Businesses face ever-shorter cycles for introductions of new or improved products and services. Faster and more flexible response to customers is now a more critical requirement. Major improvements in response time often require simplification of work units and processes and/or the ability for rapid changeover from one process to another. Cross-trained employees are vital assets in such a demanding environment.

A major success factor in meeting competitive challenges is the design-to-introduction (product generation) cycle time. To meet the demands of rapidly changing, global markets, organizations need to carry out stage-to-stage integration (concurrent engineering) of activities from research to commercialization.

All aspects of time performance are becoming increasingly important and should be among your key process measures. Other important benefits can be derived from this focus on time; time improvements often drive simultaneous improvements in organization, quality, cost, and productivity.

Focus on the Future

Pursuit of sustainable growth and market leadership requires a strong future orientation and a willingness to make long-term commitments to key stakeholders — your customers, employees, suppliers, stockholders, the public, and your community. Your organization should anticipate many factors in your strategic planning efforts, such as customers' expectations, new business and partnering opportunities, the increasingly global marketplace, technological developments, new customer and market segments, evolving regulatory requirements, community/societal expectations, and strategic changes by competitors. Short- and long-term plans, strategic objectives, and resource allocations need to reflect these influences. Major components of a future focus include developing employees and suppliers, seeking opportunities for innovation, and fulfilling public responsibilities.

Managing for Innovation

Innovation is making meaningful change to improve an organization's products, services, and processes and create new value for the organization's stakeholders. Innovation should focus on leading your organization to new dimensions of performance. Innovation is no longer strictly the purview of research and development departments. Innovation is important for key product and service processes and for support processes. Organizations should be structured in such a way that innovation becomes part of the culture and daily work.

Management by Fact

Organizations depend upon the measurement and analysis of performance. Such measurements must derive from your organization's strategy and provide critical data and information about key processes, outputs, and results. Many types of data and information are needed for performance measurement, management, and improvement. Performance measurement areas include: customer, product, and service; operations, market, and competitive comparisons; and supplier, employee, and cost and financial.

Analysis refers to extracting larger meaning from data and information to support evaluation, decision making, and operational improvement within your organization. Analysis entails using data to determine trends, projections, and cause and effect — that might not be evident without analysis. Data and analysis support a variety of purposes, such as planning, reviewing your overall performance, improving operations, and comparing your performance with competitors or with "best practices" benchmarks.

A major consideration in performance improvement involves the selection and use of performance measures or indicators. *The measures or indicators you select should best represent the factors that lead to improved customer, operational, and financial performance. A comprehensive set of measures or indicators tied to customer and/or organizational performance requirements represents a clear basis for aligning all activities with your organization's goals.* Through the analysis of data from the tracking processes, the measures or indicators themselves may be evaluated and changed to better support such goals.

Public Responsibility and Citizenship

An organization's leadership needs to stress its responsibilities to the public and needs to practice good citizenship. These responsibilities refer to basic expectations of your organization — business ethics and protection of public health, safety, and the environment. Health, safety, and the environment include your organization's operations as well as the life cycles of your products and services. Also, organizations need to emphasize resource conservation and waste reduction at the source. Planning should anticipate adverse impacts from production, distribution, transportation, use, and disposal of your products. Plans should seek to prevent problems, to provide a forthright response if problems occur, and to make available information and support needed to maintain public awareness, safety, and confidence.

For many organizations, the product design stage is critical from the point of view of public responsibility. Design decisions impact your production process and the content of municipal and industrial wastes. Effective design strategies should anticipate growing environmental demands and related factors.

Organizations should not only meet all local, state, and federal laws and regulatory requirements, they should treat these and related requirements as opportunities for continuous improvement "beyond mere compliance." This requires the use of appropriate measures in managing performance.

Practicing good citizenship refers to leadership and support — within the limits of your organization's resources — of publicly important purposes. Such purposes might include improving education, health care in the community, environmental excellence, resource conservation, community service, industry and business practices, and sharing non-proprietary information. Leadership as a corporate citizen also entails influencing other organizations, private and public, to partner for these purposes. For example, your organization could lead efforts to help define the obligations of your industry to its communities.

Focus on Results and Creating Value

An organization's performance measurements need to focus on key results. Results should be focused on creating and balancing value for all your stakeholders — customers, employees, stockholders, suppliers and partners, the public, and the community. By creating value for all your stakeholders, your organization builds loyalty and contributes to growing the economy. To meet the sometimes conflicting and changing aims that balancing value implies, organizational strategy needs to explicitly include all stakeholder requirements. This will help to ensure that actions and plans meet differing stakeholder

needs and avoid adverse impacts on any stakeholders. The use of a balanced composite of leading and lagging performance measures offers an effective means to communicate short- and longer-term priorities, to monitor actual performance, and to provide a focus for improving results.

Systems Perspective

The Baldrige Criteria provide a systems perspective for managing your organization and achieving performance excellence. The core values and the seven Baldrige Categories form the building blocks of the system. However, successful management of the overall enterprise requires synthesis and alignment. Synthesis means looking at your organization as a whole and focusing on what is important to the whole enterprise. Alignment means concentrating on key organizational linkages among requirements given in the Baldrige Categories.

Alignment is depicted through the Baldrige framework on page 6. Alignment means that your senior leaders are focused on strategic directions and on your customers. It means that your senior leaders monitor, respond to, and build on your business results. Alignment means linking your key strategies with your key processes and aligning your resources to improve overall performance and satisfy customers.

Thus, a systems perspective means managing your whole enterprise, as well as its components, to achieve performance improvement.

Criteria for Performance Excellence Framework

The Core Values and Concepts are embodied in seven Categories, as follows:

1 **Leadership**
2 **Strategic Planning**
3 **Customer and Market Focus**
4 **Information and Analysis**
5 **Human Resource Focus**
6 **Process Management**
7 **Business Results**

The figure below provides the framework connecting and integrating the Categories.

From top to bottom, the framework has three basic elements:

Strategy and Action Plans

Strategy and Action Plans (top of figure) yield the set of customer and market focused performance requirements, derived from short- and long-term strategic planning, that must be met and exceeded for your organization's strategy to succeed. Strategy and Action Plans guide overall resource decisions and drive the alignment of measures for all work units to ensure customer satisfaction and market success.

System

The system is comprised of the six Baldrige Categories in the center of the figure that define the organization, its operations, and its results.

Leadership (Category 1), Strategic Planning (Category 2), and Customer and Market Focus (Category 3) represent the leadership triad. These Categories are placed together to emphasize the importance of a leadership focus on strategy and customers. Senior leaders must set organizational direction and seek future opportunities for your organization.

If your leadership does not focus on customers, your organization as a whole will lack that focus.

Human Resource Focus (Category 5), Process Management (Category 6), and Business Results (Category 7) represent the results triad. Your organization's employees and its key processes accomplish the work of the organization that yields your business results.

All actions point toward Business Results — a composite of customer, financial, and operational performance results, including human resource results and public responsibility.

The horizontal arrow in the center of the framework links the leadership triad to the results triad, a linkage critical to organizational success. Furthermore, the arrow indicates the central relationship between Leadership (Category 1) and Business Results (Category 7). Leaders must keep their eyes on business results and must learn from them to drive improvement.

Information and Analysis

Information and Analysis (Category 4) are critical to the effective management of your organization and to a fact-based system for improving performance and competitiveness. Information and analysis serve as a foundation for the performance management system.

Criteria Structure

The seven Criteria Categories shown in the figure are subdivided into Items and Areas to Address:

Items

There are 19 Items, each focusing on a major requirement. Item titles and point values are given on page 9. The Item format is shown on page 47.

Areas to Address

Items consist of one or more Areas to Address (Areas). Organizations address their responses to the specific requirements of these Areas.

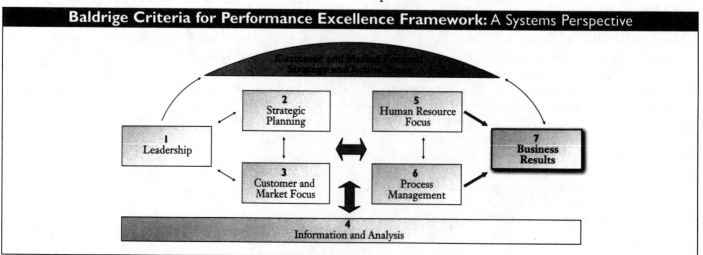

Baldrige Criteria for Performance Excellence Framework: A Systems Perspective

KEY CHARACTERISTICS OF THE CRITERIA

1. The Criteria focus on business results.

The Criteria focus on the key areas of business performance, given below.

> **Business performance areas:**
>
> (1) customer focused results;
> (2) financial and market results;
> (3) human resource results;
> (4) supplier and partner results; and
> (5) organizational effectiveness results.

The use of this composite of indicators is intended to ensure that strategies are balanced — that they do not inappropriately trade off among important stakeholders, objectives, or short- and long-term goals.

2. The Criteria are non-prescriptive and adaptable.

The Criteria are made up of results-oriented requirements. However, the Criteria *do not* prescribe:

- specific tools, techniques, technologies, systems, measures, or starting points;

- that your organization should or should not have departments for quality, planning, or other functions;

- how your organization should be structured; or

- that different units in your organization should be managed in the same way.

These factors are important and are likely to change as needs and strategies evolve. Hence, the Criteria do emphasize that such factors be evaluated as part of your organization's performance reviews.

The Criteria are non-prescriptive because:

(1) The focus is on results, not on procedures, tools, or organizational structure. Organizations are encouraged to develop and *demonstrate* creative, adaptive, and flexible approaches for meeting basic requirements. Non-prescriptive requirements are intended to foster incremental and major ("breakthrough") improvements as well as basic change.

(2) Selection of tools, techniques, systems, and organizational structure usually depends upon factors such as business type and size, your organization's stage of development, and employee capabilities and responsibilities.

(3) Focus on common requirements, rather than on common procedures, fosters better understanding, communication, sharing, and alignment, while supporting innovation and diversity in approaches.

3. The Criteria support a systems perspective to maintaining organization-wide goal alignment.

The systems perspective to goal alignment is embedded in the integrated structure of the Core Values and Concepts, the Criteria, and the results-oriented, cause-effect linkages among the Criteria Items.

Alignment in the Criteria is built around connecting and reinforcing measures derived from your organization's strategy. These measures tie directly to customer value and to overall performance. The use of measures thus channels different activities in consistent directions with less need for detailed procedures, centralized decision making, or process management. Measures thereby serve both as a communications tool and a basis for deploying consistent overall performance requirements. Such alignment ensures consistency of purpose while also supporting agility, innovation, and decentralized decision making.

A systems perspective to goal alignment, particularly when strategy and goals change over time, requires dynamic linkages among Criteria Items. In the Criteria, action-oriented cycles of learning take place via feedback between processes and results.

The learning cycles have four, clearly defined stages:

(1) planning, including design of processes, selection of measures, and deployment of requirements;

(2) execution of plans;

(3) assessment of progress, taking into account internal and external results; and

(4) revision of plans based upon assessment findings, learning, new inputs, and new requirements.

4. The Criteria support goal-based diagnosis.

The Criteria and the Scoring Guidelines make up a two-part diagnostic (assessment) system. The Criteria are a set of 19 performance-oriented requirements. The Scoring Guidelines spell out the assessment dimensions — Approach, Deployment, and Results — and the key factors used to assess against each dimension. An assessment thus provides a profile of strengths and opportunities for improvement relative to the 19 basic requirements. In this way, assessment leads to actions that contribute to performance improvement in all areas, as described in the shaded box above. This diagnostic assessment is a useful management tool that goes beyond most performance reviews and is applicable to a wide range of strategies and management systems.

The Criteria for Performance Excellence have evolved significantly over the last several years toward comprehensive coverage of strategy-driven performance, addressing the needs of all stakeholders — customers, employees, stockholders, suppliers and partners, and the public. During this period of time, other sections of the Criteria booklet have not fully kept pace with the evolving Criteria. For 2000, there are no changes to the Criteria Item requirements; revisions have been made in other important sections of the Criteria booklet.

The most significant changes in the Criteria booklet are summarized as follows:

- The Core Values and Concepts have been revised.

- The Glossary of Key Terms has been revised and expanded.

- The Category and Item Descriptions have been rewritten and reformatted.

- The Scoring Guidelines have been revised for Approach/Deployment Items.

- The Guidelines for Responding to Approach/ Deployment Items have been modified to explain the desired responses for questions that begin with *How* and for questions that begin with *What*.

Changes have been made throughout the Criteria booklet. A more detailed explanation of the most significant changes are:

Core Values and Concepts

- Many of the Core Values and Concepts have been changed to better align with the foundation for the current Criteria. The number of Core Values and Concepts remains constant at 11.

- The following Core Values and Concepts have replaced the indicated Core Values and Concepts: *Visionary Leadership* replaces Leadership, *Customer Driven* replaces Customer-Driven Quality, *Organizational and Personal Learning* replaces Continuous Improvement and Learning, *Valuing Employees and Partners* replaces Valuing Employees, *Agility* replaces Fast Response, *Focus on the Future* replaces Long-Range View of the Future, and *Focus on Results and Creating Value* replaces Results Focus. The new Core Values and Concepts are intended to provide a more holistic and current view of organizational performance excellence.

- Two of the 1999 Core Values and Concepts, Design Quality and Prevention and Partnership Development, have been incorporated into the new Core Values and Concepts.

- Two new Core Values and Concepts have been added to underpin the current Criteria: *Managing for Innovation* and *Systems Perspective*.

- Two 1999 Core Values and Concepts remain: *Management by Fact* and *Public Responsibility and Citizenship*.

Glossary of Key Terms

- The following key terms have been added to the Glossary: Analysis, Approach, Deployment, Empowerment, Results, Strategic Objectives, and Systematic. All of these terms have very specific meanings in the Baldrige context.

Category and Item Descriptions

- Each Item Description now has three parts: *Purpose*, *Requirements*, and *Comments*. This three-part presentation is intended to better aid the understanding of the Criteria Items. *Purpose* tells you what the Item is examining and why. *Requirements* summarizes the key Item requirements. *Comments* provides additional explanation and examples of how you might address the Item requirements.

Scoring Guidelines

- The word *effective* replaces the word *sound* for Approach/Deployment Items in the Scoring Guidelines. *Effective* relates to producing the desired result and to appropriateness for intended use. *Effective* is a better term in the context of a Baldrige assessment.

2000 Categories/Items	Point Values

1	**Leadership**	**125**
1.1	Organizational Leadership	85
1.2	Public Responsibility and Citizenship	40

2	**Strategic Planning**	**85**
2.1	Strategy Development	40
2.2	Strategy Deployment	45

3	**Customer and Market Focus**	**85**
3.1	Customer and Market Knowledge	40
3.2	Customer Satisfaction and Relationships	45

4	**Information and Analysis**	**85**
4.1	Measurement of Organizational Performance	40
4.2	Analysis of Organizational Performance	45

5	**Human Resource Focus**	**85**
5.1	Work Systems	35
5.2	Employee Education, Training, and Development	25
5.3	Employee Well-Being and Satisfaction	25

6	**Process Management**	**85**
6.1	Product and Service Processes	55
6.2	Support Processes	15
6.3	Supplier and Partnering Processes	15

7	**Business Results**	**450**
7.1	Customer Focused Results	115
7.2	Financial and Market Results	115
7.3	Human Resource Results	80
7.4	Supplier and Partner Results	25
7.5	Organizational Effectiveness Results	115

TOTAL POINTS	**1000**

> **Note:** The Scoring System used with the Criteria Items in a Baldrige assessment can be found on pages 44-45.

1 Leadership (125 pts.)

The *Leadership* Category examines how your organization's senior leaders address values and performance expectations, as well as a focus on customers and other stakeholders, empowerment, innovation, learning, and organizational directions. Also examined is how your organization addresses its responsibilities to the public and supports its key communities.

1.1 Organizational Leadership (85 pts.)

Approach - Deployment

Describe how senior leaders guide your organization and review organizational performance.

Within your response, include answers to the following questions:

a. **Senior Leadership Direction**

(1) How do senior leaders set, communicate, and deploy organizational values, performance expectations, and a focus on creating and balancing value for customers and other stakeholders? Include communication and deployment through your leadership structure and to all employees.

(2) How do senior leaders establish and reinforce an environment for empowerment and innovation, and encourage and support organizational and employee learning?

(3) How do senior leaders set directions and seek future opportunities for your organization?

b. **Organizational Performance Review**

(1) How do senior leaders review organizational performance and capabilities to assess organizational health, competitive performance, and progress relative to performance goals and changing organizational needs? Include the key performance measures regularly reviewed by your senior leaders.

(2) How do you translate organizational performance review findings into priorities for improvement and opportunities for innovation?

(3) What are your key recent performance review findings, priorities for improvement, and opportunities for innovation? How are they deployed throughout your organization and, as appropriate, to your suppliers/partners and key customers to ensure organizational alignment?

(4) How do senior leaders use organizational performance review findings and employee feedback to improve their leadership effectiveness and the effectiveness of management throughout the organization?

Note:

Your organizational performance results should be reported in Items 7.1, 7.2, 7.3, 7.4, and 7.5.

Item notes serve three purposes: (1) clarify terms or requirements presented in Criteria Items; (2) give instructions on responding to the Criteria Item requirements; or (3) indicate key linkages to other Items. In all cases, the intent is to help you respond to the Criteria Item requirements.

Item responses are assessed by considering the Criteria Item requirements and the maturity of your approaches, breadth of deployment, and strength of your improvement process and results relative to the Scoring System. Refer to the Scoring System information on pages 44-45.

For definitions of the following **key terms**, see pages 27-29: alignment, approach, deployment, empowerment, innovation, measures, performance, and value.

For additional description of this Item, see page 30.

1.2 Public Responsibility and Citizenship (40 pts.)

Describe how your organization addresses its responsibilities to the public and how your organization practices good citizenship.

Within your response, include answers to the following questions:

a. Responsibilities to the Public

(1) How do you address the impacts on society of your products, services, and operations? Include your key practices, measures, and targets for regulatory and legal requirements and for risks associated with your products, services, and operations.

(2) How do you anticipate public concerns with current and future products, services, and operations? How do you prepare for these concerns in a proactive manner?

(3) How do you ensure ethical business practices in all stakeholder transactions and interactions?

b. Support of Key Communities

How do your organization, your senior leaders, and your employees actively support and strengthen your key communities? Include how you identify key communities and determine areas of emphasis for organizational involvement and support.

Notes:

N1. Public responsibilities in areas critical to your business also should be addressed in Strategy Development (Item 2.1) and in Process Management (Category 6). Key results, such as results of regulatory/legal compliance or environmental improvements through use of "green" technology or other means, should be reported as Organizational Effectiveness Results (Item 7.5).

For additional description of this Item, see page 30.

N2. Areas of community support appropriate for inclusion in 1.2b might include your efforts to strengthen local community services, education, the environment, and practices of trade, business, or professional associations.

N3. Health and safety of employees are not addressed in Item 1.2; you should address these factors in Item 5.3.

The *Strategic Planning* Category examines your organization's strategy development process, including how your organization develops strategic objectives, action plans, and related human resource plans. Also examined are how plans are deployed and how performance is tracked.

2.1 Strategy Development (40 pts.)

Approach - Deployment

Describe your organization's strategy development process to strengthen organizational performance and competitive position. Summarize your key strategic objectives.

Within your response, include answers to the following questions:

a. Strategy Development Process

(1) What is your strategic planning process? Include key steps and key participants in the process.

(2) How do you consider the following key factors in your process? Include how relevant data and information are gathered and analyzed.

The factors are:

- customer and market needs/expectations, including new product/service opportunities
- your competitive environment and capabilities, including use of new technology
- financial, societal, and other potential risks
- your human resource capabilities and needs
- your operational capabilities and needs, including resource availability
- your supplier and/or partner capabilities and needs

b. Strategic Objectives

What are your key strategic objectives and your timetable for accomplishing them? In setting objectives, how do you evaluate options to assess how well they respond to the factors in 2.1a(2) most important to your performance?

Notes:

N1. Strategy development refers to your organization's approach (formal or informal) to a future-oriented basis for business decisions, resource allocations, and management. Such development might utilize various types of forecasts, projections, options, scenarios, and/or other approaches to addressing the future.

N2. You should interpret the word strategy broadly. Strategy might be built around or lead to any or all of the following: new products, services, and markets; revenue growth; cost reduction; business acquisitions; and new partnerships and alliances. Strategy might be directed toward becoming a preferred supplier, a low-cost producer, a market innovator, and/or a high-end or customized service provider.

Strategy might depend upon or require you to develop different kinds of capabilities, such as rapid response, customization, market understanding, lean or virtual manufacturing, relationships, rapid innovation, technology management, leveraging assets, business process excellence, and information management. Responses to Item 2.1 should address the key factors from your point of view.

N3. Item 2.1 addresses your overall organizational directions and strategy that might include changes in services, products, and/or product lines. However, the Item does not address product and service design; you should address these factors in Item 6.1.

For definitions of the following **key terms**, see pages 28-29: process and strategic objectives.

For additional description of this Item, see pages 31-32.

Describe your organization's strategy deployment process. Summarize your organization's action plans and related performance measures. Project the performance of these key measures into the future.

Within your response, include answers to the following questions:

a. Action Plan Development and Deployment

(1) How do you develop action plans that address your key strategic objectives? What are your key short- and longer-term action plans? Include key changes, if any, in your products/services and/or your customers/markets.

(2) What are your key human resource requirements and plans, based on your strategic objectives and action plans?

(3) How do you allocate resources to ensure accomplishment of your overall action plan?

(4) What are your key performance measures and/or indicators for tracking progress relative to your action plans?

(5) How do you communicate and deploy your strategic objectives, action plans, and performance measures/indicators to achieve overall organizational alignment?

b. Performance Projection

(1) What are your two-to-five year projections for key performance measures and/or indicators? Include key performance targets and/or goals, as appropriate.

(2) How does your projected performance compare with competitors, key benchmarks, and past performance, as appropriate? What is the basis for these comparisons?

Notes:

N1. Action plan development and deployment are closely linked to other Items in the Criteria and to the performance excellence framework on page 6. Examples of key linkages are:

- Item 1.1 for how your senior leaders set and communicate directions;

- Category 3 for gathering customer and market knowledge as input to your strategy and action plans, and for deploying action plans;

- Category 4 for information and analysis to support your development of strategy, to provide an effective performance basis for your performance measurements, and to track progress relative to your strategic objectives and action plans;

- Category 5 for your work system needs, employee education, training, and development needs, and related human resource factors resulting from action plans;

- Category 6 for process requirements resulting from your action plans; and

- Item 7.5 for accomplishments relative to your organizational strategy.

N2. Measures and/or indicators of projected performance (2.2b) might include changes resulting from new business ventures, business acquisitions, new value creation, market entry and/or shifts, and/or significant anticipated innovations in products, services, and/or technology.

For definitions of the following **key terms**, see pages 27-28: action plans, measures and indicators.

For additional description of this Item, see pages 32-33.

The *Customer and Market Focus* Category examines how your organization determines requirements, expectations, and preferences of customers and markets. Also examined is how your organization builds relationships with customers and determines their satisfaction.

3.1 Customer and Market Knowledge (40 pts.)

Approach - Deployment

Describe how your organization determines short- and longer-term requirements, expectations, and preferences of customers and markets to ensure the relevance of current products/services and to develop new opportunities.

Within your response, include answers to the following questions:

a. Customer and Market Knowledge

(1) How do you determine or target customers, customer groups, and/or market segments? How do you consider customers of competitors and other potential customers and/or markets in this determination?

(2) How do you listen and learn to determine key requirements and drivers of purchase decisions for current, former, and potential customers? If determination methods differ for different customers and/or customer groups, include the key differences.

(3) How do you determine and/or project key product/service features and their relative importance/value to customers for purposes of current and future marketing, product planning, and other business developments, as appropriate? How do you use relevant information from current and former customers, including marketing/sales information, customer retention, won/lost analysis, and complaints, in this determination?

(4) How do you keep your listening and learning methods current with business needs and directions?

Notes:

N1. If your products and services are sold to end users via other businesses such as retail stores or dealers, customer groups [3.1a(1)] should include both the end users and these intermediate businesses.

N2. Product and service features [3.1a(3)] refer to all important characteristics and to the performance of your products and services throughout their full life cycle and the full "consumption chain." The focus should be on features that bear upon customer preference and repurchase loyalty — for example, those features that differentiate your products and services from competing offerings. Those features might include factors such as price, value, delivery, customer or technical support, and the sales relationship.

For additional description of this Item, see page 33.

3.2 Customer Satisfaction and Relationships (45 pts.)   **Approach - Deployment**

Describe how your organization determines the satisfaction of customers and builds relationships to retain current business and to develop new opportunities.

Within your response, include answers to the following questions:

a. **Customer Relationships**
  (1) How do you determine key access mechanisms to facilitate the ability of customers to conduct business, seek assistance and information, and make complaints? Include a summary of your key mechanisms.

  (2) How do you determine key customer contact requirements and deploy these requirements to all employees involved in the response chain?

  (3) What is your complaint management process? Include how you ensure that complaints are resolved effectively and promptly, and that all complaints received are aggregated and analyzed for use in overall organizational improvement.

  (4) How do you build relationships with customers for repeat business and/or positive referral?

  (5) How do you keep your approaches to customer access and relationships current with business needs and directions?

b. **Customer Satisfaction Determination**
  (1) What processes, measurement methods, and data do you use to determine customer satisfaction and dissatisfaction? Include how your measurements capture actionable information that reflects customers' future business and/or potential for positive referral. Also include any significant differences in processes or methods for different customer groups and/or market segments.

  (2) How do you follow up with customers on products/services and recent transactions to receive prompt and actionable feedback?

  (3) How do you obtain and use information on customer satisfaction relative to competitors and/or benchmarks, as appropriate?

  (4) How do you keep your approaches to satisfaction determination current with business needs and directions?

Notes:

N1. Customer relationships (3.2a) might include the development of partnerships or alliances.

N2. Customer satisfaction and dissatisfaction determination (3.2b) might include any or all of the following: surveys, formal and informal feedback from customers, use of customer account data, and complaints.

N3. Customer satisfaction measurements might include both a numerical rating scale and descriptors for each unit in the scale. Actionable customer satisfaction measurements provide reliable information about customer ratings of your specific product, service, and relationship features, the linkage between

these ratings, and your customer's likely future actions — repurchase and/or positive referral. Product and service features might include overall value and price.

N4. Your customer satisfaction and dissatisfaction results and information on product/service measures that contribute to customer satisfaction or dissatisfaction should be reported in Item 7.1. These latter measures might include trends and levels in performance of customer-desired product features or customer complaint handling effectiveness (such as complaint response time, effective resolution, and percent of complaints resolved on first contact).

For additional description of this Item, see page 34.

The *Information and Analysis* Category examines your organization's performance measurement system and how your organization analyzes performance data and information.

4.1 Measurement of Organizational Performance (40 pts.)   Approach - Deployment

Describe how your organization provides effective performance measurement systems for understanding, aligning, and improving performance at all levels and in all parts of your organization.

Within your response, include answers to the following questions:

a. Measurement of Organizational Performance
   (1) How do you address the major components of an effective performance measurement system, including the following key factors?

   • selection of measures/indicators, and extent and effectiveness of their use in daily operations
   • selection and integration of measures/indicators and completeness of data to track your overall organizational performance
   • selection, and extent and effectiveness of use of key comparative data and information
   • data and information reliability
   • a cost/financial understanding of improvement options
   • correlations/projections of data to support planning

   (2) How do you keep your performance measurement system current with business needs and directions?

Notes:

N1. The term information and analysis refers to the key metrics used by your organization to measure and analyze performance. Performance measurement is used in fact-based decision making for setting and aligning organizational directions and resource use at your work unit, key process, departmental, and whole organization levels.

N2. Deployment of data and information might be via electronic or other means. Reliability [4.1a(1)] includes reliability of software and delivery systems.

N3. Comparative data and information include benchmarking and competitive comparisons. Benchmarking refers to processes and results that represent best practices and performance for similar activities, inside or outside your organization's industry. Competitive comparisons refer to performance relative to competitors in your organization's markets.

For additional description of this Item, see pages 34-35.

4.2 Analysis of Organizational Performance (45 pts.)

Describe how your organization analyzes performance data and information to assess and understand overall organizational performance.

Within your response, include answers to the following questions:

a. Analysis of Organizational Performance
   (1) How do you perform analyses to support your senior executives' organizational performance review and your organizational planning? How do you ensure that the analyses address the overall health of your organization, including your key business results and strategic objectives?

   (2) How do you ensure that the results of organizational-level analysis are linked to work group and/or functional-level operations to enable effective support for decision making?

   (3) How does analysis support daily operations throughout your organization? Include how this analysis ensures that measures align with action plans.

Notes:

N1. Analysis includes trends, projections, comparisons, and cause-effect correlations intended to support your performance reviews and the setting of priorities for resource use. Accordingly, analysis draws upon all types of data: customer-related, financial and market, operational, and competitive.

N2. Your performance results should be reported in Items 7.1, 7.2, 7.3, 7.4, and 7.5.

For a definition of the following **key term**, see page 27: analysis.

For additional description of this Item, see pages 35-36.

The *Human Resource Focus* Category examines how your organization enables employees to develop and utilize their full potential, aligned with the organization's objectives. Also examined are your organization's efforts to build and maintain a work environment and an employee support climate conducive to performance excellence, full participation, and personal and organizational growth.

5.1 Work Systems (35 pts.)

Approach - Deployment

Describe how your organization's work and job design, compensation, career progression, and related work force practices enable employees to achieve high performance in your operations.

Within your response, include answers to the following questions:

a. Work Systems

 (1) How do you design, organize, and manage work and jobs to promote cooperation and collaboration, individual initiative, innovation, and flexibility, and to keep current with business needs?

 (2) How do your managers and supervisors encourage and motivate employees to develop and utilize their full potential? Include formal and/or informal mechanisms you use to encourage and support employees in job- and career-related development/learning objectives.

 (3) How does your employee performance management system, including feedback to employees, support high performance?

 (4) How do your compensation, recognition, and related reward/incentive practices reinforce high performance?

 (5) How do you ensure effective communication, cooperation, and knowledge/skill sharing across work units, functions, and locations, as appropriate?

 (6) How do you identify characteristics and skills needed by potential employees; how do you recruit and hire new employees? How do you take into account key performance requirements, diversity of your community, and fair work force practices?

Notes:

N1. The term employees refers to your organization's permanent, temporary, and part-time personnel, as well as any contract employees supervised by your organization. Employees include managers and supervisors at all levels. You should address contract employees supervised by a contractor in Item 6.3.

N2. The term work design refers to how your employees are organized and/or organize themselves in formal and informal, temporary, or longer-term units. This might include work teams, process teams, customer action teams, problem-solving teams, centers of excellence, functional units, cross-functional teams, and departments — self-managed or managed by supervisors.

The term job design refers to responsibilities, authorities, and tasks of individuals. In some work systems, jobs might be shared by a team, based upon cross-training.

N3. Compensation and recognition include promotions and bonuses that might be based upon performance, skills acquired, and other factors. Recognition includes monetary and nonmonetary, formal and informal, and individual and group recognition.

For a definition of the following **key term**, see pages 27-28: high performance work.

For additional description of this Item, see pages 36-37.

5.2 Employee Education, Training, and Development (25 pts.)   `Approach - Deployment`

Describe how your organization's education and training support the achievement of your business objectives, build employee knowledge, skills, and capabilities, and contribute to improved employee performance.

Within your response, include answers to the following questions:

a. Employee Education, Training, and Development

(1) How does your education and training approach balance short- and longer-term organizational and employee needs, including development, learning, and career progression?

(2) How do you design education and training to keep current with business and individual needs? Include how job and organizational performance are used in education and training design and evaluation.

(3) How do you seek and use input from employees and their supervisors/managers on education and training needs, expectations, and design?

(4) How do you deliver and evaluate education and training? Include formal and informal education, training, and learning, as appropriate.

(5) How do you address key developmental and training needs, including diversity training, management/leadership development, new employee orientation, and safety, as appropriate?

(6) How do you address performance excellence in your education and training? Include how employees learn to use performance measurements, performance standards, skill standards, performance improvement, quality control methods, and benchmarking, as appropriate.

(7) How do you reinforce knowledge and skills on the job?

Note:

Education and training delivery [5.2a(4)] might occur inside or outside your organization and involve on-the-job, classroom, computer-based, distance learning, and/or other types of delivery (formal or informal).

For additional description of this Item, see pages 37-38.

5.3 Employee Well-Being and Satisfaction (25 pts.)

Describe how your organization maintains a work environment and an employee support climate that contribute to the well-being, satisfaction, and motivation of all employees.

Within your response, include answers to the following questions:

a. **Work Environment**

How do you address and improve workplace health, safety, and ergonomic factors? How do employees take part in identifying these factors and in improving workplace safety? Include performance measures and/or targets for each key environmental factor. Also include significant differences, if any, based on different work environments for employee groups and/or work units.

b. **Employee Support Climate**

(1) How do you enhance your employees' work climate via services, benefits, and policies? How are these enhancements selected and tailored to the needs of different categories and types of employees, and to individuals, as appropriate?

(2) How does your work climate consider and support the needs of a diverse work force?

c. **Employee Satisfaction**

(1) How do you determine the key factors that affect employee well-being, satisfaction, and motivation?

(2) What formal and/or informal assessment methods and measures do you use to determine employee well-being, satisfaction, and motivation? How do you tailor these methods and measures to a diverse work force and to different categories and types of employees? How do you use other indicators such as employee turnover, absenteeism, grievances, and productivity to assess and improve employee well-being, satisfaction, and motivation?

(3) How do you relate assessment findings to key business results to identify work environment and employee support climate improvement priorities?

Notes:

N1. Approaches for enhancing your employees' work climate [5.3b(1)] might include: counseling; career development and employability services; recreational or cultural activities; non-work-related education; day care; job rotation and/or sharing; special leave for family responsibilities and/or for community service; home safety training; flexible work hours; outplacement; and retiree benefits (including extended health care).

N2. Specific factors that might affect your employees' well-being, satisfaction, and motivation [5.3c(1)] include: effective employee problem or grievance resolution; safety factors; employee views of management; employee training, development, and career opportunities; employee preparation for changes in technology or the work organization; work environment and other work conditions; workload; cooperation and teamwork; recognition; benefits; communications; job security; compensation; and equal opportunity.

N3. Measures and/or indicators of well-being, satisfaction, and motivation [5.3c(2)] might include: safety; absenteeism; turnover; turnover rate for customer contact employees; grievances; strikes; other job actions; insurance costs; worker's compensation claims; and results of surveys. Your results relative to such measures and/or indicators should be reported in Item 7.3.

N4. Priority setting [5.3c(3)] might draw upon your human resource results presented in Item 7.3 and might involve addressing employee problems based on their impact on your organizational performance.

For additional description of this Item, see page 38.

The *Process Management* Category examines the key aspects of your organization's process management, including customer-focused design, product and service delivery, support, and supplier and partnering processes involving all work units.

6.1 Product and Service Processes (55 pts.)

Approach - Deployment

Describe how your organization manages key product and service design and delivery processes.

Within your response, include answers to the following questions:

a. Design Processes
   (1) What are your design processes for products/services and their related production/delivery processes?

   (2) How do you incorporate changing customer/market requirements into product/service designs and production/delivery systems and processes?

   (3) How do you incorporate new technology into products/services and into production/delivery systems and processes, as appropriate?

   (4) How do your design processes address design quality and cycle time, transfer of learning from past projects and other parts of the organization, cost control, new design technology, productivity, and other efficiency/effectiveness factors?

   (5) How do you ensure that your production/delivery process design accommodates all key operational performance requirements?

   (6) How do you coordinate and test design and production/delivery processes to ensure capability for trouble-free and timely introduction of products/services?

b. Production/Delivery Processes
   (1) What are your key production/delivery processes and their key performance requirements?

   (2) How does your day-to-day operation of key production/delivery processes ensure meeting key performance requirements?

   (3) What are your key performance measures and/or indicators used for the control and improvement of these processes? Include how real-time customer input is sought, as appropriate.

   (4) How do you improve your production/delivery processes to achieve better process performance and improvements to products/services, as appropriate? How are improvements shared with other organizational units and processes, as appropriate?

Notes:

N1. Product and service design, production, and delivery differ greatly among organizations, depending upon many factors. These factors include the nature of your products and services, technology requirements, issues of modularity and parts commonality, customer and supplier relationships and involvement, and product and service customization. Responses to Item 6.1 should address the most critical requirements for your business.

N2. Responses to Item 6.1 should include how your customers and key suppliers and partners are involved in your design processes, as appropriate.

N3. Your results of operational improvements in product and service design and delivery processes should be reported in Item 7.5. Your results of improvements in product and service performance should be reported in Item 7.1.

For definitions of the following **key terms**, see pages 27-29: cycle time and productivity.

For additional description of this Item, see pages 39-40.

6.2 Support Processes (15 pts.)

Describe how your organization manages its key support processes.

Within your response, include answers to the following questions:

a. **Support Processes**

(1) What are your key support processes?

(2) How do you determine key support process requirements, incorporating input from internal and/or external customers, as appropriate? What are the key operational requirements (such as productivity and cycle time) for the processes?

(3) How do you design these processes to meet all the key requirements?

(4) How does your day-to-day operation of key support processes ensure meeting key performance requirements? How do you determine and use in-process measures and/or customer feedback in your support processes?

(5) How do you improve your support processes to achieve better performance and to keep them current with business needs and directions, as appropriate? How are improvements shared with other organizational units and processes, as appropriate?

Notes:

N1. Your support processes are those that support your organization's products/services design and delivery processes, and business operations. This might include information and knowledge management, finance and accounting, facilities management, research and development, administration, and sales/marketing. The key support processes to be included in Item 6.2 are unique to your organization and how you operate. Focus should be on your most important processes not addressed in Items 6.1 and 6.3.

N2. Your results of improvements in key support processes and key support process performance results should be reported in Item 7.5.

For additional description of this Item, see page 40.

6.3 Supplier and Partnering Processes (15 pts.)

Describe how your organization manages its key supplier and/or partnering interactions and processes.

Within your response, include answers to the following questions:

a. Supplier and Partnering Processes

(1) What key products/services do you purchase from suppliers and/or partners?

(2) How do you incorporate performance requirements into supplier and/or partner process management? What key performance requirements must your suppliers and/or partners meet to fulfill your overall requirements?

(3) How do you ensure that your performance requirements are met? How do you provide timely and actionable feedback to suppliers and/or partners? Include the key performance measures and/or indicators and any targets you use for supplier and/or partner assessment.

(4) How do you minimize overall costs associated with inspections, tests, and process and/or performance audits?

(5) How do you provide business assistance and/or incentives to suppliers and/or partners to help them improve their overall performance and to improve their abilities to contribute to your current and longer-term performance?

(6) How do you improve your supplier and/or partner processes, including your role as supportive customer/partner, to keep current with your business needs and directions? How are improvements shared throughout your organization, as appropriate?

Notes:

N1. The term supplier refers to other organizations and to units of your parent organization that provide you with goods and services.

N2. Your supplier and partnering processes might include processes for supply chain improvement and optimization, beyond your direct suppliers and partners.

N3. If your organization selects preferred suppliers and/or partners based upon volume of business or criticality of their supplied products and/or services, include your selection criteria in the response.

N4. Your results of improvements in supplier and partnering processes and supplier/partner performance results should be reported in Item 7.4.

For additional description of this Item, see pages 40-41.

The *Business Results* Category examines your organization's performance and improvement in key business areas — customer satisfaction, product and service performance, financial and marketplace performance, human resource results, supplier and partner results, and operational performance. Also examined are performance levels relative to competitors.

7.1 Customer Focused Results (115 pts.)

Results

Summarize your organization's customer focused results, including customer satisfaction and product and service performance results. Segment your results by customer groups and market segments, as appropriate. Include appropriate comparative data.

Provide data and information to answer the following questions:

a. Customer Focused Results

(1) What are your current levels and trends in key measures and/or indicators of customer satisfaction, dissatisfaction, and satisfaction relative to competitors?

(2) What are your current levels and trends in key measures and/or indicators of customer loyalty, positive referral, customer-perceived value, and/or customer relationship building, as appropriate?

(3) What are your current levels and trends in key measures and/or indicators of product and service performance?

Notes:

N1. Customer satisfaction and dissatisfaction results reported in this Item should relate to determination methods and data described in Item 3.2.

N2. Measures and/or indicators of customer satisfaction relative to competitors might include objective information and data from your customers and from independent organizations.

For a definition of the following **key term**, see page 29: results.

For additional description of this Item, see pages 41-42.

N3. Comparative performance of your products and services and product/service performance measures that serve as indicators of customer satisfaction should be included in 7.1a(3).

N4. The combination of direct customer measures/ indicators in 7.1a(1) and 7.1a(2) with product and service performance measures/indicators in 7.1a(3) provides an opportunity to determine cause and effect relationships between your product/service attributes and evidence of customer satisfaction, loyalty, positive referral, etc.

7.2 Financial and Market Results (115 pts.)

Results

Summarize your organization's key financial and marketplace performance results, segmented by market segments, as appropriate. Include appropriate comparative data.

Provide data and information to answer the following questions:

a. Financial and Market Results

(1) What are your current levels and trends in key measures and/or indicators of financial performance, including aggregate measures of financial return and/or economic value, as appropriate?

(2) What are your current levels and trends in key measures and/or indicators of marketplace performance, including market share/position, business growth, and new markets entered, as appropriate?

Note:

Aggregate measures such as return on investment (ROI), asset utilization, operating margins, profitability, profitability by market/customer segment,

liquidity, debt to equity ratio, value added per employee, and financial activity measures are appropriate for responding to 7.2a(1).

For additional description of this Item, see page 42.

7.3 Human Resource Results (80 pts.)

Summarize your organization's human resource results, including employee well-being, satisfaction, development, and work system performance. Segment your results by types and categories of employees, as appropriate. Include appropriate comparative data.

Provide data and information to answer the following questions:

a. Human Resource Results

(1) What are your current levels and trends in key measures and/or indicators of employee well-being, satisfaction and dissatisfaction, and development?

(2) What are your current levels and trends in key measures and/or indicators of work system performance and effectiveness?

Notes:

N1. Results reported in this Item should relate to activities described in Category 5. Your results should be responsive to key process needs described in Category 6, and your organization's action plans and related human resource plans described in Item 2.2.

N2. For appropriate measures of employee well-being and satisfaction, see Notes to Item 5.3. Appropriate measures and/or indicators of employee development

might include innovation and suggestion rates, courses completed, learning, on-the-job performance improvements, and cross-training.

N3. Appropriate measures and/or indicators of work system performance and effectiveness might include job and job classification simplification, job rotation, work layout, and changing supervisory ratios.

For additional description of this Item, see page 42.

7.4 Supplier and Partner Results (25 pts.)

Summarize your organization's key supplier and partner results. Include appropriate comparative data.

Provide data and information to answer the following question:

a. Supplier and Partner Results
What are your current levels and trends in key measures and/or indicators of supplier and partner performance? Include your performance and/or cost improvements resulting from supplier and partner performance and performance management.

Note:

Results reported in this Item should relate directly to processes and performance requirements described in Item 6.3.

For additional description of this Item, see page 42.

7.5 Organizational Effectiveness Results (115 pts.)

Summarize your organization's key operational performance results that contribute to the achievement of organizational effectiveness. Include appropriate comparative data.

Provide data and information to answer the following questions:

a. Organizational Effectiveness Results

(1) What are your current levels and trends in key measures and/or indicators of key design, production, delivery, and support process performance? Include productivity, cycle time, and other appropriate measures of effectiveness and efficiency.

(2) What are your results for key measures and/or indicators of regulatory/legal compliance and citizenship? What are your results for key measures and/or indicators of accomplishment of organizational strategy?

Notes:

N1. Results reported in Item 7.5 should address your key organizational requirements and progress toward accomplishment of your key organizational performance goals as presented in the Business Overview, and in Items 1.1, 2.2, 6.1, and 6.2. Include results not reported in Items 7.1, 7.2, 7.3, and 7.4.

N2. Results reported in Item 7.5 should provide key information for analysis (Item 4.2) and review (Item 1.1)

of your organizational operational performance and should provide the operational basis for customer results (Item 7.1) and financial and market results (Item 7.2).

N3. Regulatory/legal compliance results reported in Item 7.5 should address requirements described in Item 1.2.

For additional description of this Item, see page 43.

GLOSSARY OF KEY TERMS

This Glossary of Key Terms defines and briefly describes terms used throughout the Criteria booklet that are important to performance management.

Action Plans

Action plans refer to principal organizational-level drivers, derived from short- and long-term strategic planning. In simplest terms, action plans are set to accomplish those things your organization should do well for your strategy to succeed. Action plan development represents the critical stage in planning when strategic objectives and goals are made specific so that effective organization-wide understanding and deployment are possible. Deployment of action plans requires analysis of overall resource needs and creation of aligned measures for all work units. Deployment might also require specialized training for some employees or recruitment of personnel.

An example of a strategic objective for a supplier in a highly competitive industry might be to develop and maintain a price leadership position. Action plans could entail design of efficient processes and creation of a cost accounting system, aligned for the organization as a whole. Performance requirements might include unit and/or team training in priority setting based upon costs and benefits. Organizational-level analysis and review could emphasize overall productivity growth.

Alignment

Alignment refers to consistency of plans, processes, information, resource decisions, actions, results, analysis, and learning to support key organization-wide goals. Effective alignment requires common understanding of purposes and goals and use of complementary measures and information for planning, tracking, analysis, and improvement at three levels: the organizational level; the key process level; and the work unit level.

Analysis

Analysis refers to assessments performed by an organization or its work units to provide a basis for effective decisions. Overall organizational analysis guides process management toward achieving key business results and toward attaining strategic objectives.

Despite their importance, individual facts and data do not usually provide an effective basis for actions or setting priorities. Actions depend upon understanding cause/effect relationships. Understanding such relationships comes from analysis of facts and data.

Approach

Approach refers to how an organization addresses the Baldrige Criteria Item requirements — the methods and processes used by the organization. Approaches are evaluated on the basis of the appropriateness of the approach to the Item requirements; effectiveness of use of the approach; and alignment with organizational needs. For further description, see the Scoring System on page 44.

Cycle Time

Cycle time refers to the time required to fulfill commitments or to complete tasks. Time measurements play a major role in the Criteria because of the great importance of time performance to improving competitiveness. In the Criteria booklet, cycle time refers to all aspects of time performance. Cycle time improvement could include time to market, order fulfillment time, delivery time, change-over time, and other key process times.

Deployment

Deployment refers to the extent to which an organization's approach is applied to the requirements of a Baldrige Criteria Item. Deployment is evaluated on the basis of the breadth and depth of application of the approach throughout the organization. For further description, see the Scoring System on page 44.

Empowerment

Empowerment refers to giving employees the authority and responsibility to make decisions and take actions. Empowerment results in decisions being made closest to the "front line," where work-related knowledge and understanding reside.

Empowerment is aimed at enabling employees to satisfy customers on first contact, to improve processes and increase productivity, and to better the organization's business results. Empowered employees require information to make appropriate decisions; thus, an organizational requirement is to provide that information in a timely and useful way.

High Performance Work

High performance work refers to work approaches used to *systematically* pursue ever higher levels of overall organizational and human performance, including quality, productivity, innovation rate, and time performance. High performance work results in improved service for customers and other stakeholders.

Approaches to high performance work vary in form, function, and incentive systems. Effective approaches frequently include: cooperation between management and the work force, including work force bargaining units; cooperation among work units, often involving teams; self-directed responsibility/employee empowerment; employee input to planning; individual and organizational skill building and learning; learning from other organizations; flexibility in job design and work assignments; a flattened organizational structure, where decision making is decentralized and decisions are made closest to the "front line"; and effective use of performance measures, including comparisons. Many high performance work systems use monetary and non-monetary incentives based upon factors such as organizational performance, team and/or individual contributions, and skill building. Also, high performance work approaches usually seek to align the design of organizations, work, jobs, employee development, and incentives.

Innovation

Innovation refers to making meaningful change to improve products, services, and/or processes and create new value for stakeholders. Innovation involves the adoption of an idea, process, technology, or product that is considered new or new to its proposed application.

Successful organizational innovation is a multi-step process that involves development and knowledge sharing, a decision to implement, implementation, evaluation, and learning. Although innovation is often associated with technological innovation, it is applicable to all key organizational processes that would benefit from breakthrough improvement and/or change.

Measures and Indicators

Measures and indicators refer to numerical information that quantifies input, output, and performance dimensions of processes, products, services, and the overall organization (outcomes). Measures and indicators might be simple (derived from one measurement) or composite.

The Criteria do not make a distinction between measures and indicators. However, some users of these terms prefer the term indicator: (1) when the measurement relates to performance, but is not a direct measure of such performance (e.g., the number of complaints is an indicator of dissatisfaction, but not a direct measure of it); and (2) when the measurement is a predictor ("leading indicator") of some more significant performance (e.g., increased customer satisfaction might be a leading indicator of market share gain).

Performance

Performance refers to output results obtained from processes, products, and services that permit evaluation and comparison relative to goals, standards, past results, and other organizations. Performance might be expressed in nonfinancial and financial terms.

The Criteria booklet addresses three types of performance: (1) customer focused, including key product and service performance; (2) financial and marketplace; and (3) operational.

Customer focused performance refers to performance relative to measures and indicators of customers' perceptions, reactions, and behaviors, and to measures and indicators of product and service characteristics important to customers. Examples include customer retention, complaints, customer survey results, product reliability, on-time delivery, defect levels, and service response time.

Financial and marketplace performance refers to performance using measures of cost and revenue, including asset utilization, asset growth, and market share. Examples include returns on investments, value added per employee, debt to equity ratio, returns on assets, operating margins, cash-to-cash cycle time, and other profitability and liquidity measures.

Operational performance refers to organizational, human resource, and supplier performance relative to effectiveness and efficiency measures and indicators. Examples include cycle time, productivity, waste reduction, and regulatory compliance. Operational performance might be measured at the work unit level, key process level, and organizational level.

Process

Process refers to linked activities with the purpose of producing a product or service for a customer (user) within or outside the organization. Generally, processes involve combinations of people, machines, tools, techniques, and materials in a systematic series of steps or actions. In some situations, processes might require adherence to a specific sequence of steps, with documentation (sometimes formal) of procedures and requirements, including well-defined measurement and control steps.

In many service situations, particularly when customers are directly involved in the service, process is used in a more general way — to spell out what must be done, possibly including a preferred or expected sequence. If a sequence is critical, the service needs to include information to help customers understand and follow the sequence. Service processes involving customers also require guidance to the providers of those services on handling contingencies related to customers' likely or possible actions or behaviors.

In knowledge work such as strategic planning, research, development, and analysis, process does not necessarily imply formal sequences of steps. Rather, process implies general understandings regarding competent performance such as timing, options to be included, evaluation, and reporting. Sequences might arise as part of these understandings.

Productivity

Productivity refers to measures of efficiency of the use of resources.

Although the term is often applied to single factors such as staffing (labor productivity), machines, materials, energy, and capital, the productivity concept applies as well to the total resources used in producing outputs. The use of an aggregate measure of overall productivity allows a determination of whether or not the net effect of overall changes in a process — possibly involving resource tradeoffs — is beneficial.

Results

Results refer to outcomes achieved by an organization in addressing the purposes of a Baldrige Criteria Item. Results are evaluated on the basis of current performance; performance relative to appropriate comparisons; rate, breadth, and importance of performance improvements; and relationship of results measures to key organizational performance requirements. For further description, see the Scoring System on page 44.

Strategic Objectives

Strategic objectives refer to an organization's major change opportunities and/or the fundamental challenges the organization faces. Strategic objectives are generally externally focused, relating to significant customer, market, product/service, or technological opportunities and challenges. Broadly stated, they are what an organization must change or improve to remain or become competitive. Strategic objectives set an organization's longer-term directions and guide resource allocations and redistributions.

See the definition of *action plans* on page 27 for the relationship between strategic objectives and action plans and for an example of each.

Systematic

Systematic refers to approaches that are repeatable and use data and information so that improvement and learning are possible. In other words, approaches are systematic if they build in the opportunity for evaluation and learning, and thereby permit a gain in maturity. As organizational approaches mature, they become more systematic and reflect cycles of evaluation and learning. For use of the term, see the Scoring Guidelines on page 45.

Value

Value refers to the degree of worth relative to cost and relative to possible alternatives of a product, service, process, asset, or function.

Organizations frequently use value considerations to determine the benefits of various options relative to their costs, such as the value of various product and service combinations to customers. Organizations seek to deliver value to all their stakeholders. This frequently requires balancing value for customers and other stakeholders, such as stockholders, employees, and the community.

Leadership (Category 1)

Leadership addresses how your senior leaders guide your organization in setting directions and seeking future opportunities. Primary attention is given to how your senior leaders set and deploy clear values and high performance expectations that address the needs of all stakeholders. The Category also includes your organization's responsibilities to the public and how your organization practices good citizenship.

1.1 Organizational Leadership

Purpose

This Item examines the key aspects of your organization's leadership and the roles of your senior leaders, with the aim of creating and sustaining a high performance organization.

Requirements

You are asked how your senior leaders set directions, communicate and deploy values and performance expectations, and take into account the expectations of customers and other stakeholders. This includes how leaders create an environment for innovation, learning, and knowledge sharing.

You also are asked how your senior leaders review organizational performance, what key performance measures they regularly review, and how review findings are used to drive improvement and change, including your leaders' effectiveness.

Comments

- Leadership's central roles in setting directions, creating and balancing value for all stakeholders, and driving performance are the focus of this Item. Success requires a strong future orientation and a commitment to both improvement and change. Increasingly, this requires creating an environment for learning and innovation, as well as the means for rapid and effective application of knowledge.

- The organizational review called for in this Item is intended to cover all areas of performance, thereby providing a picture of the "state of health" of your organization. This includes not only how well you are currently performing, but also how well you are moving toward the future. It is anticipated that the review findings will provide a reliable means to guide both improvement and change, tied to your organization's own key objectives, success factors, and measures. Therefore, an important component of your senior leaders' organizational review is the translation of the review findings into an action agenda, sufficiently specific for deployment throughout your organization and to your suppliers/partners and key customers.

1.2 Public Responsibility and Citizenship

Purpose

This Item examines how your organization fulfills its public responsibilities and encourages, supports, and practices good citizenship.

Requirements

You are asked how your organization addresses current and future impacts on society in a proactive manner and how it ensures ethical business practices in all stakeholder interactions. The impacts and practices are expected to cover all relevant and important areas — products, services, and operations.

You also are asked how your organization, your senior leaders, and your employees identify, support, and strengthen key communities as part of good citizenship practices.

Comments

- An integral part of performance management and improvement is proactively addressing legal and regulatory requirements and risk factors. Addressing these areas requires establishing appropriate measures and/or indicators that senior leaders track in their overall performance review. Your organization should be sensitive to issues of public concern, whether or not these issues are currently embodied in law.

- Citizenship implies going beyond a compliance orientation. Good citizenship opportunities are available to organizations of all sizes. These opportunities include employee community service that is encouraged and supported by your organization.

- Examples of organizational community involvement include: influencing the adoption of higher standards in education by communicating employability requirements to schools and school boards; partnering with other businesses and health care providers to improve health in the local community by providing education and volunteer services to address public health issues; and partnering to influence trade and business associations to engage in beneficial, co-operative activities, such as sharing best practices to improve overall U.S. global competitiveness and the environment.

Strategic Planning (Category 2)

Strategic Planning addresses strategic and action planning, and deployment of plans. The Category stresses that customer-driven quality and operational performance excellence are key strategic issues that need to be integral parts of your organization's overall planning.

Specifically:

- customer-driven quality is a strategic view of quality. The focus is on the drivers of customer satisfaction, customer retention, new markets, and market share — key factors in competitiveness, profitability, and business success; and

- operational performance improvement contributes to short-term and longer-term productivity growth and cost/price competitiveness. Building operational capability — including speed, responsiveness, and flexibility — represents an investment in strengthening your competitive fitness.

The Criteria emphasize that improvement and learning need to be embedded in work processes. The special role of strategic planning is to align work processes with your organization's strategic directions, thereby ensuring that improvement and learning reinforce organizational priorities.

The Strategic Planning Category examines how your organization:

- understands the key customer, market, and operational requirements as input to setting strategic directions. This helps to ensure that ongoing process improvements are aligned with your organization's strategic directions.

- optimizes the use of resources, ensures the availability of trained employees, and ensures bridging between short-term and longer-term requirements that may entail capital expenditures, supplier development, etc.

- ensures that deployment will be effective — that there are mechanisms to transmit requirements and achieve alignment on three basic levels: (1) the organization/executive level; (2) the key process level; and (3) the work-unit/individual-job level.

The requirements for the Strategic Planning Category are intended to encourage strategic thinking and acting — to develop a basis for a distinct competitive position in the marketplace. *These requirements do not imply formalized plans, planning systems, departments, or specific planning cycles.* Also, the Category does not imply that all your improvements could or should be planned in advance. An effective improvement system combines improvements of many types and degrees of involvement. This requires clear strategic guidance, particularly when improvement alternatives compete for limited resources. In most cases, priority setting depends heavily upon a cost rationale. However, you also might have critical requirements such as public responsibilities that are not driven by cost considerations alone.

2.1 Strategy Development

Purpose

This Item examines how your organization sets strategic directions and develops your strategic objectives, with the aim of strengthening your overall performance and competitiveness.

Requirements

You are asked to outline your organization's strategic planning process, including identifying the key participants. You are asked how you consider the key factors that affect your organization's future. These factors cover external and internal influences on your organization. You are asked to address each factor and outline how relevant data and information are gathered and analyzed.

Finally, you are asked to summarize your key strategic objectives and your timetable for accomplishing them.

Comments

■ This Item calls for basic information on the planning process and for information on all the key influences, risks, challenges, and other requirements that might affect your organization's future opportunities and directions — taking as long-term a view as possible. This approach is intended to provide a thorough and realistic context for the development of a customer- and market-focused strategy to guide ongoing decision making, resource allocation, and overall management.

■ This Item is intended to cover all types of businesses, competitive situations, strategic issues, planning approaches, and plans. The requirements explicitly call for a future-oriented basis for action, but do not imply formalized planning, planning departments, planning cycles, or a specified way of visualizing the future. Even if your organization is seeking to create an entirely new business situation, it is still necessary to set and to test the objectives that define and guide critical actions and performance.

■ This Item focuses on competitive leadership, which usually depends upon revenue growth and operational effectiveness. Competitive leadership requires a view of the future that includes not only the markets or segments in which your organization competes, but also how it competes. *How it competes* presents many options and requires that you understand your organization's and your competitors' strengths and weaknesses. Although no specific time horizon is included, the thrust of this Item is sustained competitive leadership.

■ An increasingly important part of strategic planning is projecting the competitive environment. Such projections help to detect and reduce competitive threats, to shorten reaction time, and to identify opportunities. Depending on the size and type of business, maturity of markets, pace of change, and competitive parameters (such as price or innovation rate), organizations might use a variety of modeling, scenario, or other techniques and judgments to project the competitive environment.

2.2 Strategy Deployment

Purpose

This Item examines how your organization translates your strategic objectives into action plans to accomplish the objectives and to enable assessment of progress relative to your action plans. The aim is to ensure that your strategies are deployed for goal achievement.

Requirements

You are asked how you develop action plans that address your organization's key strategic objectives. You are asked to summarize your key short- and longer-term action plans. Particular attention is given to products/services, customers/markets, human resource requirements, and resource allocations.

You also are asked to specify key measures and/or indicators used in tracking progress relative to the action plans and how you communicate and align strategic objectives, action plans, and performance.

Finally, you are asked to provide a two-to-five year projection of key performance measures and/or indicators, including key performance targets and/or goals. This projected performance is the basis for comparing past performance and performance relative to competitors and benchmarks, as appropriate.

Comments

■ This Item calls for information on how your action plans are developed and deployed. Accomplishment of action plans requires the definition of resource requirements and performance measures, as well as aligning work unit, supplier, and/or partner plans. Of central importance is how you achieve alignment and consistency — for example, via key processes and key measurements. Also, alignment and consistency are intended to provide a basis for setting and communicating priorities for ongoing improvement activities — part of the daily work of all work units. In addition, performance measures are critical to performance tracking. Critical action plan resource requirements include human resource plans that support your overall strategy.

■ Examples of possible human resource plan elements are:
- redesign of your work organization and/or jobs to increase employee empowerment and decision making;
- initiatives to promote greater labor-management cooperation, such as union partnerships;
- initiatives to foster knowledge sharing and organizational learning;
- modification of your compensation and recognition systems to recognize team, organizational, stock market, customer, or other performance attributes; and

- education and training initiatives, such as developmental programs for future leaders, partnerships with universities to help ensure the availability of future employees, and/or establishment of technology-based training capabilities.

■ Projections and comparisons in this Item are intended to encourage your organization to improve its ability to understand and track dynamic, competitive performance factors. Through this tracking process, your organization should be better prepared to take into account its rate of improvement and change relative to competitors and relative to your own targets or stretch goals. Such tracking serves as a key diagnostic management tool.

■ In addition to improvement relative to past performance and to competitors, projected performance also might include changes resulting from new business ventures, entry into new markets, product/service innovations, or other strategic thrusts.

Customer and Market Focus (Category 3)

Customer and Market Focus addresses how your organization seeks to understand the voices of customers and of the marketplace. The Category stresses relationships as an important part of an overall listening, learning, and performance excellence strategy. Your customer satisfaction and dissatisfaction results provide vital information for understanding your customers and the marketplace. In many cases, such results and trends provide the most meaningful information, not only on your customers' views but also on their marketplace behaviors — repeat business and positive referrals.

3.1 Customer and Market Knowledge

Purpose

This Item examines your organization's key processes for gaining knowledge about your current and future customers and markets, with the aim of offering relevant products and services, understanding emerging customer requirements and expectations, and keeping pace with changing markets and marketplaces.

Requirements

You are asked how you determine key customer groups and how you segment your markets. You are asked how you consider potential customers, including your competitors' customers. You are asked how you determine key requirements and drivers of purchase decisions, and how you determine key product/service features. These factors are likely to differ for different customer groups and market segments. Knowledge of customer groups and market segments allows your organization to tailor listening and learning strategies and marketplace offerings, to support your marketing strategies, and to develop new business.

Finally, you are asked how you improve your customer listening and learning strategies so that you can keep current with your changing business needs and directions.

Comments

■ In a rapidly changing competitive environment, many factors may affect customer preference and loyalty and your interface with customers in the marketplace. This makes it necessary to listen and learn on a continuous basis. To be effective as an organization, listening and learning need to be closely linked with your organization's overall business strategy and strategy-setting process.

■ A relationship strategy may be possible with some customers but not with others. Differing relationships may require very different listening and learning strategies. The use of electronic commerce is rapidly changing many marketplaces and may affect your listening and learning strategies as well as your definition of customer groups and market segments.

■ Selection of listening and learning strategies depends on your organization's key business factors. Some frequently used strategies include: focus groups with key customers; close integration with key customers; interviews with lost customers about their purchase decisions; use of the customer complaint process to understand key product and service attributes; won/lost analysis relative to competitors; and survey/feedback information, including use of the Internet.

3.2 *Customer Satisfaction and Relationships*

Purpose

This Item examines your organization's processes for determining customer satisfaction and building customer relationships, with the aim of acquiring new customers, retaining existing customers, and developing new opportunities.

Requirements

You are asked how you provide easy access for customers and potential customers to seek information or assistance and/or to comment and complain. You are asked how customer contact requirements are determined and deployed. You also are asked how your organization aggregates, analyzes, and learns from complaint information. Prompt and effective response and solutions to customer needs and desires are a source of satisfaction and loyalty.

You are asked how you build relationships with your customers since business success, business development, and product/service innovation increasingly depend on maintaining close relationships with your customers.

You are asked how you keep your approaches to all aspects of customer relationships current with changing business needs and directions since approaches to and bases for relationships may change quickly.

You also are asked about your satisfaction and dis-satisfaction determination processes and how they differ for different customer groups because satisfied customers are a requirement for loyalty, repeat business, and positive referrals.

Finally, you are asked how you follow up with customers regarding products, services, and recent transactions, and how you determine the customers' satisfaction relative to competitors so that you may improve future performance.

Comments

- This Item emphasizes how you obtain actionable information from customers. To be actionable, you should be able to tie the information to key business processes, and you should be able to determine cost/revenue implications for improvement priority setting.

- Complaint aggregation, analysis, and root cause determination should lead to effective elimination of the causes of complaints and to priority setting for process, product, and service improvements. Successful outcomes require effective deployment of information throughout the organization.

- A key aspect of customer satisfaction determination is satisfaction relative to competitors and competing or alternative offerings. Such information might be derived from your own comparative studies or from independent studies. The factors that lead to customer preference are of critical importance in understanding factors that drive markets and potentially affect longer-term competitiveness.

Information and Analysis (Category 4)

Information and Analysis is the main point within the Criteria for all key information to effectively measure performance and manage your organization, and to drive improvement of performance and competitiveness. In the simplest terms, Category 4 is the "brain center" for the alignment of your organization's operations and its strategic directions. However, since information and analysis might themselves be primary sources of competitive advantage and productivity growth, the Category also includes such strategic considerations.

4.1 *Measurement of Organizational Performance*

Purpose

This Item examines your organization's selection, management, and use of data and information for performance measurement, in support of organizational planning and performance improvement. The aim is to serve as a key foundation for your functioning as a high performing organization.

Requirements

You are asked how you establish the major components of an effective performance measurement system for your organization. You are asked how you select and use measures for tracking daily operations and how you select and integrate measures for monitoring overall organizational performance. You also are asked how you ensure data and information reliability since reliability is critical to successful monitoring of operations and to successful data integration for assessing overall performance.

You are asked how you select and use competitive comparisons and benchmarking information to help drive performance improvement.

Finally, you are asked how you keep your organization's performance measurement system current with changing business needs.

Comments

- Alignment and integration are key concepts for success-ful implementation of your performance measurement system. They are viewed in terms of extent and effectiveness of use to meet your performance assessment needs. Alignment and integration include how measures are aligned throughout your organization, how they are integrated to yield organization-wide measures, and how performance measurement requirements are deployed by your senior

leaders to track work group and process level performance on key measures targeted for organization-wide significance and/or improvement.

- Performance data and information are especially important in business networks, alliances, and supply chains. Your responses to this Item should take into account this strategic use of data and information, and should recognize the need for rapid data validation and reliability assurance given the increasing use of electronic data transfer.

- The use of competitive and comparative information is important to all organizations. The major premises for using competitive and comparative information are: (1) your organization needs to know where it stands relative to competitors and to best practices; (2) comparative and benchmarking information often provides the impetus for significant ("breakthrough") improvement or change; and (3) preparation for comparing performance information frequently leads to a better understanding of your processes and their performance. Benchmarking information also may support business analysis and decisions relating to core competencies, alliances, and outsourcing.

- Your effective selection and use of competitive comparisons and benchmarking information require: (1) determination of needs and priorities; (2) criteria for seeking appropriate sources for comparisons — from within and outside your organization's industry and markets; and (3) use of data and information to set stretch targets and to promote major, non-incremental

improvements in areas most critical to your organization's competitive strategy.

4.2 *Analysis of Organizational Performance*

Purpose

This Item examines your organization's analysis of its performance, as a basis for assessing your overall organizational health. The Item serves as a central analysis point in an integrated performance measurement and management system that relies on financial and nonfinancial data and information. The aim of analysis is to guide your organization's process management toward the achievement of key business results and strategic objectives.

Requirements

You are asked how you analyze data and information from all parts of your organization to support your senior leaders' assessment of overall organizational health, your organizational planning, and your daily operations.

Comments

- Individual facts and data do not usually provide an effective basis for organizational priority setting. This Item emphasizes that close alignment is needed between your analysis and your organizational performance review and between your analysis and your organizational planning. This ensures that analysis is relevant to decision making and that decision making is based on relevant facts.

- Action depends upon understanding cause/effect connections among processes and between processes and business/performance results. Process actions and their results may have many resource implications. Organizations have a critical need to provide an effective analytical basis for decisions because resources for improvement are limited and cause/effect connections are often unclear.

- Analyses that your organization conducts to gain an understanding of performance and needed actions may vary widely, depending upon your type of organization, size, competitive environment, and other factors. Examples of possible analyses include:

  - how product and service quality improvement correlates with key customer indicators such as customer satisfaction, customer retention, and market share;
  - cost/revenue implications of customer-related problems and problem resolution effectiveness;
  - interpretation of market share changes in terms of customer gains and losses and changes in customer satisfaction;
  - improvement trends in key operational performance indicators such as productivity, cycle time, waste reduction, new product introduction, and defect levels;
  - relationships between employee/organizational learning and value added per employee;
  - financial benefits derived from improvements in employee safety, absenteeism, and turnover;
  - benefits and costs associated with education and training;
  - benefits and costs associated with improved organizational knowledge management and sharing;
  - how the ability to identify and meet employee requirements correlates with employee retention, motivation, and productivity;
  - cost/revenue implications of employee-related problems and effective problem resolution;
  - individual or aggregate measures of productivity and quality relative to competitors;
  - cost trends relative to competitors;
  - relationships between product/service quality, operational performance indicators, and overall financial performance trends as reflected in indicators such as operating costs, revenues, asset utilization, and value added per employee;
  - allocation of resources among alternative improvement projects based on cost/revenue implications and improvement potential;
  - net earnings derived from quality/operational/human resource performance improvements;

  - comparisons among business units showing how quality and operational performance improvement affect financial performance;
  - contributions of improvement activities to cash flow, working capital use, and shareholder value;
  - profit impacts of customer retention;
  - cost/revenue implications of new market entry, including global market entry or expansion;
  - cost/revenue, customer, and productivity implications of engaging in and/or expanding electronic commerce;
  - market share versus profits; and
  - trends in economic, market, and shareholder indicators of value.

Human Resource Focus (Category 5)

Human Resource Focus addresses key human resource practices — those directed toward creating a high performance workplace and toward developing employees to enable them and your organization to adapt to change. The Category covers human resource development and management requirements in an integrated way, that is, aligned with your organization's strategic directions. Included in the focus on human resources is a focus on your work environment and your employee support climate.

To ensure the basic alignment of human resource management with overall strategy, the Criteria also include human resource planning as part of organizational planning in the Strategic Planning Category.

5.1 Work Systems

Purpose

This Item examines your organization's systems for work and job design, compensation, employee performance management, motivation, recognition, communication, and hiring, with the aim of enabling and encouraging all employees to contribute effectively and to the best of their ability. These systems are intended to foster high performance, to result in individual and organizational learning, and to enable adaptation to change.

Requirements

You are asked how you design work and jobs to allow employees to exercise discretion and decision making, resulting in high performance.

You are asked how you encourage and motivate employees, how you manage employee performance, how you compensate, recognize, and reward employees, and how you ensure effective communication and cooperation, all in support of high performance and employee well-being and loyalty.

Finally, you are asked how you profile, recruit, and hire employees who will meet your expectations and needs.

This requirement entails ensuring that the work force is reflective of your key communities. The right work force is an enabler of high performance.

Comments

- High performance work is characterized by flexibility, innovation, knowledge and skill sharing, alignment with organizational objectives, customer focus, and rapid response to changing business needs and requirements of the marketplace. The focus of this Item is on a work force capable of achieving high performance. In addition to the enabled employees and proper work system design, high performance work requires ongoing education and training, and information systems that ensure proper information flow. To help employees realize their full potential, many organizations use individual development plans developed with each employee and addressing his/her career and learning objectives.

- Factors for your consideration in work and job design include simplification of job classifications, cross-training, job rotation, use of teams (including self-directed teams), and changes in work layout and location. Also important is effective communication across functions and work units to ensure a focus on customer requirements and to ensure an environment with trust, knowledge sharing, and mutual respect.

- Compensation and recognition systems should be matched to your work systems. To be effective, compensation and recognition might be tied to demonstrated skills and/or to peer evaluations. Compensation and recognition approaches also might include profit sharing, team or unit performance, and linkage to customer satisfaction and loyalty measures or other business objectives.

5.2 *Employee Education, Training, and Development*

Purpose

This Item examines your organization's work force education, training, and on-the-job reinforcement of knowledge and skills, with the aim of meeting ongoing needs of employees and a high performance workplace.

Requirements

You are asked how education and training are designed, delivered, reinforced on the job, and evaluated, with special emphasis placed on meeting individual career progression and organizational business needs. You are asked how you consider job and organizational performance in education and training design and evaluation in support of a fact-based management system.

You are asked how employees and their supervisors participate in the needs determination, design, and evaluation of education and training, because these individuals frequently are best able to identify critical needs and evaluate success. You also are asked how employees and supervisors use performance measures and standards to ensure performance excellence in education and training.

Finally, you are asked about your organization's key developmental and training needs, including such high priority needs as management/leadership development, diversity training, and safety. Succession planning and leadership development, at all levels in increasingly diverse organizations, present a growing challenge and need.

Comments

- Depending on the nature of your organization's work and employees' responsibilities and stage of organizational and personal development, education and training needs might vary greatly. These needs might include knowledge sharing skills, communications, teamwork, problem solving, interpreting and using data, meeting customer requirements, process analysis and simplification, waste and cycle time reduction, and priority setting based on strategic alignment or cost/benefit analysis. Education needs also might include basic skills, such as reading, writing, language, and arithmetic.

- Education and training delivery might occur inside or outside your organization and could involve on-the-job, classroom, computer-based, distance learning, or other types of delivery. Training also might occur through developmental assignments within or outside your organization.

- When you evaluate education and training, you should seek effectiveness measures as a critical component of evaluation. Such measures might address impact on individual, unit, and organizational performance, impact on customer-related performance, and cost/benefit analysis of the training.

- Although this Item does not specifically ask you about training for customer contact employees, such training is increasingly important and common. It frequently includes: acquiring critical knowledge and skills with respect to your products, services, and customers; skills on how to listen to customers; recovery from problems or failures; and learning how to effectively manage customer expectations.

5.3 Employee Well-Being and Satisfaction

Purpose

This Item examines your organization's work environment, your employee support climate, and how you determine employee satisfaction, with the aim of fostering the well-being, satisfaction, and motivation of all employees, recognizing their diverse needs.

Requirements

You are asked how you ensure a safe and healthful work environment for all employees, taking into account their differing work environments and associated requirements. Special emphasis is placed on how employees contribute to identifying important factors and to improving workplace safety. You also are asked to identify appropriate measures and targets for key environmental factors so that status and progress can be tracked.

You are asked how you enhance employee well-being, satisfaction, and motivation based upon a holistic view of this key stakeholder group. Special emphasis is placed on the variety of approaches you use to satisfy a diverse work force with differing needs and expectations.

Finally, you are asked how you assess employee well-being, satisfaction, and motivation, and how you relate assessment findings to key business results to set improvement priorities.

Comments

- Most organizations, regardless of size, have many opportunities to contribute to employee well-being, satisfaction, and motivation. Some examples of services, facilities, activities, and other opportunities are personal and career counseling; career development and employability services; recreational or cultural activities; formal and informal recognition; non-work-related education; day care; special leave for family responsibilities and/or community service; flexible work hours and benefits packages; outplacement services; and retiree benefits, including extended health care and access to employee services.

- Although satisfaction with pay and promotion is important, these two factors are generally not sufficient to ensure overall employee satisfaction, motivation, and high performance. Some examples of other factors to consider are effective employee problem and grievance resolution; employee development and career opportunities; work environment and management support; workload; communication, cooperation, and teamwork; job security; appreciation of the differing needs of diverse employee groups; and organizational support for serving customers.

- In addition to direct measurement of employee satisfaction and well-being through formal or informal surveys, some other indicators of satisfaction and well-being include: absenteeism, turnover, grievances, strikes, OSHA reportables, and worker's compensation claims.

Process Management (Category 6)

Process Management is the focal point within the Criteria for all key work processes. Built into the Category are the central requirements for efficient and effective process management — effective design; a prevention orientation; linkage to suppliers and partners; operational performance; cycle time; and evaluation, continuous improvement, and organizational learning.

Flexibility, cost reduction, and cycle time reduction are increasingly important in all aspects of process management and organizational design. In simplest terms, flexibility refers to your ability to adapt quickly and effectively to changing requirements. Depending on the nature of your organization's strategy and markets, flexibility might mean rapid changeover from one product to another, rapid response to changing demands, or the ability to produce a wide range of customized services. Flexibility might demand special strategies such as implementing modular designs, sharing components, sharing manufacturing lines, and providing specialized training. Flexibility also increasingly involves outsourcing decisions, agreements with key suppliers, and novel partnering arrangements.

Cost and cycle time reduction often involve many of the same process management strategies as achieving flexibility. Thus, it is crucial to utilize key measures for these requirements in your overall process management.

6.1 Product and Service Processes

Purpose

This Item examines your organization's key product and service design and delivery processes, with the aim of improving your marketplace and operational performance.

Requirements

You are asked to identify your key design processes for products and services and their related production and delivery processes. You are asked how you address key requirements, such as customer/market requirements and new technology. You also are asked how you address key factors in design effectiveness, including cost control, cycle time, and learning from past design projects. Finally, you are asked how you ensure that design processes cover all key operational performance requirements and appropriate coordination and testing to ensure effective product/service launch.

You are asked to identify your key production/delivery processes, their key performance requirements, and key performance measures. These requirements and measures are the basis for maintaining and improving your products, services, and production/delivery processes. Finally, you are asked how you improve your production/delivery processes to achieve better processes and products/services.

Comments

- Your design approaches could differ appreciably depending upon the nature of your products/services — whether the products/services are entirely new, variants, or involve major or minor process changes. You should consider the key requirements for your products and services. Factors that might need to be considered in design include: safety; long-term performance; environmental impact; "green" manufacturing; measurement capability; process capability; manufacturability; maintainability; supplier capability; and documentation. Effective design also must consider cycle time and productivity of production and delivery processes. This might involve detailed mapping of manufacturing or service processes and redesigning ("reengineering") those processes to achieve efficiency, as well as to meet changing customer requirements.

- Many organizations need to consider requirements for suppliers and/or business partners at the design stage. Overall, effective design must take into account all stakeholders in the value chain. If many design projects are carried out in parallel, or if your organization's products utilize parts, equipment, and facilities that are used for other products, coordination of resources might be a major concern, but might offer means to significantly reduce unit costs and time to market.

- Coordination of design and production/delivery processes involves all work units and/or individuals who will take part in production/delivery and whose performance materially affects overall process outcome. This might include groups such as research and development (R&D), marketing, design, and product/process engineering.

- This Item calls for information on the management and improvement of key production/delivery processes. The information required includes a description of the key processes, their specific requirements, and how performance relative to these requirements is determined and maintained. Specific reference is made to in-process measurements and customer interactions. These measurements and interactions require the identification of critical points in processes for measurement, observation, or interaction. These activities should occur at the earliest points possible in processes to minimize problems and costs that may result from deviations from expected performance. Expected performance frequently requires setting performance levels or standards to guide decision making. When deviations occur, corrective action is required to restore the performance of the process to its design specifications. Depending on the nature of the process, the corrective action could involve technical and/or human considerations. Proper corrective action involves changes at the source (root cause) of the deviation. Such corrective action should minimize the likelihood of this type of variation occurring again or anywhere else in your organization. When customer interactions are involved, differences among customers must be considered in evaluating how well the process is performing. This might entail specific or general contingencies, depending on the customer information gathered. This is especially true of professional and personal services.

- This Item also calls for information on how processes are improved to achieve better performance. Better performance means not only better quality from your customers' perspective but also better financial and operational performance — such as productivity — from your organization's perspective. A variety of process improvement approaches are commonly used. These approaches include: (1) sharing successful strategies across your organization; (2) process analysis and research (e.g., process mapping, optimization experiments, and error proofing); (3) research and development results; (4) benchmarking; (5) using alternative technology; and (6) using information from customers of the processes — within and outside of your organization. Process improvement approaches might utilize financial data to evaluate alternatives and set priorities. Together, these approaches offer a wide range of possibilities, including complete redesign ("reengineering") of processes.

6.2 *Support Processes*

Purpose

This Item examines your organization's key support processes, with the aim of improving your overall operational performance.

Requirements

You are asked to identify your key support processes and their design requirements. You are asked how your organization's key support processes are designed to meet all your requirements and how you incorporate input from internal and external customers, as appropriate.

You also are asked how day-to-day operation of your key support processes ensures meeting the key requirements, including how in-process measures and/or customer feedback are used.

Finally, you are asked how you improve your key support processes to achieve better performance and to keep them current with your changing business needs and directions.

Comments

■ Your support processes are those that support product and/or service delivery, but are not usually designed in detail with the products and services. The support process requirements usually do not depend significantly upon product and service characteristics. Support process design requirements usually depend significantly upon your internal requirements, and they must be coordinated and integrated to ensure efficient and effective linkage and performance. Support processes might include finance and accounting, software services, sales, marketing, public relations, information services, personnel, legal services, plant and facilities management, research and development, and secretarial and other administrative services.

■ This Item calls for information on how your organization evaluates and improves the performance of your key support processes. Four approaches frequently used are: (1) process analysis and research; (2) benchmarking; (3) use of alternative technology; and (4) use of information from customers of the processes — within and outside your organization. Together, these approaches offer a wide range of possibilities, including complete redesign ("reengineering") of processes.

6.3 *Supplier and Partnering Processes*

Purpose

This Item examines your organization's key supplier and partnering processes and relationships, with the aim of improving your performance and your suppliers' performance.

Requirements

You are asked to identify the key products and services that you obtain from suppliers and partners to understand the nature and business criticality of these supplies. You are asked for your key performance requirements and measures for suppliers and partners, and how you use these requirements and measures in managing and improving performance. These performance requirements and associated measures should be the principal factors you use in making purchases (e.g., quality, timeliness, and price).

You are asked how you provide actionable feedback and how you minimize costs associated with acceptance testing, two components of a system for supplier/partner relationship building and process improvement. You also are asked how you provide your suppliers and partners with assistance and incentives, which will contribute to improvements in their performance and your performance.

Finally, you are asked how you improve your supplier and partnering processes so that you and your suppliers can keep current with your changing business needs and directions.

Comments

■ Suppliers and partners are receiving increasing focus as many organizations re-evaluate their core functions and the potential for better overall performance through strategic use of suppliers and partners. As a result, supply chain management is a growing factor in many organizations' productivity, profitability, and overall business success.

■ In identifying key suppliers and partners, you should consider goods and services used in the design, production, delivery, and use of your organization's products and services, i.e., consider both upstream and downstream suppliers and partners.

■ The Item places particular emphasis on the unique relationships that lead to high performance. Electronic data and information exchange is fostering new modes of communication and new types of relationships that can support high performance on the part of suppliers and customers. You are encouraged to focus on actions that will not only improve supplier performance, but actions that will enable them to contribute to your improved performance. In addition to electronic information exchange, such actions might include one

or more of the following: improving your procurement and supplier management processes; joint planning; customer-supplier teams; training; long-term agreements; and recognition. Your supplier management planning might include changes in supplier selection, leading to a reduction in the number of suppliers and an increase in preferred supplier and partnership agreements.

Business Results (Category 7)

The Business Results Category provides a results focus that encompasses your customers' evaluation of your organization's products and services, your overall financial and market performance, and results of all key processes and process improvement activities. Through this focus, the Criteria's dual purposes — superior value of offerings as viewed by your customers and the marketplace, and superior organizational performance reflected in your operational and financial indicators — are maintained. Category 7 thus provides "real-time" information (measures of progress) for evaluation and improvement of processes, products, and services, aligned with your overall organizational strategy. Item 4.2 calls for analysis of business results data and information to determine your overall organizational performance.

7.1 Customer Focused Results

Purpose

This Item examines your organization's customer focused performance results, with the aim of demonstrating how well your organization has been satisfying your customers and delivering product and service quality that lead to satisfaction and loyalty.

Requirements

You are asked to provide current levels, trends, and appropriate comparisons for key measures and/or indicators of customer satisfaction, dissatisfaction, and satisfaction relative to competitors. You are asked to provide data and information on customer loyalty (retention), positive referral, and customer-perceived value.

You also are asked to provide levels and trends in key measures and/or indicators of product and service performance. Such results should be for key drivers of your customers' satisfaction and retention.

Comments

- This Item focuses on the creation and use of all relevant data to determine and help predict your organization's performance as viewed by your customers. Relevant data and information include: customer satisfaction and dissatisfaction; retention, gains, and losses of customers and customer accounts; customer complaints and warranty claims; customer-perceived value based on quality and price; and awards, ratings, and recognition from customers and independent rating organizations.

- The Item includes measures of product and service performance that serve as indicators of customers' views and decision making relative to future purchases and relationships. These measures of product and service performance are derived from customer-related information gathered in Items 3.1 and 3.2 ("listening posts").

- Product and service measures appropriate for inclusion might be based upon the following: internal quality measurements; field performance of products; data collected from your customers by other organizations on ease of use or other attributes; or customer surveys on product and service performance.

- The correlation between product/service performance and customer indicators is a critical management tool — for defining and focusing on key quality and customer requirements and for identifying product/service differentiators in the marketplace. The correlation might reveal emerging or changing market segments, the changing importance of requirements, or even the potential obsolescence of offerings.

7.2 *Financial and Market Results*

Purpose

This Item examines your organization's financial and market results, with the aim of understanding your marketplace challenges and opportunities.

Requirements

You are asked to provide levels, trends, and appropriate comparisons for key financial, market, and business indicators. Overall, these results should provide a complete picture of your financial and marketplace success and challenges.

Comments

- Measures reported in this Item are those usually tracked by senior leadership on an ongoing basis to assess your organization's performance.

- Appropriate financial measures and indicators might include: revenue, profits, market position, cash-to-cash cycle time, earnings per share, and returns measures. Marketplace performance measures might include: market share, measures of business growth, new product and geographic markets entered (including exports), and percent new product sales.

7.3 *Human Resource Results*

Purpose

This Item examines your organization's human resource results, with the aim of demonstrating how well your organization has been creating and maintaining a positive, productive, learning, and caring work environment.

Requirements

You are asked to provide current levels, trends, and appropriate comparisons for key measures and/or indicators of employee well-being, satisfaction, dissatisfaction, and development.

You also are asked to provide data and information on your organization's work system performance and effectiveness.

Comments

- Results reported might include generic or organization-specific factors. Generic factors might include: safety, absenteeism, turnover, satisfaction, and complaints (grievances). For some measures, such as absenteeism and turnover, local or regional comparisons are appropriate.

- Organization-specific factors are those you assess for determining your employees' well-being and satisfaction. These factors might include: extent of training or cross-training, or extent and success of self-direction.

- Results measures reported for work system performance might include improvement in job classification, job rotation, work layout, and local decision making. Results reported might include input data, such as extent of training, but the main emphasis should be on data that show effectiveness of outcomes.

7.4 *Supplier and Partner Results*

Purpose

This Item examines your organization's supplier and partner results, with the aims of demonstrating how well your organization ensures the quality, delivery, and price of externally provided goods and services and how your suppliers/partners contribute to your improved performance.

Requirements

You are asked to provide current levels, trends, and appropriate comparisons for key measures and/or indicators of supplier and partner performance, including how their performance affects your improved performance. You should emphasize your most critical requirements for business success.

Comments

- Suppliers and partners provide goods and services "upstream" and "downstream." Data reported should reflect results by whatever means they occur — via improvements by suppliers and partners and/or through better selection of suppliers and partners.

- For purposes of this Item, providers of goods and services within your parent organization, but not in your own organization, should be included as suppliers or partners.

- Results reported might include: quality levels, cost savings, total supply chain management costs, reductions in waste, reductions in inventory, reductions in cycle time, and increases in productivity. Indicators of better connection and communication, such as achieved via electronic commerce or data exchanges, are appropriate for inclusion. Indicators of supplier and partner performance improvement via external compliance, such as ISO 9000 and Y2K readiness, also are appropriate for inclusion.

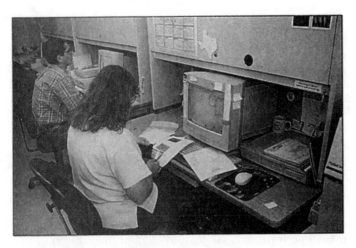

7.5 *Organizational Effectiveness Results*

Purpose

This Item examines your organization's other key operational performance results, with the aim of achieving organizational effectiveness and key organizational goals.

Requirements

You are asked to provide current levels, trends, and appropriate comparisons for key measures and/or indicators of operational and strategic performance that support the ongoing achievement of results reported in Items 7.1 through 7.4.

You also are asked to provide data and information on your organization's regulatory/legal compliance and citizenship.

Comments

- This Item encourages your organization to develop and include unique and innovative measures to track business development and operational improvement. However, all key areas of business and operational performance should be covered by measures that are relevant and important to your organization.

- Measures and/or indicators of operational effectiveness and efficiency might include: reduced emission levels, waste stream reductions, by-product use, and recycling; internal responsiveness indicators such as cycle times, production flexibility, lead times, set-up times, and time to market; business-specific indicators such as innovation rates, product/process yields, and delivery performance to request; third-party assessment results such as ISO 9000 audits; and indicators of strategic goal achievement.

- Measures should include environmental and regulatory compliance and noteworthy achievements in these areas, as appropriate. Results also should include indicators of support for key communities and other public purposes.

- If your organization has received sanctions or adverse actions under law, regulation, or contract during the past three years, the incidents and current status should be summarized.

Scoring System

The scoring of responses to Criteria Items (Items) and Award applicant feedback are based on three evaluation dimensions: (1) Approach; (2) Deployment; and (3) Results. Criteria users need to furnish information relating to these dimensions. Specific factors for these dimensions are described below. Scoring Guidelines are given on page 45.

Approach

Approach refers to how you address the Item requirements — the *method(s)* used. The factors used to evaluate approaches include:

- appropriateness of the methods to the requirements
- effectiveness of use of the methods. Degree to which the approach:
  - is repeatable, integrated, and consistently applied
  - embodies evaluation/improvement/learning cycles
  - is based on reliable information and data
- alignment with your organizational needs
- evidence of innovation

Deployment

Deployment refers to the *extent* to which your approach is applied to all requirements of the Item. The factors used to evaluate deployment include:

- use of the approach in addressing Item requirements relevant to your organization
- use of the approach by all appropriate work units

Results

Results refers to *outcomes* in achieving the purposes given in the Item. The factors used to evaluate results include:

- your current performance
- performance relative to appropriate comparisons and/or benchmarks
- rate, breadth, and importance of your performance improvements
- linkage of your results measures to key customer, market, process, and action plan performance requirements identified in your Business Overview and in Approach/Deployment Items

Item Classification and Scoring Dimensions

Items are classified according to the kinds of information and/or data you are expected to furnish relative to the three evaluation dimensions.

The two types of Items and their designations are:

1. Approach/Deployment   **Approach - Deployment**
2. Results   **Results**

Approach and Deployment are linked to emphasize that descriptions of Approach should always indicate the Deployment — consistent with the *specific requirements*
of the Item. Although Approach and Deployment dimensions are linked, feedback to Award applicants reflects strengths and/or opportunities for improvement in either or both dimensions.

Results Items call for data showing performance levels and trends on key measures and/or indicators of organizational performance. Results Items also call for data on breadth of performance improvements — how widespread your improvement results are. This is directly related to the Deployment dimension. That is, if improvement processes are widely deployed, there should be corresponding results. A score for a Results Item is thus a composite based upon overall performance, taking into account the breadth of improvements and their importance. (See next paragraph.)

"Importance" as a Scoring Factor

The three evaluation dimensions described previously are critical to evaluation and feedback. However, evaluation and feedback also must consider the importance of your reported Approach, Deployment, and Results to your key business factors. The areas of greatest importance should be identified in your Business Overview and in Items such as 2.1, 2.2, 3.1, 6.1, and 7.5. Your key customer requirements and key strategic objectives and action plans are particularly important.

Assignment of Scores to Your Responses

The following guidelines should be observed in assigning scores to your Item responses:

- All Areas to Address should be included in your Item response. Also, responses should reflect what is important to your organization;
- In assigning a score to an Item, first decide which scoring range (e.g., 50% to 60%) best fits the overall Item response. Overall "best fit" does not require total agreement with each of the statements for that scoring range. Actual score *within* the range depends upon judgment of the closeness of the Item response in relation to the statements in the next higher and next lower scoring ranges;
- An Approach/Deployment Item score of 50% represents an approach that meets the overall objectives of the Item and that is deployed to the principal activities and work units covered in the Item. Higher scores reflect maturity (cycles of improvement), integration, and broader deployment; and
- A Results Item score of 50% represents a clear indication of improvement trends and/or good levels of performance in the principal results areas covered in the Item. Higher scores reflect better improvement rates and/or levels of performance, and better comparative performance as well as broader coverage and integration with business requirements.

Scoring Guidelines

SCORE	RESULTS
0%	■ no results or poor results in areas reported
10% to 20%	■ some improvements *and/or* early good performance levels in a few areas ■ results not reported for many to most areas of importance to the organization's key business requirements
30% to 40%	■ improvements *and/or* good performance levels in many areas of importance to the organization's key business requirements ■ early stages of developing trends and obtaining comparative information ■ results reported for many to most areas of importance to the organization's key business requirements
50% to 60%	■ improvement trends *and/or* good performance levels reported for most areas of importance to the organization's key business requirements ■ no pattern of adverse trends and no poor performance levels in areas of importance to the organization's key business requirements ■ some trends *and/or* current performance levels — evaluated against relevant comparisons *and/or* benchmarks — show areas of strength *and/or* good to very good relative performance levels ■ business results address most key customer, market, and process requirements
70% to 80%	■ current performance is good to excellent in areas of importance to the organization's key business requirements ■ most improvement trends *and/or* current performance levels are sustained ■ many to most trends *and/or* current performance levels — evaluated against relevant comparisons *and/or* benchmarks — show areas of leadership and very good relative performance levels ■ business results address most key customer, market, process, and action plan requirements
90% to 100%	■ current performance is excellent in most areas of importance to the organization's key business requirements ■ excellent improvement trends *and/or* sustained excellent performance levels in most areas ■ evidence of industry and benchmark leadership demonstrated in many areas ■ business results fully address key customer, market, process, and action plan requirements

SCORE	APPROACH/DEPLOYMENT
0%	■ no systematic approach evident; anecdotal information
10% to 20%	■ beginning of a systematic approach to the basic purposes of the Item ■ major gaps exist in deployment that would inhibit progress in achieving the basic purposes of the Item ■ early stages of a transition from reacting to problems to a general improvement orientation
30% to 40%	■ an effective, systematic approach, responsive to the basic purposes of the Item ■ approach is deployed, although some areas or work units are in early stages of deployment ■ beginning of a systematic approach to evaluation and improvement of basic Item processes
50% to 60%	■ an effective, systematic approach, responsive to the overall purposes of the Item ■ approach is well-deployed, although deployment may vary in some areas or work units ■ a fact-based, systematic evaluation and improvement process is in place for basic Item processes ■ approach is aligned with basic organizational needs identified in the other Criteria Categories
70% to 80%	■ an effective, systematic approach, responsive to the multiple requirements of the Item ■ approach is well-deployed, with no significant gaps ■ a fact-based, systematic evaluation and improvement process and organizational learning/sharing are key management tools; clear evidence of refinement and improved integration as a result of organizational-level analysis and sharing ■ approach is well-integrated with organizational needs identified in the other Criteria Categories
90% to 100%	■ an effective, systematic approach, fully responsive to all the requirements of the Item ■ approach is fully deployed without significant weaknesses or gaps in any areas or work units ■ a very strong, fact-based, systematic evaluation and improvement process and extensive organizational learning/sharing are key management tools; strong refinement and integration, backed by excellent organizational-level analysis and sharing ■ approach is fully integrated with organizational needs identified in the other Criteria Categories

For a definition of the following **key term**, see page 29: systematic.

PREPARING THE BUSINESS OVERVIEW

The Business Overview is an outline of your business. It should address what is most important to the business, key influences on how the business operates, and where the business is headed. *The Business Overview is a statement of what is relevant and important to your organization and its performance.*

The Business Overview is critically important because:

- it is the most appropriate starting point for self-assessment and for writing an application. It helps you focus on key business performance requirements and business results; and

- it is used by the Examiners and Judges in all stages of application review and during the site visit.

It is strongly recommended that the Business Overview be prepared first and that it be used as a guide in self-assessment and in writing and reviewing a Baldrige application.

Guidelines for Preparing the Business Overview

The Business Overview consists of five sections as follows:

1. Basic description of your organization

This section should provide information on:

- your products and services;

- the size and location(s) of your organization and whether it is publicly or privately owned;

- your organizational culture: purpose, vision, mission, and values, as appropriate;

- your major markets: local, regional, national, or international; and principal customer types: consumers, other businesses, government, etc.;

- your employee base, including number, educational level, work force and job diversity, bargaining units, and special safety requirements;

- your major equipment, facilities, and technologies used; and

- the regulatory environment affecting you: occupational health and safety, environmental, financial, and product, etc.

If your organization is a subunit of a larger organization, describe:

- the organizational relationship to your parent and percent of employees the subunit represents;

- how your products and services relate to those of your parent and/or other units of the parent organization; and

- key support services, if any, that your parent organization provides.

2. Customer and market requirements

This section should provide information on:

- key customer and market requirements (for example, on-time delivery, low defect levels, price demands, and after-sales services) for your products and services. Briefly describe all important requirements, and note significant differences, if any, in requirements among customer groups and/or market segments. (Note any special relationships, such as partnerships, with customers or customer groups.)

3. Supplier and partnering relationships

This section should provide information on:

- types and numbers of suppliers of goods and services;

- the most important types of suppliers, dealers, and other businesses; and

- any limitations, special relationships, or special requirements that may exist with some or all suppliers and partners.

4. Competitive situation

This section should provide information on:

- numbers and types of competitors;

- your position (relative size, growth) in the industry;

- principal factors that determine your competitive success, such as productivity growth, cost reduction, and product innovation; and

- changes taking place that affect competition, such as growing global competition.

5. Business directions

This section should provide information, as appropriate, on:

- major new thrusts, such as changes in products or entry into new markets or segments;

- new business alliances;

- introduction of new technologies;

- changes in strategy; and

- unique factors.

Page Limit

For Baldrige Award applicants, the Business Overview is limited to five pages. These are not counted in the overall application page limit. Typing instructions for the Business Overview are the same as for the application. These instructions are given in the *2000 Application Forms & Instructions for Business, Education, and Health Care* booklet. Ordering information is given on page 53.

The guidelines given in this section are offered to assist you, as a Criteria user, in responding most effectively to the requirements of the 19 Criteria Items. Writing an application for the Baldrige Award involves responding to these requirements in 50 or fewer pages.

The guidelines are presented in three parts:

(1) General Guidelines regarding the Criteria booklet, including how the Items are formatted;

(2) Guidelines for Responding to Approach/Deployment Items; and

(3) Guidelines for Responding to Results Items.

General Guidelines

I. Read the entire Criteria booklet.

The main sections of the booklet provide an overall orientation to the Criteria, including how responses are to be evaluated for self-assessment or by Award Examiners. You should become thoroughly familiar with the following sections:

- Criteria for Performance Excellence (pages 10-26)

- Scoring information (pages 44-45)

- Glossary of Key Terms (pages 27-29)

- Category and Item Descriptions (pages 30-43)

2. Review the Item format and understand how to respond to the Item requirements.

The Item format (see figure below) shows the different parts of Items, the significance of each part, and where each part is placed. It is especially important to understand the Areas to Address and the Item Notes. Each Item and Area to Address is described in greater detail in a separate section (pages 30-43).

Each Item is classified either **Approach-Deployment** or **Results**, depending on the type of information required. Guidelines for responding to Approach/Deployment Items are given on pages 48-49. Guidelines for responding to Results Items are given on pages 49-50.

Item requirements are presented in question format, sometimes with modifying statements. Responses to an Item should contain answers to all questions and modifying statements; however, each question need not be separately answered. Responses to multiple questions within a single Area to Address may be grouped, as appropriate to your organization.

3. Start by preparing the Business Overview.

The Business Overview is the most appropriate starting point for initiating a self-assessment or for writing an application. The Business Overview is intended to help everyone — including Criteria users/application writers and reviewers — to understand what is most relevant and important to your organization's business. Guidelines for preparing the Business Overview are given on page 46.

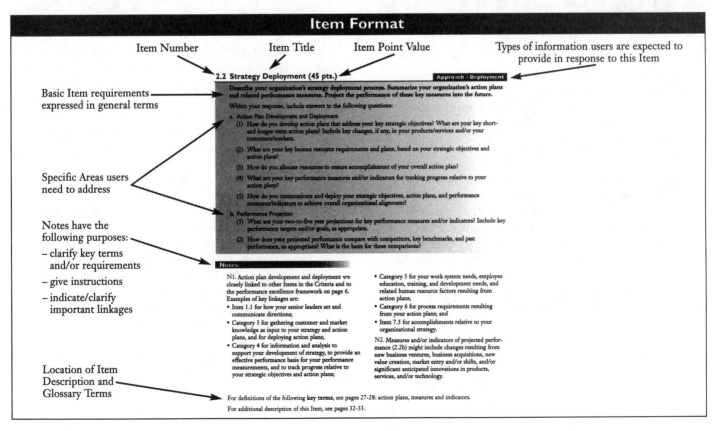

Guidelines for Responding to Approach/Deployment Items

The Criteria focus on key performance results. However, results by themselves offer little *diagnostic* value. For example, if some results are poor or are improving at rates slower than your competition's, it is important to understand *why* this is so and *what* might be done to accelerate improvement.

The purpose of Approach-Deployment Items is to permit diagnosis of your organization's most important processes — the ones that enable fast-paced performance improvement and contribute to key business results. Diagnosis and feedback depend heavily upon the *content and completeness* of Approach-Deployment Item responses. For this reason, it is important to respond to these Items by providing your key process information. Guidelines for organizing and reviewing such information follow.

1. Understand the meaning of *how*.

Items requesting information on approach include questions that begin with the word *how*. *Responses should outline your key process information such as methods, measures, deployment, and evaluation/improvement/learning factors.* Responses lacking such information, or merely providing an example, are referred to in the Scoring Guidelines as *anecdotal information*.

2. Understand the meaning of *what*.

Two types of questions in Approach/Deployment Items begin with the word *what*. The first type of question requests basic information on key processes and how they work. Although it is helpful to include *who* performs the work, merely stating *who* does not permit diagnosis or feedback. The second type of question requests information on *what* are your key findings, plans, objectives, goals, or measures. These questions set the context for showing alignment in your performance management system. For example, when you identify key strategic objectives, your action plans, human resource development plans, and some of your results measures can be expected to relate to the stated strategic objectives.

3. Write and review response(s) with the following guidelines and comments in mind:

- Show that activities are *systematic*.

  Approaches that are systematic are repeatable and use data and information so that improvement and learning are possible. In other words, approaches are systematic if they build in the opportunity for evaluation and learning, and thereby permit a gain in maturity.

- Show deployment.

  Deployment information should summarize what is done in different parts of your organization. Deployment can be shown compactly by using tables.

- Show focus and consistency.

  There are four important factors to consider regarding focus and consistency: (1) the Business Overview should make clear what is important; (2) the Strategic Planning Category, including the strategic objectives and action plans, should highlight areas of greatest focus and describe how deployment is accomplished; (3) descriptions of organizational-level analysis and review (Items 4.2 and 1.1) should show how your organization analyzes and reviews performance information to set priorities; and (4) the Process Management Category should highlight product, service, support, and supplier processes that are key to your overall performance. *Focus and consistency in the Approach-Deployment Items and tracking corresponding measures in the Results Items should improve business performance.*

- Respond fully to Item requirements.

  Missing information will be interpreted as a gap in approach and/or deployment. All Areas to Address should be addressed. Individual components of an Area to Address may be addressed individually or together.

4. Cross-reference when appropriate.

As much as possible, each Item response should be self-contained. However, responses to different Items might be mutually reinforcing. It is then appropriate to refer to the other responses, rather than to repeat information. In such cases, key process information should be given in the Item requesting this information. For example, employee education and training should be described in detail in Item 5.2. References elsewhere to education and training would then reference, but not repeat, this detail.

5. Use a compact format.

Applicants should make the best use of the 50 application pages permitted. Applicants are encouraged to use flowcharts, tables, and "bullets" to present information.

6. Refer to the Scoring Guidelines.

The evaluation of Item responses is accomplished by considering the Criteria Item requirements and the maturity of the approaches, breadth of deployment, and strength of the improvement process relative to the Scoring Guidelines. Therefore, you need to consider both the Criteria and the Scoring Guidelines.

Guidelines for Responding to Results Items

The Criteria place the greatest emphasis on results. The following information, guidelines, and example relate to effective and complete reporting of results.

1. Focus on the most critical business results.

Results reported should cover the most important requirements for your business success, highlighted in your Business Overview, and in the Strategic Planning and Process Management Categories.

2. Note the meaning of the four key requirements from the Scoring Guidelines for effective reporting of results data.

- *trends* to show directions of results and rates of change;

- *performance levels* on a meaningful measurement scale;

- *comparisons* to show how results compare with those of other, appropriately selected organizations; and

- *breadth and importance of results* to show that all important results are included.

3. Include trend data covering actual periods for tracking trends.

No minimum period of time is specified for trend data. Trends might span five years or more for some results. However, for important results, new data should be included even if trends and comparisons are not yet well established.

4. Use a compact format — graphs and tables.

Many results can be reported compactly by using graphs and tables. Graphs and tables should be labeled for easy interpretation. Results over time or compared with others should be "normalized" — presented in a way (such as use of ratios) that takes into account various size factors. For example, reporting safety trends in terms of lost workdays per 100 employees would be more meaningful than total lost workdays, if the number of employees has varied over the time period, or if you are comparing your results to organizations varying in size.

5. Integrate results into the body of the text.

Discussion of results and the results themselves should be close together in an Award application. *Trends that show a significant positive or negative change should be explained.* Use figure numbers that correspond to Items. For example, the third figure for Item 7.1 would be Figure 7.1-3. (See the example in the figure that follows.)

The following graph illustrates data an organization might present as part of a response to Item 7.1, Customer Focused Results. In the Business Overview, the organization has indicated on-time delivery as a key customer requirement.

Using the graph, the following characteristics of clear and effective data reporting are illustrated:

- A figure number is provided for reference to the graph in the text.

- Both axes and units of measure are clearly labeled.

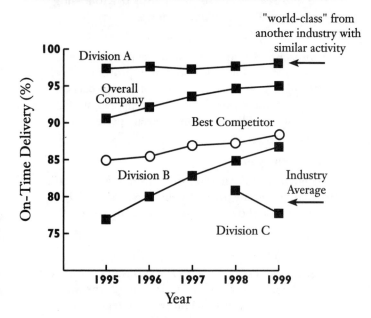

Figure 7.1-3 On-Time Delivery Performance

- Trend lines report data for a key customer requirement — on-time delivery.

- Results are presented for several years.

- Appropriate comparisons are clearly shown.

- The company shows, using a single graph, that its three divisions separately track on-time delivery.

To help interpret the Scoring Guidelines (page 45), the following comments on the graphed results would be appropriate:

- The current overall company performance level is excellent. This conclusion is supported by the comparison with competitors and with a "world-class" level.

- The company shows excellent improvement trends.

- Division A is the current performance leader — showing sustained high performance and a slightly positive trend. Division B shows rapid improvement. Its current performance is near that of the best industry competitor but trails the "world-class" level.

- Division C — a new division — is having early problems with on-time delivery. (The company briefly should explain these early problems.)

The Malcolm Baldrige National Quality Award is an annual Award to recognize U.S. organizations for performance excellence.

The Award promotes:

- awareness of performance excellence as an increasingly important element in competitiveness; and

- information sharing of successful performance strategies and the benefits derived from using these strategies.

Award Participation

The Award eligibility categories include:

- manufacturing businesses

- service businesses

- small businesses

- education institutions

- health care organizations

Copies of the Education Criteria and Health Care Criteria are available, and ordering information can be found on page 53.

Three awards may be given in each category each year.

To participate in the Award process, an organization must submit an application package that addresses the Criteria for Performance Excellence (pages 10-26). Award applicants are expected to provide information and data on their organization's key processes and results. The information and data must be adequate to demonstrate that applicants' approaches are effective and yield desired outcomes.

Application Requirements

Each applicant needs to submit an application package that consists of three parts:

- an Eligibility Determination Form showing that eligibility has been approved;

- a completed Application Form; and

- an application report consisting of a Business Overview and responses to the Criteria.

Detailed information and the necessary forms are contained in the *2000 Application Forms & Instructions for Business, Education, and Health Care* booklet. Ordering instructions for this booklet are given on page 53.

Application Review

Applications are reviewed and evaluated by members of the Board of Examiners, in accord with strict rules regarding conflict of interest, in a four-stage process:

Stage 1 - independent review and evaluation by at least five members of the Board

Stage 2 - consensus review and evaluation for applications that score well in Stage 1

Stage 3 - site visits to applicants that score well in Stage 2

Stage 4 - Judges' review and recommendations of Award recipients

Feedback to Applicants

The feedback report, a tool for continuous improvement, is a written assessment by an evaluation team of leading U.S. experts. Each Award applicant receives a feedback report at the conclusion of the review process.

The feedback report contains an applicant-specific listing of strengths and opportunities for improvement based on the Criteria for Performance Excellence. Used by companies, education institutions, and health care organizations as part of their strategic planning processes, the feedback report helps organizations focus on their customers and improve productivity. The feedback system is one of the most important components of the Baldrige Award process; it provides a pathway for continuous improvement.

Feedback reports are mailed at various times during the Award cycle, based on the stage of review an application reaches in the evaluation process. Strict confidentiality is observed at all times and in every aspect of application review and feedback.

Award Recipients

Award recipients may publicize and advertise their Awards. Recipients are expected to share information about their successful performance strategies with other U.S. organizations.

If your organization is applying in the Education or Health Care Category, refer to the appropriate sector-specific Criteria booklet and the *2000 Application Forms & Instructions for Business, Education, and Health Care*. Ordering information is on page 53.

SUMMARY OF BUSINESS ELIGIBILITY CATEGORIES AND RESTRICTIONS

If You are Considering Applying For the Award:

- These Criteria should be used only for the business eligibility categories (manufacturing, service, and small business).

- The following is only a summary of the eligibility rules for the business categories. Summaries of the eligibility rules for the education and health care categories are in the respective Criteria booklets. For-profit health care organizations or education institutions can apply under the service category using these Criteria or under the health care or education categories, using their respective Criteria. If there is a question on eligibility, check the complete eligibility rules in the 2000 *Application Forms & Instructions for Business, Education, and Health Care*, or call the Baldrige National Quality Program Office at (301) 975-2036.

- Whatever your Award Eligibility Category, you will need to obtain a copy of the 2000 *Application Forms & Instructions for Business, Education, and Health Care* before proceeding. Ordering instructions are given on page 53.

Basic Eligibility

Public Law 100-107 establishes the three business eligibility categories of the Award: manufacturing, service, and small business. Any for-profit business and some subunits head-quartered in the United States or its territories, including U.S. subunits of foreign companies, may apply for the Award. Eligibility is intended to be as open as possible. For example, publicly or privately owned, domestic or foreign owned entities, joint ventures, corporations, sole proprietorships, and holding companies may apply. Not eligible in the business category are: local, state, and federal government agencies; trade associations; professional societies; and not-for-profit organizations.

Business Award Eligibility Categories

Manufacturing: Companies or some subunits (see section below on subunits) that produce and sell manufactured products or manufacturing processes, and producers of agricultural, mining, or construction products.

Service: Companies or some subunits (see section below on subunits) that sell services.

Small Business: Companies or some subunits engaged in manufacturing and/or the provision of services that are comprised of 500 or fewer employees.

Subunits

A subunit is a unit or division of a larger (parent) company. Subunits of companies in the manufacturing, service, or small business eligibility categories might be eligible. The subunit must have more than 500 employees, or have more than 25% of the employees of the parent, or have been independent prior to being acquired by its parent. In the last case, it must continue to operate largely independently under its own identity.

The subunit must be self-sufficient enough to be examined in all seven Criteria Categories, and it must be a discrete business entity that is readily distinguishable from other parts of the parent organization. It cannot be primarily an internal supplier to other units in the parent company or a business support function (sales, distribution, legal services, etc.).

Other Restrictions on Eligibility

Location: Although an applicant may have facilities outside the United States or its territories or receive support from its parent, in the event of a site visit, the applicant must ensure that the appropriate people and materials are available for examination in the United States to document the operational practices associated with all of its major business functions. In the event that the applicant receives the Award, it must be able to share information on the seven Criteria Categories at the Quest for Excellence Conference and at its U.S. facilities. Sharing beyond the Quest for Excellence Conference is on a voluntary basis.

Multiple-Application Restrictions: A subunit and its parent may not both apply for Awards in the same year. In some cases, more than one subunit of a parent may apply. If the employee size of the parent, including all of its subunits, is:

- 0-1000 parent employees, 1 applicant per parent per category may apply;

- 1001-20,000 parent employees, 2 applicants per parent per category may apply;

- Over 20,000 parent employees, 2 applicants per parent per category for the first 20,000, plus 1 per 20,000 or fraction thereof above 20,000 per parent per category may apply.

Future Eligibility Restrictions: If an organization or a subunit that has more than 50% of the total employees of the parent receives an Award, the organization and all its subunits are ineligible to apply for another Award for a period of five years. If a subunit receives an Award, that subunit and all its subunits are ineligible to apply for another Award for a period of five years. After five years, Award recipients are eligible to reapply for the Award or to reapply "for feedback only."

Eligibility Determination

To ensure that Award recipients meet all reasonable requirements and expectations in representing the Award throughout the United States, potential applicants must have their eligibility approved prior to applying for the Award. Potential applicants for the 2000 Award are encouraged to submit their Eligibility Determination Forms as early as possible after they are available, but no later than April 6, 2000. This form is contained in the 2000 *Application Forms & Instructions for Business, Education, and Health Care.*

How to Order Copies of Baldrige Program Materials

Note: If you are planning to apply for the Award, you will need the *2000 Application Forms & Instructions for Business, Education, and Health Care* in addition to the Criteria booklet.

Individual Orders

Individual copies of the Criteria booklets and the Application Forms & Instructions can be obtained free of charge from:

Baldrige National Quality Program
National Institute of Standards and Technology
Administration Building, Room A635
100 Bureau Drive, Stop 1020
Gaithersburg, MD 20899-1020
Telephone: (301) 975-2036
Fax: (301) 948-3716
E-mail: nqp@nist.gov

Bulk Orders

Multiple copies of the *2000 Criteria for Performance Excellence* booklets may be ordered in packets of 10 for $29.95 plus shipping and handling from the American Society for Quality (ASQ).

2000 Business Criteria — Item Number T1101
2000 Education Criteria — Item Number T1103
2000 Health Care Criteria — Item Number T1102

How to Order

ASQ offers four convenient ways to order:

- For fastest service, call toll free (800) 248-1946 in the United States and Canada (in Mexico, dial toll free 95-800-248-1946). Have item numbers, your credit card or purchase order number, and (if applicable) ASQ member number ready.

- Or fax your completed order form to ASQ at (414) 272-1734.

- Or mail your order to: ASQ Customer Service Department, P.O. Box 3066, Milwaukee, WI 53201-3066.

- Or order online by accessing ASQ's website at http://www.asq.org.

Payment

Your payment options include: Check, money order, U.S. purchase order, VISA, MasterCard, or American Express. Payment must be made in U.S. currency; checks and money orders must be drawn on a U.S. financial institution. All international orders must be prepaid. Please make checks payable to ASQ.

Shipping Fees

The following shipping and processing schedule applies to all orders:

Order Amount	U.S. Charges	Canadian Charges
0 - $34.99	$ 4.00	$ 9.00
$35.00 - $99.99	6.25	11.25
Over $100.00	12.50*	17.50

- There is an additional charge of 25% of the total order amount for shipments outside the United States/Canada.

- Orders shipped within the continental United States and Canada where UPS service is available will be shipped UPS.

- Please allow one to two weeks for delivery. International customers, please allow six to eight weeks for delivery.

- Your credit card will not be charged until your items are shipped. Shipping and processing are charged one time, up front, for the entire order.

* If actual shipping charges exceed $12.50 ($17.50 Canadian), ASQ will invoice the customer for the additional expense.

Baldrige Educational Materials

Each year, the Baldrige National Quality Program develops materials for training members of the Board of Examiners and for sharing information on the successful performance excellence strategies of the Award recipients. The following items are a sample of the educational materials that may be ordered from ASQ.

▪ Case Studies

The case studies are used to prepare Examiners for the interpretation of the Criteria and the Scoring System. The case studies, when used with the Criteria, illustrate the Award application and review process. The case study packet is illustrative of an application for the Baldrige Award and is useful in understanding the benefits of the Baldrige process, as well as for self-assessment, planning, training, and other uses.

1999 Business Case Study Packet: Collin Technologies (Based on the *1999 Criteria for Performance Excellence*)

Item Number T1079: $49.95 plus shipping and handling

1998 Business Case Study Packet: Gemini Home Health Services (Based on the *1998 Criteria for Performance Excellence*)

Item Number T1083: $49.95 plus shipping and handling

Education Case Study Packet: Ridgecrest School District (Based on the *1995 Education Pilot Criteria*)

Item Number T1023: $7.28 plus shipping and handling

Health Care Case Study Packet: Pinnacle Health Plan (Based on the *1995 Health Care Pilot Criteria*)

Item Number T1029: $7.28 plus shipping and handling

▪ Award Recipients' Videos

The Award recipients' videos are a valuable resource for gaining a better understanding of performance excellence and quality achievement. The videos provide background information on the Baldrige National Quality Program, highlights from the annual Award ceremony, and interviews with representatives from the Award recipients' organizations. Information on the 1999 Award recipients video is provided below. Videos about Award recipients from other years also are available from ASQ.

1999 — Item Number T1086 $ 20.00
(Available March 2000)

▪ How to Order

To order a Case Study Packet (Collin Technologies, Gemini Home Health Services, Ridgecrest School District, or Pinnacle Health Plan), bulk orders of the 2000 Criteria booklet, or the Award recipients' videos, contact:

ASQ Customer Service Department
P.O. Box 3066
Milwaukee, WI 53201-3066
Telephone: (800) 248-1946
Fax: (414) 272-1734
E-mail: asq@asq.org
Web Address: http://www.asq.org

FEES FOR THE 2000 AWARD CYCLE

Eligibility Determination Fees

The eligibility determination fee is $100 for all potential business applicants. This fee is nonrefundable.

Application Fees

- manufacturing business category — $4500
- service business category — $4500
- small business category — $1500
- supplemental sections — $1500

Detailed information on fees is given in the *2000 Application Forms & Instructions for Business, Education, and Health Care* booklet.

Note: There will be an increase in fees in 2001.

Site Visit Review Fees

Site visit review fees will be set when the visits are scheduled. Fees depend upon the number of Examiners assigned and the duration of the visit. Site visit review fees for applicants in the small business category will be charged at one-half of the rate charged for applicants in the manufacturing and service categories. These fees are paid only by those applicants reaching the site visit stage.

Eligibility Determination Forms due — April 6, 2000
Award Applications due — May 31, 2000

The Baldrige National Quality Program welcomes your comments on the Criteria or any of the Baldrige Award processes. Please address your comments to:

2000 Criteria for Performance Excellence
Baldrige National Quality Program
National Institute of Standards and Technology
Administration Building, Room A635
100 Bureau Drive, Stop 1020
Gaithersburg, MD 20899-1020

or   E-mail: nqp@nist.gov

or   Web Address: http://www.quality.nist.gov

The Malcolm Baldrige National Quality Award was created by Public Law 100-107, signed into law on August 20, 1987. Public Law 100-107 led to the creation of a new public-private partnership. Principal support for the program comes from the Foundation for the Malcolm Baldrige National Quality Award, established in 1988.

The Award is named for Malcolm Baldrige, who served as Secretary of Commerce from 1981 until his death in 1987. His managerial excellence contributed to long-term improvement in efficiency and effectiveness of government.

The Findings and Purposes Section of Public Law 100-107 states that:

" 1. the leadership of the United States in product and process quality has been challenged strongly (and sometimes successfully) by foreign competition, and our Nation's productivity growth has improved less than our competitors' over the last two decades.

2. American business and industry are beginning to understand that poor quality costs companies as much as 20 percent of sales revenues nationally and that improved quality of goods and services goes hand in hand with improved productivity, lower costs, and increased profitability.

3. strategic planning for quality and quality improvement programs, through a commitment to excellence in manufacturing and services, are becoming more and more essential to the well-being of our Nation's economy and our ability to compete effectively in the global marketplace.

4. improved management understanding of the factory floor, worker involvement in quality, and greater emphasis on statistical process control can lead to dramatic improvements in the cost and quality of manufactured products.

5. the concept of quality improvement is directly applicable to small companies as well as large, to service industries as well as manufacturing, and to the public sector as well as private enterprise.

6. in order to be successful, quality improvement programs must be management-led and customer-oriented, and this may require fundamental changes in the way companies and agencies do business.

7. several major industrial nations have successfully coupled rigorous private-sector quality audits with national awards giving special recognition to those enterprises the audits identify as the very best; and

8. a national quality award program of this kind in the United States would help improve quality and productivity by:

   A. helping to stimulate American companies to improve quality and productivity for the pride of recognition while obtaining a competitive edge through increased profits;

   B. recognizing the achievements of those companies that improve the quality of their goods and services and providing an example to others;

   C. establishing guidelines and criteria that can be used by business, industrial, governmental, and other organizations in evaluating their own quality improvement efforts; and

   D. providing specific guidance for other American organizations that wish to learn how to manage for high quality by making available detailed information on how winning organizations were able to change their cultures and achieve eminence."

The Baldrige National Quality Program thanks the following 1998 Award recipients for the use of the photographs in this booklet: Boeing Airlift and Tanker Programs, Solar Turbines Incorporated, and Texas Nameplate Company, Inc.

Baldrige National Quality Program

United States Department of Commerce
Technology Administration
National Institute of Standards and Technology
Baldrige National Quality Program
Administration Building, Room A635
100 Bureau Drive, Stop 1020
Gaithersburg, MD 20899-1020

The National Institute of Standards and Technology (NIST) is a non-regulatory federal agency within the Commerce Department's Technology Administration. NIST's primary mission is to strengthen the U.S. economy and improve the quality of life by working with industry to develop and apply technology, measurements, and standards. The Baldrige National Quality Program at NIST manages the Malcolm Baldrige National Quality Award.

Call the Baldrige National Quality Program for:

- information on applying for the Baldrige Award
- information on the Malcolm Baldrige National Quality Award process and eligibility requirements
- information on becoming a Baldrige Examiner
- information on the Baldrige Award recipients
- individual copies of the Criteria for Business, Education, and Health Care (no cost)
- information on other Baldrige National Quality Program materials

Telephone: (301) 975-2036; Fax: (301) 948-3716; E-mail: nqp@nist.gov
Web Address: http://www.quality.nist.gov

American Society for Quality
611 East Wisconsin Avenue
P.O. Box 3005
Milwaukee, WI 53201-3005

The American Society for Quality (ASQ) advances individual and organizational performance excellence worldwide by providing opportunities for learning, quality improvement, and knowledge exchange. ASQ administers the Malcolm Baldrige National Quality Award under contract to NIST.

Call ASQ to order:

- bulk copies of the Criteria
- case studies
- Award recipients' videos

Telephone: (800) 248-1946; Fax: (414) 272-1734; E-mail: asq@asq.org
Web Address: http://www.asq.org

excellence

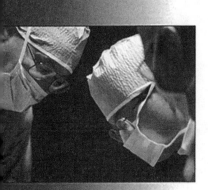

Application Forms & Instructions

for Business, Education, and Health Care

accomplishment

recognition

Malcolm Baldrige
National
Quality
Award

The Award, composed of two solid crystal prismatic forms, stands 14 inches tall. The crystal is held in a base of black anodized aluminum with the Award recipient's name engraved on the base. A 22-karat, gold-plated medallion is captured in the front section of the crystal. The medal bears the inscriptions: "Malcolm Baldrige National Quality Award" and "The Quest for Excellence" on one side and the Presidential Seal on the other.

The President of the United States traditionally presents the Awards at a special ceremony in Washington, DC.

Awards are made annually to recognize U.S. organizations for performance excellence. The Award eligibility categories include:

- manufacturing businesses
- service businesses
- small businesses
- education organizations
- health care organizations

Award recipients may publicize and advertise their Awards. Recipients are expected to share information about their successful performance strategies with other U.S. organizations.

Changes to the Eligibility Rules

To increase the opportunity for feedback for more organizations and in response to applicant requests to allow more subunits in organizations to take advantage of the Award process, the multiple application restriction has been modified. In some cases, more than one subunit of a parent organization may apply for the Award. For more information, refer to page 8 of this booklet.

Crystal by Steuben

The Malcolm Baldrige National Quality Award logo and the phrases "Quest for Excellence" and "Performance Excellence" are trademarks and service marks of the National Institute of Standards and Technology.

Contents

If you plan to apply for the Award in 2000, you will also need the appropriate *2000 Criteria for Performance Excellence* (Business, Education, or Health Care) for your particular organization. Ordering information is given on page 24.

Eligibility Determination Package due — April 6, 2000
Award Application Package due — May 31, 2000

What is the purpose of this booklet?

The purpose of this booklet is to provide eligibility and application instructions and forms to organizations interested in applying for the Malcolm Baldrige National Quality Award.

What is the Malcolm Baldrige National Quality Award?

The Malcolm Baldrige National Quality Award, created by public law in 1987, is the highest level of national recognition for performance excellence that a U.S. organization can receive.

The major focus of the Award is on results, including customer satisfaction. It is *not* given for specific products or services. To receive an Award, an organization must have a system that ensures continuous improvement in the delivery of products and/or services and provides a way of satisfying and responding to stakeholders.

Up to three Awards may be given annually in each of five eligibility categories: manufacturing businesses, service businesses, small businesses, education organizations, and health care organizations.

Why was the Award established?

The Award was established to promote the awareness of performance excellence as an increasingly important element in competitiveness. Not only does it recognize excellent organizations, the Award also aims to increase the understanding of the requirements for performance excellence. To accomplish this, the Award promotes information sharing on successful performance strategies and the benefits derived from implementation of these strategies.

Who may participate?

Organizations that may apply include: privately and publicly owned for-profit businesses headquartered in the United States and its territories; for-profit and not-for-profit public, private, and government education organizations that provide educational services to students in the United States and its territories; and for-profit and not-for-profit public, private, and government health care organizations, which are located in the United States and its territories, and are primarily engaged in providing medical, surgical, or other health services directly to persons. Subunits of organizations may apply if they meet certain requirements.

Who is involved with the Award process?

National Institute of Standards and Technology (NIST): The Department of Commerce is responsible for the Baldrige National Quality Program and the Award. NIST, an agency of the Department's Technology Administration, manages the Baldrige Program.

American Society for Quality (ASQ): ASQ assists in administering the Award Program under contract to NIST.

Board of Examiners: The Board of Examiners evaluates Award applications and prepares feedback reports for the applicants. The Board consists of leading U.S. business, health care, and education experts.

Judges: The Panel of Judges, part of the Board of Examiners, selects Award applicants to undergo site visits and recommends Award recipients. Judges are appointed by the Secretary of Commerce from all sectors of the U.S. economy.

Board of Overseers: The Board is appointed by the Secretary of Commerce and is the advisory organization on the Baldrige National Quality Program to the Department of Commerce. The Board consists of distinguished leaders from all sectors of the U.S. economy.

The Foundation for the Malcolm Baldrige National Quality Award: The Foundation raises funds to permanently endow the Award Program and manages the endowment.

Some of the seven Baldrige Categories have different names in the Business, Education, and Health Care Criteria. How do the Education and Health Care Criteria Categories differ from the seven Business Categories?

There is a very close alignment among all three Criteria and their related Categories. Three of the Categories — Category 1: Leadership; Category 2: Strategic Planning; and Category 4: Information and Analysis — have the same title in all three Criteria. The other four Categories have different titles that reflect differences in terminology among the three sectors. For example, in the Business Criteria, Category 3 is called "Customer and Market Focus." That same Category is called "Student and Stakeholder Focus" in the Education Criteria and "Focus on Patients, Other Customers, and Markets" in the Health Care Criteria.

What is the basis for the Criteria?

Criteria are developed from the state-of-the-art learnings of private and public sector organizations that are working to achieve organizational performance excellence. The Criteria reflect validated, leading-edge practices for achieving performance excellence.

How do applicants benefit from applying for the Award?

Each applicant gains an outside perspective on its organization based on 300 to 1,000 hours of review by members of the Board of Examiners. The results of this review are distilled in a feedback report, outlining strengths and opportunities for improvement based on the Criteria. Feedback reports are often used by organizations as part of their strategic planning process to focus on their customers and to improve results, as well as to help energize and guide their organizational improvement efforts.

How are Award recipients selected?

Award applications are reviewed by a team from the Board of Examiners. High-scoring applicants receive site visits. The Panel of Judges recommends Award recipients from among the site-visited organizations. The Secretary of Commerce then makes the final selection of Award recipients.

What does an organization receive if it is an Award recipient?

Each Award recipient receives a crystal trophy bearing a gold-plated medallion with the inscriptions "Malcolm Baldrige National Quality Award" and "The Quest for Excellence." The President of the United States traditionally presents the Awards at a special ceremony in Washington, DC. Award recipients may publicize and advertise their Awards.

Is the identity of applicants and the information submitted made available to the public?

The identity of all applicants remains confidential unless they receive an Award. Information submitted by applicants is also treated as confidential.

What is expected of Award recipients?

Award recipients are required to share information about their exceptional performance practices with other U.S. organizations. However, recipients are not required to share proprietary information, even if such information was part of their Award application. The principal mechanisms for sharing information are the annual Quest for Excellence Conference, highlighted on the inside back cover, and several one-day regional conferences. Sharing beyond the Quest for Excellence Conference is on a voluntary basis.

How do organizations apply?

Applying for the Award is a two-step process. The first step is eligibility determination, which involves establishing that the organization meets eligibility requirements. Instructions and forms for establishing eligibility begin on page 6.

Once eligibility has been determined, the second step consists of preparing and completing an application form and an application report. The application report must summarize the organization's practices and results in response to the requirements delineated in the Items of the Criteria for Performance Excellence. Award application instructions and forms begin on page 19.

Eligibility Determination
(Package postmarked to ASQ by *April 6, 2000*)

Prepare and submit the Eligibility Determination Package postmarked no later than April 6, 2000, to establish eligibility in one of five Award categories: manufacturing, service, small business, education, or health care. Remember to submit the nonrefundable Eligibility Determination Fee along with the Eligibility Determination Package. (See box on page 5.)

Note: *In the event of multiple submissions from one parent organization, while all may be found eligible, the number of applicants for the Award will be determined by Rule VI.C., found on page 8.*

Award Application
(Package postmarked to ASQ by *May 31, 2000*)

Prepare and submit 25 copies of the application report with the application fee(s) postmarked no later than May 31, 2000. The application fee, which must be included as part of the Award Application Package, covers expenses associated with the review of applications and the development of feedback reports. Fees are detailed on page 5.

Stage 1: Independent Review
(*June - August 2000*)

The application report is reviewed independently by members of the Board of Examiners. At the conclusion of this review, the Panel of Judges determines which applications advance to Stage 2: Consensus Review. At each stage, applicants receive every reasonable consideration to advance to the next stage.

Stage 2: Consensus Review
(*August - September 2000*)

The application report is reviewed jointly by a team of Examiners, led by a Senior Examiner. At the conclusion of this review, the Panel of Judges determines which applicants should receive site visits.

Stage 3: Site Visit Review
(*October - November 2000*)

A team of four to eight members of the Board of Examiners, led by a Senior Examiner, conducts on-site verification and clarification of the application report. Site visits primarily consist of a review of pertinent records and data, and interviews with executives and employees. No site visits are conducted outside of the United States or its territories. Following the site visit, the site visit review team submits its report to the Panel of Judges.

If an organization is chosen for a site visit, the organization is responsible for paying a site visit review fee, which helps to cover expenses associated with the site visit. Additional information on site visit fees is given on page 5.

Stage 4: Judges' Final Review
(*November 2000*)

The Panel of Judges conducts final reviews and presents Award recipient recommendations to the Director of NIST, who conveys the recommendations to the Secretary of Commerce. The Secretary of Commerce makes the final determination of Award recipients.

Role Model Determination: The Secretary of Commerce and the Director of NIST are responsible for determining that recommended Award recipients are appropriate role models and, therefore, should be approved for the Malcolm Baldrige National Quality Award. The purpose of this determination is to help ensure that the Award's integrity is preserved.

In determining role models, NIST conducts records checks on potential Award recipients to ensure compliance with legal and regulatory requirements. The records checked include those of the Internal Revenue Service, the Federal Bureau of Investigation, the Bureau of Export Administration, the General Services Administration, and local police and judicial offices in the applicant's headquarters jurisdiction. No new or independent investigations are conducted.

Feedback Reports
(September 2000 - December 2000)

Each applicant, including Award recipients, receives a feedback report. Feedback reports are received after it is determined that the applicant will not move to the next stage of consideration for the Award or that the applicant is an Award recipient. Feedback reports are prepared by members of the Board of Examiners based on applicants' responses to the Criteria for Performance Excellence. The feedback reports contain applicant-specific listings of strengths and opportunities for improvement based on the Criteria for Performance Excellence.

Award Ceremony
(Winter 2001)

The President of the United States traditionally presents the Awards at a special ceremony in Washington, DC.

Fees for the 2000 and 2001 Award Cycles

Eligibility Determination Fee
For the 2000 Award Cycle, a nonrefundable fee of $100 must be submitted to ASQ along with the Eligibility Determination Package postmarked no later than April 6, 2000. The eligibility fee will be $150 in 2001.

Application Fee
The chart below shows the application fees for 2000 and 2001. For the 2000 Award cycle, the appropriate fee(s) must be submitted to ASQ with the Award Application Package postmarked no later than May 31, 2000.

	MANUFACTURING	SERVICE	SMALL BUSINESS	EDUCATION			HEALTH CARE	
	ALL	ALL	ALL	>500 EMPLOYEES & FOR-PROFIT	<500 EMPLOYEES & FOR-PROFIT	NOT-FOR-PROFIT	>500 EMPLOYEES	<500 EMPLOYEES
2000	$4500	$4500	$1500	$4500	$1500	$300	$4500	$1500
2001	$5000	$5000	$2000	$5000	$2000	$500	$5000	$2000

Site Visit Review Fee
This fee is paid only by applicants receiving site visits. The fee is set when visits are scheduled and is dependent on a number of factors, including the number of sites to be visited, the number of Examiners assigned, and the duration of the visit. The fee is due to ASQ two weeks after completion of the site visit.

The site visit fee for small businesses, for-profit education organizations, and for-profit and not-for-profit health care organizations with fewer than 500 employees is one-half the rate required of applicants with more than 500 employees in the manufacturing, service, for-profit education, and health care sectors. These fees are expected to remain the same in 2001. In 2000, the site visit fee for not-for-profit educational organizations is $1200. In 2001, that fee will be $1500.

I. Purpose

The purpose of this section is to provide applicants with instructions for preparing the Eligibility Determination Package, which is the first step in applying for the Malcolm Baldrige National Quality Award. These instructions describe the considerations that are used to determine eligibility and explain how to complete the Eligibility Determination Form.

II. Objective

The objective of the Eligibility Determination Package is to provide sufficient information to establish whether the organization is eligible to apply for the Award. In addition, the completed Eligibility Determination Package represents a useful profile of the organization. For this reason, it is included in the application report and is often the first information about the applicant read by Examiners. This information is also used to avoid conflicts of interest when assigning applications to Examiners.

III. Submission Requirements

A. Eligibility Determination Package

1. The Eligibility Determination Form must be filled out completely and signed. All information provided is considered confidential.

2. The applicant must attach a line and box organization chart to the form. Each box within the chart should include the name of the head of the unit or division it describes.

3. If the applying organization is a subunit of a larger organization, the following must also be attached:

   ■ a copy of the relevant section/pages of an official publication supporting the subunit designation; and

   ■ line and box organization chart(s) showing the relationship of the applicant to the highest management level of the parent organization, *including all intervening and/or subunit levels.* Include the names of intervening and/or subunit levels and their leaders. This information is used to identify multiple applications from one parent.

B. Letter of Transmittal

A transmittal letter on the applicant's stationery signed by the applicant's Highest-Ranking Official must accompany the Eligibility Determination Package. The letter merely needs to state that the organization is submitting its eligibility application.

C. Fee

A check or money order for the $100 nonrefundable fee must be attached to the Eligibility Determination Package. The fee must be payable to "The Malcolm Baldrige National Quality Award."

D. Submission

Potential applicants for the 2000 Award are encouraged to submit the Eligibility Determination Package as soon as possible. **The package must be postmarked no later than April 6, 2000.**

IV. Eligibility Determination

The Eligibility Determination Package will be reviewed promptly. If clarification is required, the designated Eligibility Contact Point or alternate will be contacted. ASQ will notify applicants of their eligibility status within 14 days of receipt of the package or request additional information, if necessary. ASQ will return the form showing the eligibility determination decision for inclusion in the Award Application Package.

V. Eligibility Categories

Public Law 100-107 established the three business eligibility categories of the Award: manufacturing, service, and small business. On October 30, 1998, President Clinton signed legislation expanding the eligibility categories to include education and health care organizations. Eligibility for the Award is intended to be as open as possible.

A. Business

Any for-profit business headquartered in the United States or its territories, including U.S. subunits of foreign companies, may apply for the Award. For-profit businesses include publicly or privately owned, domestic or foreign owned companies; joint ventures; corporations; sole proprietorships; partnerships; and holding companies.

Note: *Local, state, and federal government agencies, not-for-profit organizations, trade associations, and professional societies are not eligible for the business categories.*

The three business categories are defined as follows:

1. Manufacturing

Companies and some subunits (see VI. Restrictions on Eligibility, Part B) that produce and sell manufactured products or manufacturing processes, and those companies that produce agricultural, mining, or construction products. (See NAICS codes on page 18.)

2. **Service**

Companies and some subunits that sell services.

Note: *Where an applicant is both a manufacturer and a service provider, the larger percentage of sales will determine the appropriate eligibility category.*

3. **Small Business**

Companies with no more than 500 employees engaged in manufacturing and/or the provision of services.

B. **Education**

Participation is open to for-profit and not-for-profit public, private, and government organizations and some subunits — including U.S. subunits of foreign organizations — that provide education services to students in the United States and its territories. Eligibility is intended to be as open as possible. For example, eligible organizations include: elementary and secondary schools and school districts; colleges, universities, and university systems; schools or colleges within universities; professional schools; community colleges; and technical schools.

Departments within schools or colleges are ineligible.

Note: *For-profit education organizations may choose to apply under the service or small business category, as appropriate, using the Business Criteria, or under the education category, using the Education Criteria.*

C. **Health Care**

Participation is open to for-profit and not-for-profit public, private, and government organizations and some subunits — including U.S. subunits of foreign organizations — located in the United States and its territories. These organizations must be primarily engaged in providing medical, surgical, or other health services directly to persons. Eligibility is intended to be as open as possible. For example, eligible organizations include: hospitals, health maintenance organizations, long-term care facilities, health care practitioner offices, home health agencies, and dialysis and ambulatory surgery centers.

Organizations that do not directly provide health services to persons, such as social service agencies, health insurance companies, or medical/dental laboratories, are ineligible under this category. However, such organizations — if they are for-profit — might be eligible under the service or small business categories.

Note: *For-profit health care organizations may choose to apply under the service or small business category, as appropriate, using the Business Criteria, or under the health care category, using the Health Care Criteria.*

Note: *When an applicant is both an education organization and a provider of health care services to persons, the larger percentage of its budget will determine the appropriate eligibility category.*

VI. Restrictions on Eligibility

The following restrictions and conditions ensure fairness and consistency:

A. **Conditions**

1. The applicant must have been in existence prior to April 6, 1999.

2. All subordinate elements of the applicant's organization must be included in the application.

3. An applicant is eligible only if the operational practices associated with all of its major organizational functions are examinable in the United States or its territories. If an applicant has some activities performed outside its immediate organization (e.g., by overseas components of the applicant, a parent organization, or other subunits), it must ensure that:

■ in the event of a site visit, the appropriate personnel and materials will be available for examination in the United States to document operational practices in all major organizational functions; and

■ in the event the applicant wins the Award, the applicant will be able to share information on the seven Criteria Categories at the Quest for Excellence Conference and at its U.S. facilities. Sharing beyond the Quest for Excellence Conference is on a voluntary basis.

B. **Subunits**

For purposes of the 2000 Award Application, a subunit means a unit or division of a larger organization. The larger organization that owns or has organizational or financial control of a subunit will be referred to as the "parent." A parent means the highest level of a company or an organization that would be eligible to apply for the Award.

1. A subunit must be self-sufficient enough to be examined in all seven Criteria Categories.

2. A subunit must have a clear definition of organization as reflected in organization literature, such as organization charts, administrative manuals, and annual reports; be recognizable as a discrete entity; and be easily distinguishable from the parent or other subunits of the parent.

3. The subunit must function as a business or operational entity, not as a collection of activities aggregated for the purposes of writing an Award application.

4. In the business eligibility categories, a subunit is ineligible if less than 50 percent of its products or services are sold or provided to customers/users outside the applicant's organization, its parent organization, and other organizations that own or have financial or organizational control of the applicant or parent.

5. Subunits performing solely support functions are ineligible.

   Examples of business support functions could be: sales, marketing, distribution, finance and accounting, human resources, environmental services, health and safety of employees, purchasing, legal services, and research and development.

   Examples of education support functions could be: academic resource and development centers, student advising units, counseling units, food services, health services, housing, libraries, safety, information technology resources, environmental services, finance and accounting, human resources, public relations, and purchasing.

   Examples of health care support functions could be: housekeeping, radiology, member services, finance and accounting, billing, human resources, purchasing, legal services, and research and development.

6. In the business eligibility categories, a subunit must satisfy at least one of the following conditions:

   ■ it must have more than 500 employees; OR

   ■ it must have at least 25 percent of all employees in the worldwide operations of the parent; OR

   ■ it must have been independent prior to being acquired by the parent and continue to operate independently under its own identity.

C. Multiple-Application Restrictions

1. A subunit and its parent may not apply for Awards in the same year.

2. All subunits may apply for eligibility determination. In some cases, more than one subunit of a parent may apply for the Award. If the employee size of the parent, including all of its subunits, is:

   ■ 0-1000 parent employees, 1 applicant per parent per category may apply for the Award;

   ■ 1001-20,000 parent employees, 2 applicants per parent per category may apply for the Award;

   ■ over 20,000 parent employees, 2 applicants per parent per category for the first 20,000, plus 1 per 20,000 or fraction thereof above 20,000 per parent per category may apply for the Award.

3. In the event of multiple submissions for the Award from subunits of the same parent beyond the limits noted in VI.C.2., the parent organization will be given the option of deciding which subunit(s) will represent it in the Award process. Alternatively, if the parent organization does not choose a representative subunit(s), the earliest postmarked application(s) for the Award will be determined to be the applicant(s) for the Award.

D. Restrictions on Award Recipients

If an organization or a subunit that has more than 50 percent of the total employees of the parent receives an Award, the organization and all its subunits are ineligible to apply for another Award for a period of five years. If a subunit receives an Award, that subunit and all its subunits are ineligible to apply for another Award for a period of five years. After five years, Award recipients are eligible to reapply for the Award or to reapply "for feedback only."

VII. Other Requirements

A. Site Visit Requirements

If some activities are performed outside the applicant's organization (for example, by an overseas component of the applicant, the parent organization, or its other subunits), the applicant, if selected for a site visit, must make available in the United States sufficient personnel, documentation, and facilities to allow a full examination of its operational practices for all major functions of its worldwide operations.

B. Award Recipient Information Sharing Requirement

In the event that the applicant receives the Award, the applicant must be able to share nonproprietary information on the seven Criteria Categories at the Quest for Excellence Conference and at its U.S. facilities. Sharing beyond the Quest for Excellence Conference is on a voluntary basis.

Instructions

1. **Applicant**

   Provide the applicant's official name, which will be used to make the role model determination. (See page 5.) Also, provide any other names by which the applicant may be known publicly, and its previous name if there has been a name change within the last five years. Provide the address of the applicant's headquarters. Indicate whether or not the applicant has existed for at least one year, or prior to April 6, 1999. If the answer is "No," briefly explain.

   Attach a line and box organization chart for the applying organization. Each box within the chart should include the name of the head of the unit or division it describes.

2. **For-Profit/Not-For-Profit Designation**

   Check the appropriate response.

3. **Industrial Classification**

   Using the three- or four-digit NAICS codes listed on page 18, provide up to three codes that best describe the applicant's products and/or services.

4. **Award Category**

   Based on the information given on pages 6 through 8, indicate which of the five Award categories is appropriate and which of the three Criteria (Business, Education, or Health Care) will be used to prepare the application.

5. **Size and Location of Applicant**

   a. Estimate the number of employees as of April 6, 2000.

   b. Check the appropriate financial descriptor (sales, revenues, or budgets) and the appropriate range for the preceding fiscal year.

   c. Indicate the number of sites the applicant has. Offices or other work areas located near each other need not be counted as separate sites if they are considered one location for business and personnel purposes.

   d. State the approximate percent (to the nearest whole number) of the applicant's employees who are located in the United States or its territories.

   e. State the approximate percent (to the nearest whole number) of the applicant's physical assets located in the United States or its territories.

   f. Check the appropriate response.

   g. Check the appropriate response.

6. **Site Listing and Descriptors**

   a. Provide the complete address of each site. In cases where many sites perform the same function, aggregate the sites under one listing and make a summary statement about the locations instead of listing an address for each one. If a site visit is to be conducted, a more detailed listing will be requested when the visit is planned. If the applicant has foreign sites, these sites must be included. Duplicate the Site Listing and Descriptors page if all sites cannot be listed on a single page. The application report must address activities in foreign sites in the appropriate Items. No site visits will be conducted at facilities outside the United States or its territories.

   b. Provide the **number** of the applicant's employees at each site. Circle the appropriate financial descriptor (sales, revenues, or budgets). Provide the approximate **percent** of sales, revenues, or budgets accounted for by the output of each site. Use "Not Applicable" (N/A) for percent of sales, when appropriate.

   c. Describe the types of all major products or services that constitute the output of each site. It may be necessary to state the relationship between the output of the site and the applicant's final products and services. It is not necessary to list every product or service.

7. **Key Business/Organization Factors**

   Provide the following information:

   a. List of key competitors

   b. Description of applicant's products, services, and technologies

   c. List of key customers/users

   d. Description of major markets (local, regional, national, and international)

   e. List of key suppliers

   f. The name of the organization's financial auditor

   g. Description of the importance of suppliers, dealers, distributors, and franchises

   Note: *The lists of key competitors, customers/users, and suppliers (including the financial auditor) are used to consider conflicts of interest in assigning Examiners.*

8. **Subunits**

   If the applicant is a subunit of a larger organization, then responses to 8a through 8j are required; otherwise, go to question 9.

a. Provide the name and address of the parent and the name and title of the Highest-Ranking Official of the highest ownership level of the parent. Provide the number of worldwide employees of the parent, including all subunits. Do not include joint ventures.

Business applicants only:
b. Check the appropriate response.
c. Check the appropriate response.
d. Check the appropriate response.

e. Check the appropriate response. If two or more subunits from the parent are planning to apply for eligibility, provide a brief explanation.

f. **Business applicants only:** Check the appropriate response. If the answer is "No," briefly describe these customers/users and their relationship to the applicant.

g. Submit a short official document, such as an annual report or the appropriate page(s) from an organization publication, that shows the organization of the parent and its relationship to the applying unit. This publication must show that the applying unit has existed for at least one year. Provide the title and a copy of this document.

h. Briefly describe the applying unit's organizational structure and management links to the parent.

Attach line and box organization chart(s) showing the relationship of the applicant to the highest management level of the parent, including all intervening levels.

i. Check the appropriate response. If "Yes" is checked, provide a brief description of the market and product or service similarity and the organizational relationships of all units providing the same or similar products and services as well as the approximate sales, revenues, or budgets for each of those units. Also, if "Yes" is checked, explain how the applicant is distinguishable from the parent and its other subunits.

j. Briefly describe the major support functions provided to the applicant by the parent or by other subunits of the parent.

9. **Supplemental Sections**

Check the appropriate response. If "No" is checked, the Eligibility Contact Point may be contacted. Applicants may have two or more diverse product and/or service lines (i.e., in different NAICS codes) with customers, types of employees, technology, planning, and quality systems that are so different that the application report alone does not allow sufficient detail for a fair examination. Such applicants may submit one or more supplemental sections in addition to the application report. (See page 19.) The use of supplemental sections must be approved during the eligibility determination process and is mandatory once approved.

10. **Eligibility Contact Point**

During the review of the 2000 Eligibility Determination Form and associated materials, it may be necessary to contact the applicant for additional information. Please designate a person who is knowledgeable about the organization and its structure and who will be available to answer inquiries during the month following submission of the Eligibility Determination Form.

11. **Alternate Eligibility Contact Point**

In the event that the Eligibility Contact Point is not available, an Alternate Eligibility Contact Point will be needed to answer questions or convey a message to the Eligibility Contact Point. Please designate a person who is available during regular business hours.

12. **Signature**

Provide the necessary contact information and the signature of the applicant's Highest-Ranking Official.

Eligibility Determination Package Preparation Instructions

The 2000 Eligibility Determination Form may be duplicated. In addition, page 2 of the 2000 Eligibility Determination Form (Item 6, Site Listing and Descriptors) should be duplicated if all sites cannot be listed on a single page. All other responses should be included in the space provided on the forms.

Use the check list on page 17 to ensure that all components of the Eligibility Determination Package have been addressed. Send a letter of transmittal on the applicant's stationery along with the completed form, associated materials, and fee to:
Malcolm Baldrige National Quality Award
c/o ASQ — Baldrige Award Administration
611 East Wisconsin Avenue • Milwaukee, WI 53202
(414) 298-8789, Extension 7205

To avoid delay, applicants are encouraged to submit their completed Eligibility Determination Package **as soon as possible. The package must be postmarked no later than April 6, 2000.** All items should be answered. Incomplete forms will cause a delay in determination. All information is considered confidential.

Eligibility Determination

ASQ will return your form with the official eligibility determination checked in the appropriate box. An approved 2000 Eligibility Determination Form must accompany each of the 25 copies of the application report.

The 2000 Eligibility Determination Package must be postmarked on or before April 6, 2000, to be considered for the 2000 Award. If a question arises about the deadline having been met, a dated receipt from the postal or overnight carrier will be required. Applicants are encouraged to submit the form well ahead of the deadline to avoid delays.

Malcolm Baldrige National Quality Award

1 Applicant

Official Name _____

Other Name _____

Prior Name _____

Headquarters Address _____

_____

_____

Has the applicant officially or legally existed for at least one year, or prior to April 6, 1999? (Check one.) ___Yes ___No (Briefly explain.)

Attach a line and box organization chart for the applying organization, including the name of the head of each unit or division.

2 For-Profit/Not-For-Profit Designation

The applicant is a for-profit organization____; a not-for-profit organization____. (Check one.)

3 Industrial Classification

List up to three of the most descriptive three- or four-digit NAICS codes. (See page 18.)

_____   _____   _____

4 Award Category (Check one.)

___ Manufacturing   ___ Service
___ Small Business
___ Education   ___ Health Care

Criteria being used (Check one.)

___ Business   ___ Education   ___ Health Care

5 Size and Location of Applicant

a. Total number of employees (business), faculty/staff (education), staff (health care) _____

b. Preceding fiscal year:
   Check one financial descriptor.
   ___Sales ___ Revenues ___ Budgets
   Check amount.
   ___ 0-$1M ___ $1M-$10M ___ $10M-$100M
   ___ $100M-$500M ___ $500M-$1B ___ Over $1B

c. Number of sites in U.S./territories ___Overseas ___

d. Percent employees in U.S./territories _____

e. Percent physical assets in U.S./territories _____

f. If some activities are performed outside the applicant's organization (e.g., by an overseas component of the applicant, the parent organization, or its other subunits), will the applicant, if selected for a site visit, make available in the United States sufficient personnel, documentation, and facilities to allow a full examination of its operational practices for all major functions of its worldwide operations?
   ___Yes ___ No ___ Not Applicable

g. In the event the applicant receives an Award, can the applicant make available sufficient personnel and documentation to share its practices at the Quest for Excellence Conference and at its U.S. facilities?
   ___Yes ___ No

6 Site Listing and Descriptors

Please refer to the instructions on page 9 to complete the Site Listing and Descriptors form on the next page (12). It is important that the totals for the number of employees, faculty and staff; percent of sales, revenues, and budgets; and sites on the form match the totals provided in 5.a., 5.b., and 5.c. above. For example, if you report 600 employees in 5.a., the total number of employees provided in the Site Listing and Descriptors form should be 600.

OMB Clearance #0693-0006
Expiration Date: October 31, 2002

This form may be copied and attached to, or bound with, other application materials.

Malcolm Baldrige National Quality Award

6 Site Listing and Descriptors

a. Address of Site	b. Size of Site		c. Description of Products or Services
	Number of Employees, Faculty, and Staff	**Percent** of Sales, Revenues, or Budgets (Circle one.)	

Provide all the information for each site, except where multiple sites produce similar products or services. For such multiple site cases, see 5.c. on page 9.

Use as many copies of this page as necessary to cover all sites.

Malcolm Baldrige National Quality Award

7 **Key Business/Organization Factors**

List or provide a brief description of the following key business/organization factors.

a. List of key competitors

b. Description of the applicant's products, services, and technologies

c. List of key customers/users

d. Description of the major markets (local, regional, national, and international)

Malcolm Baldrige National Quality Award

7 **Key Business/Organization Factors** (Continued)

    e.   List of key suppliers

    f.   The name of the organization's financial auditor

    g.   Description of the importance of the applicant's suppliers, dealers, distributors, and franchises

8 **Subunits**

Is the applicant a subsidiary, unit, division, or like organization of a larger parent? (Check one.)

    ___Yes (Continue.)   ___No (Go to Item 9.)

a. Parent Organization

    Name _____

    Address _____

    _____

    _____

    Highest-Ranking Official

    Name _____

    Title _____

Number of worldwide employees of the parent

_____

b. **Business Only:** Does the applicant have more than 500 employees?
(Check one.) ___Yes ___No

c. **Business Only:** Does the applicant comprise over 25 percent of the worldwide employees of the parent?
(Check one.) ___Yes ___No

d. **Business Only:** Was the applicant independent prior to being acquired, and does it continue to operate independently under its own identity?
(Check one.) ___Yes ___No

e. Does the applicant's parent or another subunit of the parent intend to apply for eligibility?
(Check one.)
    ___Yes (Briefly explain.) ___No ___Do not know

Malcolm Baldrige National Quality Award

8 **Subunits** (Continued)

f. **Business Only:** Are over 50 percent of the applicant's products or services sold or provided to customers/users outside the applicant's organization, its parent, and other organizations that own or have financial or organizational control of the applicant or parent?

(Check one.) ___Yes ___No (Briefly explain.)

g. Name the official document supporting the subunit designation.

_____

_____

Include a copy of the document with this form.

h. Briefly describe the organizational structure and management links to the parent.

Attach line and box organization chart(s) showing the relationship of the applicant to the highest management level of the parent, including all intervening levels. Each box within the chart should include the name of the head of the unit or division it describes.

i. Do other units within the parent provide similar products or services?

(Check one.) ___Yes (Briefly explain.) ___No

If "Yes," also explain how the applicant is distinguishable from the parent and its other subunits.

j. Briefly describe the major support functions provided to the applicant by the parent or by other subunits of the parent.

Malcolm Baldrige National Quality Award

9 Supplemental Sections

Does the applicant have: (a) a single performance system that supports all of its product and/or service lines; and (b) products or services that are essentially similar in terms of customers/users, technology, types of employees, and planning?

(Check one.)

___Yes (Go to Item 10.)

___No (Briefly describe the differences in the products and/or services covered in terms of differences in customers, technology, types of employees, and planning. The Eligibility Contact Point will be asked for more information if necessary.)

10 Eligibility Contact Point

Mr.
Mrs.
Ms.
Name Dr. _____

Title _____

Applicant Name _____

Mailing Address _____

_____

_____

Overnight
Mailing Address (Do not indicate a P.O. Box number.)

_____

_____

Telephone No. _____

Fax No. _____

11 Alternate Eligibility Contact Point

Mr.
Mrs.
Ms.
Name Dr. _____

Telephone No. _____

Fax No. _____

12 Signature, Highest-Ranking Official

Date _____

X _____

Mr.
Mrs.
Ms.
Name Dr. _____

Title _____

Applicant Name _____

Address _____

_____

_____

Telephone No. _____

Fax No. _____

DO NOT WRITE BELOW THIS LINE

2000 Eligibility Determination

☐ Manufacturing   ☐ Education

☐ Service   ☐ Health Care

☐ Small Business

- -

☐ Ineligible

_____

Award Administration

For Official Use Only

2000 Eligibility Determination Package Check List

1. Eligibility Determination Form:

a. Have all questions been answered completely?

___Yes ___No

b. Is a line and box organization chart included that shows all components of the applicant's organization and the name of the head of each unit or division?

___Yes ___No

c. If the applicant is a subunit of a larger organization,

- are line and box organization charts included that show the relationship of the applicant to the highest management level of the parent? Are all intervening levels and the names of the heads of each unit included?

___Yes ___No

- are relevant sections/pages of an official document supporting the subunit designation included?

___Yes ___No

d. Is the Eligibility Determination Form signed by the Highest-Ranking Official?

___Yes ___No

2. Letter of Transmittal:

Is the Eligibility Determination Package accompanied by a letter on the applicant's stationery and signed by the Highest-Ranking Official?

___Yes ___No

3. Fee:

Is a check or money order included for the $100 nonrefundable eligibility determination fee made payable to: **The Malcolm Baldrige National Quality Award?**

___Yes ___No

If you have checked "No" for any question on this list, please recheck the instructions on pages 6-10 before submitting your Eligibility Determination Package.

The Baldrige National Quality Program welcomes your comments on the *2000 Application Forms & Instructions for Business, Education, and Health Care*, the Criteria, or the Award processes. Please address your comments to:

2000 Application Forms & Instructions for Business, Education, and Health Care
National Institute of Standards and Technology
Baldrige National Quality Program
Administration Building, Room A635
100 Bureau Drive, Stop 1020
Gaithersburg, Maryland 20899-1020

or E-mail: nqp@nist.gov

or Web Address: http://www.quality.nist.gov

North American Industry Classification System (NAICS) Codes

Please insert NAICS codes most relevant to your organization's products and/or services on the first page of the Eligibility Determination Form. If you wish to access the NAICS codes on-line, connect to "http://www.census.gov," select "subjects A to Z," select "N," select "NAICS (North American Industry Classification System)."

Code	Sector	Code	Sector	Code	Sector
111	Crop Production	335	Electrical Equipment, Appliance and Component Manufacturing		5223 Activities Related to Credit Intermediation
112	Animal Production			523	Securities, Commodity Contracts and Other Intermediation
113	Forestry and Logging		3353 Electrical Equipment Manufacturing-Power Distribution and Specialty Transformer; Motor and Generator; Switchgear; and Relay and Industrial Control Manufacturing		
114	Fishing, Hunting and Trapping				5231 Securities and Commodity Contracts Intermediation
115	Support Activities for Agriculture and Forestry				5232 Securities and Commodity Exchanges
211	Oil and Gas Extraction				5239 Other Financial Investment Activities
212	Mining (except Oil and Gas)		3359 Other Electrical Equipment and Component Manufacturing-Battery; Communication and Energy Wire and Cable; and Wiring Device Manufacturing	524	Insurance Carriers and Related Activities
213	Support Activities for Mining			525	Funds, Trusts and Other Financial Vehicles (U.S. Organizations)
221	Utilities				
233	Building, Developing and General Contracting				5251 Insurance and Employee Benefit Funds
234	Heavy Construction	336	Transportation Equipment Manufacturing		
235	Special Trade Contractors	337	Furniture and Related Product Manufacturing		5259 Other Investment Pools and Funds
311	Food Manufacturing			531	Real Estate
312	Beverage and Tobacco Product Manufacturing	339	Miscellaneous Manufacturing	532	Rental and Leasing Services
313	Textile Mills	421	Wholesale Trade, Durable Goods	533	Owners and Lessors of Other Non-Financial Assets
314	Textile Product Mills	422	Wholesale Trade, Nondurable Goods		
315	Apparel Manufacturing	441	Motor Vehicle and Parts Dealers	541	Professional, Scientific and Technical Services
316	Leather and Allied Product Manufacturing	442	Furniture and Home Furnishings Stores		
321	Wood Product Manufacturing	443	Electronics and Appliance Stores	551	Management of Companies and Enterprises
322	Paper Manufacturing	444	Building Material and Garden Equipment and Supplies Stores		
323	Printing and Related Support Activities			561	Administrative and Support Services
324	Petroleum and Coal Products Manufacturing	445	Food and Beverage Stores	562	Waste Management and Remediation Services
325	Chemical Manufacturing	446	Health and Personal Care Stores		
326	Plastics and Rubber Products Manufacturing	447	Gasoline Stations	611	Educational Services
327	Nonmetallic Mineral Product Manufacturing	448	Clothing and Clothing Accessories Stores	621	Ambulatory Health Care Services
				622	Hospitals
331	Primary Metal Manufacturing	451	Sporting Goods, Hobby, Book and Music Stores	623	Nursing and Residential Care Facilities
332	Fabricated Metal Product Manufacturing	452	General Merchandise Stores	624	Social Assistance
333	Machinery Manufacturing	453	Miscellaneous Store Retailers	711	Performing Arts, Spectator Sports and Related Industries
	3331 Agriculture, Construction, and Mining Machinery Manufacturing	454	Nonstore Retailers		
		481	Air Transportation	712	Museums, Historical Sites and Similar Institutions
	3332 Industrial Machinery Manufacturing	482	Rail Transportation		
		483	Water Transportation	713	Amusement, Gambling and Recreation Institutions
	3333 Commercial and Service Industry Machinery Manufacturing	484	Truck Transportation		
		485	Transit and Ground Passenger Transportation	721	Accommodations (hotels)
	3334 Ventilation, Heating, Air-Conditioning and Commercial Refrigeration Equipment Manufacturing			722	Food Services and Drinking Places
		486	Pipeline Transportation	811	Repair and Maintenance
		487	Scenic and Sightseeing Transportation	812	Personal and Laundry Services
	3335 Metalworking Machinery Manufacturing	488	Support Activities for Transportation	813	Religious, Grant Making, Civic, and Professional and Similar Organizations
		491	Postal Service		
	3336 Engine, Turbine, and Power Transmission Equipment	492	Couriers and Messengers		
		493	Warehousing and Storage Facilities	921	Executive, Legislative, Public Finance and General
	3339 Other General Purpose Machinery Manufacturing	511	Publishing Industries		
		512	Motion Picture and Sound Recording Industries	922	Justice, Public Order, Safety
334	Computer and Electronic Product Manufacturing			923	Administration of Human Resource Programs
		513	Broadcasting and Telecommunications		
	3341 Computer and Peripheral Equipment Manufacturing	514	Information Services and Data Processing Services	924	Administration of Environmental Quality Programs
	3342 Communications Equipment Manufacturing	521	Monetary Authorities-Central Bank	925	Administration of Housing Programs, Urban Planning
		522	Credit Intermediation and Related Activities	926	Administration of Economic Programs
	3344 Semiconductor and Other Electronic Component Manufacturing		5221 Depository Credit Intermediation	927	Space Research and Technology
				928	National Security and International Affairs
			5222 Non-Depository Credit Intermediation	999	Unclassified Establishments

Instructions for responding to the Criteria and writing the Business/Organization Overview are included in each of the three Criteria Booklets. Use the Criteria appropriate to your eligibility category (Business, Education, or Health Care).

I. Purpose

The purpose of this section is to provide eligible applicants with instructions for preparing the Award Application Package. These instructions describe content, format, assembly, and submission requirements.

II. Objective

The objective of the Award Application Package is to allow the applicant to provide sufficient information to permit a rigorous evaluation by the Board of Examiners. Information is required on the applicant's performance management system and on the results of its processes. All information provided is considered confidential.

III. Content Requirements

A. Application Report - All Applicants

Only an application report is required if an applicant has a single performance system that supports all of its product and/or service lines, and if the products or services are essentially similar in terms of customers, technology, types of employees, planning, and quality systems. **This is the case with most applicants.**

An application report must contain the following in the order listed:

- Front Cover — blank (no text, pictures, or figures) to help ensure confidentiality
- Title Page
- Labeled Tabs or Dividers
- Table of Contents
- Approved 2000 Eligibility Determination Form
- Organization Chart(s)
- 2000 Application Form
- Business/Organization Overview (5 pages or less)
- Glossary of Terms and Abbreviations
- Responses Addressing All Criteria Items (50 pages or less)

- Summary of Supplemental Sections, if applicable (2 pages or less — see information below under "B. Supplemental Sections")
- Back Cover — blank

All units/subunits of the applicant must be included in the application report [and/or supplemental section(s)].

B. Supplemental Sections

In order to maintain an equivalent level of detail for all sizes and types of applicants, certain applicants may need to provide supplemental sections. Supplemental sections are intended to permit applicants with the most complex organizations and performance systems to describe them in sufficient detail to permit a rigorous examination. Supplemental sections may be required if the applicant has two or more diverse product and/or service lines (i.e., in different NAICS codes) with customers, technology, types of employees, planning, and quality systems that are so different that the application report alone will not allow sufficient detail for a fair examination.

The use of supplemental sections must be approved during eligibility determination. Once supplemental sections are approved, they must be submitted by the applicant. If both an application report and supplemental section(s) are submitted, the application report should cover the largest aggregation of similar product and/or service lines that are supported by a single performance system.

Together, the application report and the supplemental section(s) must cover all products and/or services and all performance systems of the applicant.

Each supplemental section must contain:

- Front Cover — blank (no text, pictures, or figures)
- Title Page
- Labeled Tabs or Dividers
- Table of Contents
- Organization Chart
- Summary of Supplemental Sections (2 pages or less)
- Business/Organization Overview (5 pages or less)
- Glossary of Terms and Abbreviations
- Responses Addressing All Criteria Items (35 pages or less)
- Back Cover — blank

IV. Format Requirements

The application report and supplemental section(s), if any, must meet the page limit, typing, and format requirements indicated below.

A. Page Limits and Exclusions

1. The Business/Organization Overview for the application report and each supplemental section is limited to five single-sided pages. If the Business/Organization Overview exceeds the five-page limit, the excess pages will be counted as part of the page count for the Responses Addressing All Criteria Items. Guidelines for preparing the Business/Organization Overview can be found in each of the Criteria booklets.

2. The Responses Addressing All Criteria Items are limited to 50 single-sided pages, which must include all pictures, graphs, figures, tables, and appendices. The responses must contain the same Category and Item numerical designations as the 2000 Criteria. Applicants should denote the Areas to Address with letters a, b, c, and so forth, corresponding to each Area, such as 4.2a.

3. The covers, dividers, tab separators, Table of Contents, Organization Chart(s), Eligibility Determination Form, Application Form, and Glossary of Terms and Abbreviations that contain only the subject material will not be counted as part of the page limit in either the application report or supplemental section(s). However, if these pages contain any additional material, such as text, quotations, graphs, figures, data tables, or pictures, they will be considered part of the 50 pages of the Responses Addressing All Criteria Items. Each page will be counted as part of the total page count for that portion of the Application Package.

4. If the Responses Addressing All Criteria Items exceed the 50-page limit, the Official Contact Point will be asked to identify which pages will be removed.

5. The Summary of Supplemental Sections, if applicable, is limited to two single-sided pages. If the summary exceeds the two-page limit, the excess will be counted as part of the page count for the Responses Addressing All Criteria Items.

6. In supplemental sections, the Responses Addressing All Criteria Items are limited to 35 single-sided pages.

B. Paper size: standard 8 1/2 by 11 inch

C. Typing

1. Font Size

- fixed pitch font of 12 or fewer characters per inch OR

- proportional spacing font of point size 10 or larger

   A typical document produced in Times Roman 10 point font will satisfy this requirement.

2. Line Spacing – Equivalent of two points of lead between lines. Note: *One point of lead equals 1/72, or 0.0138 inch.*

3. Font Style – Any font style may be used that meets the font size and line spacing requirements, but Helvetica and Times Roman or equivalent styles are preferred.

4. Type used in picture captions, graphs, figures, data tables, and appendices also must meet the requirements for font size and line spacing. If the table or graph is reduced from its original size for inclusion, applicants must use larger type sizes in preparing the original so that the reduced material in the application report meets the font size requirements.

   Font style and/or size need not be uniform throughout the application report so long as all styles and sizes meet the requirements.

D. Format

1. The number of lines per page must not exceed 60, including the page headings. A blank line separating paragraphs is counted as a line.

2. A margin of at least 3/4 inch on the side of the page that is bound or fastened and at least 1/2 inch on the opposite side of the page is preferred.

3. Pages set up in a two-column format are preferred. Pages may be printed on both sides.

4. Text pages should have portrait orientation. Graphs, figures, and data tables may have either portrait or landscape orientation.

E. Numbering

The pages of the Responses Addressing All Criteria Items must be numbered consecutively from start to finish; e.g., 1, ..., 50. Blank pages should not be numbered. All figures should be numbered.

V. Assembly Requirements

A. All components of the application report and supplemental section(s) must be securely fastened to prevent separation during handling. The use of clips or binders with easily opened pressure-sensitive clips is discouraged. Supplemental section(s) must be bound separately from the application report.

B. The use of bulky binders or similar heavy covers is discouraged.

C. Video and audio tapes or other information aids are not acceptable.

VI. Submission Requirements

A. Applicants must submit a 2000 Award Application Package containing:

1. Twenty-five individually bound copies of the complete application report and, if appropriate, twenty-five individually bound copies of each supplemental section.

2. A check or money order covering the application fees for the application report and, if appropriate, each supplemental section. (See No. 5 of the Application Form Instructions on page 22 for specific fees.) The check or money order should be made payable to **The Malcolm Baldrige National Quality Award**.

B. The 2000 Award Application Package must be postmarked or consigned to an overnight delivery service no later than May 31, 2000, to be eligible for a 2000 Award. If a question arises about the deadline having been met, the applicant will be asked to supply a dated receipt from the postal or overnight carrier.

The Baldrige National Quality Program reserves the right to return incomplete submissions or submissions that do not meet the requirements given in the sections entitled "Content Requirements" and "Format Requirements" along with the application fee.

Send the complete 2000 Award Application Package to:

Malcolm Baldrige National Quality Award
c/o ASQ — Baldrige Award Administration
611 East Wisconsin Avenue
Milwaukee, WI 53202
(414) 298-8789, Extension 7205

VII. Description of Application Report Parts

Each copy of the application report must contain:

A. **Front Cover** — blank (no text, pictures, or figures).

B. **Title Page** with the name of the applicant and, optionally, the applicant's address, pictures, and logo; the date; a statement indicating that this is an application for the 2000 Malcolm Baldrige National Quality Award; and/or a statement regarding confidentiality of content. No further information or text about the applicant may be included on this page.

C. **Labeled Tabs or Dividers** separating the sections of the report and containing only the title of the section. No further information or text about the applicant may be included on the Tabs or Dividers.

D. **Table of Contents** indicating the page number of the following: the approved 2000 Eligibility Determination Form, the Organization Chart(s), the 2000 Application Form, the Business/Organization Overview, the Glossary of Terms and Abbreviations, and each Category and Item. Areas to Address, tables, and figures need not be included in the Table of Contents.

E. **2000 Eligibility Determination Form** approved by ASQ, including all Site Listing and Descriptors pages and, if the applicant is a subunit, line and box organization chart(s) of the parent/holding company showing where the applicant fits into the overall organization.

F. **Line and box organization chart(s) of the applicant** with sufficient detail for Examiners to understand the relationships among the applicant's subunits.

G. **2000 Application Form** (see page 23) signed by the applicant, indicating that the applicant agrees to the terms and conditions of the Award process and, if chosen, agrees to host a site visit; facilitate an open and unbiased examination; pay reasonable costs associated with the site visit; and, if selected as an Award recipient, share information on successful performance excellence strategies with other U.S. organizations.

H. **Business/Organization Overview** outlining the applicant's organization, addressing what is most important to the organization as well as the key business/organization factors that influence how the organization operates and where it is headed. A vital part of the overall application, the Business/Organization Overview is used by the Examiners in all stages of the application review.

I. **Glossary of Terms and Abbreviations** used in the application report and each supplemental section.

J. **Responses Addressing All Criteria Items**

- Respond to each Item as a whole. Address the set of Areas with an emphasis that reflects the applicant's organization and performance system. To facilitate review by the Board of Examiners, respond to the Areas in the order given in the Items. Address activities in foreign sites in the appropriate Items.

- If an Area to Address does not pertain to the applicant's organization or performance system, provide a statement of one or two sentences explaining why the Area is not applicable. The Item/Area designator should be used as described under format requirements.

K. If applicable, provide a **Summary of Supplemental Sections** — a brief description of each supplemental section, including the products, services, and NAICS codes.

L. **Back Cover** — blank.

Instructions

Provide all information requested. A copy of the 2000 Application Form must be included in each of the 25 copies of the application report, as described on page 19.

1. Applicant

Provide the official name and mailing address of the organization applying for the Award.

2. Award Category

From the approved 2000 Eligibility Determination Form, indicate the eligibility category under which the applicant was approved and which Criteria are being used.

3. Official Contact Point

As the examination proceeds, the applicant may need to be contacted for additional information or for arrangements for a site visit. Further communications between the applicant and the American Society for Quality (ASQ) or the Baldrige National Quality Program will be limited to this Official Contact Point. This person should have both in-depth knowledge of the organization and a good understanding of the organization's application. Designate a person with authority who will be available to provide additional information, to answer inquiries, or to arrange a site visit.

If the Official Contact Point changes during the course of the application process, please inform ASQ.

4. Alternate Official Contact Point

In the event that the Official Contact Point is not available, the Alternate Official Contact Point will be contacted to answer questions or to convey a message to the Official Contact Point. Please designate a person who is available during regular business hours.

5. Fee

Fee payment must be submitted with the application. The fees for the application report are: $4500 for manufacturing, service, for-profit education institutions, and for-profit and not-for-profit health care organizations with more than 500 employees; $1500 for small businesses, for-profit education institutions, and for-profit and not-for-profit health care organizations with fewer than 500 employees; and $300 for not-for-profit education institutions. A fee of $1500 is required for supplemental sections.

6. Release Statement

Please read this section carefully. A signed application indicates that the applicant agrees to the terms and conditions stated therein.

7. Signature, Highest-Ranking Official

The applicant's Highest-Ranking Official must sign in the space provided, indicating that the applicant will comply with the terms and conditions stated in the document. Type that person's name, title, address, and telephone number, as indicated.

Malcolm Baldrige National Quality Award

1 Applicant

Name _____

Mailing Address _____

_____

_____

2 Award Category (Check one.)

___ Manufacturing ___ Service ___ Small Business
___ Education ___ Health Care

For small businesses, indicate whether the larger percentage of sales is in service or manufacturing. (Check one.)

___ Service ___ Manufacturing

Criteria being used (Check one.)

___ Business ___ Education ___ Health Care

3 Official Contact Point

Mr.
Mrs.
Ms.
Name Dr. _____

Title _____

Applicant Name _____

Mailing Address _____

_____

Overnight
Mailing Address (Do not use P.O. Box number.)

_____

_____

Telephone No. _____

Fax No. _____

4 Alternate Official Contact Point

Mr.
Mrs.
Ms.
Name Dr. _____

Telephone No. _____

Fax No. _____

5 Fee (See page 5 for instructions.)

Enclosed is $_____ to cover one application report and _____ supplemental sections.

Make check or money order payable to:

The Malcolm Baldrige National Quality Award

6 Release Statement

We understand that this application will be reviewed by members of the Board of Examiners.

Should our organization be selected for a site visit, we agree to host the site visit and to facilitate an open and unbiased examination. We understand that the organization must pay reasonable costs associated with a site visit.

If our organization is selected to receive an Award, we agree to share nonproprietary information on our successful performance excellence strategies with other U.S. organizations.

7 Signature, Highest-Ranking Official

Date _____

X _____

Mr.
Mrs.
Ms.
Name Dr. _____

Title _____

Applicant Name _____

Mailing Address _____

_____

_____

Telephone No. _____

OMB Clearance #0693-0006
Expiration Date: October 31, 2002

This form may be copied and attached to, or bound with, other application materials.

Award Materials

Individual Orders

Individual copies of the Criteria booklets and the *2000 Application Forms & Instructions for Business, Education, and Health Care* can be obtained free of charge from the Baldrige National Quality Program at NIST. Telephone: (301) 975-2036; Fax: (301) 948-3716; E-mail: nqp@nist.gov.

Bulk Orders

Multiple copies of the *2000 Criteria for Performance Excellence* booklets may be ordered in packets of 10 for $29.95 plus shipping and handling from the American Society for Quality (ASQ).

2000 Business Criteria — Item Number T1101
2000 Education Criteria — Item Number T1103
2000 Health Care Criteria — Item Number T1102

How to Order

ASQ offers four convenient ways to order:

- For fastest service, call toll free (800) 248-1946 in the United States and Canada (in Mexico, dial toll free 95-800-248-1946). Have item numbers, your credit card or purchase order number, and (if applicable) ASQ member number ready.

- Or fax your completed order form to ASQ at (414) 272-1734.

- Or mail your order to ASQ Customer Service Department, P.O. Box 3066, Milwaukee, WI 53201-3066.

- Or order online from ASQ's website at http://www.asq.org.

Payment

Your payment options include: check, money order, U.S. purchase order, VISA, MasterCard, or American Express. Payment must be made in U.S. currency; checks and money orders must be drawn on a U.S. financial institution. All international orders must be prepaid. Please make checks payable to ASQ.

Shipping Fees

The following shipping and processing schedule applies to all orders:

Order Amount	U.S. Charges	Canadian Charges
0 – $34.99	$ 4.00	$ 9.00
$35.00 – $99.99	6.25	11.25
Over $100.00	12.50*	17.50

- There is an additional charge of 25 percent of the total order amount for shipments outside the United States/Canada.

- Orders shipped within the continental United States and Canada where UPS service is available will be shipped UPS.

- Please allow one to two weeks for delivery. International customers, please allow six to eight weeks for delivery.

- Your credit card will not be charged until your items are shipped. Shipping and processing are charged one time, up front, for the entire order.

* *If actual shipping charges exceed $12.50 ($17.50 Canadian), ASQ will invoice the customer for the additional expense.*

Baldrige Educational Materials

Each year, the Baldrige National Quality Program develops materials for training members of the Board of Examiners and for sharing information on the successful performance excellence strategies of the Award recipients. The items listed below are a sample of the educational materials that may be ordered from ASQ.

- **Case Studies** The case studies are used to prepare Examiners for the interpretation of the Criteria and the Scoring System. The case studies, when used with the Criteria, illustrate the Award application and review process. The case study packet is illustrative of an application for the Baldrige Award and is useful in understanding the benefits of the Baldrige process, as well as for self-assessment, planning, training, and other uses.

  - **1999 Business Case Study Packet: Collin Technologies** *(Based on the 1999 Criteria for Performance Excellence)* Item Number T1079: $49.95 plus shipping and handling

  - **1998 Business Case Study Packet: Gemini Home Health Services** *(Based on the 1998 Criteria for Performance Excellence)* Item Number T1083: $49.95 plus shipping and handling

  - **Education Case Study Packet: Ridgecrest School District** *(Based on the 1995 Education Pilot Criteria)* Item Number T1023: $7.28 plus shipping and handling

  - **Health Care Case Study Packet: Pinnacle Health Plan** *(Based on the 1995 Health Care Pilot Criteria)* Item Number T1029: $7.28 plus shipping and handling

- **Award Recipients' Videos** The Award recipients' videos are a valuable resource for gaining a better understanding of performance excellence and quality achievement. The videos provide background information on the Baldrige National Quality Program, highlights from the annual Award ceremony, and interviews with representatives from the Award recipients' organizations. Information on the 1999 Award recipients' video is provided below. Videos about Award recipients from other years also are available from ASQ.

  - **1999 Award Recipients' Video** Item Number T1086: $20.00 plus shipping and handling *(Available March 2000)*

Quest For Excellence XII Conference

Each year, Quest for Excellence, the official conference of the Malcolm Baldrige National Quality Award, provides a forum for Baldrige Award recipients to share their exceptional performance practices with worldwide leaders in business, education, health care, and not-for-profit organizations. Quest for Excellence XII will showcase the 1999 recipients.

For the last 11 years, executives, managers, and quality leaders have come to this conference to learn how these role model organizations have achieved performance excellence. CEOs and other leaders from the Award recipients who are transforming their organizations give presentations covering all seven Categories of the Baldrige Criteria, their journey to performance

excellence, and their lessons learned. Conference attendees will have the opportunity to ask questions of the Award recipients. This three-day conference is designed to maximize learning and networking opportunities.

The Quest for Excellence XII Conference will be held March 12-15, 2000, at the Marriott Wardman Park Hotel in Washington, DC. For further information, contact the National Institute of Standards and Technology (NIST), Baldrige National Quality Program, Administration Building, Room A635, 100 Bureau Drive, Stop 1020, Gaithersburg, MD 20899-1020; telephone: (301) 975-2036; fax: (301) 948-3716; or E-mail: nqp@nist.gov.

Paperwork Reduction Act Statement

Notwithstanding any other provision of the law, no person is required to respond to, nor shall any person be subject to a penalty for failure to comply with, a collection of information subject to the requirements of the Paperwork Reduction Act, unless that collection of information displays a currently valid OMB Control Number.

The reason for collecting this information is to allow organizations to apply for the Malcolm Baldrige National Quality Award (Award). The information obtained will assist in determining the winners. Responses to the collection of information are required to be considered for the Award. Confidentiality of the submitted information is covered under the Freedom of Information Act to the extent possible under the law.

The public reporting burden for this collection is estimated to average 100 hours for the initial response of the first-time applicant (this includes the time for

reviewing instructions, searching existing data sources, gathering and maintaining the relevant data, and completing and reviewing the collection of information). As the organization reapplies for the Award in future years, it is possible that this burden will change, in either direction, based on the feedback the respondent gains from their first application.

Send comments regarding this burden estimate or any other aspect of this collection of information, including suggestions for reducing this burden, to:

Dr. Harry Hertz, Director, Baldrige National Quality Program, NIST, Administration Building, Room A635, 100 Bureau Drive, Stop 1020, Gaithersburg, MD 20899-1020, and to the Office of Information and Regulatory Affairs, Office of Management and Budget, Washington, DC 20503.

Baldrige National Quality Program

United States Department of Commerce
Technology Administration
National Institute of Standards and Technology
Baldrige National Quality Program
Administration Building, Room A635
100 Bureau Drive, Stop 1020
Gaithersburg, MD 20899-1020

The National Institute of Standards and Technology (NIST) is a non-regulatory federal agency within the Commerce Department's Technology Administration. NIST's primary mission is to strengthen the U.S. economy and improve the quality of life by working with industry to develop and apply technology, measurements, and standards. The Baldrige National Quality Program at NIST manages the Malcolm Baldrige National Quality Award.

Call the Baldrige National Quality Program for:

* information on applying for the Baldrige Award
* information on the Malcolm Baldrige National Quality Award process and eligibility requirements
* information on becoming a Baldrige Examiner
* information on the Baldrige Award recipients
* individual copies of the Criteria for Business, Education, and Health Care (no cost)
* information on other Baldrige National Quality Program materials

Telephone: (301) 975-2036; Fax: (301) 948-3716; E-mail: nqp@nist.gov
Web Address: http://www.quality.nist.gov

American Society for Quality
611 East Wisconsin Avenue
P.O. Box 3005
Milwaukee, WI 53201-3005

The American Society for Quality (ASQ) advances individual and organizational performance excellence worldwide by providing opportunities for learning, quality improvement, and knowledge exchange. ASQ administers the Malcolm Baldrige National Quality Award under contract to NIST.

Call ASQ to order:

* bulk copies of the Criteria
* case studies
* Award recipients' videos

Telephone: (800) 248-1946; Fax: (414) 272-1734; E-mail: asq@asq.org
Web Address: http://www.asq.org

Design: RCW Communication Design, Inc.

✪ printed on recycled paper

Books from Productivity, Inc.

Productivity, Inc. publishes books that empower individuals and companies to achieve excellence in quality, productivity, and the creative involvement of all employees. Through steadfast efforts to support the vision and strategy of continuous improvement, Productivity delivers today's leading-edge tools and techniques gathered directly from industry leaders around the world. Call toll-free (800) 394-6868 for our free catalog.

5S FOR OPERATORS
5 Pillars of the Visual Workplace
Productivity Development Team

Operator books are based on the principles of adult learning to meet the reading needs of a shopfloor audience. Written at the appropriate reading level, these books are heavily illustrated with photos and drawings. The text is set up with one concept for every two to four pages so that it can be easily read in chunks; headers and assists in the margin make the significance of each section stand out. Each chapter summarizes main concepts and tools at the beginning and lists application questions at the end. This particular book presents the main concepts and tools from Hirano's *5 Pillars of the Visual Workplace*. Hirano discusses how the 5S theory fosters efficiency, maintenance, and continuous improvement in all areas of the company, from the plant floor to the sales office. It explains why the 5S's are important and gives the who, what, where, and how of 5S implementation.
ISBN 1-56327-123-0 /136 pages, illustrated / $25.00 / Order 5SOP

BECOMING LEAN
Inside Stories of U.S. Manufacturers
Jeffrey Liker

Most other books on lean management focus on technical methods and offer a picture of what a lean system should look like. Some provide snapshots of before and after. This is the first book to provide technical descriptions of successful solutions and performance improvements. The first book to include powerful first-hand accounts of the complete process of change, its impact on the entire organization, and the rewards and benefits of becoming lean. At the heart of this book you will find the stories of American manufacturers who have successfully implemented lean methods. Authors offer personalized accounts of their organization's lean transformation, including struggles and successes, frustrations and surprises. Now you have a unique opportunity to go inside their implementation process to see what worked, what didn't, and why. Many of these executives and managers who led the charge to becoming lean in their organizations tell their stories here for the first time!
ISBN 1-56327-173-7/ 350 pages / $35.00 / Order LEAN

QUICK RESPONSE MANUFACTURING
A Companywide Approach to Reducing Lead Times
Rajan Suri

Quick Response Manufacturing (QRM) is an expansion of time-based competition (TBC) strategies, which use speed for a competitive advantage. Essentially, QRM stems from a single principle: to reduce lead times. But unlike other time-based competition strategies, QRM is an approach for the entire organization, from the front desk to the shop floor, from purchasing to sales. In order to truly succeed with speed-based competition, you must adopt the approach throughout the organization.
ISBN 1-56327-201-6/ 560 pages / $50.00 / Order QRM

Productivity, Inc., Dept. BK, P.O. Box 13390, Portland, OR 97213-0390
Telephone: 1-800-394-6868   Fax: 1-800-394-6286

FAST TRACK TO WASTE-FREE MANUFACTURING:
Straight Talk from a Plant Manager
John W. Davis

Batch, or mass, manufacturing is still the preferred system of production for most U.S.-based industry. But to survive, let alone become globally competitive, companies will have to put aside their old habitual mass manufacturing paradigms and completely change their existing system of production. In Fast Track to *Waste-Free Manufacturing: Straight Talk from a Plant Manager*, John Davis details a new and proven system called Waste-Free Manufacturing (WFM) that rapidly deploys the lean process. He covers nearly every aspect of the lean revolution and provides essential tools and techniques you will need to implement WFM. Drawing from more than 30 years of manufacturing experience, John Davis gives you tools and techniques for eliminating anything that cannot be clearly established as value added.
ISBN: 1-56327-212-1 / 425 pages / $45.00 / Order WFM

TO ORDER: Write, phone, or fax Productivity, Inc., Dept. BK, P.O. Box 13390, Portland, OR 97213-0390, phone 1-800-394-6868, fax 1-800-394-6286.

Outside the U.S. phone (503) 235-0600; fax (503) 235-0909

Send check or charge to your credit card (American Express, Visa, MasterCard accepted).

U.S. ORDERS: Add $5 shipping for first book, $2 each additional for UPS surface delivery. Add $5 for each AV program containing 1 or 2 tapes; add $15 for each AV program containing 3 or more tapes. We offer attractive quantity discounts for bulk purchases of individual or mixed titles; call for more information.

ORDER BY E-MAIL: Order 24 hours a day from anywhere in the world. Use either address:
  To order: **info@productivityinc.com**
  To view the online catalog and/or order: **http://www.productivityinc.com/**

QUANTITY DISCOUNTS: For information on quantity discounts, please contact our sales department.

INTERNATIONAL ORDERS: Write, phone, or fax for quote and indicate shipping method desired. For international callers, the telephone number is 503-235-0600 and the fax number is 503-235-0909. Prepayment in U.S. dollars must accompany your order (checks must be drawn on U.S. banks). When quote is returned with payment, your order will be shipped promptly by the method requested.

NOTE: Prices are in U.S. dollars and are subject to change without notice.

Productivity, Inc. Consulting, Training, Workshops, and Conferences
EDUCATION...IMPLEMENTATION...RESULTS

Productivity, Inc. is the leading American consulting, training, and publishing company focusing on delivering improvement technology to the global manufacturing industry.

Productivity, Inc. prides itself on delivering today's leading performance improvement tools and methodologies to enhance rapid, ongoing, measurable results. Whether you need assistance with long-term planning or focused, results-driven training, Productivity, Inc.'s world-class consultants can enhance your pursuit of competitive advantage. In concert with your management team, Productivity, Inc. will focus on implementing the principles of Value-Adding Management, Total Quality Management, Just-in-Time, and Total Productive Maintenance. Each approach is supported by Productivity's wide array of team-based tools: Standardization, One-Piece Flow, Hoshin Planning, Quick Changeover, Mistake-Proofing, Kanban, Problem Solving with CEDAC, Visual Workplace, Visual Office, Autonomous Maintenance, Overall Equipment Effectiveness, Design of Experiments, Quality Function Deployment, Ergonomics, and more! And, based on continuing research, Productivity, Inc. expands its offering every year.

Productivity, Inc.'s conferences provide an excellent opportunity to interact with the best of the best. Each year our national conferences bring together the leading practitioners of world-class, high-performance strategies. Our workshops, forums, plant tours, and master series are scheduled throughout the U.S. to provide the opportunity for continuous improvement in key areas of lean management and production.

Productivity, Inc. is known for significant improvement on the shop floor and the bottom line. Through years of repeat business, an expanding and loyal client base continues to recommend Productivity, Inc. to their colleagues. Contact Productivity, Inc. to learn how we can tailor our services to fit your needs.